THE UNIVERSITY OF NEW MEXICO PRESS

SOUTH AFRICA
An Imperial Dilemma

Non-Europeans and the British Nation
1902-1914

By BENJAMIN SACKS

The publication
of this book was assisted
by a grant from
the Ford Foundation

Manufactured
in the United States
of America by
the University of New Mexico
Printing Plant,
Albuquerque

Library of Congress
Catalog Card No. 66-29015

First Edition

CONTENTS

PREFACE

Scholarly studies on South Africa for the decade prior to World War I are not lacking. Geoffrey Barker Pyrah's *Imperial Policy and South Africa, 1902-10* (1955) emphasizes British officialdom with a minimum on public opinion. Leonard Monteath Thompson's *The Unification of South Africa, 1902-1910* (1960) focuses upon the point of view of South Africa with a minimum on the British position. Nicholas Mansergh's *South Africa, 1906-1961: The Price of Magnanimity* (1962), is concerned with the fact that Great Britain sacrificed the interests of the non-Europeans (and possibly the British colonial stock) in an effort to reconcile the Boers to British rule. All devote considerable attention to the native problem and the first two treat moderately the British Indian problem.

This book presents the British point of view but stresses public opinion as well as the role of officialdom. Moreover, it is concerned with all the episodes involving non-Europeans during the years from 1902 to 1914. There are chapters devoted to the Chinese coolie experiment, the Zulu disturbances, the native and integration, and the British Indian and integration. It is hoped that this study will make some contribution to the growing literature on the subject.

Considering the remoteness of South Africa, the question may be raised as to the completeness of information available to the British public. But facilities for keeping up with developments were ample. Modern communication advances in telegraph and wireless enabled history in the making to be relayed quickly across vast expanses of sea and land. The press subscribed to the daily dispatches sent out by international news agencies. Several newspapers had correspondents reporting on the spot. Journalists were engaged to cover special topics and events. British people from all walks of life toured South Africa to see things for themselves. Travel books recounting observations were published by the dozen. The antislavery and trade-union movements, for example, had branches or counterparts in South Africa to keep them informed. Ties of blood and friendship produced a steady ex-change of letters containing intimate confidences about colonial events. Scores of Blue Books were printed revealing the details of cor-respondence between officialdom and civil servants overseas. The constitutional device of the daily question-and-answer hour in the House of Commons, designed to inquire into the administration of laws, was a rich source of information.

The matter of terminology for white, black, and yellow peoples in South Africa requires clarification. The word Kaffir (Kafir) is used most often in the literature to identify the Bantu, although strictly speaking it meant the Xosa (and originally it was an Arabic word for an unbeliever). Many native tribes resent this nomenclature as imply-ing the white man's contempt for aborigines. After 1919, and certainly since World War II, the more acceptably dignified appellations of native and Bantu have been used. The latter term has been adopted for legislative and administrative purposes. Natives themselves prefer the term African as reflecting a more exalted nationalistic stature. No-tices designating separate facilities and amenities have employed the identifying labels of European and non-European. More recently, partly because of the refusal of American visitors to regard themselves as Europeans, the notices are being changed to read white and non-white. In the case of whites, the labels of English, British, or Anglo-Saxon as against Dutch or Boer (a Dutch word for farmer) are used to distinguish between the two European stocks. By the twentieth century, Boer and Afrikaner are interchangeable in the literature, al-though the Boer would insist today that Afrikaner represents an em-bracing South African culture which it is hoped would sweep Briton as well as Boer into its vortex. Afrikaans refers to the language of the Boers and, while its roots may be traced to the Dutch tongue, it has acquired a maturity of its own, especially for speaking. As for the Chinese and Indians who make up part of the scene, synonymous words of reference will be Asiatic and Oriental as encountered in the documentary records.

Some practices in style and footnote citations require clarification. The use of parentheses in titles of persons indicates that the individual acquired his title at a later date. Abbrevations have been used for several of the important documentary sources. The letters *P.P.* mean parliamentary (or sessional) papers and the attached letters, Cd., mean command paper (a report of statistical data, investigations, or recommendations) submitted to the House of Commons; *P.R.O.* stands for Public Record Office, and c.o. for Colonial Office papers and dispatches.

Library depositories in the United States possess a large amount of the printed material. British sources such as sessional papers, parliamentary debates, periodicals, and personal reminiscences can be found in any number of academic, public, and research institutions. The Library of Congress contains almost a complete file of the cosmopolitan English dailies for the years from 1902 to 1914. An excellent collection of religious and labor weeklies is available; but they are dispersed in various libraries and can be best located through reference to Gregory's *Union List of Serials*. The pamphlet literature that has trickled across the Atlantic Ocean is spotty and scattered. South African source materials, utilized to confirm the many statements and claims circulating in British circles, are mainly concentrated in the Boston, New York, and Washington, D.C., areas and comprise a very respectable lot.

The remainder of the material was gathered in London. The Public Record Office houses a variety of colonial documents open now for use through 1914. The sessional papers (Blue Books) can now be supplemented by a series of volumes entitled *African (South) Confidential Prints*. The latter are complementary, containing communications withheld from publication at the time because of the possible repercussions for imperial relations. The British Colonial Office papers and dispatches include both kinds of correspondence plus the minutes of the staff and numerous letters from societies and organizations. Excellent collections of the pamphlet literature are located in the libraries at the Commonwealth Relations Office and the Colonial Office. The Royal Commonwealth Society boasts a wealth of South African sources and extensive holdings in secondary works. The British Museum and its newspaper depository at Colindale filled in many a gap, especially as a reservoir of bibliographical aids. The London School of Economics and Political Science provided ready access to government publications and standard treatises. A debt of gratitude is owed to all for permission to utilize their facilities.

Acknowledgments are due many for making this study possible. The willingness of individuals in London acquainted with the South African scene to discuss events provided stimulation and insight. The assistance of my previous academic connection, the University of New Mexico, was extensive. A sabbatical leave in 1961 afforded time to pursue my research. The University Research Committee granted financial aid to make possible a return visit abroad during the summer of 1963. The University Library staff was indefatigable in matters of reference information and interlibrary loans.

The assistance of Arizona State University, whose faculty I have recently joined, is equally appreciated. A reduced teaching load gave me the leisure to write the final draft of the manuscript. Its Library staff located materials in other depositories. Its Research Committee financially assisted the typing of the final copy and provided funds for travel for editorial consultation. A major role was played by Roland Dickey, director of the University of New Mexico Press, and Gus Blaisdell, editor, in resolving many problems of writing and organization. The responsibility for the content– data, arrangement, interpretation—is, of course, my own.

BENJAMIN SACKS

Department of History
Arizona State University
Tempe, Arizona
May, 1966

1

Historical Introduction

THE NON-EUROPEANS

White settlements in South Africa date back to the middle
of the seventeenth century. The Dutch East India Company was in
need of a refreshment station for vessels engaged in trade with the
Far East. The Cape of Good Hope was conveniently situated for
taking on fresh water and provisions. Hence it was that a contingent of
Dutch farmers and their families were sent out to raise vegetables and
cattle. Subsequently, their numbers were augmented by new emigrants
including French Huguenots, Germans, and Scandinavians. Intermarriage brought assimilation with the dominant Dutch stock. At
the close of the eighteenth century, the European component would
appear to have been well over 25,000.[1]

An early group of nomads encountered were the Bushmen, a pigmy
race of aboriginals. They would seem to have been utterly devoid of
human sensibilities. Family ties and loyalties were tenuous and the
sick and aged were callously abandoned. They regarded the cattle of
the Europeans as fair prey, and with their poisoned arrows made life
precarious for the white settlers. The Boer policy was one of extermination against the Bushmen, driving them deep into the rocky fastness
of neighboring mountains or beyond into desert country. Despite the
fact that the Bushmen and their Stone Age weapons were no match
for the Boers, the conflict was frequently renewed in all parts of
European grazing land. By the close of the eighteenth century the
resistance had been broken. Thereafter, Bushmen retreated to pursue
a nomadic existence, often on the periphery of the white communities.
When caught pilfering or loitering, they were brought in to work on
Boer farms. Children of the Bushmen were prize catches as appren-

tices. Today descendants are still to be found in remote areas but their chief attraction is for students of primitive culture.

Hottentots were taller in stature and more advanced in their cultural habits than the Bushmen. They forged implements of copper and were a pastoral people tending domesticated cattle and sheep. They practiced polygamy, observed closer family ties, and spoke a click language. They too preyed upon the white settlements but fell easy victims to the Boers and their superior arms. The fate of the Hottentots was not extermination for, unlike the Bushmen, they submitted quickly to white domination. Left to shift for themselves, the Hottentots became detribalized hangers-on, bartering away their cattle for beads, tobacco, and liquor. The Boers reduced them to humble dependency, exploiting their labor to the point of servitude and describing them contemptuously as "dull, stupid, lazy, and stinking." At the close of the eighteenth century the Hottentots numbered about 18,000 although some estimates go much higher.

Reliance upon slaves as a source of labor was not a major factor until the close of the seventeenth century. The background would appear to have been a combination of circumstances. On the one hand, an expansion of the white communities created a demand for more labor; on the other, the decimation of the indigenous people as a result of war and smallpox reduced the available supply. The earliest contingent of slaves dates back to the 1660's and consisted of Malays transported as prisoners to expiate acts of crime. Only retention of the Moslem religion preserved the identity of their Oriental past and assured some degree of racial separateness. The greater number, purchased through Arab slave dealers, came from French Madagascar and Portuguese East Africa (Mozambique). The Boers treated them as chattels although manumission was possible. In terms of numbers, the estimates are 300 in 1687, 1,100 in 1708, and 30,000 in 1800.

The Cape Coloured constituted a unique element of the non-European population. Several generations of intermarriage and irregular physical relations between Bushmen, Hottentots, slaves, and Europeans sired this half-caste progeny. The white man's participation is attributed to extenuating circumstances. Sailors and soldiers were lonely sojourners separated for long periods from their families. Colonists, unaccompanied by their wives, spent months at a time in remote areas grazing famished flocks and herds. European males exceeded females in number. Some Cape Coloured bore a close resemblance to whites in facial features, pigmentation, and texture of hair. Many inherited the ability to grasp Western skills. But their role in society was still identified with that of the non-Europeans, and they were employed by the Boers in the most menial occupations. By the end of the eighteenth century the Boers were discountenancing marriage with non-Europeans to keep their own stock pure. They disavowed the nation of half-breeds whom they had helped to bring into existence as "bad blood" and the evil product of miscegenation. In later census reports, the Cape Coloured are carried under the heading of "mixed and other Coloured People."

The Bantu entered the picture in the eighteenth century. The name Bantu itself is a philological and perhaps ethnological abstraction, suggesting people with the black woolly hair and thick lips of the Negroid. Included in this great family are the Basuto, Zulu, Xosa, Bechuana, Matabele, Fingo, Swazi, and Mashona. Each tribe had a paramount chief and possessed a well-defined system of courts. They were cattle people, and agriculture was incidental in their economy. While the paramount chief controlled land rights, every family was entitled to share in pasturage. The Bantu would appear to have had their origin either in the Great Lakes or in the interior regions of the Gold Coast. The move south was in search of new grazing lands. Their arrival in the vicinity of the Great Fish, Keiskamma, and Kei rivers coincided with the movement of the Boers eastward from the Cape settlements. The Bantu were fearsome fighters, more so than any the Boers had previously encountered, although internecine rivalries weakened their fighting abilities. A series of bloody and destructive frontier wars followed. The Boer commando was fashioned to cope with the marauders. At the close of the eighteenth century the two foes were locked in a death struggle for land.

ADVENT OF THE BRITISH

British acquisition of Cape Colony served to focus attention upon the plight of non-Europeans. Great Britain had temporarily occupied the territory during the French Revolution as a result of Gallic domination of Holland and the fear that thereby British trade to India might be jeopardized. The resurgence of France under Napoleon

Bonaparte prompted a second occupation, confirmed on a permanent basis in 1815 at the Congress of Vienna.

What projected the status of native peoples quickly to the fore was the aggressive antislavery movement at home led by William Wilberforce and Thomas Clarkson. The humanitarian impulse demanded that the United Kingdom set for itself the goal of a free society in Cape Colony. The *Act of 1807*, which had abolished the slave trade in the British Empire, was forthwith extended to the newly acquired offspring. If the ultimate object was eradication of slavery root and branch, the first step was to cut off the source of supply. British colonial authorities lost no time in compliance. In 1816 they directed that a central registry be compiled of those already enslaved so that illicit shipments of Negroes might be more effectively prevented in the future. Henceforth any slaveholder who could not prove registration would be required to set free his chattel.

In the meantime, pending the day of emancipation, an effort was made to improve the lot of those enslaved. An ordinance was enacted in 1823 to ensure fair treatment for those on the registry. Fieldwork was forbidden on Sunday. Adequate clothing and wholesome food were to be available. Hours of work were set at ten in the winter and twelve in the summer and extra time at harvest was to be paid for. Children from three to ten years of age were allowed at least three days weekly for attendance at school. Nor could those below eight years of age be separated from their parents. A master guilty of ill-treatment (described euphemistically as domestic correction) was punishable by forced public sale of his abused slave. In 1826 the so-called *Nineteenth Ordinance* took the further steps of providing a guardian of slaves and permitting testimony by slaves against masters in criminal court.

The end came in 1833 when Great Britain abolished slavery throughout the Empire with compensation for owners. In Cape Colony it meant freedom for the 39,000 slaves on the register at the time. A four-year period of apprenticeship was set in order for owners to adjust themselves to a free-labor economy.

The deteriorative status of the Hottentots posed a danger to the principle of a free society, especially with the curtailment of slave labor. British missionaries, led by the formidable Congregational clergyman, Dr. John Philip, set up stations or institutions on public land to provide Hottentots with a home and training in agriculture and crafts. But it was equally imperative to bring to the attention of the authorities the growing nature of servitude for those dependent upon the white settlers. The Dutch constabulary were pictured as the compliant agents of ruthless Boer farmers. A pass system had been devised to limit the movement of Hottentots, including the necessity to get permission from one's employer to seek another job. Unduly long periods of apprenticeship were imposed upon children, thus assuring a source of cheap labor and thereby binding parents to remain at work alongside their offspring. Courts accepted lengthy oral contracts upon the word of an employer. Even lengthier written contracts were recognized, regardless of the illiterate worker's understanding when he signed. To top all, harsh disciplinary punishments were meted out at the request of Boer masters.

As early as 1809, the second Earl of Caledon, Governor of Cape Colony, issued a code (sometimes called the Magna Charta of the Hottentots) to regulate the use of their labor. It required registration of contracts enduring for more than one month, specified regular payment of wages, and outlawed claims to personal services on the ground of debts owed. Magistrates were dispatched to enforce these conditions. What weakened their effectiveness was the problem of vagrancy. The Hottentot must have a domicile and could not leave it without a certificate until a new master spoke for him. In short, the pass system checked the opportunity of Hottentots to negotiate freely with Boer farmers. Nevertheless, the magistrates proceeded with their responsibility, summoning the proud and patriarchal Boers to answer for misconduct toward servants. The Black Circuit of 1812 was especially famous and brought a number of indictments with penalties. The aftermath was a resentful and brooding Boer community. When one of the farmers was killed resisting arrest, Slachter's Nek Rebellion of 1815 followed. Five Boers were publicly hanged for defying British authority.

Missionaries pressed the plight of the Hottentots relentlessly and, in 1828, procured the passage of the *Fiftieth Ordinance* sweeping away the tentacles of forced labor. Pass laws were repealed. The period of apprenticeship was reduced, to be contracted for by parents instead of being automatic because a family was on the premises. Nor could apprenticeship be indefinite. A limitation of seven years was set, not to

extend beyond the age of sixteen for girls and eighteen for boys nor
beyond the expiration of their parents' contract. Maximum terms for
oral and written contracts were pared, ranging from one month, if a
private agreement, to twelve months, if drawn up in the presence of a
clerk or justice of peace. The right accorded Hottentots to purchase
land in Cape Colony signified their legal status as free individuals in
the European community. Subsequently, the disallowance of a new
pass law in 1834, however much it might have been needed to cope
with an excess of vagrancy, reaffirmed the emancipation of the Hottentots. Even the *Master and Servant Acts* (1842 and 1856), extending
the terms of oral and written contracts to one and three years respectively, did not violate the essential fact of free status, for they applied
to whites as well as to blacks.

British authorities, prodded by Dr. Philip, intervened in the clashes
between Boer and Bantu as well. A buffer area (constantly shifting its
boundaries) was designated on the eastern frontier. Both were forbidden entrance into this neutral zone. The Boers complained that they
were denied the right to take suitable measures of reprisal against the
Bantu for theft of their cattle, massacre of their families, and destruction of their homes. Baron Glenelg, Secretary of State for the Colonies,
had little sympathy for the Boer point of view, considering that the
Bantu had been left with little land for their own survival. Writing in
1835, he observed that "in the conduct which [had been] pursued towards the Kaffir nation by the Colonists . . . through a long series of
years, the Kaffirs had an ample justification of the war into which
they rushed."[2]

Admittedly, the Great Trek of 1836 involved more than a protest
against British meddling in Boer relations with non-Europeans. Democratic institutions were replaced by a centralized administration. The
civil service was staffed from the ranks of the Anglo-Saxon stock to
the exclusion of the Boers. English common law was substituted for
the Dutch legal system, and the English language designated as the
medium of the courts. The Boers considered the monetary compensation for the loss of their slaves inadequate. The award had been far
below the assessed valuation and the need for cash to hire labor compelled the liquidation of bonds on the local stock market at a considerable loss. But, by and large, the explosive factor was the refusal of

British authorities to acquiesce in the Boer thesis that the native had been meant to be the servant of the white man. Peter Retief, intrepid Boer leader, stated bluntly the motivation which drove his people into the interior to escape British jurisdiction:

> We are resolved . . . that we will uphold the just principles of liberty; but whilst we will take care that no one shall be held in a state of slavery, it is our determination to maintain such regulations as may suppress crime and preserve proper relations between master and servant.[3]

The Great Trek lasted from 1836 to 1843 and embraced more than 12,000 people. It has been likened to the wandering of the Children of Israel, the voyage of the Pilgrim Fathers, the opening of the American West, and the Mormon migration to the Rockies. The trail led beyond the Orange and Vaal rivers and across the passes of the Drakensburg Mountains. Apart from the adversities of nature, the struggle against ambush by hostile Bantu reached heroic proportions. Equally troublesome were the missionaries who did not intend that the Boers should have a free hand with natives in their new habitat. Sources of information indicated that Boer farmers were up to their old tricks of ensnaring native labor. Traffic in indentured apprentices and blackbirding children seemed to be the order of the day. The home government was reminded of the Anglo-Saxon dedication to humanitarian principles. The result was successive proclamations of the Queen's sovereignty over Natal in 1843 and over Orange Free State and the Transvaal in 1848. The title of High Commissioner was bestowed upon the Governor of Cape Colony to administer these outlying districts.

Shortly, however, Great Britain restored independence to Orange Free State and the Transvaal (but not to Natal because of its greater strategic value). The decision was prompted by the prospect of patrolling a vast hinterland in the face of already extensive imperial obligations over the surface of the earth. So, in 1852, by the *Sand River Convention*, the South African Republic (Transvaal) was recognized as a sovereign state and, in 1854, by the *Bloemfontein Convention*, Orange Free State was accorded the same status. A major condition called for no slavery or traffic in slaves. An excellent explanation of this about-face action by Great Britain is contained in a letter which Henry Labouchere (Baron Taunton), Secretary of State for the Colonies, wrote in July 1858 to Queen Victoria:

> It is certainly true . . . that the existence of these Free States may complicate our relations with the Kaffirs, and possibly be a source of danger to the security of British dominion in South Africa. But the latter danger seems very remote. They possess no portion of the sea coast, and are engaged in a constant struggle with the barbarous tribes in their neighborhood.
>
> To retain and protect these territories would have involved an immense expenditure and have been attended with great difficulties. Besides, the same question would have speedily recurred, as these emigrant Boers would soon have gone further into the interior and again have asserted their independence.[4]

BELEAGUERED NON-EUROPEANS

British policy in Cape Colony reflected the new blueprint to bestow self-government upon all white offspring. But the political status of non-Europeans left much to be desired. True, the receipt of representative government in 1853 was accompanied (at British insistence) by a liberal franchise granted to adult males regardless of color who possessed property valued at £25 or earned £50 annually in wages or £25 with keep. Nor is there much to cavil with in the measure of 1887 (responsible government had been granted in 1872), stating that no person could be registered as a voter if he shared in tribal occupation of lands or buildings. However, an amendment in 1892, raising the property requirement to £75, eliminating the income bracket of £25 with keep, and adding an educational test of writing out one's name, address, and occupation put a different complexion on matters. The intent was to meet the threat of overwhelming numbers of Bantu whose lands had been incorporated into Cape Colony. As colonial whites saw it, the alternative could be an ultimate swamping of the electorate by a native registration.

The receipt of representative government in Natal in 1856 was also accompanied by a liberal franchise. Adult males regardless of color qualified who possessed property worth £50 or rented property for £10 annually or resided for three years in a district and had a yearly income of £96. But in 1865 a series of amendments revealed a growing animus toward political rights for non-Europeans. These included a residential provision of twelve years, exemption from native law for seven years, an educational test, and a recommendation of three European electors prior to being placed on the voting register. When Natal received responsible government in 1893 (delayed for a long time partly because of an unsatisfactory native policy), the voting statistics showed how effectively the native had been eliminated: 99 per cent of adult white males, 50 Cape Coloured, 6 natives. And the fact to be pondered was that in Natal, where British settlers greatly outnumbered Boers, one would have assumed a resounding triumph for the Anglo-Saxon tradition of human dignity.

Nor did the juridical freedom possessed by non-Europeans in Cape Colony and Natal stimulate any improvement in their social status. For most, the story became that of hangers-on and slum dwellers on fringes of the European settlements. Only some Cape Coloured were able to penetrate into the semiskilled and professional classes, and then mainly in Cape Colony. No doubt their longer contact with Western civilization and their proficiency in the use of the Dutch and English languages were assets. In Natal the requirement in the grant of responsible government that an annual sum of £10,000 be appropriated for the welfare of natives and the designation of the governor as paramount chief effected little. As Professor William Miller Macmillan of the University of Witwatersrand remarks, the violence of the controversy which preceded their de jure liberation caused a reaction among the colonists, leaving the economic condition of non-Europeans in neglect.[5]

The Bantu in particular found themselves subject to a host of disabilities. They had to carry an identification pass, observe curfew laws, and submit to separate (and inferior) amenities and travel facilities. Their economic options were to live in such locations as British intervention had salvaged for them, or to work for European farmers under conditions not far removed from servitude, or to seek menial jobs in the towns. An especially keen analysis was written in January 1873 by Sir Anthony Musgrave, Lieutenant Governor of Natal and quoted verbatim by Cornelius de Kieweit, an American student of the South African scene:

It is obvious to the casual observer that none of the most common domestic occupations of life could proceed among the European population for a day without the assistance of Kafirs. The contrast in this respect between South Africa and British North America is very striking to one who has the opportunity to compare the two places. In North America the population is obliged in all things to be self reliant; they have no servile race to help them. Here, the Europeans of whatever rank of life, are served by Kafirs; who cook for them, wash for them, wait upon them, act as nurse maids for their children; in short do all the manifold services required by those who do little or nothing for themselves. A mechanic going to execute any little job of work; it may be a Blacksmith or a Carpenter, will have one or two Kafirs to carry his tools for him and generally to render him assistance. . . .[6]

Whether the *Glen Grey Act* passed by Cape Colony in 1894 would point the way to a better future for non-Europeans remained to be seen. The idea was to mark off a native district where natives could receive instruction in Western culture without having to meet the strangling competition of the white man.* Farming would be on the basis of individual tenure. Local self-government in such matters as roads, schools, and sanitation would provide excellent training in democracy. The dubious feature related to a special 10s. tax imposed upon any native not in possession of a land allocation or not in service beyond the district boundary for at least three months in the preceding year. Since farming plots were not sufficient to go around, the danger of a pseudosegregation policy subservient to the labor needs of the white community was very real.** At any rate, the act was implemented and applied in the Transkeian Territories where perhaps 800,000 natives lived at the time.

The plight of non-Europeans was worse in the two Dutch Republics of Orange Free State and the Transvaal. It is true that both adhered to the stipulation (incorporated in the restoration of their

*Sir Theophilus Shepstone, native administrator, and his son Henrique promoted the idea of a native affairs department for Natal and urged plans for large reserves to be set aside.

**If the reputed aim was to assure cheap labor for the Kimberley diamond mines, few natives were ever able to satisfy their many cash needs without seeking work in the white community. The provision came to be a nuisance to enforce on the few occasions necessary and was repealed in 1905.

independence in the 1850's) of no practices partaking of slavery. Nor could it be said that this status had been subsequently impaired in connection with developments in the Transvaal. Reannexed by Great Britain in 1877, on the ground that Boer embroilment in native wars imperiled the security of South Africa, the independence of the Transvaal was acknowledged for a second time in 1881 after the British defeat at Majuba Hill. Both the *Pretoria Convention of 1881* and the *London Convention of 1884* (a revision of the former omitting the words "British suzerainty" and eliminating the Crown's veto over native legislation) reaffirmed the prohibition against slavery. Indeed, further guarantees were inserted that allowed natives to acquire land (to be held in trust by a native location commission) and granted freedom of movement consistent with the maintenance of public order and pass laws.

However, as the spirit of native administration revealed itself, the non-Europeans became second-class citizens. They remained outside the circle of burghers and were excluded from all skilled work. Pass laws operated severely and justice was hard to obtain against a white man in court. Separate amenities of an inferior quality were marked off for non-Europeans. European speculators and Dutch farmers encroached steadily upon native locations. In time a vicious cycle set in: insufficient acreage and backward methods of cultivation in the locations led to overcrowded conditions and exhaustion of the soil. Given these conditions, coupled with taxes to be paid in cash, the native had no alternative but to seek work in the white community at whatever terms were offered. Extremely low wages were justified on the basis of the simple wants of the natives. While in London during 1876 to discuss colonial matters with the fourth Earl of Carnarvon, Secretary of State for the Colonies, Jan Hendrik Brand, President of Orange Free State, told him that "we have no native question; we have settled that already. The whites are to the natives as two to one."[7]

The question arises as to why Great Britain did not take a more active part in combating the drift of South Africa away from the Anglo-Saxon tradition of a free society. Perhaps the answer reposed in the desire for political amalgamation of the four white communities as a better approach to the exploitation of the economic and military potential of the subcontinent. Past experiences had shown

how resentful the colonists were on the native question and to raise
the issue aggressively could ruin the imperial goal. Moreover, hope
was entertained that union would be a better springboard from which
to promote justice for the native and to bring out the finer sensibilities of colonial whites. Thus, at a cabinet meeting in 1874, Lord
Carnarvon listed forcefully the advantages of federation:

> European immigration and capital flow slowly into countries under
> small and isolated Governments whose financial solvency is questionable,
> and where there is no adequate security for property and no confidence in
> prudent legislation. Federation would greatly improve and cheapen the
> administration of affairs in almost every branch and greatly lessen the
> probability of a demand for aid in the shape of Imperial money or troops.
> But the most immediately urgent reason for general union is the . . .
> formidable character of the native question, and the [need for a] uniform,
> wise and strong policy in dealing with it. . . . The policy of establishing
> through Confederation a great South African dominion is indeed recom-
> mended by other considerations connected with the advance of civiliza-
> tion in Africa and the general interests of the Empire; but it is in respect
> of its influence on the solution of the native question that the Confedera-
> tion has become a matter of immediate concern to Parliament and the
> United Kingdom.[8]

What rendered the chances of federation increasingly remote were
territorial rivalries between Great Britain and the Dutch Republics.
Orange Free State was offended by what it described as the mischievous intervention of Great Britain to circumscribe its rightful claims
to adjacent lands. Annexation of Basutoland was sought in retaliation
for the long and expensive wars incurred by the raids of the great
chieftain Moshesh. When the tide turned against him in his quest
for more land to feed his people, Moshesh appealed to Great Britain.
The Imperial State intervened in 1868 and accepted jurisdiction over
Basutoland, turning over administrative responsibility to Cape Colony.
The latter found the cost of policing too burdensome and in 1884
transferred custody back to the mother country. Basutoland received
the status of a protectorate. But to Orange Free State it was a standing reminder of blunted aspirations.

A second episode related to Griqualand West and centered about the discovery of diamond mines in the 1860's. Orange Free State sought to incorporate this valuable mineral deposit into its domains. Pressure from those staking out claims, largely British adventurers, stirred the British Colonial Office to action. In 1871 a Liberal government headed by William Ewart Gladstone annexed the territory, turning it over in 1880 to Cape Colony. So the Kimberley diamond mines, named after the incumbent Secretary of State for the Colonies, were likewise lost to Orange Free State.

The Transvaal was similarly offended by British moves to prevent its legitimate expansion (let alone its temporary loss of sovereignty from 1877 to 1881). Granted that the Portuguese diplomatic victory in 1875 to gain possession of Delagoa Bay did not preclude the Transvaal from negotiating an agreement for the construction of a railway to the harbor of Lourenço Marques. But the maneuvers of Great Britain to force a hasty submission of the dispute to arbitration had closed the door to the dream of the Transvaal for an outlet of its own to the sea. Expansion to the north was also denied when the British government entered into an agreement with the tribes of Matabeleland that promised no cession of land without the prior sanction of Great Britain. To add insult to injury, the British South Africa Company, headed by Cecil Rhodes, already wealthy by virtue of his diamond mines ventures, was given a charter to develop the resources of Matabeleland. Finally, any hope of reaching the sea at Tongaland to the south of Delagoa Bay was dashed when Great Britain would only allow the Transvaal to administer Swaziland, but not to annex it.

If these vigorous demonstrations of British paramountcy in diplomatic duels with the Dutch Republics put a damper upon the chances for a South African union, a corollary effect was an increasing hesitancy on the part of the British to intervene in native matters. Great Britain did not give up hope for an eventual union and trusted that the merits of federation would override the irritations of transitory territorial squabbles. But to press the case of the native too strongly—either in its own self-governing Cape Colony and Natal or in the adjacent independent states of Orange Free State and the Transvaal—ran counter to the deep convictions of the white settlers. So, in the closing decades of the nineteenth century, nothing of moment could be done for the native. As Professor Colin Rhys Lovell of the University of Southern California puts it, frontier apartheid was permitted to crystallize without much resistance on the part of Great Britain.[9]

THE BRITISH INDIAN

The British Indian constituted a belated addition to the non-European population of South Africa. The story had its genesis in the 1860's when indentured Indian coolies were brought to Natal to work on sugar plantations, because the Zulus were difficult to recruit, undependable, and inefficient. The British Colonial Office itself was a partner in the resort to Indian coolies, suggesting the success of similar experiments elsewhere in the Empire. The original agreement with Indian authorities called for an indenture of three years. If the coolie wished to stay as a free person, he must reindenture for a fourth year. Later the coolie was offered a further reward—if he worked on the sugar plantations for five years more—either a free passage home or the equivalent of its value in public land. Many ex-indentured coolies chose to remain and entered other occupations—coal mines, railways, hotels. A number of free Indians came over to provide professional services for their lower-class compatriots—doctors, lawyers, priests, traders.[10]

European shopkeepers soon stirred trouble, complaining that Indian hawkers took trade away from them. The lower standards of living endurable among Asiatics was assigned as the reason for their devastating competition. Although opposed by planters needing coolie labor, a series of measures followed by which Natal hoped to force the ex-indentured and free Indians to return to their homeland. In 1895 a law decreed that every Indian coolie over sixteen years of age who failed to reindenture would be subject to an annual tax of £3, a heavy financial burden indeed. In 1896 a law deprived free Indians of the vote on the ground that descendants of countries lacking representative institutions based on a parliamentary franchise (as was the case in India) did not meet the requirements for Natal citizenship. In 1897 a law denied licenses to trade unless accounts could be kept in English. Also in 1897, a law defined a prohibited immigrant to include "any person who, when asked to do so by an officer appointed under this

Act, shall fail to himself write out and sign in the characters of any language of Europe an application." Despite these restrictive measures the numbers of Indian residents continued to mount, totaling 110,000 in 1899 apportioned thus: 40,000 indentured, 60,000 ex-indentured, 10,000 free immigrants.

Cape Colony was only moderately affected by the influx of British Indians. An estimated 2,500, and mostly merchants, did make their way to its territory. While they were permitted to engage in trade and to own fixed property, indications were not wanting that trouble was ahead. Their price cutting caused friction and in many municipalities efforts were made to revoke their licenses. Indian hawkers by the score were denied renewals. Equally as frustrating was a law requiring the payment of £1 for reentry after each visit outside and the duration of absence could not be longer than one year. This growing animosity had gone so far in the city of East London as to cause the enactment of anti-Indian bylaws. Use of sidewalks and benches in public parks were prohibited. Passes were required after dark. Special sections in tram cars were designated.

No less inhospitable were the two Dutch Republics. Scarcely a dozen Indians had opened shops in Orange Free State in the 1880's when the European settlers started a powerful agitation. The Volksraad passed a stringent law expelling all Indian traders at a nominal compensation which resulted in an estimated loss of £9,000 to these harassed merchants. Henceforth their numbers would be restricted to a handful allowed to engage as hotel waiters, cooks, and domestic servants. Nor was it intended to make their lot a happy one. In 1890 a ban was imposed upon their right to hold fixed property or to become merchants and farmers. In 1899 the immigration laws were tightened: as in Natal in 1897, the category of prohibited persons was made to include those persons who failed to write out and sign in the characters of any European language the application form set forth. The obvious result was revealed in the *Census of 1904* which recorded only two hundred fifty-three Asiatics in Orange Free State.

The Transvaal was in easy proximity to Natal and so got the overflow, thus becoming a second area of British Indian concentration in South Africa. They entered as free individuals and engaged in trade. Even earlier than in Natal the white shopkeepers began to complain of their unfair competition. But for President Paul Kruger to do something it was necessary to deal with Great Britain because Article XIV of the *London Convention of 1884* stated that "all persons other than a native had to be allowed full right of movement, residence, and trade with the Transvaal." When the British government agreed to accept reasonable measures with the right to interpret its own assent, Kruger felt that the road was clear to restrictive legislation. *Law No. 3 of 1885* followed, excluding Asiatics from the franchise, exacting a compulsory registration fee of £3, decreeing separate locations for residence (albeit on sanitary grounds), and forbidding acquisition of fixed property outside locations. A court decision later permitted Kruger to confine Asiatic trading to specified locations.

Great Britain directed its severest strictures against Natal and the Transvaal. Pressure was strong from the India Office, for the animosity aroused against the Imperial State in that treasured possession must be pacified. While the British Colonial Office toned down some of the more extreme proposals against British Indians in Natal, the theory of self-government made it hesitant to exercise the power of disallowance. More vigorous were the protests lodged against violations of a gentleman's agreement between the Transvaal and Great Britain. Melius de Villiers, Chief Justice of Orange Free State, was selected as arbitrator to determine whether *Law No. 3 of 1885* did breach the *London Convention of 1884* and he interpreted the provisions as applying only to Europeans.[11] However, the British government continued to maintain diplomatic pressure on behalf of Indian residents in the Transvaal. What eased the situation was the halfhearted enforcement of these humiliating conditions, mainly because Kruger did not care to add to his many other difficulties with Great Britain. The result was that the Indian population kept increasing—an estimated total of 13,000 on the eve of the Boer War.

The British Indians in South Africa did not let matters rest thus. Their champion was Mahatma Gandhi, a London-trained lawyer who had come out in 1893 to represent a client in a commercial transaction. The indignities to which he was subjected on the railways and at hotels influenced him to remain and defend the rights of his countrymen. Petitions and telegrams flowed in a steady stream to the British Colonial Office protesting infringements of their status as British subjects. When Alfred Milner (baronet in 1901 and viscount in 1902) arrived in 1897 as Governor of Cape Colony and High Commissioner, the issue had reached an acute stage. His impression was that "we shall have to bend to the blast, if it is not to break us."[12] The only possible course seemed to be to intervene in specific cases of harsh treatment. Representations were frequent, especially to the Transvaal over its segregation laws and its denial of trading licenses to Indians.[13] Indeed, the British government made the plight of Indians a casus belli against the Transvaal. The fifth Marquess of Lansdowne, Secretary of State for Foreign Affairs, stated this fact frankly at Sheffield, when speaking of the negotiations leading up to the Boer War:

> I do not know that anything fills me with more indignation than its treatment of these Indians. And the harm is not confined to the sufferers on the spot, for what do you imagine would be the effect produced in India when these poor people return to their country to report to their friends that the Government of the Empress, so mighty and irresistible in India, with its population of 300,000,000 is powerless to secure redress at the hands of a small South African State.[14]

THE BOER WAR IN BRITISH CIRCLES

The immediate roots of the Boer War are to be traced to the discovery of gold along the Witwatersrand in 1886. The gold mining industry expanded rapidly and thousands of Uitlanders—Americans, Australians, Cornishmen, Englishmen, Scotsmen—flocked to the land of glittering promise. If the Transvaal at first welcomed the boom of a revived economy and a replenished treasury, the Boers soon had second thoughts. The phenomenal rise of Johannesburg dwarfing Pretoria and presaging the triumph of Anglo-Saxon culture disturbed Kruger. Uitlanders would outnumber Boers and achieve political predominance. The consequence was a series of amendments to the franchise laws in the 1890's, culminating in a fourteen-year residential requirement. In addition, the gold mining companies were subject to harassments—an extortionate dynamite monopoly, high taxes, excessive living costs, and native labor shortages partly owing to an uncontrolled liquor traffic. Kruger also sought closer connections with Germany, favoring capital and merchants from that country in the development of railways and commerce.

The situation worsened with the Jameson Raid of 1896. This effort to achieve a redress of grievances by physical force was a fiasco. Kruger suppressed it easily and, with great relish, turned the captured leaders over to Great Britain for punishment. More importantly, Kruger used the threatened coup as justification for further repressive measures. Ordinances were enacted calling for expulsion of persons dangerous to the public peace, imposing restrictions upon open-air meetings and the press, and specifying Dutch as the language in the schools. Great Britain interceded in behalf of Uitlander (and mineowner). Protracted negotiations between Lord Milner and Kruger were conducted in a tense atmosphere during the summer of 1899. Endless proposals were exchanged. The treatment of non-Europeans was raised although not as forcefully as the case of the aggrieved whites. A rupture came in September when the diplomatic parleys collapsed amidst ominous troop movements by both sides. The outbreak of war in October found the Transvaal joined by Orange Free State which saw its own future equally threatened.

The Conservative government in London affirmed that the salvation of human rights in South Africa could only be secured by an end to Boer independence. It was a just war which sought to liberate fellow countrymen oppressed by a corrupt Dutch oligarchy. The third Marquess of Salisbury, Prime Minister, dissolved the House of Commons, although it had two years more to run, and appealed to the electorate for an endorsement of the war against the Boers. The Khaki Election of October 1900 gave the Conservatives a sweeping victory, 402 seats to 189 for the Liberals.

Conservative organs manifested patriotic enthusiasm and were united in lending support to the prosecution of the war. The *Daily Mail*, brought out in 1896 by Sir Alfred Charles William Harmsworth (Viscount Northcliffe), as the first of the halfpenny newspapers, led the way as a trumpeter of imperialism. *The Times* was under the editorship of George Earl Buckle who served later as a coauthor of a standard biography of Benjamin Disraeli (Earl of Beaconsfield), illustrious in the annals of the Conservative party. Originally a Liberal supporter, the *Daily Telegraph* abandoned that affiliation after the Irish Home Rule proposals of Gladstone. The *Morning Post* had been a high Tory newspaper for over a century and of excellent literary quality. The *Standard* was well known for its staunch adherence to Church, Crown, House of Lords, and the City. The *Pall Mall Gazette* was an evening newspaper, ending its connection with the Liberals in 1892 when purchased by William Waldorf Astor of the wealthy American family.

The Liberal party was bitterly divided over the morality of the Boer War. The *Annual Register* noted that (in the voting divisions related to the prosecution of the military campaigns) sixty-two Liberals supported and sixty-eight Liberals opposed the measures submitted. In addition, it estimated some thirty Liberals as refusing to commit themselves and still another twenty-seven Liberals as now joining one side and then another side.[15]

Sir Henry Campbell-Bannerman, titular leader of His Majesty's Opposition, led the pro-Boer wing in Parliament. Others included Sir William Venables Harcourt, arch foe of imperialism, John Morley (Viscount), distinguished scholar, David Lloyd George, fiery Welsh pacifist, and Sir Wilfrid Lawson, patriarch of Puritan Radicalism. They labeled the conflict a manifestation of jingoism and for the benefit of mineowners and financiers. Their official mouthpiece was the *Daily News*, purchased in 1901 and promptly staffed with personnel of their own thinking. The *Manchester Guardian*, published by Charles Prestwich Scott, was outspoken against British diplomacy leading up to the outbreak of war. If the *Westminster Gazette*, an evening newspaper under the editorship of John Alfred Spender, took a middle-of-the-road position, its sympathy lay with the Boers. However, as the war progressed, the pro-Boer Liberals turned their attention more to the future, feeling that the war once begun should be seen through to victory. The vital business was to assure that the climate of triumph would be such as to reconcile the Boers to life under the Union Jack.

The fifth Earl of Rosebery, for a time successor to Gladstone as titular head of the Liberal party, led a wing supporting the British fight against the Boers. Lord Rosebery had been part of a group who had won the Liberal party over to a more responsive position on imperialism as a worthy instrument to spread civilization. He was ably seconded in his defense of the Boer War by Herbert Henry Asquith (Earl of Oxford and Asquith), Sir Henry Fowler (Viscount of Wolverhampton), Sir Edward Grey (Viscount of Fallodon), and Richard Burdon Haldane (Viscount of Cloan). Their thesis was that no compromise could halt the reactionary policy of Kruger, who must bear the larger share of guilt. The *Daily Chronicle* constituted the major exponent of their views, after Henry William Massingham resigned as editor, when the ownership decreed loyal cooperation in the war effort. However, the Conservative government did not escape criticism at the hands of this pro-imperialist Liberal group. It was censured for failing to be militarily prepared in the face of an obviously inevitable conflict.

The Labour movement for the most part opposed the Boer War. To be sure, the Trades Union Congress, after passing a pro-Boer resolution in 1900 "by a small majority," refused to adopt a similar statement in 1901 by a large majority of 724,000 to 330,000.[16] But the Labour Representation Committee, formed in 1899 to pursue independent political action for social reform as the immediate goal and socialism as the ultimate goal, termed the conflict one of predatory capitalism. The motion adopted at the first annual conference, held in February 1901, pronounced the war "to be mainly due to the corrupt agitation of the Transvaal mineowners, having for its object the acquisition of monopolies and a cheap supply of coloured and European labour." A truce to hostilities was urged pending submission of the issues to arbitration under the articles of *The Hague Convention of 1899*.[17]

The socialist movement also opposed the Boer War. *Justice*, weekly organ of the Social Democratic Federation, Marxian in its collectivist approach and headed by Henry Mayers Hyndman, voiced displeasure at the diplomacy leading up to the outbreak of war. The *Clarion*, a popular socialist weekly edited by Robert Blatchford, denounced British arrogance in seeking to crush the two small Dutch Republics. The Independent Labour Party, counting among its spokesmen J. Keir Hardie, J. Ramsay MacDonald, and Philip Snowden, stated its case against the war in the *Independent Labour Party News*, a monthly issue, and the *Labour Leader*, a weekly organ. MacDonald was particularly militant, declaring that "I am against the war. I think it deplorable. I do not believe in the maxim 'my country right or wrong' but 'my country.' "[18] This so-called unpatriotic and pacifist stand cost him whatever chance he might have had to win Leicester during the Khaki Election of 1900.

Only the Fabian Society, exponent of an evolutionary socialism stressing practical applications in the municipal arena, took a different stand. At first its leaders, among whom were Sidney and Beatrice Webb, George Bernard Shaw, and H. G. Wells, preferred that the organization avoid embroilment in the matter.[19] Later, however, a special pamphlet was written by Shaw, entitled *Fabianism and the Empire*, which defended the merits of imperialism and the righteousness of the Boer War.[20] MacDonald resigned his membership in the society, including a seat on its executive. Years later, in 1916, when reviewing *The History of the Fabian Society* by Edward R. Pease, secretary of the society, MacDonald commented fully on his reasons:

> I left when the Society declared that the aggressive war in South Africa did not concern it. . . . A Socialist society which for reasons of self-preservation condones the South African War might be admirable for drafting gas and water programs, but it was evidently quite useless for educating the people into independence of thought and strength of judgment without which gas and water are of no importance.
> . . . Then came their tract on Imperialism defending it—A Great Power was bound to govern it in the interests of civilization and 'such mighty forces as gold mines' should not be left to the control of 'small communities of frontiersmen.' And so on—Never has a militarist and exploiting international capitalism received such a brilliant defence. . . .[21]

AN IMPERIAL QUANDARY

The military details of the Boer War form no part of this study. The Boers, led by Commandant-General Louis Botha and General Jan Christiaan Smuts, put up a courageous struggle. But, eventually, superior British numbers, the use of concentration camps for the families of the enemy, and barbed wire entanglements overcame the guerrilla tactics of the Boers. After three years of desperate fighting, peace was concluded on May 31, 1902 at Vereeniging. The astonishing thing about the treaty is the spirit of moderation in the terms given the Boers. Assuredly, Orange Free State and the Transvaal had to acknowledge British sovereignty. No doubt too the Boers would say that the havoc wrought during the war should be the entire financial responsibility of Great Britain. Nevertheless, the Imperial State could not be described as otherwise than generous in accepting the obligation of repatriating the Boers and their families from concentration camps and of rehabilitating their devastated farms. Moreover, the Imperial State accorded the use of the Dutch language in schools where desired and in courts of law when vital for the effective dispensation of justice. Furthermore, Great Britain promised that at the earliest possible date military rule would be replaced by civil government. Then, as soon as circumstances permitted, representative institutions leading to self-government would be granted. The reason for all this lenient treatment may be sought in Great Britain's hope that a reconciled Boer population would bring the desired political federation of South Africa.

What appears most disconcerting is the decision at Vereeniging to hold over the matter of a native franchise until responsible government. Not only had Lord Milner made the lot of natives in the Transvaal the subject of complaints before the war (and in the diplomacy leading to the outbreak of the war), but Joseph Chamberlain, Secretary of State for the Colonies, had indicated a determination to protect their interests during an early and abortive attempt at peace negotiations in 1901. On February 27, preliminary to a meeting the next day between the two military leaders, Horatio Herbert Kitchener (first Earl) and Botha, Chamberlain wrote to Lord Milner thus:

> Botha must not be allowed to suppose that there will be absolutely no change as to the status of natives, but we do not contemplate making them masters of the whites. He might be referred to the laws of Cape Colony and Natal which have not endangered the status or interests of whites.[22]

After the two generals had met on February 28 at Middleburg, there followed an exchange of views between Chamberlain and Lord Milner on the exact terms of peace to be offered the Boers. While Botha would be accommodated in his desire for the colonial whites to be protected from an overwhelming number of native voters, legal equality for all men would be affirmed. Chamberlain observed "that we cannot consent to purchase a shameful peace by leaving the coloured population in the position in which they stood before the war with not even the ordinary civil rights which the Government of the Cape Colony has long conceded them." Lord Milner preferred the word "Kaffirs" to "coloured population" because "it is the aboriginal native of whom Botha is afraid" whereas "I do not see why respectable coloured persons, who are a small number, should be placed under any disadvantage at all." As finally authorized, the terms included the statement that no "franchise to Kaffirs" would be given "before representative Government . . . and if then given it will be so limited as to secure the just predominance of the white race." Moreover, it was stipulated that the "legal position of coloured persons would be similar to that which they held in Cape Colony." Chamberlain would appear to have used the words "Kaffirs" and "coloured persons" interchangeably.[23]

What then is the explanation (a year later in the *Treaty of Vereeniging*) for omitting any guarantee of legal rights to natives and deferring a native franchise until after the grant of responsible government? Perhaps the answer is to be found in a minute of the Natal cabinet, dated March 28, 1901, addressed to Lord Milner. The latter had requested both Cape Colony and Natal to present a statement of their views on the future peace settlement. As loyal participants during the military ordeal, they merited a share in the councils of the Imperial State. The most significant passages were in the Natal response, stressing that natives should not be given any political rights in the two enemy states pending the latter's rehabilitation. To do otherwise would alienate Briton and Boer colonials alike, provoke racial bitterness, and make good government difficult. The assumption in the mother country that colonists were unjust and harsh to the native had worked great harm in relations between the two white stocks. At the moment, the natives' greatest need was to be taught habits of steady industry.[24]

The views of the Natal government served to emphasize the dilemma confronting the Imperial State. The question of non-Europeans had to be considered in the light of imperial interests in South Africa. It was important to have the support of the colonists and they insisted upon white supremacy. The fact that the predominant British stock in Natal held the same convictions as the Boers meant that the mother country would be alone in any crusade for equality between white and black. Lord Milner pointed out this significant fact as far back as November 18, 1897, in a letter to Asquith. The latter had enunciated in a political speech at Wormit, in Fifeshire, two principles of action in South Africa: 1) restoration of good relations between Dutch and English colonials and 2) protection of natives against oppression and wrong.[25] Lord Milner argued that the Liberal party failed to realize the irreconcilability of the two objectives. His key sentence was "that you might indeed unite English and Dutch by protecting the black man, but you would unite them against yourself [Great Britain]. . . . There is the whole crux of the South African position."[26]

The Liberal party remained entrapped between doctrinal adherence to democratic institutions for white offspring and a humanitarian concern for native peoples. This dichotomy of thinking is to be encountered in comments of party leaders during the war years. Thus, Asquith wrote to Campbell-Bannerman on June 23, 1901, that there should be due protection for the aborigines in any future scheme of autonomy bestowed upon the conquered Dutch Republics.[27] Again, the Marquess of Ripon, Secretary of State for the Colonies in Gladstone's last ministry (from 1892 to 1895), wrote to Campbell-Bannerman on January 19, 1901 to the effect that the governor should be appointed as paramount chief with powers to assure fair treatment.[28] On the other hand, Campbell-Bannerman noted the dedication of the Imperial State to the noble goal of self-government for colonial communities. Thus, in notes penned during 1901, he observed that "Mr. Chamberlain thinks we are strong enough for a military occupation of indefinite length and perhaps we are; but it is not the English way to govern white men as a subject race and England will be involved in a moral catastrophe, worse than all her losses if we make the attempt."[29]

DeKieweit contends that the mold for the post-Boer War years had already been set:

> When at the end of the Great Boer War, South Africa lay helpless at her feet, Great Britain could only think how she might most speedily raise the stricken Republics and reconcile them to herself. In such an aim there was no longer any real room for a courageous native policy.[30]

Speculate as one may on this point of view, this much can be said—the Boer War had projected anew the challenge of South Africa. The British nation had been made aware that the conquest of Orange Free State and the Transvaal afforded an opportunity once more to resolve the problem of a white community and a vast non-European population.

THE BRITISH COLONIAL OFFICE

Some observations are in order concerning the British Colonial Office, responsible for the administration of imperial possessions. At its head was the Secretary of State for the Colonies with cabinet rank in His Majesty's government. He was assisted at the political level by the Parliamentary Under-Secretary of State for the Colonies, usually a member of the other legislative chamber. The British civil service staff was headed by the Permanent Under-Secretary for the Colonies who served as chief adviser to the Secretary of State for the Colonies. The affairs of the various overseas territories were dealt with in separate departments according to geographical areas. The South African Department (until 1910 when the Dominions Department, created in 1907, took over) handled the correspondence with Cape Colony, Natal, Orange River Colony (later Orange Free State again), and the Transvaal. Its personnel was recruited through examinations and consisted of assistant secretaries, principal clerks, and first- and second-class clerks.[31]

The British Colonial Office was the custodian of the "Colonial Regulations" printed in the annual edition of the *Colonial Office List*. The enforcement and interpretation of regulations accumulated over many decades and, based upon Parliamentary enactments, gave continuity to the administration of the British Empire. The daily breath of life was imparted by the minute paper, initiated by any matter which required the attention of, or a decision by, the British government. The pertinent communication or memorandum was minuted with observations by junior and senior civil servants until it reached the seat of authority. After the Secretary of State for the Colonies or his deputy, the Parliamentary Under-Secretary, rendered a judgment and initialed it, the minute paper was returned for preparation of a draft statement by a junior clerk. The proposed answer proceeded again through the various echelons until the magic words "for signature" were inscribed at the political level. In short, the Secretary of State for the Colonies had at his command the counsel of civil servants well versed in the constitutional and legal history of the British Empire.

For the period from 1902 to 1914 the position of Permanent Under-

Secretary for the Colonies was occupied by Sir Montagu Frederick Ommanney (1900-07), Sir Francis John Stephens Hopwood (1907-11) and later to be Baron Southborough, and Sir John Anderson (1911-16), later Viscount Waverly. Their educational backgrounds varied, Ommanney obtaining his schooling at Cheltenham and Woolwich (to become at first an engineer), Hopwood at King Edward VI at Louth (to become at first a solicitor), and Anderson at Aberdeen University. Only Hopwood had traveled in South Africa, serving in 1906 on a committee headed by Sir Joseph West Ridgeway, veteran colonial administrator, to consider constitutions for the Transvaal and Orange River Colony. Only Anderson went up through the ranks of the British Colonial Office, as a second-class clerk in 1879, a first-class clerk in 1896, and a principal clerk in 1897. But all three had previously held responsible positions before their appointments as Permanent Under-Secretary for the Colonies. Ommanney was Crown Agent for the Colonies from 1877 to 1900. Hopwood had been posted in the legal section of the Board of Trade. Anderson had been Governor of the Straits Settlement and High Commissioner of the Federated Malay States from 1904 until 1911. Both Hopwood and Anderson served in other distinguished capacities, the former as a civil lord of the Admiralty concerned with contracts during World War I and the latter as Lord President of the Council during World War II.

Nor were the biographical facts any less notable for those who held the rank of an assistant under-secretary of state in the South African Department. These included Sir Frederick Graham (1897-1907), Hugh Bertram Cox (1897-1911), Sir George Vandeleur Fiddes (1906-16), and Sir Hartmann Wolfgang Just (1907-16). All were university-trained, Graham at Edinburgh, Cox at Christ Church, Oxford, Fiddes at Brasenose College, Oxford, and Just at Corpus Christi College, Oxford. All save Cox rose through the ranks, each serving in turn as second-class clerk, first-class clerk, and principal clerk. Cox had a varied career before entering the British Colonial Office, serving as legal counsel in the Board of Treasury and as a member of several diplomatic missions. Both Fiddes and Just were personally acquainted with South Africa. Fiddes was private secretary to Lord Milner from 1897 to 1900 and secretary to the Transvaal administration from 1900 to 1902. Just traveled as private secretary with Chamberlain when he went on his trip to South Africa in 1902. Both Fiddes and Just later served with distinction in other offices, the former as Permanent Under-Secretary of State for the Colonies from 1916 to 1921 and the latter as secretary to the Imperial Conference and as an assistant under-secretary in the Dominions Division of the British Colonial Office.

The principal clerks in the South African Department whose observations are most often encountered in Minute Papers were Sir Henry Charles Miller Lambert, Sir Douglas Orme Malcolm, Sir William Arthur Robinson, Arthur Berriedale Keith, and Roland Venables Vernon. All possessed excellent educational backgrounds, attending preparatory schools and graduating from Oxford University, the first two from New College, the third from Queen's College, and the last two from Balliol College. All entered the British Colonial Office as second-class clerks and rose to the grade of principal clerk during the years under consideration. Only Malcolm spent any time in South Africa, posted as private secretary to the second Earl of Selborne, successor to Lord Milner as Governor of the Transvaal and Orange River Colony and High Commissioner of South Africa from 1905 to 1910. But Lambert gained valuable experience as private secretary for Chamberlain on the Select Committee of the House of Commons, appointed in 1896 to study the genesis of the Jameson Raid. Most of them occupied positions of distinction in later years. Malcolm retired from the British Colonial Office in 1912 to become a director of the British South Africa Company and then its president during the transformation of its territory into Rhodesia. Keith left the British Colonial Office in 1914 to become Regius Professor of Sanskrit and Comparative Philology at Edinburgh University and author of many books on the constitutional history of the British Empire. Lambert served as an assistant under-secretary for the colonies from 1916 to 1921 and as Acting Permanent Under-Secretary of State for the Colonies in 1924 and 1925. Robinson transferred to the Ministry of Health, becoming Permanent Under-Secretary from 1920 to 1935.

2

The Chinese Coolie Experiment
Initial Phase

A LABOR SHORTAGE

The Witwatersrand goldfields extend for an aggregate of sixty-two miles, running east and west and bisected by Johannesburg. The scene to the naked eye is that of a series of reefs or ridge-like hills. The glittering metal is not to be found in rich nuggets, nor in alluvial deposits, nor in veins. Rather, it is encrusted in solid quartzite formations, dropping down obliquely to depths not fathomed even today. When bared openly in a mine face, the quartzite formation resembles pebble beds or *blankets* (a Dutch word meaning an almond confectionery type of coloring). The gold is distributed uniformly and finely in continuous layers of the conglomerated rock.[1]

Extraction of the particles of gold is expensive, requiring heavy machinery and electric power. Dynamite charges are planted in rock-drilled holes and the shattered ore is brought to the surface and deposited on revolving tables for elimination of worthless rock. The gold-flecked ore is taken to a mill where stamp batteries pound and grind as water flows over it until nothing but a powdered pulp is left. This sediment is then run over copper plates treated with mercury and the resultant chemical reaction gathers in from one-half to two-thirds of the gold particles. The remainder, still locked in the pyrites and other minerals, is recovered by the cyanide process. A solution of cyanide of potassium dissolves the gold dust and causes it to precipitate on zinc shavings in the form of a fine brown mud. This is smelted with suitable fluxes and the gold settles to the bottom. What remains of the pounded rock is washed away to form great mounds of cyanide tailings.

A visitor to Johannesburg is forcibly reminded of the gold rush days by the surrounding hills, yellowish in color, heaped with slag tossed up from thousands of feet below the surface.

Large outlays of money, more than a wealthy person could muster, were needed to carry on such deep-level mining operations. The joint stock company, eventually numbering over one hundred, was the answer to the accumulation of capital. In time the holding company made its appearance, buying up a large segment of mining properties. The advantages were greater economy in operation and a hedge against a drop in the fortunes of any one single mine. In short, the shareholder had a better guarantee of good and continuous dividends. The more important holding companies were as follows: 1) Wernher, Beit, and Company, associated with Eckstein and Company, 2) Consolidated Goldfields of South Africa Gold Trust Limited, associated with the Cecil Rhodes interests, 3) Johannesburg Consolidated Investment Company managed by the Barnato brothers, 4) J. B. Robinson Group, 5) S. Neuman and Company, 6) General Mining and Financing Corporation led by the Albu Group, 7) A. Goerz and Company, 8) Farrar and Anglo-French Group, and 9) Messrs. Lewis and Marks.

Direct responsibility for technical operations was assumed by each individual mine. A manager, assisted by a staff of shift bosses and overseers, supervised all work. Skilled white miners were hired to break the ground at so much per fathom, with cost of materials and wages of the unskilled help paid by management. Some mines preferred to retain control of the entire operation, employing all the personnel on a payroll basis. Native peoples south of the Zambesi river were recruited for the exacting physical tasks underground. The British government was receptive to the use of the Basuto. Natal and Cape Colony had no objection to their Bantu males entering into engagements. Orange Free State cooperated with the Transvaal to make its African population available. However, the majority of the natives came from Portuguese East Africa where the authorities charged a fee per head for recruits. The usual labor contract called for a specified tour of duty not less than six months and up to a year or two. Residence was in compounds on mining premises, families having to remain behind. Passes to go into town were permitted occasionally but for a maximum of forty-eight hours. All amenities were furnished—food, lodging, medical care.

Gold mining on the Rand was only temporarily disrupted by the Boer War. Operations were resumed during the summer of 1901 after the British occupation of Johannesburg. Ambitious plans were made to open poorer as well as richer mines and to step up exploration of adjoining reefs. To make an intensive exploitation of the less productive mines financially feasible, the Transvaal Chamber of Mines (the mineowners' association) announced a reduction in the native monthly wage from 50s. to 30s. But the immediate aftermath of the Boer War was disappointing in figures of native employment. Whereas in July 1899, prior to the outbreak of the war, natives in service numbered 111,697, the count in July 1903 stood at 55,507.* As the mineowners surveyed the situation, a labor shortage loomed, nullifying any prospect to accelerate the tempo of gold production.

Mining interests beseeched the British Colonial Office to do something about the labor shortage. In its papers and dispatches are letters from Sidney H. Farrar on behalf of the company headed by his brother Sir George Farrar; from (Sir) Lionel Phillips, associated with Eckstein and Company; and from (Sir) Francis Drummond Chaplin, manager for the Consolidated Goldfields of South Africa Gold Trust Limited. Their solution was to have Chamberlain press the Foreign Office for permission to recruit in British East and Central Africa and Nyasaland. As an alternative, the use of Asiatics was broached. The reaction at Whitehall was cool and cautious.[2]

When Chamberlain broke precedent as Secretary of State for the Colonies to make a personal tour of South Africa from December 1902 through February 1903, he discussed the matter with Lord Milner whose duties as High Commissioner included the administration of the two conquered colonies. Chamberlain observed "that it would raise a storm at home" to bring over Asiatic coolies. Furthermore, answering rumors that he would approve of such importation if mineowners bore a portion of the war debt, Chamberlain declared in a public address at Johannesburg "that anything of that sort would be discreditable to the mining interests; it would be almost treasonable on my part; and I destroy it in a sentence." He suggested that if natives were offered higher wages, married quarters, and limited supplies of Kaffir beer, they would flock to the mines in adequate numbers. How-

*Comprehensive tables of mining statistics have been compiled in Appendix A.

ever, he confided privately to Lord Milner that he was prepared to review the situation if the local white population favored labor from the outside. The Transvaal was destined to be self-governing and so any step taken should have popular support. Of course, he hastened to say, no evidence was yet forthcoming of that kind and, indeed, protest meetings in Johannesburg and Pretoria against any scheme of Asiatic labor was testimony to the contrary.[3]

Lord Milner was not long in swinging to the side of the mineowners. He regarded as significant the action taken in March 1903 at the Bloemfontein Conference, convened by representatives from Natal, Cape Colony, Orange River Colony, the Transvaal, and Rhodesia, primarily to discuss customs and railway rates. The matter of manpower shortage was raised and a resolution was carried unanimously:

> that the permanent settlement in South Africa of Asiatic races would be injurious and should not be permitted; but that, if industrial development positively requires it, the introduction of unskilled labourers under a system of Government control only, by which provision is made for indenture and repatriation at the termination thereof, should be permissible.[4]

Accordingly, in July 1903, Lord Milner appointed a commission to investigate overall labor needs of the Transvaal with special reference to the gold mines. The twelve members were drawn from the ranks of mining, business, finance, agriculture, and labor. The chairman was Andrew Mackie Niven, a stockbroker and representative of the Witwatersrand Deep Limited mine on the Transvaal Chamber of Mines. Among associates connected with mining enterprises were George Henry Goch, a director of the Village Main Reef mine, Sir George Farrar, Samual Evans of Eckstein and Company, C. F. B. Tainton, a director of the East Rand Deep Limited mine, John W. Philip, a member of the Stock Exchange and Labour Importation Association (recruiting natives), and David Forbes, mining engineer. The rest were from diverse walks of life—Johannes Cornelis Brink, a member of the Transvaal Legislative Council, Lieutenant Colonel James Donaldson (replacement for W. Leslie Daniels, president of the Johannesburg Chamber of Trade) active in commerce, E. P. Perrow, president of the Transvaal Miners' Association, Peter Whiteside, secretary of the Engine Drivers' Society, John William Quinn, member of the Johannesburg Town Council and a confectionery merchant. The British Colonial Office had no objection to the nominees save that "one only (Brink) is a Dutchman and David Forbes is semi-Dutch . . . and the report may therefore be misleading as a guide of public opinion. . . ."[5]

The Transvaal Labour Commission met for an aggregate of thirty-two days, holding sessions intermittently from July 21 to October 6, 1903. Some ninety-two individuals were heard from all parts of Africa —native affairs administrators, recruiting agents, missionaries, farmers, mineowners, tribal chieftains. Advertisements to publicize the inquiry were placed in principal newspapers throughout South Africa and in East African centers as far as Beira, Zanzibar, and Mombasa. The information sought concerned the availability of native labor and the special conditions affecting their willingness to work on the Rand. Witnesses were asked to hand in written statements before testifying so that the cross-examination could be conducted more expeditiously. The findings were submitted in November 1903 and were published in several Blue Books.[6]

A Majority Report was signed by all save Quinn and Whiteside. As these ten members assimilated the evidence collected, the gold mines needed 142,500 natives for the various processes involved in the maximum use of 7,145 stamps available, as against 46,500 natives currently employed and utilizing only 3,725 stamps. In addition, 30,000 natives were needed for exploration projects designed to open new mines, as against 9,000 natives currently employed. To put it another way, where in August 1899 some 6,240 stamps were at work producing gold valued at £1,720,097 or equal to an annual rate of £20,650,884, in July 1903 the 3,725 stamps at work produced gold valued at £1,068,-717 or equal to an annual rate of £12,827,004. Furthermore, given favorable conditions of labor, there was reason to believe that 11,120 new stamps could be erected within the next five years, thereby providing work for an additional 196,000 laborers. In short, gold mines could use 172,500 natives at the moment and a total of 368,500 ultimately.[7]

No less critical were labor shortages in other areas of the Transvaal economy. Some 9,000 natives were engaged in the coal mines whereas when the gold mines were operating at maximum capacity the expanded fuel needs would require 17,700 natives. Acreage awaiting cultivation was estimated to call for an agricultural labor force of 80,000, yet at the moment only 27,500 natives were in the fields or out on the ranges. A staff of 12,400 carried on railway maintenance while the current workload justified a complement of 16,000. Plans for new railway construction would require a force of 40,000 natives, a sharp contrast to the 4,000 on the payroll. For the rest, it was roughly predicted that smaller but equally vital industrial enterprises would hire about 70,000 natives and would obviously need more manpower in order to keep pace with the quickened tempo anticipated in the Transvaal.

Emphasis was placed upon the calculations of Jacobus Nicholas De Jongh, testifying in behalf of the Transvaal Chamber of Mines, that not more than 235,000 adult native males were procurable in the combined regions of Central and South Africa. The population of this area was 13,597,691, broken down into 6,326,511 south and 7,271,180 north of the Zambesi River. A block numbering 8,925,461 natives could be subtracted as unable to withstand the rigor of the colder weather on the Rand. Employable males in the age bracket from fifteen to forty in the remaining block of 4,672,230 natives could not supply more than 10 per cent or 467,223. The average period of work annually engaged in by natives was never more than six months, owing to homesickness and the exhausting nature of underground work. So only an equivalent of 235,000 natives constituted the potential labor market in Africa against a host of demands for workers from all branches of the economy. Importation of labor from outside of Africa seemed the solution for the hard-pressed gold mines.[8]

A Minority Report was submitted by Quinn and Whiteside. They argued that the testimony of mineowners, upon which their ten associates relied, was motivated by the selfish desire to make the greatest profit in the shortest time. A different set of figures offered by some witnesses seemed to them to be more in keeping with technological data and the achievement of a stable economy. The essential premise was that from ten to twelve rather than twenty natives were sufficient to keep a stamp in operation. Calculating on this basis, the gold mines required only 85,000 natives for production plus 18,250 for exploration projects. Comparable adjustments could likewise be made for other industries. Coal mines should be able to meet commitments with a force of 12,000. Railway maintenance and construction of new lines

could be efficiently implemented with a force of 20,000. The index of
farm acreage suggested a reasonable performance with a force of
55,000. In short, adding the estimated 70,000 engaged in other enterprises, the figure of 270,000 natives for all labor requisites seemed
nearer the truth.[9]

Optimism was expressed that an adequate pool of native labor did
exist in Africa. The number of adult native males available for work
was much greater than the figure of 235,000 arrived at by spokesmen
for the mineowners. A fairer ratio would be 1 in 8 of the 13,597,691
native population qualifying as eligible workers. That meant, in round
numbers, a labor potential of 1,500,000. Chamberlain's suggestion was
recalled—that if conditions of work were made attractive there would
be no dearth of recruits. Other possibilities were greater use of labor-
saving machinery and extended experiments with unskilled white
labor. In the meantime it was heartening news to read the statistics
of gold output. Whereas in January 1903 the value of gold production
amounted to £846,490, in October 1903 it had risen to £1,208,669 or
at an annual rate of £14,500,000, not far off the prewar mark of
£16,000,000 for 1898 (last full year of operation before the Boer
War). The people of the Transvaal should not allow themselves to
be stampeded into regrettable actions by the jeremiads of mineowners.
An excessively rapid exhaustion of the gold mines could leave the
Transvaal economy in a state of imbalance.

Lord Milner accepted the Majority Report as a truer evaluation of
the status of the gold mines. He was equally impressed with the conditions proposed for recruitment of labor abroad. H. Ross Skinner, an
agent of the Transvaal Chamber of Mines, had been dispatched on a
journey around the world to inquire into sources of labor, the terms
under which they should be hired, and their suitability for mining.
His travels from February to September 1903 took him to California,
British Columbia, Malay Peninsula, Japan, and China. His report recommended China as the most likely place to find satisfactory recruits,
but the experiences of Canada and the United States with the unas-
similable Oriental advised against privileges of citizenship. Chinese
coolies should be brought in as indentured servants, restricted in
movement and occupation, and repatriated at the termination of the
contract. Such an arrangement would forestall any permanently undesirable social problems.[10]

When Lord Milner traveled to England in October 1903 on an extended leave, he took with him the unpublished testimony of the Transvaal Labour Commission. He spared no pains to present a substantial case before responsible British statesmen. A grave economic depression gripped the Transvaal; its cause could be traced to a labor shortage in the gold mines. He impressed the issue at stake upon Arthur James Balfour (Earl of Balfour), nephew and successor to the ailing Lord Salisbury as Prime Minister, and upon Alfred Lyttelton, newly appointed Secretary of State for the Colonies upon the resignation of Chamberlain. The Conservative government must weigh the possible political advantage accruing to the Liberal party in the cry of "slavery" versus the prosperity of a colony entrusted to its charge. Certainly, a stagnant Transvaal economy would lessen any chance of increasing Anglo-Saxon stock in order to offset the Boer preponderance.[11]

Liberal members were sought out in the hope of concerting a nonpartisan policy. Cecil Headlam, editor of the *Milner Papers*, tells us that Lord Milner found Campbell-Bannerman and Lawson unalterably opposed. Whether or not their antipathy exasperated Lord Milner, he nevertheless charged them with desiring to assure the Boers a positive role in South Africa whereas an influx of Asiatics would promote the ascendancy of the British stock on the Rand. His conversations with Grey and Haldane at a dinner party given by the Asquiths were more satisfactory. They expressed themselves as prepared to prevent the issue of indentured Asiatic labor from being exploited for party gain.* They saw nothing incompatible between the goal of an imperial moral standard and a temporary proposal aimed to strengthen the Transvaal economy along with due consideration for imported labor.[12]

Lord Milner was back in South Africa by December 1903 and threw himself unreservedly into the fight to win approval for Chinese coolies. He cited petitions signed by thousands of colonial whites, one with 47,000 names of males over sixteen years of age. He sent newspaper clippings to the British Colonial Office describing demonstrations

---

*Haldane alone would appear to have kept faith. His name is missing from the division on a motion by Herbert Louis Samuel (Viscount), Liberal M.P., on February 17, 1904, to postpone action on the use of Asiatics until colonial opinion had been formally ascertained. *Commons*, Feb. 17, 1904, p. 122. Cf. Pyrah (1955), p. 189; Sommer (1960), p. 141.

held in favor of the experiment. He discounted the protestations of
the anti-Asiatic White League as the voice of a small minority.
Most significant of all was the endorsement given the proposal by the
Transvaal Legislative Council on December 30 by a vote of twenty-
two to four. This body had been set up in May 1903 as a modest
instalment of representative government. Besides Lord Milner ex of-
ficio, there were thirteen official and thirteen unofficial members, all
nominated by him. The former were drawn from his staff and the
latter from the citizenry. Here was an accurate barometer of public
opinion.[13]

Lord Milner challenged the views expressed by General Botha de-
precating the reinforcement of an overwhelming black population with
yellow hordes just for the benefit of mining companies and dividends.[14] He accused Boer leaders of malice aforethought in their opposition—in their desire to retard the Transvaal economy in order to
impede British immigration and to cause friction between the colonial
Anglo-Saxon and his fellow countrymen in the British Isles. Lord
Milner countered these dissentient statements with resolutions from
Boer communities and associations accepting Asiatics as a temporary
necessity albeit undesirable as a permanent policy.[15]

The staff at the British Colonial Office had mixed views on the
predicament of the gold mines. Ommanney preferred the Minority
Report as "offering a more reasonable [scheme of] development." If
the mines were in trouble, the cause was overcapitalized stock. At the
same time he was inclined to accept the warning in the Majority
Report that "to go against it [Asiatic labor] would be to alienate the
most powerful interest on our side and the only one which can place
the Transvaal on a sound footing." Fiddes drew up a long memorandum in November 1903 stressing the economic consequences of a
depressed mining industry. The estimated budgetary deficiency for
the Transvaal Crown Colony by 1905-06 was put at £300,000 and was
only to be met by increased revenue from the mines. At a conservative
computation of 10s. per ton profit, 2,000 idle stamps meant £500
daily loss to the local treasury. The blow to shareholders would be
equally shattering and affect the British economy. Already it was calculated that the market value of the mines had shrunk 25 per cent
since December 1902. Where perhaps one-third to one-half of the

mining shares before 1899 were owned on the Continent, now about four-fifths were in the hands of British investors and held on borrowed money.[16]

However, the British Colonial Office maintained an attitude of correctness toward steps taken to anticipate approval of Asiatic labor. When, in March 1903, letters of introduction to British consular agents were asked for by Skinner to facilitate his inquiries, Chamberlain had no objection: "but on the understanding this does not commit to approval of the idea of Chinese nor to make any arrangements." When the Transvaal government, in November 1903, asked for permission to temporarily employ William Evans, Protector of the Chinese at the Straits Settlements, as adviser on pertinent regulations, Lyttelton agreed: "but it must be kept quiet and does not commit us as to the Chinese." The sternest criticism was for the hasty action of Lord Milner in preparing a draft ordinance before colonial public opinion had been fully ascertained; in the event that a strong anti-Chinese sentiment existed, the arrival of coolies could provoke a violent reaction.[17]

The intense hostility of Cape Colony to Asiatic labor was well known. Its legislature in July 1903 had passed a resolution strongly disapproving such a proposal. It was undesirable to add another colored race to the already heterogeneous population in South Africa. The effort to civilize natives along the lines of good work habits without compulsion would be checked. Sufficient labor south of the Equator could be found if fair wages, good housing, and ample food were provided. A discordant note would be introduced into the federation movement. Indeed, in 1904, so intense was the conviction of Cape Colony, that a *Chinese Exclusion Act* was placed on the statute book to forestall any influx of Asiatics from the Transvaal if the proposal went through. The British Colonial Office preferred to mark time as to whether it was "a question for South Africa or the two new colonies."[18]

Fiddes anticipated that Australia, Canada, and other parts of the British Empire might be offended. But the principle of self-government carried with it a corresponding obligation not to interfere in the internal affairs of other members. Canada had twice expressed an opinion on home rule for Ireland and had been invited by the British government in diplomatic language to mind its own business.* On the other hand, Rhodesia favored it, the British South Africa Company actually hoping for a similar contingent of indentured Asiatics for work in its mines. At the Bloemfontein Conference in March 1903, Rhodesia had brought in the resolution sanctioning resort to Asiatic labor if necessary.[19]

The move of Richard John Seddon, Premier of New Zealand, on January 11, 1904, inviting other British self-governing communities to join in a protest against the Transvaal proposal did not distress Lyttelton. The only affirmative response was from Alfred Deakin, Prime Minister of Australia, and the final outcome was the dispatch on January 19 of separate telegrams by the two countries. They were similar in content, emphasizing the grave perils—racial, social, political, sanitary—which were certain to accompany the introduction of an alien element. Lyttelton's reply was a masterpiece of tactfulness. He acknowledged the right of component parts of the Empire to render an opinion on so important a question, especially in view of their military assistance during the Boer War. But he went on to explain that the policy of the Imperial State was to treat the Transvaal as though it were self-governing and on that basis to allow it the freedom to deal with its own domestic problems.[20]

CASE FOR THE CHINESE

Conservative circles in the British Isles endorsed the Majority Report and its recommendation for Asiatic labor. A thriving gold industry was the keystone of the Transvaal economy. The contrast between an annual budget of £200,000 before the discovery of gold and £7,000,000 currently was an obvious index.** Bond issues to the tune of £35,000,000 were to be floated for roads, railway lines, and irrigation facilities. The municipality of Johannesburg had borrowed £3,000,000 to carry out urgent utility improvements—sewerage, water mains, street paving, hospitals, and electric power stations. The Imperial

*The two occasions were in 1882 and 1903 when the Canadian Parliament memorialized the British government on the desirability of self-government for Ireland. P.P., 1882, XLV, Cd. 3294, 1903, XLIV, Cd. 1697.

**The Transvaal revenue had been on the decline, dropping from £328,000 in 1883-84 to £218,000 in 1885-86. DeKock (1936), pp. 51-52.

State was pressing for a war contribution of £30,000,000 from the Transvaal. It was quite evident that the gold output which had reached an annual rate of £20,000,000 in 1899 would have to be doubled to provide the necessary revenue for these obligations. Yet at the moment gold production was at the pace of £14,000,000 annually. Ian Zachary Malcolm, Conservative M.P. and previously private secretary to Lord Salisbury, averred "that gold was to the Transvaal what cane fields used to be to the West Indies, . . . cod fishing . . . to Newfoundland, [and] . . . tea to Ceylon."[21]

References were frequent to a commercial report by (Sir) Henry Birchenough, dispatched in 1903 as special trade commissioner to South Africa, as to the economic benefits for Great Britain of a bustling Rand industry. Where British exports in 1893 amounted to £9,000,000, they had risen in 1902 to £26,000,000. Where South Africa stood sixth on the list of customers in 1893, its purchases in 1903 surpassed those of America, Germany, France, and Australia and were second only to India. Especially attractive was the estimate that every new stamp erected meant £1,600 worth of machinery and every stamp at work meant £330 worth of material annually. Horace Weldon, Transvaal mining engineer, held out an inviting prospect to Birchenough. A proposed addition of 8,000 stamps by 1908 would require £12,800,000 worth of new machinery. In terms of expendable stores imported to service 8,000 new stamps plus the existing 6,500 stamps (correctly, 7,145), the annual purchases should total £5,500,000. The *Morning Post* noted that the 200,000 Rand shareholders were mostly British and their daily losses now amounted to £10,000 because of curtailed operations. A drop of £3,000,000 annually in dividends spent mainly at home was not to be taken lightly. Nor should the deleterious effect of a diminished gold supply upon London as the center of world credit be overlooked.[22]

The Boer War was blamed for the failure of natives to flock back in large numbers to the mines. The British army had paid natives as much as £5 monthly to do transport work, more than they had ever earned on the Rand. Many retired to the reservations to indulge natural habits of idleness or used their wealth to purchase additional wives for farming chores. The Witwatersrand Native Labour Association, organized in 1900 by the mineowners to coordinate recruitment of workers, was unflagging in its efforts to obtain natives and, by 1904, had spent the large sum of £450,000. Particularly commendable were the half-way houses and shelters set up along the itinerary to assure good food and lodgings for Portuguese East African coolies whose numbers exceeded all others.* If Charles Sydney Goldmann, Conservative M.P. after 1910 and active in South African gold mining enterprises, conceded that the reduction in the native wage monthly from 50s. to 30s. in 1901 upon the reopening of the gold mines had contributed to the labor shortage, the cherished hope was to enable poorer mines to be exploited. Unfortunately the extravagant wages received by natives during the military campaigns had nullified this worthy aim. At any rate mineowners had hiked wages in 1903 and no significant increase in native workers had followed.[23]

Sir Clement Kinloch-Cooke, Conservative M.P. after 1910 and editor of the *Empire Review*, did not minimize the excessive deathrate of 71 per 1,000 (for 1903) as a deterrent frightening away the native worker. But it was the result of an extraordinary epidemic of influenza. In the period from November 1902 to April 1903, before the scourge hit, the deathrate averaged 57.5 per 1,000. This figure compared favorably with 57.2 per 1,000 for 1902 in the Kimberley diamond mines where the recruits were the Basuto, inured to high plateau regions and subject to the salutary measure of bathing after work (while stripped down to prevent diamond thefts). Still there was no intent to gloss over the need to improve the medical record on the Rand. The native continued to be too casual in his habits and, after emerging from the shaft, did not remain in his quarters sufficiently long to cool off. The risk of phthisis from lung inhalation of metallic dust was multiplied by failure to use wet-drilling and safety devices. The ninth Duke of Marlborough, Parliamentary Under-Secretary for the Colonies, was confident that planned improvements—change houses, bathing facilities, sanitation—would soon bear fruit. Indeed, by June 1904, he took heart in a comparison of deathrates per 1,000 for the first four months in 1903 and 1904 respectively: January—61 and 59; February—44 and 37; March—49 and 36; April—52 and 32.**

---

*Portuguese East Africa in 1903 supplied 45,158 out of the 85,377 natives on the Rand. *Witwatersrand Native Labour Association*, Report, 1904, p. 3.

**The months listed represent the warmer part of the year which were less harmful to the health of the native workers.

The native had no reason to be apprehensive of his health while working in the gold mines.[24]

The merits of Chinese coolies as workers were extolled. Experiences elsewhere demonstrated the contribution which they could make to the economic development of a country. They had benefited Canada, Ceylon, Borneo, Singapore, Australia, New Zealand, and the United States. Their role had been magnificent in making accessible the resources of the Malay Peninsula. In less than thirty years a forest of jungles had been transformed into flourishing settlements possessed of railways, roads, telegraphs, and a trade of £10,000,000 per annum. They had helped to complete the first transcontinental railroad in America and no one could speak too highly of them. The Canadian Pacific Railroad could not have been cut through British Columbia without their labor. If Australia had continued to employ the Chinese, a transcontinental railroad could have been constructed long ago and the Northern Territory opened up for exploitation. A derivative value for South Africa could be the rehabilitation of the native as a worker. The presence of the Chinese as a competitor would spur the native to establish the worth of his hire.[25]

Granted that some restrictive conditions were imperative. The complicated social skein in South Africa made it impossible to admit Chinese coolies as free men. Their use must be as a temporary expedient, for no sound imperialist could contemplate dumping tens of thousands of "pig-tails" upon the Transvaal save as sojourners. If regret was expressed at the refusal of Lord Curzon (Marquess Curzon of Kedleston), Viceroy of India, to permit recruitment on such a basis, the reason was duly appreciated. India was protesting the disabilities imposed upon those of its people resident in South Africa.* As a member of the British Empire, India claimed the traditional liberties of an Englishman for its emigrants entering other territories under the Union Jack. The incident which sealed the chance to tap India for

*Lord Curzon wrote thus in 1904: "We are not in the least anxious for Indians to go to the Transvaal at all. The relief thereby given to our Indian problem [an overcrowded population] is infinitesimal and we only lay up for ourselves a crop of trouble in the future. Outside the Government of India itself, where the Imperial sentiment is strong, I know of no class, community, or individual in India, who wants the Indian to have anything to do with the Transvaal. The bitter example of Natal is before them." Calpin (1949), p. 62.

labor was a request of the Transvaal for 10,000 coolies to work on railway construction. Lord Curzon would only give his approval contingent upon repeal of the disabilities against Indians domiciled there. When the Transvaal was not prepared to make concessions, the negotiations collapsed. That left the Far East as still the best source for a labor supply.[26]

A strong denial was entered against the charge of excessive moral weakness. Orientals were not to be distinguished from other races as practitioners of vice. Some were imbibers of spirits but no more immoderately than Occidentals. The *Morning Post* understood that the opium habit was a necessary prophylactic against malaria in the scourged plains of China, done in solitude and seldom led to breaches of the law. If a Chinese indulged often in petty gambling, he was not the horse-racing addict that the British worker had become. Horace Annesley Vachell, novelist, playwright, and onetime California rancher, told readers of the *Spectator* of his own observations while on the Pacific coast as an employer of Chinese cooks, woodcutters, and laundrymen. The Chinese belonged to companies who saw to their wellbeing and kept them in touch with kinfolk in China. Perhaps some did wallow in sin but the white man in San Francisco had his Tigertown-caged women, dives, gambling hells, and opium dens too.[27]

The real objection of those with malicious tongues, commented Charles Stuart Wortley, Parliamentary Under-Secretary for the Home Department in past Salisbury cabinets, was that the Chinese worked harder and for less wages. He turned for confirmation to Gladstone,* a fountain of wisdom to thousands:

> Why is the Chinaman thus taxed [heavily upon his advent in the white man's country]? Not because a superior race resents the contact—you may say contamination—of the inferior; not because civilization recoils from companionship with a people who are considered to be uncivilized. But the Chinaman comes in to compete with the young [white] labourer, . . . he does more work for the money, . . . is less exacting. . . . It is not for his vices but for his virtues that he is so [meanly] treated.[28]

*Gladstone delivered this address before the Cobden Club on May 12, 1890, scolding the Australian colonies for their hostility to Chinese immigration. *The Times*, May 13, 1890, 11b.

Popular sentiment in the Transvaal was described as rallying behind the mineowners. Lyttelton confessed himself impressed by the vote of twenty-two to four cast in the Legislative Council for a resolution endorsing the use of Chinese coolies. Apart from the unanimous approval of the thirteen official members, the nine affirmative votes in the unofficial group included four Boers, two mining men, two merchants, and one British farmer, a respectable cross-section of the citizenry.[29] Reference was had to the petition in January 1904 with the signatures of 47,000 adult white males favoring Chinese coolies, representing seventy per cent of those eligible to sign it.[30] Much was made of a pronouncement of the Free Church Council of Johannesburg on March 5, 1904, by a vote of thirty to one, as adding moral weight to the proposal. It read "that while expressing no opinion on the economic questions involved, this meeting strongly deprecates the Free Church Council's [England and Wales] agitation against Chinese labour and thinks that fuller knowledge will modify the latter's views regarding the conditions of service which are voluntary and similar to conditions which have long prevailed in South Africa."[31] No less valued was the commendation of the Rt. Rev. William Marlborough Carter (Bishop of Pretoria)[32] on March 10, 1904 "that the importation of unskilled Asiatic labour under government regulations was the only solution of the present difficulties."[33]

The British nation was assured that Chinese coolies would not spell doom for the federation movement. The apparent opposition in Cape Colony stemmed from political expediency. An election campaign was on and the rival parties (Bond and Progressives) were running so close as to enhance the importance of the non-European vote in several constituencies. Clever politicians were bidding for their ballots by coming out against the Chinese as a threat to the livelihood of unskilled native labor.[34] A more accurate index of South African opinion could be found in the action of the Natal Legislative Assembly voting thirty to two that the Transvaal be left to handle the problem of a labor shortage.* Lyttelton regarded as no less indicative the sentiment expressed at the Bloemfontein Conference in March

---

*The Natal resolution was prompted by receipt of the telegram from New Zealand inviting a joint protest against the proposed use of Asiatic labor in the Transvaal. P. R. O., c.o. 179/229; *The Times,* Jan. 14, 1904, 3c (news item).

1903 attended by representatives from Cape Colony, Natal, Orange River Colony, the Transvaal, and Rhodesia. A resolution was passed unanimously recognizing a possible dearth of workers and accepting use of Asiatic labor under restricted conditions if circumstances warranted it.[35]

Conservatives gave short shrift to the memorials from Australia and New Zealand. No one would challenge their right to pursue a white policy: otherwise a few million whites would be pitted against 400,000,000 Asiatics. But they could show more tolerance because aliens had been used when an emergency required it. Queensland had brought in Kanakas from the South Sea Islands for work on sugar plantations.[36] Western Australia had passed an act (in 1884) permitting the engagement of indentured workers from any Asiatic or African country.[37] Kinloch-Cooke understood that in New Zealand the Labour party had put pressure on Seddon. Still that gentleman should realize political appeasement in his own land was hardly a compensation for strained relations with other member states under the Union Jack. Similarly, the backdrop for Deakin's participation was an Australian Labour party insistent upon the supremacy of white labor. The fourth Baron Harris, a past Parliamentary Under-Secretary for India and a director of the South Africa Gold Trust Limited, commented tartly that Australia and New Zealand were entitled to exclude colored labor if they wished but they were not good judges of what was necessary in another part of the British Empire.[38]

CASE AGAINST THE CHINESE

Liberal and Labour circles acquainted the British nation with the merits of the Minority Report. A figure of ten to twelve "boys," instead of twenty per stamp, went to the core of the matter and significantly reduced the necessary complement of unskilled labor. The productive capacity of natives could be increased several fold by a strict enforcement of liquor laws and encouragement of labor-saving devices. Furthermore, an upswing in natives was to be recorded, justifying the plea for patience. The monthly returns of the Transvaal Chamber of Mines showed a native force of 35,624 in December 1903, 52,487 in June 1903, and 69,000 in January 1904. Carrying the figures to May 1904, a going rate of 78,000 compared favorably with pre-Boer War marks. For the rest, if additional numbers had to be found, Sir Harry Hamilton Johnston, well-known African explorer and student of native culture, was convinced that the vast hinterland of the "dark continent" could be tapped profitably.[39]

Equally significant was the upswing in gold production. A figure of 2,866,827 ounces of fine gold for 1903 compared favorably with that of 1,691,519 ounces for 1902. If the ratio of progress continued during 1904, then the total should approximate the 4,295,602 ounces mined in 1898. In value the gold extracted came to £7,269,888 in 1902 and £12,589,247 in 1903. Carrying the figures to March 1904, the output monthly was £1,654,258 or at an annual rate of £15,750,000, practically equaling that of 1898 (although not yet the figure of £20,000,000 annually based upon the production record for August 1899). The fifth Earl Spencer, First Lord of the Admiralty in the last Gladstone ministry, reminded the public that Lord Milner himself had acknowledged the production gains. In reply to a deputation from the anti-Asiatic White League in June 1903, before he had come out strongly in favor of Chinese labor, Lord Milner had said that the gold output was already greater than for 1895-96 and steadily rising.[40]

The *Westminster Gazette* argued that the best interest of the colony was not to work out the mines in feverish haste but to prolong production until permanent industries could be built up. A minimum of sixty years would allow normal exploitation within the framework of a balanced economy. The alternative was a deserted mining camp and the relapse of South Africa into a cattle country and the Dutch as the only white inhabitants. One need but recall the tribulations of Spain after its wealth in the mines of Central and South America had dried up. In the meanwhile, the Spanish citizenry had lost the incentive to develop its own natural resources and when the day of reckoning came Spain declined rapidly. The *Labour Leader* preferred to have the Transvaal take over the mines and operate them as a state enterprise. Organic evolution could then be guided toward a sounder community life. In this connection, the request of the Balfour government that the mineowners underwrite one-third of the £30,000,000 war indemnity sought from the Transvaal was eyed suspiciously. Naturally, the mineowners could plead importation of Chinese labor as the only means to increase gold production and thereby meet the requested financial burden.[41]

Campbell-Bannerman disliked centering an empire around economic advantages. The Conservative party's emphasis upon orders for machinery and dividends for shareholders smacked of predatory colonialism. Surely these material gains should not invite indifference to the shabby motives of the holding companies. Their aim was not so much to work mines for honest production as to attract investors for gold shares. In the case of the poorer mines, Chinese labor could create a false sense of prosperity for a short time and stimulate a rise in the value of their stock, thus enabling the holding companies to unload shares upon the public at a profit. Even the better Rand mines were not immune from the need for cheap labor, burdened as they were with the obligations of overcapitalized stock. Excessively high dividends had been declared in the past in order to push up the market value of gold shares. Those who purchased shares at higher figures expected comparable returns from their investments. The mining structure remained in the grip of men seeking desperately by sensational means to buttress the strength of "Kaffirs," the vernacular for shares of stock in gold mining companies.[42]

The diabolical strategy of mineowners to establish a case for Asiatic labor was laid bare. The reduction of the native wage in 1901 from 50s. to 30s. per month could promote a scarcity of labor and rush the Transvaal into a decision on Chinese coolies. Unfortunately for mineowners, the natives were given £5 a month to drive army transports and a greater labor shortage followed than was desired. The seemingly generous move of mineowners to raise the wage scale in 1903 was only to avoid a collapse of mining operations. Even at that, it was not a full restoration, comparing an average wage in March 1904 of 42s. 5d. with the prevailing rate in 1899 of 47s. 1d. When the aftermath of the wage raise in 1903 brought a steady increase in native labor, averaging between 1,500 and 3,000 monthly, the faucet of recruitment would appear to have been deliberately shut off. Between August 1903 and February 1904 the number of natives on the Rand remained almost constant, obviously to provide the Transvaal Labour Commission with data of a pessimistic kind.* John Burns, a Lib-Lab M.P., quoted William Grant, past Native Labour Commissioner to the Transvaal Chamber of Mines,** as saying that the labor shortage had been arranged to support the Transvaal's demand for Asiatics.[43]

Conditions at the gold mines frightened away native labor. The Witwatersrand Native Labour Association allocated recruits on a pro rata basis and so individual mines had no incentive to earn a reputation for good treatment. References were numerous to a Blue Book which contained the report of a committee of tribal representatives sent from Cape Colony in September 1903 to check the causes of why their people were loath to work on the Rand. Despite the obtrusive presence of management at the interviews, those from the Transkeian Territories were wrought up enough to describe the long hours, deceitful wage promises, unfit sleeping quarters, indifferent medical care, and physical abuse.[44] The *Manchester Guardian* regarded as discouraging the high rate of mortality from accidents, pneumonia, dietetic diseases, and phthisis. Unlike the Conservatives, whose interpretation of mortality statistics focused upon the encouraging note of steady improvement, it would go no further than to quote the appalling deathrate of 71 per 1,000 for 1903. This contrasted painfully with the 1903 record per 1,000 in the Kimberley diamond mines of 32.03 and in Rhodesia of 37.24.[45] Little wonder that natives preferred surface jobs in other occupations to work in the Rand deathtrap.[46]

It was to be doubted whether the advent of Chinese coolies would bring the economic benefits so confidently heralded. Local merchants would not profit, for the Chinese consumed only rice and salt fish. Their auxiliary wants would be few and the greater part of their wages would be remitted to the old country for enjoyment after repatriation. The argument advanced that starving Chinese coolies were being rescued from poverty at home by removal to the gold reefs was a cheap rationalization. Easing the condition of a few would not make a dent in the plight of the millions anchored in China. If this samaritan plea

*Labour recruitment figures for the pertinent months are as follows (*P.P.*, 1907, LVII, Cd. 3528, pp. 136-37): June 1902 (28,613), Dec. 1902 (42,305), June 1903 (60,200), Aug. 1903 (63,382), Jan. 1904 (67,994).

**The comment of William Grant would not seem to have been that emphatic: "The outcome today is the absolute result either of ignorance or design. I go as far as that." *P.P.*, 1904, XXXIX, Cd. 1897, p. 337.

to think of saving the Chinese from the horrors of life in their ancient land were sincere, then it was an act of cruelty on the part of mine-owners to acquiesce in their repatriation at the end of the contract period. Only the forces of avaricious capitalism stood to gain and the talk of prosperity all around was simply balderdash.[47]

The advent of Chinese coolies on the Rand must end in disaster for the Transvaal. That was not to reflect against the Chinese as they lived in their own land. A people best developed a personality under its own skies. China was as much wronged as South Africa when the family life of the Oriental was uprooted. The tragedy of Ireland had been the degeneration of its children when they migrated to the United States and so too the Israelites in their wanderings. It was not likely that the natives could stand aloof and the inevitable contact would produce a mixed race with low morals. Such a hybrid progeny might even be a more formidable menace to colonial whites, for the Chinese strain possessed greater powers of organization and tenacity. William Alexander McArthur, Liberal M.P., recalled his years in Australia (he had been born in Sydney) and how the Chinese were a plague spot, bringing with them almost every possible Oriental vice. Chinatown was the starting point of moral deterioration for the white community. The Chinese gambled, committed murder, and sold their women into prostitution. The first man who brought a cargo of blacks from Africa to Virginia in the seventeenth century could not dream that there would be nine million blacks in the United States today or that a bloody civil war would be fought over the slavery question. South Africa should take heed lest it suffer a similar fate.[48]

Certainly, the harness of servitude to be placed upon the Chinese coolies did not comport with the exalted ideals of Western civilization. They would enter as pariahs and dwell amidst circumstances akin to a penal colony. And to think that British children were taught to blame Spain because its silver mines in the new world had been worked with forced labor. William Sanders, active in the Fabian Society, commented upon the irony of Great Britain pouring out money and lives to bring freedom to oppressed Uitlanders, only to be confronted with the reintroduction of human enslavement. It was revolting to hear of such conditions as compounds, pass certificates, and compulsory repatriation.[49]

Perhaps the most elaborate thoughts penned on the inherent immorality of indentured labor were those of the *Church Times*, an Anglican weekly journal: *

What is being done is nothing less than the erection of a social order that shall be based on the principle of colour servitude. . . . Slavery in its mildest form is an evil, corrupting by the dishonour in which it places labour. But in certain stages of social development it appears to have some incidental advantages and populations otherwise irreclaimable have been raised through its operation. To bring about this effect it must be so ordered that the slave, if manumitted, or his descendants, can rise by personal worth to the level of his master. This was the redeeming feature of the brute slavery of ancient Rome. . . . But there is the one form of slavery which has no hope—the slavery of colour. . . . In the greater part of the United States this principle was firmly held. . . . The result was to demoralize labour. . . . The mining magnates of South Africa demand a slave system of this kind. . . . They are definitely bondsmen, imported under contracts. The safeguards of compounds and return to [their] country are probably inspired by the experience of the United States. . . . Even if the Chinese are returned it will degrade the coloured races of the colony and increase the difficulties of a stable social order.[50]

The image of a colonial public opinion solidly in favor of Asiatic labor was challenged. The vote of twenty-two to four in the Transvaal Legislative Council had been a foregone conclusion. As a nominated body, and influenced by Lord Milner, it recorded the wishes of the mineowners. Four adverse votes in the ranks of unofficial members suggested a strong undercurrent of hostile sentiment. The *Clarion* expressed skepticism as to the spontaneity of petitions supporting the case of the mineowners. Reports had it that the instruction to whites was "sign or sack." Samuel referred to the treatment accorded such well-known figures as Frederic Hugh Page Creswell, manager of the Village Main Reef mine, William Flavelle Monypenny, editor of the *Johannesburg Star*,** and Wilfred John Wybergh, Commissioner of

*The religious press, whatever its political leanings, joined forces with Liberals and Labourities against the use of indentured Asiatics.

**The editorial of Monypenny announcing his resignation is as follows: "To the policy of Chinese immigration, to which the Chamber of Mines has decided to devote its energies, the present editor . . . remains resolutely opposed and declines in any way to identify himself with such an experiment. To the ideal of a white South Africa, which,

Mines,* as lending credence to this impression. All three had been ousted from their posts because of opposition to the Chinese. The only way to ascertain the true nature of public opinion in the Transvaal was by a referendum or an election after the grant of responsible government.[51]

The fourth Baron Stanley of Alderley, an exponent of liberalism in the House of Lords, discounted the pro-Asiatic stand of the Free Church Council of Johannesburg. Its reactionary attitude was not surprising in view of the generous contributions of mineowners to their churches. It had been the same in the American South with clergymen defending the slave economy of their parishioners—the white plantation aristocracy. A better guide to spiritual righteousness was a letter written by the Rt. Rev. Arthur Chandler (Bishop of Bloemfontein) condemning the use of indentured labor as a degradation of human dignity.[52] Nor should the fact be ignored that the Boers, with few exceptions, regarded Asiatics with pronounced disapproval. In interviews and deputations, leading Boers had condemned the proposal. The final outcome could wreck reconciliation efforts, for the Boers would interpret the action as an entrenchment of a British mineowning plutocracy.[53]

Campbell-Bannerman feared that the Chinese coolie issue would split South Africa and weaken the federation movement. The disapproval voiced by the Cape Colony Legislature in July 1903 was a stern admonition. Nor was it true that Bond and Progressives had spoken out against Asiatics during the election in January 1904 only as a clever bid for the native vote. Public opinion among whites had hardened against the proposal and to espouse Asiatic importation would have been political suicide. As for the vote of thirty to two in the Natal Legislative Assembly supporting the right of the Transvaal to take its own counsel, that was not surprising. Since Natal resorted

to whatever qualifications it may necessarily be subject, is something very different from the ideal of a Chinese South Africa, he resolutely clings, with perfect faith that whatever its enemies may do today that ideal will inevitably prevail. But as the financial houses which control the mining industry of the Transvaal have for the present enrolled themselves among its enemies the present editor of the *Star* withdraws." *Johannesburg Star*, weekly edition, Dec. 5, 1903, 9d.

*The British Colonial Office understood that Wybergh had resigned under pressure for inefficient administration of his department. Resignation was permitted to save face and he had taken advantage of the Asiatic question to connect his resignation with his dissenting views on that subject. *P.R.O.*, c.o. 879/90, No. 715, c.o. 251/59.

to indentured Indian coolies, it could not easily deny a similar privilege to the Transvaal. Furthermore, Natal was beholden to the patronage of the Transvaal for trade in transit from its port at Durban. Lord Ripon had a different interpretation of the qualified sanction accorded Asiatic labor at the Bloemfontein Conference. The resolution was at best a grudging one and prefaced with the pronouncement that Asiatics on a permanent basis would be injurious to the best interests of South Africa. The controversy had planted "an apple of division between northern and southern colonies . . . and may lead to civil war as in America."[54]

Stress was placed upon the memorials of New Zealand and Australia as threatening an imperial crisis. Both had a special right to protest on the ground that they shed blood and incurred financial burdens during the Boer War in behalf of the oppressed Uitlanders. A force of 17,000 from the Australian states, 1,000 from the Commonwealth, and 6,000 from New Zealand was a sizeable contingent. The Earl of Carrington, Lord Chamberlain in the last Gladstone ministry, recalled his impressions as Governor-General of New South Wales of the deeply rooted hostility there to the Chinese. In May 1888, three ships, each carrying several hundred Chinese coolies on board, tried to dock at Sydney. The whole population turned out with swords and staves and the Chinese were not allowed to come ashore.[55] The most recent resolution passed by a vote of fifty-four to five in the House of Representatives on March 22, 1904 (and unanimously in the Senate on March 16), requesting a canvass of the Transvaal white population on the proposition, showed that Australia had not changed its mind. The second Baron of Tweedmouth, Liberal M.P. prior to 1894, believed that Canada held similar convictions although Sir Wilfrid Laurier, Prime Minister, had refrained from joining the Australasian states in their protest. At the request of British Columbia, he had raised the poll tax on immigrant Chinese from $100 to $500.[56] The appearance of Chinese coolies in the Transvaal could have a chilling effect upon the unity of the British Empire.[57]

USE OF WHITES

Conservative circles did not regard the alternative solution of unskilled white labor as feasible. A major impediment was its expensiveness on the basis of the standard of living expected of whites. A realistic family budget for a man, wife, and three children averaged £24 monthly.* At the very least, simply for a married couple, a wage of 12s. a day would have to be paid. Goldmann asserted that few mines could afford such a stipend. In 1899, eight outstanding deep-level mines spent £512,803 for skilled white labor and £410,696 for unskilled native labor. The total cost, including materials, came to £1,626,008 or 25s. 6d. per ton. Assuming the substitution of 6,943 unskilled whites at 12s. per day as equal in productivity to 13,877 natives at 2s. 4d. per day, the wages items would rise to £1,098,932. If the cost of skilled whites and materials remained constant, the total bill would come to £2,214,244 or 35s. 7d. per ton. In short, where the average profit of these eight mines in 1899 was 16s. 8d. per ton at world prices, use of unskilled whites would reduce it by one-third, a risky margin if the market value of gold dropped. As for the introduction of machine drills to make white labor more economical, Goldmann did not believe this technologically sound, especially on the western slope of the Rand where fissures were too narrow for their effective application.[58]

Lyttelton referred to a trial with 900 English navvies during 1903 on railway construction to point up the prohibitive cost of unskilled whites. After seven months the expense was found to be so high that their services were discontinued. If they had been retained to lay the entire seven hundred miles of track, the deficit above estimates would have been £1,400,000. As it was, for the time they were employed the budget ran over by £115,000.[59] Even more illuminating and pertinent was the experiment at the Village Main Reef mine where Creswell hired unskilled whites (along with natives) for the period from June 1902 to December 1903. They were paid 10s. a day plus food and lodging and yet the turnover was astonishing. Nearly 5,000 whites passed through the register for an average term of service of one month, and never more than 400 were on hand at any one moment.[60] Kinloch-Cooke contrasted the performance of the City and Surburban mine

---

*The Emigrants' Information Office (*Colonial Handbook*, No. 11, May 1904, pp. 25-26) issued some facts on living conditions for whites in the Transvaal: £24 10s. monthly minimum for a man, wife, and three children; £12 to £20 monthly rent for a five-room house; £3 10s. monthly rent for a single room; £8 to £13 monthly for board and lodging for one person.

using only natives with that of the mixed force employed by Creswell at the Village Main Reef mine. For the month of September 1903 the former crushed 16,500 tons at a profit of 23s. 4d. per ton while the latter crushed 18,045 tons at a profit of 7s. 3d. per ton.[61] The sacrifice of dividends to shareholders in the Village Main Reef mine was £3,000 per month per 100 stamps. If the experiment had been tried on the entire Rand, the annual loss would have been over £1,000,000.[62]

The tradition of racial supremacy operated as a potent obstacle to the use of whites for physical labor. The English navvies on railway construction got disgusted because white inhabitants roundly abused them for working alongside natives. Demobilized soldiers who sought work in the Transvaal left within three months, resenting the label of "white Kaffirs." Lord Selborne, shortly to replace Lord Milner in South Africa, in 1905, recounted a story told him by Lieutenant-Colonel Alexander Weston Jarvis, formerly a Conservative M.P. whose service during the Boer War as a yeomanry officer was marked with distinction. Colonel Jarvis had found that only one out of one hundred fifty men prepared to settle in South Africa would accept "Kaffir's work" and he quit after six weeks. Humanitarian and Negrophile alike might regret this prejudice but menial labor in a native environment proved distasteful to whites. Resort to the use of the less racially-conscious whites from the Continent was equally undesirable. Both Hungarians and Italians were unruly, liked alcohol too well, and would be a discordant element.* Their low standards of morality and sanitation would expose Europeans to depreciation in the eyes of natives. Whites held their primacy in South Africa by virtue of being the dominant race and to work with colored labor on equal terms would be to court disaster.[63]

However, confidence was expressed that the advent of Chinese coolies would increase the number of whites in the Transvaal. There would be a need for battery men, cyanide hands, carpenters, and shift bosses to go along with the contemplated army of foreigners. All of these jobs were of the skilled variety in which whites could properly

---

*This appraisal would appear to have been in response to letters carried in Conservative newspapers. An example is that of Herbert Reade, assistant secretary to the Board of Customs and Excise, who noted the use of Italians on the Cape-Natal railway line and of Hungarians in the coal mines of Pennsylvania and Alabama. *Morning Post*, Jan. 27, Feb. 7, 1903.

be employed. Kinloch-Cooke, applying the pre-Boer War yardstick of seven natives to one white, calculated that if the desired maximum of 50,000 were brought in, then 7,000 more skilled whites would be hired. That could easily mean a count of 800 whites for every 1,000 Chinese when women and children were included. In addition, increases in auxiliary classes of artisans and tradesmen to service the wants of an expanding white population would be needed. Indeed, the quickened volume of business generated by a booming Rand might enable railways to reduce import rates and thereby widen the circle of jobs financially possible for the white man as his living costs went down. A cycle of events could be set in motion for the greater employment of whites with due regard to racial dignity. But, unless the current labor shortage was rectified at an early date, the number of skilled whites on the Rand could dwindle.[64]

Liberal and Labour circles regarded the moment as portentous for the destiny of South Africa. The Asiatic question would decide its future as a white man's country in the image of Australia and Canada, or as a land where all the work was done by servile hands. In particular, the opportunity was present to achieve a preponderance of voting strength for British stock, thus assuring a community with a vigorous democratic life. Climate should be no obstacle considering how well British troops had held up during the severe test of long marches across the sun-scorched veldt. Gold mines were of no value to a country except as a means to an end. An influx of whites into California for the gold rush had meant that afterwards its vacant lands would be peopled by the right kind of settlers. Australia had pursued a white policy and, after the first flush of gold mining fever passed, many remained to engage in agriculture and crafts. MacDonald felt the urgency of a concerted effort on behalf of the white population already present. When he had been in South Africa during 1902, he saw jobless mechanics roaming the streets of Johannesburg. Unless something were done for them soon, an exodus of whites was inevitable.[65]

Admittedly, whites must be paid more but they were also more dependable and productive. One should never lose sight of the economic axiom that those industries which offered lucrative wages were soon made their own by white men, and employers never regretted it. A high wage bill was often the best stimulus to an enterprise, for it forced maximum application of new techniques and machinery. The *Investors' Review* touched upon the tremendous profits yielded by some of the Rand gold mines. Imagine any English business that paid dividends of 2,120 per cent as the Johannesburg Pioneer had done or the Wemmer of 472 per cent or the Bonanza of 165 per cent.* Surely, these and other mines could afford to employ the white man and still earn respectable profits. As for those mining properties so poor that they could only be worked by cheap labor, the answer should be that human beings were not a commodity to sacrifice upon the altar of private property. Honest wages and due dignity for the white worker would vanquish the labor difficulty in South Africa.[66]

Nor, for that matter, was the high cost of living insoluble. No doubt to maintain a standard in keeping with Western habits did involve greater expenditures for material things in South Africa. One must be chastened by the figures quoted for house rents and food. A family of four needed a sum of £20 monthly to make ends meet. Samuel believed some relief could be obtained if steamship and storage "rings" were broken. These monopolies boosted transportation rates for supplies far beyond a reasonable gain.** Once the first inroads were notched against their strangling effect, an entire sequence of beneficial developments would be set in motion. Whites could accept lesser wages. In turn a growing influx of whites would stimulate local produce for the home market and at cheaper prices. Housing projects on a large scale could be initiated with attendant savings inherent in mass production. The challenge was to start the ball rolling.[67]

Samuel defended the accomplishments of Creswell with unskilled

---

*The official figures cite dividends over the years from 1887 to 1905 of 2,107½ per cent for the Johannesburg Pioneer, 1,237 per cent for Wemmer, and 627½ per cent for Bonanza. *Transvaal Chamber of Mines*, Report, 1905, p. 216.

**Birchenough has an excellent description of the shipping ring and some comparisons of living costs between England and Johannesburg (*P.P.*, 1904, LXI, Cd. 1844, pp. 38, 62-64).

	ENGLAND	JOHANNESBURG
4 lbs. of bread	4d. to 5½d.	1s.
7 lbs. of oatmeal	10d.	3s. 6d.
7 lbs. of flour	1s. 6d.	1s. 9d.
1 lb. of tea	1s. 6d.	2s. 6d.
1 lb. of candles	4½d.	9d.
1 lb. of bacon	8½d.	1s. 4d.

whites in the face of the obstacles thrown across his path. He had to
deal with discharged soldiers who did not take kindly to the work and
with mineowners who displayed a distinct bias from the start. Yet a
comparison of costs in July 1899 (using only natives) with those in
July 1903 (using a mixed force) showed excellent results.[68] In the
cyanide works it was per ton 5.3d. and 4.9d. respectively. In the stamp
mill it was per ton 4.8d. and 4.2d respectively. In machine drill contract work per ton it was 6s. 4d. and 6s. 9d. respectively.* In the case
of the English navvies employed on railway construction, the men
were bad to begin with and simply would not work. The report of en-
gineers on the job was "that these men are not navvies at all, and are
determined to loaf through their year's agreement . . . and appear to
have come out with the intention of doing no work."[69] The Daily
News offered a comparison of the detailed cost of the Roodepoort
mine on the Rand and the Scottish Gympie mine in Queensland, the
former employing colored and the latter white labor. Over a four
months' stretch the costs per ton on the Roodepoort were £1 6s. 11.14d
and on the Scottish Gympie £1 8s. 2.52d., an insignificant difference
considering the stake of a white community. What made the achievement of the Australian mine more remarkable was the fact that in
depth of shaft, softness of ore, and gold content per ton of ore, the
advantages were all on the side of the Rand mine.[70]

Whether Asiatic labor would measurably increase the number of
whites was deemed highly problematical. Whereas on the Rand the
ratio figured out currently at one white to five blacks, experience with
Chinese coolies indicated a ratio of one white to fifty yellow men. The
Chinese were clever enough not to require the supervision bestowed
upon natives. Even when overseers were necessary, it should be obvious that the Chinese would have to be given bosses of their own
race who understood their language. Sir Hiram Stevens Maxim, in-
ventor of the automatic system of firearms and a transplanted American, noted the persistence with which the Chinese sought to remain
in the countries of their engagements. In the United States their lower
standard of living had driven white men out of one occupation after

*Creswell's critics, testifying before the Transvaal Labour Commission, credited his
good showing to reduced cost of explosives, elimination of sorting, and lower native
wages. P.P., 1904, XXXIX, Cd. 1897, p. 583.

another. They acquired and cultivated plots of ground and competed with local gardeners. Belatedly, American communities tried to contain them by heavy taxes and boycotts, but the Chinese could not be budged.[71] Maxim depicted their doughty qualities:

> The heathen Chinese has a large and highly-developed brain, the push and resource of a live Yankee, the financial and business ability of the Jew, the coolness and acquisitiveness of the canny Scot, and the patient and temperate habits of the Turks, all rolled into one. He has the strength and toughness of a mule, the appetite and digestive powers of an ostrich and the staying qualities of a steam engine.[72]

The *Westminster Gazette* accused the mineowners of envisaging an industry carried on by docile black labor with a limited number of highly paid whites. The case was given away in a report (submitted in January 1903 by the Transvaal Chamber of Mines to Lord Milner) of the need to guard against any "opening for that trail of the serpent, the formation of labour unions."[73] Lord Carrington offered a companion piece of evidence, summarizing a memorandum read before a meeting of directors of the South Africa Gold Trust Limited, on February 9, 1903, by Charles Dunell Rudd, a partner of Cecil Rhodes. The essence was that even if 100,000 whites could do the work of 200,000 blacks there was the undesirable consequence "that they would simply hold the government in the hollow of their hands."[74] Most frequently cited is a letter, dated July 3, 1902, sent to Creswell by Percy Tarbutt, chairman of the Village Main Reef mine, disapproving his experiment.[75] The significant paragraph is as follows:

> I [Tarbutt] have consulted the Consolidated Goldfields people and one of the members of the Board of the Village Main Reef has consulted Wernher, Beit and Company, and the feeling seems to be that if a large number of white men are employed on the Rand . . . the same troubles will arise as are now prevalent in the Australian colonies, i.e., that the combination of the labouring classes will become so strong as to be able to dictate, not only on questions of wages, but also on political questions by the power of their votes when a representative government is established.[76]

LABOUR IMPORTATION ORDINANCE OF 1904

On January 16, 1904, Lyttelton made known the decision of the British government to sanction the importation of Chinese coolies. Lord Milner lost no time in framing an ordinance, his staff having been at work on the details since November 1903. Passage through the Transvaal Legislative Council took almost one month, from the first reading on January 19 to the third reading on February 10. It was reviewed in the British Parliament between February 11 and March 4. Subsequently, in the House of Lords on March 18 and March 21 and in the House of Commons on March 21, a belated but vain effort was made by Liberal and Labour M.P.'s to censure the Conservative government for approval of an ordinance indifferent to human dignity. Royal assent was given on May 11. The final chapter related to negotiations with China, since under the *Convention of 1860* the Foreign Office would have to secure the consent of Chinese authorities. This was accomplished on May 13, 1904.[77]

As enacted, a Transvaal Emigrant Agent and a Chinese Inspector were to be stationed at the point of embarkation to explain the conditions of work to recruits. Regulations were prescribed for medical examinations and comfort on board ship. Durban was designated as the port of debarkation. Allocation of coolies would be limited to those mines granted licenses and with suitable housing accommodations on the premises. The contract was for three years plus renewal for another three years if mutually agreed upon. Repatriation was mandatory at the termination of the contract. The coolies would be restricted to unskilled labor on the Rand and a schedule of fifty-five prohibited trades was drawn up. They were forbidden to hold fixed property, must reside in compounds, and could not venture outside the compounds without a permit or for more than forty-eight hours. An identification card was to be carried at all times and to be shown on demand by the constabulary. The courts were to be accessible for registering complaints or seeking redress. Wages were to be the subject of further review but must be on a scale comparable to those paid natives and with an option for piecework. Transportation expenses were to be met by mineowners for those wives and children desirous of accompanying the coolies.

The British Colonial Office played an active role to secure an ordinance of the most humane nature. Lord Milner was bombarded with inquiries on recruitment procedures, safeguards during the voyage, adequate inspection in the mines, wage rates, and wholesome living conditions. Several conferences were held with representatives from the Foreign Office and the Chinese Embassy to iron out amendments requested by the latter. Some were incorporated in the *Ordinance* and others were pledged by word of mouth. A Chinese consular agent would have the right to visit mines and make representations for well-being. The employer would have no right to administer corporal punishment. It would be unlawful to transfer a coolie from one employer to another without his consent. Repatriation must take place at the original port of embarkation to avoid any coolie being stranded far from home. Quite troublesome were the terms of compensation to the Chinese government for administrative costs. The concern of the British Colonial Office was to avoid setting a precedent of high charges that might influence future recruitment on other occasions when the applicants might be less easily able to bear the expense. The compromise effected set £3 per head for the first 10,000 and £2 per head in excess of that number.[78]

Conservative circles approved wholeheartedly of the *Ordinance*. Advertisements would be circulated throughout Chinese villages publicizing the general conditions. Particulars would be explained and a certification obtained that the contract had been entered into voluntarily. Careful arrangements should assure comfort and sanitation on board ship, including the presence of an adequate medical staff. The compounds would extend over two square miles and promises were held out of garden plots and free seed. It was admirable to know that the plans called for hospitals, bathhouses, and gymnasia, all morale building facilities. The menu for the daily fare was impressive: one and one-half pounds of rice, one-half pound of fish, one-half pound of vegetables, and several ounces of tea. Their life would be a far cry from the cruelties practiced by Cortez in Mexico and Pizarro in Peru. Mineowners were well aware that unless they treated the Chinese considerately, the flow of recruits would lag. As for the anxiety manifested by Dr. Randall Thomas Davidson (Archbishop of Canterbury) of the moral implications if Chinese womenfolk did not come, Lyttelton promised that a concerted effort would be made to bring over their families.[79]

Aspersions of slavery were not suffered in silence. The sacrifice of personal liberty would be temporary, incurred voluntarily, and with full knowledge of the terms. This was a far cry from the status of chattel, abolished in 1833. Then, blacks were forcibly impressed, herded aboard ship like cattle, sold to the highest bidder, deprived of legal rights, and lashed with the whip. Some restrictions were necessary in lands where white men lived among hordes of semisavages. In many respects the conditions were identical with those under which natives labored on the Rand. Lord Selborne noted how well the *Ordinance* came off in a comparison with that of British Guiana (1895) and yet no one described the latter as partaking of slavery.[80] Whereas in British Guiana an Indian coolie could be transferred from one employer to another without his consent, that was prohibited in the Transvaal; in British Guiana the pay was approximately 1s. a day, in the Transvaal the prospect was 2s. a day plus food and lodging. True, the Indian coolie could remain and engage in other occupations. But British Guiana was a country where white men served only as entrepreneurs and welcomed others as a labor force. In the Transvaal, however, the white man had a chance to establish a community of his own and such concessions were impossible.[81]

Many persons at home were pictured as being in a status not unlike that of indentured Chinese coolies. Soldiers and sailors had to serve for a definite period. If a recruit sought to break his contract before the term of enlistment was up, he must tender a penalty payment. Men in the armed forces were confined to barracks and required to live in army quarters. The soldier was rarely given a forty-eight hour leave and only three per cent of them were allowed to marry. Balfour wondered if the lot of mercantile marine sailors would be labeled "slavery," since contracts were for the length of the voyage and some of these sea journeys often took three years. The general practice of English commercial houses in India and China was to article young clerks for periods from three to five years under agreements replete with restrictions. In many trades the custom of placing apprentices on a contract basis was widespread. Domestic servants in London were off work for no more than a few hours a week. All jobs entailed some limitations on human freedom.[82]

The Imperial State should not set itself in opposition to the wishes of the Transvaal. That would be to repeat the error of one hundred thirty years ago in respect of the American colonies. It had proved fatal then to override what kinfolk had deemed vital to their welfare. To interfere with settlers on the spot could provoke a demand for independence. Downing Street should cease to meddle in colonial domestic matters. *The Times* summed up the proper imperial role to be that of giving each offspring the widest latitude to manage local affairs in a manner dictated by its own interests. Only thus could the mother country prepare for cordial relations with the Transvaal when the day came for this wealthy colony to assume the responsibilities of self-government.[83]

Liberal and Labour circles saw nothing in the *Ordinance* to make importation of Chinese coolies palatable. It would be a physical impossibility to discuss thirty-five clauses and fourteen penalties with each recruit. Agents abroad would be concerned to round up the greatest number of recruits and any explanation of conditions would be perfunctory. If a Chinese decided not to sign, upon becoming suspicious that the work would be disagreeable, he could be left stranded at the port of embarkation without money and hundreds of miles from home. Deplorable, to say the least, was the denial of the privilege to engage in trade or to hold fixed property. What stimulation could there be if the lowest types of physical jobs remained their lot. Worse, the statement leaving wages as a subject for regulations was too general and uncertain and lent credence to the charge that mineowners were after cheap labor. Most depressing for those devoted to human dignity was the restricted life in the compounds, notably a mere forty-eight hour leave for trips outside the premises.[84]

The permission for families to come over at the expense of the mineowners sounded too much like a pious declamation. The contingencies were many—if the coolie asked for his wife, if she were willing to go, if the importer stirred himself. More likely the deciding factor would be the expense, and preference would be shown for single men. Experience even suggested that the Chinese coolie would be reluctant to bring along his family. As of 1901, for the Straits Settlements and the Federated Malay States, there were 462,375 Chinese males and 63,719 Chinese females and many of the latter were unmarried.*

*The official census figures of 1901 list 219,844 males and 62,729 females for the Straits Settlements and 273,475 males and 27,158 females for the Federated Malay States. P.P., 1905, CII, Cd. 2660, pp. 123, 128.

Major John Edward Bernard Seely (successively Colonel, Major-General and Baron Mottistone), who resigned his seat as a Conservative M.P. on the Chinese coolie issue and joined the Liberal party,† visualized what would happen if a desired forty per cent ratio of women really came to pass. On the basis of an ultimate 50,000 indentured Chinese coolies and reckoning three children to a family, eventually 250,000 Chinese would be assembled on the Rand. It was hard to believe that the intention to bring over an appreciable number of families could be sincere. In the meanwhile, one shuddered to envisage a crowded compound, some men crouched in corners smoking opium, others gambling, and still others seated in a circle watching a dance totally lacking in decency. Such cheap labor was dearly bought.[85]

No essential difference seemed to mark the status of an indentured coolie and a slave. True, the Chinese entered into the engagement voluntarily but that was like the old days when a man could sell himself into slavery to pay his debts. Certainly, to be kept under lock and key constituted a negation of liberty. Asquith called to mind Lord Milner's denunciation of Kruger for fixing the plight of a helot upon the Uitlander.* That statement now appeared hypocritical and stood forth as an excuse for the unworthier motive of protecting British interests in the gold mines. No guarantee was present that a Chinese coolie would have the benefit of a master's concern for his personal welfare. The mineowner was not apt to be solicitous for "property" only his temporarily. At least the plantation owner in America had a spur lest his chattel depreciate in value upon the auction market. Forsaken was the charter of human freedom fought for so arduously a century ago by William Wilberforce, redoubtable antislavery crusader.[86]

The religious press dwelt at length upon the indentured Chinese as a prototype of servitude.** The *Pilot*, an Anglican weekly, would

†Major Seely had fought in the Boer War and numbered Creswell as a fellow officer and perhaps had been imbued with the latter's hopes for a white South Africa. Seely (1930), pp. 102-05.

*Lord Milner's words were as follows: "The spectacle of thousands of British subjects kept permanently in the position of helots, constantly chafing under undoubted grievances . . . does steadily undermine the influence of Great Britain and the respect for the British Government within its own dominions." Headlam (1931), I, pp. 353-55.

**Religious circles were greatly wrought up over the moral consequences of bringing in thousands of Chinese coolies without their womenfolk. *Lords*, Feb. 12, 1904, pp.

not go so far as to say that the contract conformed to the image enshrined in "Uncle Tom." But it was a limited form of slavery without the alleviations of the old plantation life. The Chinese were being permitted to forego the attributes of liberty for a potage of gold. It should not be forgotten that English law forbade men to sell themselves even in order to escape starvation. The fact that any one who harbored or concealed a Chinese committed a breach of the Ordinance implied a sort of Fugitive Slave Law. The *Catholic Times* minced no words in defining the contract as a reintroduction of slavery under the Union Jack. Roman Catholics prided themselves on the long centuries during which the Papacy had fought slavery as a sin against God. The money magnates should pay decent wages and accord human dignity to labor of whatever color. The *Methodist Times* believed that it would be better if the prosperity of South Africa were delayed a generation than to let it become a community based on slavery. The British nation would do well to remember the fable of Atalanta, in the Greek myth, who stopped to pick up the golden apples and lost the race. The spirit of the *Ordinance* was un-Christian, condemning men to the status of mere "muscular machines."[87]

Sir Henry Fowler contested the favorable comparison drawn in Conservative circles between the *Ordinance* of the Transvaal and that of British Guiana. He recalled his own role in 1894 as Secretary of State for the Colonies in the further amendment of the latter to increase the privileges of the Indian coolie. These included a minimum wage, a forty-eight hour leave once a fortnight, and the right to hold fixed property. At the conclusion of his contract the Indian coolie was encouraged to stay and take his place as a member of the community. Over two hundred of the two hundred forty-six clauses were devoted to the protection of the Indian coolie. In contrast, all thirty-five clauses of the Transvaal *Ordinance* were concerned with assuring that the Chinese coolie carry out his contract of service. The *Daily Chronicle* declared that the refusal of India to permit the use of its people on railway work (so long as their countrymen in the Transvaal endured disabilities) spoke volumes. A study of ordinances in vogue everywhere in the British Empire—West Indies, Mauritius, Ceylon—would prove

174-75 (Bishop of Rochester); *Methodist Times*, Mar. 10, 1904; *Pilot*, Mar. 26, 1904; *The Times*, Feb. 8, 1904, 8b (Bishop of Worcester).

that the opportunity existed to better one's self.[88] That could not be said of the Transvaal *Ordinance*.[89]

The British nation was called upon to heed a proud heritage of uprooting slavery. There was the case of the Kanakas brought to Queensland in 1863 for labor on sugar plantations. When the abuses of "blackbirding" were disclosed, so great had been the adverse publicity that Australia (in 1904) forbade their use entirely.[90] The scandalous treatment of Chinese coolies on the guano deposits of Chincha Islands owned by Peru was ended by an appeal of Great Britain to the Chinese government for no more shipments of recruits.[91] So flagrant were the breaches of recruitment at the Portuguese port of Macao—kidnapping, cruelty, overcrowded ships—that the British government interceded in 1873, practically issuing an ultimatum to Portugal before the situation was rectified.[92] Three separate occasions could be listed with the Transvaal itself when the Imperial State had made it a condition of independence that there be no slavery: *Sand River Convention of 1852, Pretoria Convention of 1881, London Convention of 1884.* To bring the role of Great Britain up to date there was the recent quarrel with the Kruger regime. The Boer War had been fought to vindicate human rights in the Transvaal at a cost of twenty-five thousand lives and £250,000,000.[93]

Equally at stake was the current effort of Great Britain to promote an exemplary standard of moral conduct among nations. Indifference in this instance would expose the conscience of the country in its efforts to further a tradition of justice throughout the world. It would sound hollow to condemn the harsh tyranny of Russia, to pass resolutions against Turkish cruelties, and to circularize other states over abuses in the Congo Free State and yet to disclaim any responsibility for the ugly head of servitude rearing itself in an imperial territory. It was a matter of humiliation to have the Chinese minister in London insist upon amendments to the Transvaal *Ordinance.* An Englishman must bow his head in shame to learn that his government needed prodding to forbid corporal punishment or the transfer of a coolie as if he were a mere chattel. The obvious inference could be drawn that the lives of the Chinese counted for little in the Western world. British relations with the Orient would not be enhanced, for educated Chinese and Japanese also had tender sensibilities.[94]

3

The Chinese Coolie Experiment
Later Phase

THE ORDINANCE IN OPERATION

No time was lost in recruiting Chinese coolies for the Transvaal. On May 25, 1904, the first shipload sailed from Hong Kong with a contingent of 1,052 on board, two having absconded before the vessel left port. The *Tweedale*, weighing 2,800 tons, arrived at Durban on June 18, 1904, losing three coolies enroute. For three days the men underwent a complete medical check. The inspection was passed by 1,006 who were then placed on board closely guarded trains, unloaded on June 22 at Johannesburg, and assigned to the New Comet mine. From then on a steady stream of ships carried coolies across the sea to South Africa. The greater number were obtained in northern China and eventually embarkation was concentrated at the ports of Chifu and Chinwangtao. By the close of 1904, the number on the Rand totaled 21,000, rising to 41,000 in June 1905. When the Balfour government yielded power in December 1905, the count stood at 48,000. William Evans, Superintendent of the Foreign Labour Department set up to administer the *Ordinance*,* understood that the maximum figure envisaged was 55,000. Thereafter, unless circumstances altered, an occasional shipload for replenishment would suffice.[1]

A series of regulations were made known in June 1904. The original wages provision called for a minimum pay of 1s. per day for a ten-hour working day with higher rewards based on piecework. Lyttelton secured a change requiring that, if in six months the average monthly

---

*William Evans returned to the Straits Settlements after a year and was replaced in June 1905 by James William Jamieson, a commercial attaché in China.

pay did not equal 50s. under piecework, then the basic wage would be hiked to 1s. 6d. per day. Otherwise, he explained, if wages averaged 30s. a month, it could be charged that the coolie had been brought in to undercut the native. The option of a three-year renewal of contracts was clarified to require a full explanation in the presence of the superintendent's staff. A coolie desirous of breaking his contract must pay all transportation expenses both ways. An itemized list of the amenities to be supplied the coolie in the compound was set forth— free lodging, water, fuel, medical aid, food rations. The generous quota of holidays with pay included Sundays, Christmas, Good Friday, and Chinese festival days (New Year, Dragon Boat, Full Moon, Winter Solstice).[2]

Subsequently, the British Colonial Office maintained a check on the stipends earned by the coolies. When six months had rolled around for the first batch employed at the New Comet mine, the results were disappointing. Their pay did not come to more than 1s. per day, attributed to the poor quality of the early coolie shipments. Nevertheless, Lyttelton insisted that the minimum be raised to 1s. 6d. per day as pledged. Whether the mineowners should be allowed to couple it with a production norm of thirty-six inches rock-drilling was duly weighed. Ommanney recognized that the Chinese could not be discharged and some lever in the form of a wage deduction was desirable against shirkers. Perhaps the mineowners should be given the right to require a minimum amount of drilling for a daily wage of 1s. 6d. but warned at the same time of costly court expense if its legality were contested. At any rate, the Chinese could always appeal abuses through the Superintendent of the Foreign Labour Department. As for those on piecework contracts, the Transvaal authorities were instructed to keep close check on the adequacy of their rewards.[3]

(Sir) Douglas Orme Malcolm, shortly to accompany Lord Selborne to South Africa as his private secretary, gathered information for Lyttelton's use in the House of Commons, to explain the fewness of wives in early shiploads. Elsewhere the facts showed that coolies simply would not avail themselves of the opportunity to bring their families with them. In Australasia, an examination of census reports between the 1860's and 1880's, before immigration restrictions were imposed, disclosed how small was the ratio of females to males among the Chinese: New South Wales (2 females and 12,986 males);

Queensland (13 females and 10,399 males); Victoria (8 females and 24,724 males); Tasmania (2 females and 842 males); South Australia (5 females and 4,146 males); Western Australia (no females and 145 males); New Zealand (16 females and 5,017 males). The census for the Straits Settlements in 1901 disclosed that of every 1,000 Chinese present there were 821 males and 179 females and yet here they could make a permanent home. A *Royal Commission Report on Chinese and Japanese Immigration into British Columbia* (1902) listed Victoria with 141 females and 3,132 males and Vancouver with 27 females and 2,053 males.[4]

Lambert took a prosaic view of the moral implications of an exclusive Chinese male population in the compounds. If the reports of Evans were true, that the Chinese were resorting to native prostitutes, "it is a natural and comparatively harmless solution of the difficulty." It was a "lesser evil than the importation of white women which has gone on for years in South Africa [for the white miners] despite the efforts of Governments to stop it." The vital point is that "we have been assured" the prosperity of the Transvaal depended on the gold mines and to go on a moral crusade was to bite off one's nose. Coolie labor was necessary "and we can hardly throw it over . . . for the sake of a moral ideal which I fear has little justification in the existing facts of any country in the world." At least the Chinese would not appear to practice incontinency nor indulge in sodomy judging from the *Royal Commission Report on Chinese and Japanese Immigration into British Columbia* (1902). From 1878 to 1901, out of seven hundred thirty-seven prison inmates, one hundred fifty-one were Chinese and only three were convicted of offenses under the heading of immorality. These figures should offer the Archbishop of Canterbury some comfort that extreme social evils did not necessarily attend the importation of Chinese coolies.[5]

Persistent reports of coolies being maltreated were checked. Time and again in the House of Commons, Lyttelton assured members that such accounts were inaccurate. If lashes were inflicted, it was done in accordance with the promises to China and in the presence of the governor or deputy governor of the prison. Sentence was delivered by a magistrate and confirmed by a judge of the High Court. It was then humiliating to learn from Lord Selborne (in August 1905) that illegal flogging had occurred. Mineowners had become exasperated by the petty offenses of the coolies and found discipline difficult and time-consuming through the slow processes of the courts. The upshot had been a meeting between representatives of the mines and Evans. Permission was granted managers to mete out light punishment for minor infractions such as dilatoriness, insanitary practices, gambling, and fighting. Apparently excessive lashings were frequent, especially between March and April 1905, after Evans had departed and before his successor, Jamieson, had arrived on the scene. When the facts came to light, Sir Arthur Lawley, Lieutenant-Governor of the Transvaal, issued on June 13, 1905, a circular canceling the de facto authority of the mines to handle disciplinary cases.[6]

An inquiry was instituted by the British Colonial Office to determine responsibility. The presence of Evans in London led to an interview on September 29, 1905. While Evans was not sure of the date, he insisted that Lord Milner had been informed of the step taken. When contacted, Lord Milner stated that he had no recollection of the matter but was not prepared to doubt Evans' word. Nor would he seek exoneration when Lord Selborne confessed himself unable to find written documents relating to the affair which Evans said were in the files of the Foreign Labour Department. Evans asserted that he had not delegated powers, but had only given permission to the mines for mild discipline in minor infractions. When coolies did complain of brutality and the facts substantiated the charge, he had procured the dismissal of the guilty parties and in some instances even prosecuted them. The British Colonial Office regretted the failure of local authorities to appreciate the gravity of their action. The distinction between slight corporal punishment and flogging was illegal and one "which public opinion here will not tolerate for a moment." And the Chinese government could make things very embarrassing in view of the solemn pledge given that there would be no corporal punishment save through due process of law.[7]

For the moment, if Lord Selborne was pressed to carry on a further inquiry into Evans' story, the promulgation on September 22 of an amendment, (No. 27 of 1905), for more effective discipline in a legal manner had to be considered. Jurisdiction was conferred on the superintendent and his staff to try any offense summarily triable by a resident magistrate if committed on the premises of the mine. The mineowner was to provide a lockup pending trial and an inspector must visit each compound once every forty-eight hours. Any infliction of corporal punishment must be confirmed by the Supreme Court. A fine could be levied against the head boy for failing to report any offense committed by a coolie in his gang. A collective fine could be levied against the entire gang if the offense were concealed as the result of conspiracy among the coolies. For the sale of opium to coolies or its possession by the latter, a maximum fine of £20 or three months' imprisonment could be imposed.[8]

The British Colonial Office staff was somewhat disconcerted that Lord Selborne should give the amendment a quick assent. While a tentative approval had been previously given the general proposal, the "finished product" was not entirely pleasing. The threat of a fine would encourage a head coolie to offer false testimony. Resort to a collective fine was questioned "as it hits the innocent as well as the guilty." Keith predicted that the ban against opium would be a source of trouble, for the Chinese had become accustomed to its use. Still there was nothing to justify withholding consent. It should be accepted on the ground of urgency and so defended in the face of a probable attack by the anti-Chinese party.[9]

Whether the background was maltreatment or the presence of bad characters, a wave of disturbances occasioned by Chinese deserters created a perilous situation. Lord Selborne held meetings with Boer leaders, Botha and Smuts among others, whose people were the most directly affected by the assaults in the countryside. Farmers were furnished with firearms, albeit a security of £20 had to be deposited for their eventual return. A ring of posts was set up around the mines, never more than five miles apart and manned by additional constabulary. Subsequently, in October 1905, several regulations were issued under No. 27 of 1905. A roll call would be held every Sunday to check resident Chinese in the compounds. Fees were to be paid for bringing in Chinese deserters, ranging from 1s. per mile for one Chinese to 3s. per mile for eight or more Chinese. Hardened criminals would be repatriated and Chinese authorities asked to prevent their reenlistment for work in the Transvaal. Only in reference to the last-mentioned proposal did Lyttelton offer any objection. Chinese judicial methods were barbaric, including the use of torture, and British public opinion would be against such practices. He would go no further than to seek the "benevolent cooperation" of the Chinese government.[10]

The British Colonial Office staff discussed the ethical issue invoked in connection with the contracts of future recruits and the
omission of the amendment imposing new penalties. Just reflected
that "it is very good for us if no one raises the objection regarding the
alteration of the contract by legislation." But brushing off the obligation to acquaint a recruit with the full details of his contract was expediency of the worst kind, solely in the interest of mineowners. Graham argued that to insist upon the technicality of having contract
changes subject to renegotiation with the Chinese authorities would
prevent "the smallest amendment and place us in an impossible position." He agreed that the duty was there to warn the coolie of any
fresh legislation "but to do so will frighten many away." A more practical reconciliation of conscience might be to prohibit any new restrictions which could not fully be justified for the benefit of all
concerned. Ommanney would hew to the strict legal line, feeling that
"we have gone as far as we can in adding new penalties in the contract
and we should not let the impression get abroad that future contracts
are mere waste paper." Lyttelton regarded the fact that the governor
was required to reserve for review by the British Colonial Office any
laws affecting the coolie as sufficient protection.[11]

Lord Selborne and Lyttelton engaged in a lengthy correspondence
over the causes of the disturbances. No doubt the illegal floggings had
aroused the resentment of the Chinese and provoked retaliation. The
baneful influence of the gambler and the thief, seeking to batten upon
the innocence of their countrymen, played their part. But more than
anything else, the lack of rapport between the white miners and the
Chinese constituted the real difficulty. The barrier of a foreign tongue,
indifference to their Oriental customs, and abusive language provoked
misunderstandings and ill will. Often an impatient management applied violence to get its commands across. When the coolie deserted in
desperation and wandered about in hunger, an inability to communicate his desire for food to the farmer brought altercations. The evident solution must be more compound managers and government
inspectors fully conversant with North Chinese dialects. Lyttelton
would have Lord Selborne spare no expense to increase the number of
such experts.[12]

Conservative circles expressed satisfaction with the way the experiment proceeded in 1904 and 1905. An answer was ready at hand for a critical pamphlet written by the Rev. Arnold Foster, Wesleyan Methodist missionary stationed in Wuchang, Central China.[13] Apparently Foster had read in the March 28, 1904 issue of the *China Times*, a Tientsin newspaper, a copy of the contract terms which failed to mention that there were no opportunities in the skilled trades or to buy land, that there was confinement to compounds, and that passes were limited to forty-eight hours. Granted the truth of his observations, the omissions were not purposely intended. The fault rested in the hastiness with which the advertisement was drawn up for quick circulation. The document seen by the Rev. Arnold Foster was probably drafted before the final terms were settled. However, by June 1904, when recruitment went into high gear, the formal contract had been made freely accessible to the Chinese. A worthier indication of the intention to treat the coolies handsomely was the amended wages regulation, calling for a minimum pay of 1s. 6d. per day, if earnings were below that after six months, and for the opportunity for still greater earnings through piecework.[14]

The compounds were pictured as quite comfortable, featuring spacious open areas and boasting excellent sanitary arrangements. Frequent references were made to the commendations of Thomas Burt, Lib-Lab M.P. and trade unionist, and so a source of information which the working class should accept as trustworthy. Burt stated "that I have inspected the compounds, kitchens, dining halls, . . . hospitals and having seen the food supplied to them, I do not think . . . there can be any reasonable complaint."[15] An Imperial South African Association pamphlet, an organization founded in 1896 to promote federation under the Union Jack and currently under the presidency of the fourteenth Baron Windsor, First Commissioner of Works, regarded as significant the change in the views of John William Quinn, one of the two authors of the Minority Report. At a banquet in Johannesburg during January 1905, Quinn confessed "that he renounced for the future all opposition to Chinese Labour. . . . The situation had now changed. . . . The Ordinance is passed, the Chinese are here, and the people seem contented. The question, therefore, is finished."[16]

(Sir) Lionel Phillips, previously associated with Eckstein and Com-

pany, Conservative M.P. after 1910, and one of four participants in
the Jameson Raid condemned to death and then released, submitted
his observations on a recent visit to South Africa:

> The Chinese have a love of plants and of birds that is pleasant to wit-
> ness. It is not uncommon to see a number of them gathered round some
> simple flower of the veld, which they touch and smell, but do not pick,
> and which they often end by digging up to plant in front of their bed-
> room in the compound. Many of them keep birds, over which they appear
> to exercise great influence.
>
> The tastes of the Chinamen [are] far more exalted than those of the
> Kaffirs and [they] purchase watches and clocks. . . . Indian hawkers do a
> roaring trade with them in fruit and in mineral waters, especially of the
> coloured variety, pink lemonade being particularly in favour.
>
> On several occasions I went out to see the coolies have their dinner.
> . . . At the Glen Deep, Limited, for instance, they have a dining room
> capable of seating 1,500 at a time. The order and cleanliness that prevails
> is beyond criticism. In the adjoining kitchen huge vessels, some contain-
> ing well-cooked rice, and others stewed meat and vegetables, emit fumes
> of a most appetising description. . . . No limit is placed upon the
> quantity of rice or tea which the coolies require, and the rations of meat
> are in every respect adequate. . . .[17]

Not too much concern was manifested at the arrival of only two
wives and twenty-six children during the first year. Lyttelton quoted
Evans to the effect that he did not anticipate any large contingent of
families unless restrictions on the rights of coolies to stay, to buy land,
and to engage in trade were removed. But the fact that over 4,000
coolies had registered as married men, with the privilege reserved to
bring their families over in the future, suggested any judgment now
would be premature. Perhaps a Chinese wanted to familarize himself
with conditions in a new land before pulling up stakes in the old country. However, Lyttelton affirmed that he would resist any requirement
that a forty per cent quota of wives must accompany the coolies. The
basis should be an opportunity to do so if the coolies so desired. The
Archbishop of Canterbury was not comforted by the conflicting
opinions and the disappointing statistics and continued to express
regret over the absence of their families. If it was indeed a fact that a

Chinese coolie would not take his wife with him, then the grave moral consequences should be reviewed.[18]

Accounts of lawlessness were dismissed as grossly exaggerated. It would be surprising if a few breaches of the law did not occur among the Chinese assembled on the Rand. There were bad characters even in the crew of a first-class battleship in the Royal Navy. Occasional desertions were known to take place in the British Army. Sir Frederick Milner, Conservative M.P., referred to statistics quoted by Sir Richard Solomon, Attorney-General for the Transvaal.[19] Speaking before the Transvaal Legislative Council in September 1905, he noted that with 45,000 Chinese present only five hundred forty-nine convictions were cited for offenses other than violations of labor regulations and only 68 served jail sentences exceeding six months. In the case of desertions, which were listed as three hundred for the first three months (during the fall of 1904), the offense amounted to absence from the premises without taking the trouble to apply for a permit. What should be borne in mind was that as larger numbers arrived disturbances would be fewer. The newcomers would find compatriots ready to teach them the ropes and so were less likely to go astray.[20]

Nor was the failure of employed whites to increase in proportion to coolies disturbing. The managerial staff had to be kept intact despite the labor shortage because key men were difficult to replace and such personnel were necessary however small the number of laborers. But once the balance was struck between officialdom and unskilled, the ratio of whites would rise. Lyttelton passed along an added explanation he had received from Lord Milner. As coolies arrived on the Rand, the hand drill replaced the machine drill and its white operator. The latter had been a temporary expedient during the labor shortage, for it was an undesirable technique on narrow reefs. Only fifteen of the active seventy-one gold mines could advantageously use machine drills to break ore. The objections were several: 1) possible collapse of the roof under the impact of blasting operations with danger of injury to the worker, 2) the expense of sorting large quantities of waste rock, 3) the greater chance of contracting phthisis from a heavy bombardment of dust. Certainly, in an absolute sense, there had been an increase of whites on the Rand from 13,500 in June 1904, before the arrival of the Chinese, to 15,500 in January 1905 with 27,000 Chinese present, and to 18,500 in October 1905 with 45,000 Chinese present.[21]

An even more positive case could be made out coupling the advent
of the coolie with an accelerated tempo of native recruitment. While
in June 1904 there were 68,174 natives at work in the mines, the figure
rose to 76,611 in December 1904, to 81,445 in February 1905, and to
97,721 in the spring of 1905. Raymond William Schumacher, an associate in Eckstein and Company, attributed the abrupt decline to
87,119 in October 1905 to the unfavorable climate created by the
threat of the Liberal party to end the Chinese coolie experiment if
voted into office. Naturally the natives sensed a possibility to apply
bargaining pressure. But once confusion had cleared away (presumably
by a Liberal defeat at the polls), the trend would be upwards again.
At any rate, an absolute increase in natives had been recorded and
could be explained by the competition of the Chinese. Then, too, the
coming of the Chinese had released many natives for work on farms,
railways, and public projects.* In this connection Sir Gilbert Parker,
Conservative M.P. and an arch imperialist, pointed out the respective
expense of native and coolie recruitment, giving a lie to the charge
that the Asiatic came cheaper. Where it cost £10 15s. per native, it
was £14 10s. plus £6 return passage (correctly, an overall £16 11s. 3d.)
per Chinese. In addition, the food cost was 5¾d. per day for the
native compared to 11d. per day for the coolie.[22]

The most impressive of all the credits flowing from the presence of
the Chinese was a revived economic life in the Transvaal. The *National Review* published an article by Chaplin comparing the performance in May 1904 of fifty-seven mines, working 4,810 stamps for
an output of 306,586 fine ounces of gold with that in November 1904
when sixty mines, working 5,235 stamps, produced 327,090 fine ounces
of gold. In monetary value the monthly output in October 1905 was
at the rate of £20,000,000 per annum, matching the high-water mark
in August 1899 just prior to the Boer War. Great Britain shared in the
prosperity to the tune of £3,250,000 worth of orders for new machinery
and materials. The additional 2,500 whites employed by February
1905 meant, on the basis of £1 per day wages, a further sum of nearly

*Lord Selborne, in a dispatch to Lyttelton, September 18, 1905, noted the advantages
that would accrue to natives from the new hospitals set up and shared by native and
coolie alike and from the influence which should bear fruit of the up-to-date Chinese
compounds and their excellent facilities for hot water, baths, and sanitation. P.R.O.,
c.o. 291/85.

£900,000 per year put in circulation. Dr. J. C. Pearson, now practicing in Brighton but for thirty years a physician in South Africa, asserted that the Chinese were filling the coffers of local merchants. On a recent visit he had personally observed their liberal purchases of watches, musical instruments, fruits, and cigarettes. One would do well to remember that the native saved his money to buy cattle and wives for the kraal.[23]

Liberals and Labourites were confirmed in their premonitions that the *Ordinance* would operate as an instrument of enslavement. Rev. Arnold Foster's statements were proof enough of the manner in which recruitment would be carried on. The advertisement which he had read in a Tientsin newspaper maintained discreet silence on the nature of the work, the severe penalties for contract violations, and the provision of compulsory repatriation. A writer who went by the name of "English Witness" did not believe it was possible for the coolie to enter upon an engagement with his eyes open. The recruiting agent had a long and complicated document to administer and to explain it fully to the thousands being hired in haste would be beyond practicality. And, for that matter, the experiences of a military recruiter indicated that the technique was more like a barrister with only one side of the story to tell. The hardships of a soldier's life were never mentioned; rather the splendid chance to serve king and country and to be admired by the female species for the handsomely fitted uniforms. As for the amended regulation raising the minimum wage to 1s. 6d. per day if the average fell below that after six months, that burst the bubble of glowing promises of 2s. per day. More, the insistence upon a production norm of thirty-six inches rock-drilling meant that the coolie would have a greater challenge to make the same wage as a native free from that requirement.[24]

Thomas Burt was embarrassed by the way Conservatives had turned his description of the excellent living conditions in compounds to their own advantage. When considered in the full context of his observations, the perspective was different. Much of the life bore a likeness to convict labor at Dartmoor in Kent. A person might be sumptuously fed and comfortably housed and yet not be necessarily compensated for the loss of his freedom. The sentinel at every gate and a three years' confinement in a compound reflected a penal institution. Baron Stanmore, a Gladstonian Liberal and veteran colonial administrator, commented "that to read accounts of how well fed and housed they are is like reading accounts of his old Inspector-General of Prisons in Ceylon." The latter always boasted with pride how sanitary the jails were, as if prisoners should take special solace in that as the end aim in life. Hordes of able-bodied males, huddled in close barracks and guarded during work and leisure hours, were inevitably degraded by the terms of their service. An indentured labor system, be it ever so well administered, sinned against the fundamental laws of civilization because it treated mortals primarily as machines.[25]

Serious indeed were the stories circulating of physical abuse meted out to coolies. Burt quoted a passage from a letter sent him by a friend whose testimony he valued highly:

> Flogging . . . by the mine officials is resorted to for the most trivial offenses. I have personally seen coolies covered with weals from calf to buttock, inflicted in the compound by the . . . manager and his head coolies. This is an everyday occurrence, numbers being flogged indiscriminately without any form of trial whatever. . . .

The *Westminster Review* called attention to the charge of Frank C. Boland, Johannesburg journalist, that "the average number of coolies flogged daily for one month early this year [1905] was 42, Sundays included . . . and during the first quarter of this year no fewer than 56 coolies were whipped after 8 P.M. one evening, . . . the dose averaging from five to fifteen strokes."[26] The *Daily Chronicle* regarded the resignation of Thomas A. See, Chinese adviser on the East Rand, in protest against the maltreatment of his countrymen as damaging. His article in its columns on July 31, 1905, was a terrible indictment of the mineowners.* Even if it were true that the coolie violated his contrac-

---

*See started work in October 1904 and quit in March 1905. After his resignation he traveled to England and was invited by the *Daily Chronicle* to communicate his experiences to its readers. See claimed that fifty per cent of the first batch of coolies were ignorant of what they were to do and others thought that they were to be soldiers. When he left, their status was deteriorating rapidly. The rations were no longer good and the amount cut down. Many were the violations for which they were fined and whipped, and weeping was not infrequent. It was not surprising that the coolie should prefer to have his family stay at home. *Daily Chronicle*, July 31, 1905, p. 6. The British Colonial Office placed little credence in his story, referring to a letter written by him in which he offered to remain in the employ of the mineowners if they outbid the Chinese community who had commissioned him to visit England in their behalf. P.R.O., c.o. 291/92.

tual obligations, it could not justify the medieval cruelty of flailing him with "a strip of black leather at the end of a three foot wooden handle [sjambok]."[27]

That embittered Chinese coolies should throw caution aside and launch a reign of terror was not surprising. White settlers on dispersed farms were in mortal fear of assault and pillage. It was a daily sight to see a mounted policeman riding in the direction of the prison, followed by a string of Chinese deserters. Hundreds of Chinese prisoners were put to work on the roads. The countermeasures taken were a poignant commentary on the prevailing hysteria. Squadrons of extra constabulary were posted around the Rand to forestall escapes. It was something to read the announcement that the Transvaal government would issue arms and ammunition to farmers with the instruction "that they are not to hesitate to shoot."[28] As of July 1905, with 43,000 Chinese on hand, the count was 2,500 convictions for crime, 1,600 repatriated for cause, 1,700 charged with desertion, and 620 dead. The *Daily Chronicle* challenged the emphasis placed by Sir Richard Solomon (and so well played up by Conservatives) upon the low ratio of one-seventh of one per cent for offenses exceeding six months' imprisonment up to July 1905. More pertinent were the 2,475 cases with less than six months' imprisonment and the 21,205 cases of unlawful absence from work. This was proof enough of the criminal character of the recruits and they should be shipped home at once before the situation got entirely out of control.[29]

A moral crisis was seen to be in the making. A total of two women and twenty-six children in the first year did not speak well for the assurances given the Archbishop of Canterbury. The fact that only 4,000 out of 43,000 Chinese coolies had bothered to register their families for future passage suggested intentional recruitment of those who would not. In the meanwhile, related Thomas Naylor, special correspondent sent by the *Daily Chronicle* to investigate on the spot, there was much fraternization between coolies and native women. Large quantities of opium were reported as being imported.* Once such a vice as opium smoking gained a foothold, it would be difficult

*A committee was appointed to inquire into the extent of opium smoking on mine premises. The outcome was the inclusion in No. 27 of 1905 of severe penalties for the sale of opium to Chinese coolies or their possession of it. P.P., 1906, LXXX, Cd. 3025, p. 82, Cd. 2786, p. 59.

to curb the spread to natives. Opium dens were reputed to be springing up in Johannesburg, adding the depravities of the Orient to those inherited from the jungle atmosphere of a mining camp. The *Speaker* wrote with a heavy hand of the havoc being wrought:

> No man of this generation who can picture the hideous life that is lived on the Rand, the brawls of exiled people crimped and cheated out of their homes, the repulsive confusions of race, and the dark foundations of debased labour upon which, we are told, the ruined Transvaal can alone be built, will ever again speak of Imperialism without remembering that he has seen the death that is in it.[30]

Naylor questioned whether the Chinese were really good workers. He cited the testimony of Herbert Hoover, at that time a mining engineer and later to become President of the United States. Hoover had visited South Africa in 1904 to study mining developments. On the day when he toured the New Comet mine where the first batch of coolies were employed, he was informed that sixty-five were in the hospital and one hundred ninety-seven absent from the job. That number constituted over one-fifth of the contingent. Hoover described those he saw rock drilling as "a very poor lot, indeed, and certainly not worth the trouble and expense of bringing out." Highly paid whites were in his estimation far more efficient than the Chinese on the Rand.[31]

The achievement in terms of employed whites did not seem very remarkable. In September 1904, after three months of Chinese labor, the extra 100 whites taken on along with the contingent of 1,000 Chinese, meant a ratio of 1 to 10. This was to be contrasted with the fact that in 1903 there were 174 whites to every 1,000 natives, rising by August 1904 to 183 whites for every 1,000 natives. Worse, in the succeeding months as the Chinese poured in, a steady drop was to be recorded for whites as against 1,000 colored (natives and Chinese): 170 (September), 158 (October), 150 (November), 143 (December). A year later, by November 1905, the situation remained unimproved. Where in June 1904 there were 13,143 whites and 74,632 natives (or 2 whites to every 11 natives), on October 31, 1905, an additional 4,946 whites were employed while natives increased to 96,392 and Chinese to 45,956 (or a ratio of 2 whites to every 27 colored). One must lament with Creswell the evidence that prior to June 1904 the whites were steadily reducing the ratio between themselves and the natives.[32]

What made the statistics more pathetic was the fact that many of the extra whites were employed on a temporary basis to construct compounds. The predictions had come true that Chinese overseers would be preferred to whites and that the presence of cheap labor would favor the hand drill over the machine drill and its white operator. The statement issued in January 1905 by the Emigrants' Information Office that no demand existed for white miners in the Transvaal and that many on the spot were unemployed was depressing.[33] Further, none of the 127,000 (correctly, 119,504) British emigrants in 1904 going to different parts of the Empire went to the Transvaal.[34] John Atkinson Hobson, Liberal in party affiliation and a critic of imperialism, predicted a sad future for the Transvaal:

> The effect . . . is to . . . diminish the demand for white settlers. . . . In the end, when the mines are worked out, the Hebrew mining speculators, American and Scotch engineers, and German traders will evacuate the country they have sacked, leaving behind them a population of Boers spoiled in large part by their contact with a gambling and luxuriant European civilization.[35]

ADVENT OF THE LIBERAL GOVERNMENT

When Balfour handed in his resignation on December 4, 1905, a Liberal government became a reality. Campbell-Bannerman accepted the task of forming a cabinet. At the British Colonial Office a new team took over, replacing Lyttelton and the Duke of Marlborough. The ninth Earl of Elgin and Kincardine, Viceroy of India from 1894 to 1899, was named Secretary of State for the Colonies, and (Sir) Winston Churchill, already boasting an escapade as a newspaper correspondent during the Boer War, succeeded as Parliamentary Under-Secretary of State for the Colonies. Subsequently, in January 1906, a general election was fought and a sweeping victory achieved at the polls, firmly establishing the Liberal party in power.

That a Liberal government would be committed to undoing the *Ordinance* had been made known on numerous occasions. At the opening session of the House of Commons on February 16, 1904, Samuel moved an amendment to the King's Address denouncing the draft ordinance. At the annual meeting of the National Liberal Federation, May 12-14, 1904, in Manchester, a resolution was unanimously passed "that the proposal is inconsistent with the common law of England, destructive of the love of liberty, inimical to the true interests of South Africa, and likely to weaken the bond of union between the several portions of the Empire." At Dundee, on November 18, 1904, Campbell-Bannerman went on record that "if and when the time comes for us to take over the responsibility of government, we shall approach the question from the point of view of the permanent interests of the country and not merely from the point of view of the temporary exigencies of those who financed the gold mines."[36]

Campbell-Bannerman spelled out his views when called to account by Frederic Mackarness, Liberal M.P., barrister, and past advocate of the Cape Supreme Court, for stating in the summer of 1905 that a Liberal government would leave the decision of Chinese labor to a self-governing Transvaal. Mackarness expressed alarm at the possibility that if the Transvaal endorsed it then indentured coolies would stay. Surely, an experiment which had produced flogging and riots and fostered an atmosphere of moral turpitude should not be tolerated under any circumstances. If there "is any one thing that would make liberals hesitate to grant full self-government to the new Colonies, it would be the prospect of their using [it] to perpetuate such a state of things." Campbell-Bannerman reassured Mackarness that his words in Parliament on July 27, 1905, did not mean to absolve Great Britain "from any further liabilities." It should be "a standing assumption in all our dealings with every part of the Empire that nothing of the nature of slavery is to be tolerated." Therefore, it followed that the status of Chinese coolies "together with the conditions under which they are recruited and brought into the country must under any circumstances remain a matter of Imperial concern." This duty was doubly imposed in the case of the Transvaal because "a British government has made itself immediately and directly responsible for setting up the present system of Chinese labour with all its hateful features."[37]

Unanimity was by no means present in Liberal ranks. (Sir) Arthur Basil Markham, a mining engineer by profession, felt so angry at the description of the *Ordinance* as slavery that he placed his resignation in the hands of the party. However, it was not accepted and in the general election of 1906, he won an unopposed seat. As he saw it, no one considered the British Guiana *Ordinance* as partaking of servitude and the Transvaal *Ordinance* was superior in many respects. The period of indenture in British Guiana lasted five years compared to three in the Transvaal. The Indian coolie had to wait ten years for a return passage and then must pay one-fourth of the cost while the Chinese coolie had his passage paid in full after three years. The confinement area in British Guiana averaged five acres where in the Transvaal it was two square miles. Captain Malcolm Kincaid-Smith, whose military career included service in India and the Boer War, declined to make use of election placards depicting the mineowners as "slave driver masters." His sources of information indicated that such insidious phraseology gave an erroneous impression of compound conditions. Eustace Fiennes, whose military career included service in Egypt and the Boer War and who had been connected with Rand gold mining enterprises, personally saw to it that "the horrible pictures representing the Chinese as slaves . . . polluting the walls in other constituencies were burnt in my committee room." The restrictions on liberty were no more onerous than the pass system under which natives lived, and the generous provisions for food, lodging, and earnings were far better than available in their own country. The Liberal party took no disciplinary action, granting its members indulgence to speak their minds.[38]

At the outset the Liberal government was confronted with the disconcerting news that during November and December 1905 licenses had been issued for 16,199 more indentured coolies. This action nullified the announcement on December 20 that the further importation of Chinese coolies would be arrested. Churchill thought it would be interesting to know if the mineowners had advance information in November of Balfour's pending resignation. Lord Selborne was not beyond reproach in the light of Lyttelton's telegram on October 27 to the effect that "I think it would be good policy for the mineowners voluntarily to put a complete stop to importation for the next six months."[39] That suggestion should have prompted delay when, over the period from November 12-18, licenses were issued for 2,000 daily. Later, in February 1906, it was revealed that Lawley had received Lyttelton's telegram and had sanctioned the licenses. But Lord Selborne

did not seek to evade responsibility, asserting that he would have done
the same since Lyttelton had left the decision to the men on the spot.
Churchill was not pacified and would stricture Lawley for failing to
consult with the governor and the Secretary of State for the Colonies
given the unusual circumstances. Lord Elgin felt that Lyttelton should
have defined his wishes more precisely but that Lawley ought to be
told "that an expression of opinion should be received of necessity
with caution."[40]

Lord Selborne urged acceptance of the licenses, arguing that the request had been planned many months ahead. The mineowners had incurred large outlays of money for machinery and accommodations in
anticipation of their arrival. The new licenses were also partly the
result of the uncertainty as to whether the first batches of coolies
would be allowed the option of another three-year reindenture. He
called attention to the advice of the Transvaal law officers that cancellation was illegal and would be subject to court action. At cabinet sessions Asquith stressed the possible financial liabilities, arguing that "it
would involve the British taxpayer . . . in large claims for compensation, . . . and would not be regarded as necessary to fulfill your
pledge." Lord Elgin agreed, adding that the licenses "could only be
revoked by ex post facto legislation which would be arbitrary in character." If the decision was to let the licenses stand,* the mineowners
were to be told that the Imperial State repudiated any assumption of
a permanently available supply of Chinese coolies and that the future
of the Ordinance would be left to an elective assembly.[41]

Meanwhile the Liberal government proposed to remove the stigma
of servitude associated with the Ordinance. If dissatisfied coolies were
offered a free passage home before the termination of their contracts,
that should erase the sting of forced labor. Objections were voiced
among the staff in the British Colonial Office. It would be costly to
the Imperial State, a disastrous blow to the mining industry, and a set-
back to prosperity in South Africa. The Transvaal government would
be particularly vulnerable in the event that replacements could be obtained only in Portuguese East Africa. The latter would demand railway concessions for traffic through Delagoa Bay at the expense of
Capetown and Durban and to the detriment of the cost of living in

*On July 6, 1906, Lord Elgin announced that the cutoff date for implementing these
new licenses would be November 30, 1906. *Lords*, July 6, 1906, p. 346.

the Transvaal. Lord Selborne doubted that many coolies were really unhappy and the greater likelihood was of the offer being used for a short holiday. Churchill defended the repatriation scheme, pointing out that unless something like this were done "Parliament will demand more drastic measures to end an immoral contract." Given careful screening and an interim delay in processing an application, the necessary tests of sincerity were at hand.[42]

A reluctant Lord Selborne prepared the details of an adequate repatriation scheme. A minimum disruption to the mining industry should be kept in the forefront. He outlined a series of conditions assuring that there would be no capricious exploitation of the invitation to break the contract and receive free passage home. The coolie should share some of the cost if possible, preferably by working until the day of his departure and turning over one-half of his wages. Stress should be placed upon continued good behavior while awaiting embarkation. Any attempt to re-engage in China for work in the Transvaal by those repatriated under the scheme should be severely punished. Churchill had no objections to the plan save the idea of having the offer circularized by word of mouth in each mine. Naturally mineowners would be happy "to whittle it away by mere mutterings." Their very protest that one-third of the Chinese would apply "conforms to the figures of desertions and fortifies our suspicions regarding the impropriety and even harshness of the indentured system on the Rand." Unless notices were posted in every compound for all to see, there would be few applications.[43]

Early returns on the repatriation program were disappointing. At the close of May 1906, after a fortnight, Lord Selborne reported the receipt of twelve applications (rising to fifty-five by July). His inquiries had brought assurances from inspectors that the notice was nailed up in every compound. He had personally visited several mines and contacted 8,000 Chinese and they were perfectly content to stay. The fact of the matter was that almost 4,000 had already been sent home—3,000 physically unsuited and 500 discontented—and so not many were left who wanted repatriation. Churchill felt that, apart from pressures operating to make the offer appear "as a hoax," the wording of the notice left a lot to be desired.[44] The requirement that the amount of money saved be stated on the application frightened many who feared it would be drawn upon to pay for their return passage.

Nor could it have been salutary to translate the notice into Chinese, applying such customary Oriental expressions as the equivalent of "tremblingly obey." [45]

During July the notice was redrafted, requiring only one month of work after application and one-half of the month's wages and omitting the admonitions.[46] Churchill declared himself satisfied with the number of three hundred seventy-five applications by August as a fulfillment of the promise to Parliament that none would be kept on the Rand against their will. Thereafter the tribulations were with Lord Selborne who persisted in constantly raising administrative perplexities. On one occasion Lord Elgin was provoked to the point of observing "that it is really impossible to meet all these conundrums." How should malingerers awaiting departure be handled? Should undesirables being repatriated be put on the same ship, when their thieving proclivities risked the savings of those under the legitimate repatriation program? Should every successful applicant be searched at embarkation for savings which he failed to declare in order to avoid sharing the cost of his passage? Nor was it easy to secure ships, provide overseers aboard, and meet health regulations. Nevertheless, when the Transvaal became a self-governing colony in January 1907, the number of applications had risen to 1,550 of whom 766 were processed and the others rejected or withdrawn.[47]

A companion approach to soften the sting of servitude was humane administration. Allegations by Boland of continued illegal floggings brought pressure for an investigation. Lord Selborne doubted the accuracy of the charges, noting that Boland offered no assistance on the previous occasion and gave Jamieson "to understand his business as a journalist was not to help the Government stop improper proceedings but to manufacture from them sensational articles for publication." Lord Elgin questioned the governor's contention that he had no evidence on which to go to court. Promises of legal proceedings when proof was available "will not be deemed sufficient in the absence of any single prosecution by the Government which can be pointed to as proof of the vigilance of its officers." Keith felt that Lord Selborne was not quite fair to Boland whose disclosures "in the English press were far more useful in stopping outrages than any mere private representations would have been." Certainly, the so-called Chinese police, recruited as indentured coolies and assigned to constabulary duty because of military experience, were not paragons. They were reputed to sell opium and loan money at high interest rates and to enforce exploitation of their countrymen with severe whippings. Enough inspectors conversant in North Chinese dialects should be hired to enable a tour at least once every forty-eight hours.[48]

The idea of setting up a commission to investigate the charges of illegal flogging was seriously entertained. Lord Selborne welcomed such a step to end the circulation of malicious stories. The trouble would be to run down the facts in each case, especially if Chinese overseers who would be the key witnesses had left the country. Not a few of the accusations were of the trumped-up variety. There was the well-known incident of H. J. Pless, an American who served as a compound manager at the Nourse Deep mine and from whom Boland had received information. According to the affidavit of a hospital attendant who had boarded with him, Pless had said that he photographed a flogging perpetrated by him "for fun" and in the hope of writing a financially remunerative book with regard to "slave driving on the Rand." Lord Elgin answered that he did not have in mind a commission to investigate what had been done in the past but to ascertain if illegal flogging had been effectively stopped at present. After all, a firm pledge had been given to the Chinese government on this point. What caused the project of a commission to be dropped was the possibility of delaying responsible government for the Transvaal. If a commission report were devastating, then Great Britain would have to carry on indefinitely until the cancer was removed. Ommanney believed that Lord Selborne's assurance of no more irregularities should be accepted at face value. A few Chinese police assaults on coolies here and there did not merit sweeping measures.[49]

Churchill sympathized with the Dutch farmers who requested compensation for damage done by marauding Chinese. The mineowners should be liable, "as would be the owner of a savage or wild beast which he had imported." It was difficult to square the tales of Chinese contentment with the 715 cited cases of desertion and absent without leave for November 1905. At that rate, the average came to 8,580 per annum out of 47,000 or eighteen per cent. Still there remained an obligation to see that the badgered Chinese were given a fair trial. Lord Selborne vouched that the inspectors held open court regularly and sentences of maximum punishment were reviewed by the Supreme

Court. However, despite a record of not one case of a fine having been imposed on a boss boy or of a collective fine upon a gang for failing to report offenses, Lord Elgin eliminated these penalties. For the rest, if the suggestion of Lord Selborne to construct fences as a means of establishing limits for the Chinese was rejected as a restriction on liberty of movement, the issuance of pass permits specifying the destination of Chinese coolies obtained approval. Thus they could not easily wander off in another direction without being quickly intercepted by the constabulary.[50]

Charges of moral turpitude on the Rand brought an investigation during the summer of 1906. Mackarness claimed that information sent him by a correspondent in the Transvaal merited further inquiry. John Alexander Bucknill, barrister and legal adviser to the Crown Colony, undertook the mission. He examined twenty-six witnesses and studied fifteen statements from medical men. The British Colonial Office received his report in November and the Liberal government deemed it so delicate in content as to warrant confidential treatment.* Lord Selborne denied the existence of organized vice in the compounds and believed the number implicated was exaggerated. So far one hundred nine cases had been uncovered, of whom thirty-seven were repatriated and seventy-two were awaiting shipment. But only two had been actually convicted and the rest of the charges were based on suspicion. Churchill hastened to assure Lord Selborne that the honor and reputation of himself and his staff were not impugned. All that could be expected was prompt repatriation of any Chinese suspected of unnatural vice.[51]

The Liberal government acknowledged a responsibility to find replacements for the coolies. The favored solution was an end to the monopoly of recruitment possessed by the Witwatersrand Native Labour Association, supposed to have created an artificial labor shortage. Support was lent in April 1906 to the application of the J. B. Robinson Group for a separate license to recruit in Portuguese East Africa. The willingness of this company to cancel a permit for 3,000 more Chinese coolies brought commendation. Lord Selborne reacted hostilely to a resumption of independent recruitment, recalling the evils of the old touting system. The poorer mines would suffer, since only the more

*The Bucknill Report is not to be found in the dispatches and papers at the Public Record Office.

prosperous mines had the resources to bid for the services of the natives on a competitive basis. Lord Selborne singled out A. E. Wilson,
agent for the Transvaal Mining Labour Company, as J. B. Robinson
Group's recruiting organization was called, as a particularly unreliable
official. However, Lord Elgin refused to back down save to put pressure upon the J. B. Robinson Group for a more acceptable agent (G.
G. Holmes). Lord Selborne obeyed reluctantly, sending off to the
Portuguese authorities a most nominal letter that the Transvaal had no
objection to separate recruitment privileges for the J. B. Robinson
Group.[52]

The game of cat and mouse played by Senhor Sousa Ribiero, Governor of Mozambique, was frustrating. First, he denied a license to the
J. B. Robinson Group on the ground that the risks to native welfare
were too great. Then he was prepared to grant a license but would
restrict the canvassing of recruits to only one agent, a hopelessly slow
process. Later he interposed the objection that other large mining
groups might want to leave the Witwatersrand Native Labour Association and he would be confronted with innumerable requests for
licenses. Churchill was highly incensed at the dilatory tactics of
Ribiero. Lord Selborne came in for a share of the blame in coupling
his issuance of a certificate to the Transvaal Mining Labour Company
with the comment that "it is a mere matter of form." Ruminations
among the staff at the British Colonial Office were not above suspect-
ing some collusion between Ribiero and the big companies behind
the Witwatersrand Native Labour Association.[53]

Sir Edward Grey, Secretary of State for Foreign Affairs, exerted diplomatic pressure in Lisbon at the request of Churchill. The Portuguese
government suggested the desirability of a joint committee to study
the whole problem of recruitment in Mozambique. Lord Elgin was
amenable but insisted that if licenses were frozen during the interim
an exception should be made in the case of the Transvaal Mining
Labour Company. Proposals and counterproposals followed with no
change in the status quo. By November, Churchill became convinced
that His Majesty's government was being trifled with. When Lord
Selborne included in one of his dispatches a comradely exchange of
letters between F. Perry, chairman of the Witwatersrand Native
Labour Association, and Ribiero, Churchill labeled it "a cynical admission of the impudent trick played upon us." On still another oc-

casion when Ribiero put forward qualms about adequate health precautions, Churchill observed acidly that "Sir E. Grey ought to see the way in which our diplomacy has been paralyzed by this pertinacious Portuguese." So furious did Churchill become, blaming the impasse upon the wily Witwatersrand Native Labour Association, that he urged the Foreign Office to have Portugal give three months' notice for the withdrawal of its monopoly.[54]

Liberals and Labourites were disappointed with the decision of Campbell-Bannerman to honor the Ordinance for the time being. Irritation was manifested over his meek acquiescence in the eleventh-hour grant of licenses for 16,199 Chinese during the last two months of 1905. It should be obvious that the scheming mineowners had resolved to tie in advance the hands of an incoming Liberal government. The Daily Chronicle traced the telltale skullduggery by a recital of license permits for several pertinent months in 1905: July (1,529), August (2,211), September (nil), October (2,351), November (13,199), December (3,000). Acceptance of this brazen fait accompli meant that the Chinese coolie experiment must be endured for several more years.[55]

The gesture to repatriate any Chinese so desirous before his contract had run out was more satisfactory. Good behavior and eligibility limited to those who had served at least six months were reasonable conditions. The offer should go far to endow the coolie with a sense of being free. Those enticed to the gold mines by false promises now had an escape route while others, who were prepared to stay, were furnished with a bargaining lever for better working conditions. But exultation turned to dismay at the small number of applications, as reported by Lord Selborne. The Manchester Guardian gathered that the failure was due to the inquisitorial procedure followed. The coolie had to tell how much he had saved and whether he could contribute toward the cost of passage home. There was also some cause to think that the cooperation of mineowners had been wanting. Placards to publicize the scheme would not appear to have been scrupulously posted and cases of intimidation had been reported. The new version, announced on July 5, eliminated the minatory and hortatory statements and reduced the contribution of the coolie to a maximum of one-half of the month's wages. These changes reflected a sincere and genuine intention to make the repatriation program meaningful.[56]

Two disclosures were stressed to justify a quick end to the Chinese coolie experiment. The first related to the revelation that Lord Milner had knowingly permitted corporal punishment to be inflicted by the mineowners. Mackarness was not prepared to let "sleeping dogs lie" and castigated the late Conservative government. It should bow its head in shame for breaking a solemn pledge to Chinese authorities. A formal censure was proposed on March 21 by William Pollard Byles, Liberal M.P. The British Empire needed proof that the day of tyrannical rule had passed. Churchill insisted upon an amendment condemning the illegal floggings but omitting the mention of any individual. While he did not condone the ill-considered stewardship of Lord Milner, he felt that great political parties should avoid recriminations with private persons. However, Churchill drew a storm of protest from Conservative benches when he remarked somewhat patronizingly that Lord Milner had served the country well over the years and retired "honourably poor."[57]

The second disclosure related to the findings of Bucknill that moral turpitude did prevail in the compounds. What a story it must be to require confidential treatment. One could only guess at the tragic legacy of contamination left in the Transvaal from 50,000 Chinese cooped up in compounds and bereft of their womenfolk. The gold discovered in the wasteland of the Rand had brought with it the curse of the Nibelung Ring. The long struggle between the avarice of nuggets and the integrity of the British Empire had ended in the triumph of temptation. The Rt. Rev. John Percival (Bishop of Hereford) demanded that these "unclean *ergastula*" be swept out at once so that a newly elected Transvaal Legislature would not be saddled with a disagreeable burden. Churchill promised that the guilty would be promptly repatriated and expressed confidence in the ability of the men on the spot to do the right thing.[58]

The *Westminster Gazette* warned that time was of the essence if South Africa was yet to be saved as a white man's country. The Transvaal was fast becoming a colony of alien labor which lived under abnormal conditions, vowed no allegiance to the community, and had no permanent interest in it. The *Daily News* commented grimly on the growing roots of a parasitic society in which white men were disinclined to engage in manual effort. How salutary would have been an influx of whites, redressing the balance of larger Bantu numbers and reducing the tension of life amidst savage hordes. As it was, the statistical story could only spread gloom. Where there had once been ten whites to every fifty-nine Kaffirs before the advent of the Chinese, the tally in November 1906 reckoned seven whites to every fifty-nine colored (Chinese and natives).[59]

Whether maximum employment of even native labor could ever be achieved (as long as the coolies remained) was problematical. Until the Chinese had numbered over 40,000 there had been a steady increase in natives: 87,000 in January 1905 and 102,000 in March 1905. The decline back to 87,000 by December 1905 coincided with the heavy accumulation of Chinese during that year. Sir William Butler, who resigned his command in July 1899 because he could not go along with the case made for the Uitlanders, readily acknowledged that more needed to be done for natives—reduction of deathrate, an increased wage rate, decent living conditions. Locations along the Rand should be set up where their families could come and live with them. To cut the mortality rate due to phthisis, he would provide regular relief by a day-off and a day-on shift system. Some cheer was derived from the announcement that the J. B. Robinson Group would be allowed to recruit independently in Portuguese East Africa and would voluntarily surrender licenses for 3,000 Chinese. That should stimulate a flagging recruitment campaign strangled by the monopoly of the Witwatersrand Native Labour Association.[60]

Conservatives cast for themselves the role of stalking horses, girded to defend the continuation of the Ordinance. Balfour denounced the cheap politics of the Liberal party during the General Election of January 1906, distributing posters of Chinese coolies in chains and being flogged. This was sheer hypocrisy, considering that Campbell-Bannerman meant to throw the responsibility for terminating the Ordinance on a self-governing Transvaal. If the Liberal government really believed that it was slavery, they should have the courage to back up their placards with action. In self-defense the Conservative party published a pamphlet entitled, Is It Slavery?, which contained some pleasant photographs meant to belie the image of indentured coolies laboring in chains or dwelling amidst squalid conditions.[61]

The sixth Marquess of Londonderry, Lord President of the Council in the late Balfour ministry, refused to accept in any charitable spirit a new distinction being drawn by Liberals that the Ordinance carried a stigma of servility rather than enslavement. He chided the Earl of Crewe, to be his successor in office, for saying that slavery was a "descriptive term"* and Churchill for confessing that his indictment was a "terminological inexactitude."** As malicious as the glib charges of slavery had been, this shift to the status of servility was no more defensible. No one could describe as a prototype of servility a worker who went in with eyes open, got a high wage, and received a free return passage at the end of his contract. One was not aware of any general outcry against the use of Portuguese East African natives who had to accept repatriation as an alternative to re-engagement. Liberal leaders should either cease calling the *Ordinance* even by the less offensive nomenclature of servitude or abolish indentured labor everywhere in the British Empire.[62]

The offer of free repatriation sooner than the contractual agreement allowed was denounced as nothing less than criminal. The result must be to unsettle the minds of the Chinese and to weaken discipline among them, because they were now fortified by the knowledge of an easy way out. Concern was expressed for the licenses granted in November and December 1905 to recruit 16,900 coolies. They would be brought in supposedly for three years and yet would have the right to ask for an earlier repatriation. If mineowners had to bear the cost of transporting Chinese coolies to South Africa, they ought to be allowed a three-year stint of work from them. Needless to say, much elation was derived from the meager response to the repatriation program. The trickle of applications testified to the happy frame of mind among the coolies. The tabulation of a mere eight hundred sent back in 1907 should be enough of an answer to those who claimed that the Chinese were unhappy.[63]

Lord Selborne's estimate that if the Chinese coolies were sent home the money spent in the Transvaal would be reduced by £4,000,000 annually was given considerable publicity.[64] The specific amount of £4,259,382 was broken down thus: 1) coolie wages—£975,504; 2) local

---

*Lord Crewe asserted that he had never used the phrase himself nor did he ever regard the *Ordinance* as one of slavery. *Lords*, Feb. 19, 1904, p. 64.

**Churchill's full statement was that if the *Ordinance* "did not constitute a state of slavery . . . in the extreme acceptance of the word without some risk of terminological inexactitude," still that did not mean it was "a proper contract." His objection was to the essence of "the idea that men are to be treated as if they were implements." *Commons*, Feb. 22, 1906, pp. 555, 570.

stores expenditures—£1,479,500; 3) white men's wages—£1,804,378. A stern competition could be expected to spring up between mining and agriculture for the available natives once the Chinese were gone. The former, with its greater staying powers, would inevitably force the latter to the wall. The Transvaal could anticipate trouble to fund its debt if curtailed Rand operations led to diminished revenue. Indeed, the entire South African economy would court disaster. Both Cape Colony and Natal subsisted in large measure as intermediaries between the Transvaal and overseas countries. The second Viscount Ridley, Conservative M.P. before he succeeded to the peerage in 1904, noted that Lord Selborne had envisaged the future plans of the gold mines to call for an expenditure of £12,000,000 (correctly, £12,283,868) for machinery in the new mills to be erected. For the rest, the jeremiads were loud in relation to the drop sure to come in the stock market value of "Kaffirs" and the staggering blow that London would suffer as the financial center of world credit if gold shipments lagged.[65]

South Africa, as a white man's country, was held to be in the balance by Conservatives as well as Liberals. From their vantage point no more discouraging news was possible than the abandonment of the Chinese coolie experiment. The mischief was already evident in the reduction of whites on the Rand by 1,000 between April and September 1906. True, the decrease took place in fourteen nonproducing mines, but the point was that mineowners were hedging on capital outlays because of the uncertainty of the labor supply. The real stake centered in the 6,000 whites on the Rand (added since the coming of the Chinese) and the survival of 17,000 whites in other trades. Nor should the value of a possible reconciliation of Boers to a partnership with Anglo-Saxons be overlooked. This would further strengthen the white man's position in South Africa. The Boer might aspire to an independent Dutch Republic, but he also relished a substantial bank account. If the British regime spelled good times, he would give it his loyalty.[66]

The Imperial South African Association published a pamphlet by Robert Raine, successor to Creswell at the Village Main Reef mine, answering the latter's claim that the failure to further his experiment with whites had cost the Rand much. Raine had taken over in November 1903 and found that white labor did not produce good results. For the period from June to October 1903, contractors using unskilled whites at 10s. per day were in debt to the company, at a loss of £3,357 to shareholders. Where the mines dispensed with contractors and hired both skilled and unskilled labor, the results were no better. Cash grants had to be given in order for the men to earn a monthly average of £12 13s., at a loss of £3,966 to shareholders. Raine took whites off the rock-drilling machines and put them to shoveling and tramming. But assignment to "Kaffir work" was not popular and, during the next ten months, 1,916 white men passed through the company register, averaging a force of one hundred thirty per month at a stay of twenty days per individual. In contrast, skilled white miners, once again given a gang of native "boys," were stimulated to increase their productivity by the prospect that no dead weight would pull down their earnings. In December 1904 their average monthly rate was up to £48 12s. 5d. from a low of £18 0s. 1d. when Creswell left. Comparing the cost per ton milled for 1903 and 1904, the averages were 26s. and 19s. respectively, a marked achievement. In the light of these facts it was difficult to follow Creswell's thinking that an increase in unskilled whites would compensate in productivity for the absence of Chinese coolies and a force of natives.[67]

John Saxon Mills, past editor of the *Cape Times* and now living in London, believed that the return of natives to the mines in increased numbers had been due to the competition of the coolies. Natives had come to realize that mineowners might use the labor shortage to obtain coolies on a permanent basis. The difference between 70,608 natives in May 1904 and 98,598 in April 1905 could be taken as proof of this contention. The drop to 87,000 natives in October 1905 was owing to the threat of the Liberal party to repatriate all Chinese at once if voted into office and not to the advent of large numbers of Chinese crowding out the demand for native labor. Natives sensed the prospect of resuming their monopoly in the unskilled labor market and holding out for arrogant wage demands. Moreover, the presence of the Chinese could be credited with the improvement recorded in deathrates among natives, declining per 1,000 from 53 (correctly, 52.68 in July 1905 to 34.73 (correctly, 32.99) in March 1906.* The arrival of the Chinese had eased the labor shortage and so only

*Again, the reader will recall the milder weather during the winter months in Johannesburg.

robust natives were hired and the rest were released for surface work in agriculture, railroad construction, and irrigation projects. To rely anew upon natives would invite indiscriminate recruiting again throughout Africa and those drawn from the tropical areas would fall easy victims to the rigors of cold and high altitude on the Rand.[68]

Lord Harris voiced dismay over the proposal for the J. B. Robinson Group to recruit independently in Portuguese East Africa. That would revive the evil practices of the touting system with its false promises and ruthless pressures. The Witwatersrand Native Labour Association was formed primarily to assist the poorest mining properties to obtain labor and the scale of remuneration had been adjusted to their operational costs. Wealthier mines had foregone selfish advantages but now they would be compelled to seek similar privileges to protect themselves against such a redoubtable rival as the J. B. Robinson Group. Poorer mines would have to be closed, for native wages were already high and to pay even more was out of the question. Certainly, Portuguese East Africa, recalling previous unhappy experiences with the touting system, would capitulate only to pressure from the British government. The existing arrangement had been a very satisfactory one, assuring selected recruits, excellent traveling facilities, and good living accommodations in the compounds.[69]

Lord Milner was defended against charges of misconduct in office, necessary not only to protect a meritorious civil servant but also to neutralize the possible whipping up of public opinion for a quick exit of Chinese coolies. William Evans, with a record of twenty years' honorable service in the Malay States, had advised Lord Milner to permit a limited amount of corporal punishment because the delay in getting breaches of law before the courts weakened discipline. Flogging in itself was not an abuse of human beings; if it was, similar traditions in the British Navy and public schools (caning) should also stand condemned. Corrective measures must accompany the restrictive circumstances under which the Chinese were admitted or the social mores of the white community would be endangered. Lord Milner felt impelled in the House of Lords to tell his side of the story. He had agreed to mild flogging only for acts of violence and disturbances of peace but not for refusal to work or desertion. What apparently happened was that his intentions had been misapplied. If he had remained in South Africa, he most assuredly would have stopped it. The error was one of administration and not of the heart.[70]

No attempt was made to minimize the seriousness of the Bucknill Report. Lyttelton acknowledged that the accounts of immorality, if true, were not to be condoned. But it should be remembered that an offer had been made to bring over the families of the coolies. It was to be lamented that no advantage had been taken of the opportunity. *The Times* could not see in vice per se a proof that the indentured Chinese had been forced into a corrupt environment. The unsavory indulgences presumably disclosed by Bucknill would appear to be habitually practiced in parts of China entirely detached from any such unusual external factor as celibate compounds. If sin there be, then prompt repatriation of the reprobates, rather than "sensationalism," was the way to deal with the problem effectually. The most tormented soul was the Archbishop of Canterbury. He would remind critics who flaunted in his face the approval he had bestowed upon the *Ordinance* that it had been given grudgingly and with the words "a regrettable necessity." Furthermore, he had thereafter persistently raised the matter of the absence of womenfolk. And if the Bucknill Report had any substance to it, he was for appropriate action being taken at once to send the Chinese home.[71]

DEPARTURE OF THE CHINESE

The fact that a self-governing Transvaal would render the final verdict on the use of Chinese coolies focused attention upon the constitution drafted at the close of 1906. Clause 50 dealt with the *Labour Importation Ordinance of 1904* and its amendments. Section 1 stated that after December 6, 1906, the date of the promulgation of the Letters Patent, no more licenses were to be issued and no contracts made under the authority of the *Ordinance* could be renewed. Section 2 stated that one year from the date of the first meeting of the Transvaal Legislature the *Ordinance* and all its amendments were to be repealed and cease to have effect. Section 3 stated that the Transvaal Legislature could make bylaws to accelerate the end of the *Ordinance* or to regulate it. Finally, a reservation was included to disallow any new ordinance which failed to meet the dictum of no servile conditions.[72]

Liberals and Labourites regarded the basis of representation for the legislature as the vulnerable point in the implementation of Clause 50. Whether allocation of seats should be computed on the basis of the total white population or the voting register of adult white males was pivotal. Calculations indicated that out of the proposed sixty seats the Rand would get twenty-four if the former and thirty-three if the latter.* Unmarried adult white males were in a majority and largely concentrated on the Rand and subject to the influence of the mineowners. So the Chinese would stay if a voting register of adult male whites was adopted. True, a population count might give political control to the Boers, for they had large families, but that chance would have to be taken. At least the Boers had a permanent stake in South Africa and were known to want the Chinese out of the country. The *Westminster Gazette* would go even further to help increase the voting strength of the Boers by extending the franchise to white women, justifiable in itself by their exposure to the peril of Chinese deserters. The final decision was a compromise, an allocation of thirty-four seats to the Rand, six to Pretoria, and twenty-nine to the rest of the Transvaal for a total of sixty-nine seats.[73]

Conservatives described the strategy of the Liberal government as nothing less than diabolical. Clause 50 would guarantee the termination of the *Ordinance*. A population count over a voters' register for representation in the legislature would put the Boers in power and assure the exit of the Chinese. Campbell-Bannerman should be aware of overplaying his hand and risking not only the collapse of the gold mines but also the ultimate hostility of a colonial community forced to go along with an unhappy bargain. Nor were the Boers quite so opposed to the Chinese coolie experiment as he thought. A far more accurate reflection of Boer sentiment, however, was to be gleaned from a clause in an agreement made on March 15, 1905, between Het Volk (pledged to Boer reconciliation with Great Britain under self-

---

*The statistical basis for these calculations may be found in the *Daily News* (March 13, 1906): a) Rand—white population (122,000), registered voters (47,412), square miles (1,653); b) Rest of the Transvaal—white population (177,000), registered voters (43,436), square miles (111,196).

government) and the Responsible Government (pledged to seek self-government and emphasizing a membership open to both Boer and Briton):

> We are of the opinion that although 'Het Volk' is opposed in principle to the introduction of Chinese labour into this Colony, the Labour Ordinance should be left operative for a period of five years. In the meanwhile, we are of the opinion that the terms of the Ordinance should be strictly carried out. Importation of Chinese should be restricted to the number that is absolutely necessary and Kaffir labour should be utilized as much as possible.[74]

The Letters Patent were issued in December 1906 and the first Transvaal election was held on February 20, 1907. The returns were a triumph for the Boers: Het Volk (37), Progressives (21), Nationalists (6), Labour party (3), Independents (2). A coalition government was formed with Het Volk as the nucleus and including all other parties save the British-supported Progressives. Botha and Smuts were named Prime Minister and Colonial Secretary respectively.

Upon the occasion of the inaugural session of the Transvaal Legislature on March 21, 1907, General Botha expressed the hope that Chinese coolies could be dispensed with at the earliest moment. He indicated that their repatriation should be accompanied by adequate replacements of men or machinery. It was not, however, until General Botha returned from attendance at an Imperial Conference in London during April that a specific plan of action was formulated. He recommended in June to the Transvaal Legislature that the coolies be sent home as their contracts expired with no re-engagement for a second three-year period. In the meanwhile the *Ordinance* and its amendments should be continued until all had been repatriated. The Transvaal Legislature responded favorably and on August 2 passed the *Indentured Labour Laws Temporary Continuance Act No. 19 of 1907*.[75]

For the statistical story of the Chinese exodus, reference is made to the *Annual Register*. The first steamer departed in July 1907, carrying 2,000 Chinese coolies whose indentures had expired (in anticipation of legislative action). Thereafter the number fell steadily, dropping from a highwater mark of 53,736 in February 1907 to 35,676 in De-

cember 1907, to 17,000 in August 1908, and to 5,370 in July 1909. The
last group left on February 28, 1910 and the Rand was back to natives
for its unskilled labor supply.[76]

The British Colonial Office followed developments closely, tying
together the loose ends of its own responsibilities. Lord Elgin held out
for leaving up the repatriation notices posted in the compounds. It
would be a safeguard for good administration and a guarantee of relief
to any maltreated Chinese coolie. The continuance of the *Ordinance*
until the contracts of all indentured coolies had expired was accepted
with equanimity. Despite the fact that it meant extending the *Ordinance* beyond the fixed date of one year after the first meeting of the
Transvaal Legislature, the purpose seemed commendable. Unless the
Chinese were kept under control and not allowed to roam as free individuals, the good order of the country could be jeopardized. While
Churchill was distressed to learn that the Chinese were frequenting
brothels, he viewed the punishments of whipping and twelve months'
imprisonment with hard labor as severe. Those who were responsible
for assembling over 50,000 Chinese without womenfolk had "no right
. . . to clear their consciences by imposing ferocious sentences upon
the unhappy victims of their greed." As for the troublesome problem of
some forty Chinese serving long sentences for brutal crimes, the desire to rid the Transvaal of all the Chinese led Lord Elgin to have
them sent for the rest of their terms to Wei-hai-wei off the Chinese
coast where the British possessed a treaty of concession.[77]

The appointment of a commission to inquire into the best means of
recruitment in Portuguese East Africa remained an active issue. But
frustration continued to mark the negotiations with Lisbon. Endless
time was consumed in framing the terms of reference. Discussion went
round and round as to the best possible agency: 1) Witwatersrand
Native Labour Association, 2) Free Recruiting, 3) Transvaal Government, 4) Mozambique. When the Witwatersrand Native Labour
Association was eliminated from consideration, the Portuguese government insisted that the termination of its monopoly should not be
announced until the commission met. Furthermore, the Portuguese
government repudiated in advance any scheme of free recruitment.
The British Colonial Office patiently acceded to one point after another, only to find the ground shifting at each turn. In the meanwhile, to add insult to injury, the J. B. Robinson Group was limited

to one license and, after six months of operation, by February 1907, could show twenty-three natives recruited.[78]

The delays were protracted long enough to bring a self-governing Transvaal on the scene. Lord Selborne informed Whitehall that his ministers did not wish to proceed with the proposed commission of enquiry. Instead the Transvaal would appoint a commission to examine recruitment prospects throughout the subcontinent. But matters did not proceed any more expeditiously and the months passed without any noticeable action. The end came in August 1907 when the Transvaal announced that it had composed differences between the Witwatersrand Native Labour Association and the J. B. Robinson Group allowing the former to continue as the sole recruiting agency. What the thoughts of the British Colonial Office were after all its strenuous efforts may be suggested from the observation of Vernon that "after the prolonged and vigorous campaign of mutual recriminations this denouement is rather amusing . . . and the lion and lamb become partners."[79]

Conservatives were keenly disappointed by General Botha's statement in June 1907 that the Chinese coolies would be repatriated upon expiry of their original contracts. Mineowners would never have imported Chinese coolies if they had known that the advantage of seasoned workers for a second round of three years would not be afforded. Arthur Griffith-Boscawen, Conservative M.P., believed that most of the difficulties relating to maltreatment and immorality had been resolved and the undesirables weeded out and sent home. He pictured the Chinese as he saw them on a recent visit to the Rand—contented and happy, wearing Panama hats, riding bicycles along Main Reef Road, and driving about Johannesburg in cabs. Stores were enjoying excellent trade. Expenditures upon schools, railways, and irrigation projects were evident to the naked eye. The Chinese experiment (which would have ceased before many years as improved rock drills were devised) should have been allowed to lapse by natural stages. Lord Harris put in a word for shareholders, noting that three hundred eighty-seven representative securities had depreciated between May and June 1907 by no less than £68,000,000.* It was to be hoped that

*Only 15 of the 387 representative securities were South African gold mining companies and these fell from an aggregate value of £76,028,000 to £69,813,000. *Bankers' Insurance Managers' and Agents,* July 1907, pp. 30-32.

the Transvaal would yet come to its senses and remember its manifold responsibilities.[80]

General Botha had grasped at straws in his decision to end the *Ordinance*. There really was no difference in principle between Chinese coolies and Portuguese East African natives. Both were indentured, came from a distance, lived in compounds, and were not accompanied by their womenfolk. Both posed the same social and moral dangers and if one could be accepted with clear conscience so could the other. The *Morning Post* was sure that the difficulties connected with procuring an adequate supply of native labor had not yet been dispelled. Natives would not seem to have learned the lesson of dependability and many still averaged six months' work over a two-year period. At that rate, to get the equivalent of 50,000 Chinese, it would be necessary to corral 200,000 natives, an utter impossibility considering that the maximum ever obtained was 100,000 natives. Nor could it be reiterated too often that the presence of Chinese coolies had brought a drop in the native deathrate in the gold mines. It had gone down to 37 per 1,000 by March 1907 although not to the remarkable low of 11 per 1,000 achieved by the Chinese.[81] This cheerful figure would not be long maintained once frantic efforts had to be made again to recruit natives from tropical Africa.[82]

Lyttelton saw a connection between the guarantee by the Imperial State of a £5,000,000 loan for the Transvaal and General Botha's sudden shift to accelerate the repatriation of the Chinese.[83] His emphasis in March 1907 upon replacements contrasted strangely with silence on that prerequisite after obtaining his loan in London while attending the Imperial Conference in April. Perhaps the Liberal government had been motivated by the wish to head off a possible deal between the Transvaal and the mineowners that would allow the Chinese to stay.* The Transvaal would have had no difficulty raising what money it required in London banking circles. Liberty to administer the valuable collateral of the gold mines on the economic principle of free enterprise would have been sufficient. As it was, General Botha

---

*Churchill defended the loan as an ordinary transaction to help the Transvaal avoid paying higher interest but he was frankly glad if it made the Transvaal "independent of the influence and control of those great mining corporations." *Commons*, June 20, 1907, pp. 727-28.

would find the loan hardly worth the price of a sluggish gold mining industry and diminished state revenue.[84]

During 1908, as the exodus of Chinese coolies proceeded steadily, Conservatives dwelt upon the incongruities of the situation. Was it not gross knavery for the Liberal party to raise such a hue and cry over slavery on the Rand and yet acquiesce in permitting the *Ordinance* to run its full course with all the supposedly objectionable features of human indignity?* Were not natives from Portuguese East Africa being brought in without their families, prohibited from owning land, and subject to repatriation? Did not the desperate search for replacements in Madagascar and Nyasaland seem a wasteful and stupid strategy to compensate for Chinese coolies who were on the spot and willing to stay?[85] The *Pall Mall Gazette* prepared the nation for sharp rises in mortality rates. Whereas in 1907 the deathrate from disease per 1,000 was 11 for the Chinese and 26.9 for the natives south of latitude 22°, the incidence for the few natives north of latitude 22° was 69.9.[86] The Transvaal would rue the day when the services of Chinese coolies were terminated.[87]

Even when the contrary fact became obvious that natives on the Rand were increasing, an explanation was found elsewhere than in the departure of the Chinese. Parker readily acknowledged the presence of 119,000 natives in 1908 compared to 88,030 in 1905. However, he attributed it to the release of 20,000 men from the Kimberley diamond mines (in the throes of a temporary depression), 17,500 from the railways (because of stagnant trade conditions), and a prolonged drought in agricultural areas. But when all these branches of the economy once again reached the same level of activity as in 1905, the latent scarcity of labor would be an urgent matter again.[88]

Liberals received with mixed emotions General Botha's statement in March 1907 that repatriation must be accompanied by replacements. On the one hand, there were those like the *Manchester Guardian* expressing wonderment as to how gradual it would be. It was a keen disappointment to have waited a whole year for the Transvaal to make this rather equivocal decision. A demand would now be

---

*Churchill answered this taunt by recalling that in 1833 the abolition of slavery was cushioned for plantation owners, faced with a labor shortage, by attaching a period of apprenticeship for the newly emancipated blacks. *Commons*, Mar. 23, 1908, pp. 120-22.

launched for a renewal of licenses to tide over gold mines pending
the search for a new source of labor. Perhaps this was the retribution
to be expected after the Liberal government had refused to do anything on its own initiative. On the other hand, there were those like
the *Daily News* and the *Tribune* who accepted General Botha's words
as a sincere intention to repatriate the Chinese. The challenge was to
make suggestions for finding substitutes. Use of machinery and a concerted effort to recruit natives would help. More drastic inspection for
security against accidents and better health conditions would make
the Rand as popular with natives as were the Kimberley diamond
mines.[89]

Liberal commentators were unanimous in accepting General Botha's
further announcement in June 1907, that the Chinese would be repatriated upon the expiration of their indentured terms, as the beginning of the end of the coolie experiment. It could be assumed General
Botha was satisfied that an energetic recruiting campaign and superior
tools would produce the necessary output. The approval of his request
by a vote of forty-five to twenty-one in the Transvaal Legislature
could well be interpreted as a declaration by the local citizenry of its
desire to rid the colony of a social cancer. Mammon and Moloch had
been vanquished by an enfranchised people. The Liberal government
had scored a victory and its action was an illustration of legitimate imperial pressure upon an offspring to prevent any labor system partaking
of the nature of slavery.[90]

The guarantee of a £5,000,000 loan by the Imperial State should be
applauded. The opposition spoke with ill grace when it labeled the
loan a bribe to the Transvaal for ending the use of Chinese coolies.
Could not Chamberlain's withdrawal of his objection to the *Ordinance* (upon the assent of mineowners to underwrite a part of the
Transvaal war debt) be called the same thing? The loan had enabled
the Botha government to keep out of the clutches of the gold mining
interests. The latter had probably hoped to exert influence in the London money market against the Transvaal procuring the loan except on
the promise of retaining the Chinese. The *Manchester Guardian* commended the "bargain" as highly creditable to both negotiating parties.
It was an appropriate reply to the threat of the mineowners to close
the mines and to strangle the Transvaal economy should the Chinese
be sent home. If Lord Salisbury could spend over £200,000,000 to

wrest control of the Transvaal from the Kruger regime for the benefit of the Rand, then Campbell-Bannerman could sanction a loan of £5,000,000 so that Briton and Boer alike might come into their own as the lawful masters.[91]

Labour commentators, mainly the socialist wing, were sharply critical of the mother country's role in the affair. Not only had the Liberal government shifted the responsibility to the Transvaal but it had practically placed the seal of approval upon the equally condemnable alternative of cheap native labor. The *New Age* refused to hail the future as bright for a worthy white community even if a plentiful supply of natives was on hand. Both the mineowners and the ruling Boers had one interest in common and that was to reduce the Anglo-Saxon element in the population. The former aimed to avoid "the trail of the serpent of trade unionism" and the latter the roots of a dominant British culture. Frederick William Jowett, Labour M.P. and active in the Independent Labour party, would go further and declare a plague on both historic parties. Where Conservatives were for the yellow variety of servile labor, Liberals were for the black species. The assumption of the desirability of cheap muscular bodies bespoke the full arrogance of capitalism.[92]

Subsequently, the steady decline in the number of Chinese coolies on the Rand was followed with evident relish. One could await with equanimity a timetable that would leave 10,000 at the close of 1908 and the dispatch of the rest within eighteen months after that date. Some thoughts were offered as to the kind of balance sheet left by the experiment. The *Methodist Times* concluded that it was not often that mistakes of so grave a character could be repaired with so little loss to those guilty of them. Lord Stanhope of Chester (tenth Earl of Chesterfield), a staunch Liberal, was not so optimistic that the serious crimes of the Chinese would leave the Transvaal unmarked. Already native women who had had physical relations with the Chinese could be seen haunting the streets of Johannesburg with their telltale offspring. The *Daily Chronicle* was thankful that the repatriation schedule was being settled in good time so that no apple of discord would be thrown into the current proceedings for a South African union.[93]

When the last group of Chinese left in February 1910, statistics were cited to deny the jeremiads poured forth by Conservatives. Between May 1904 and September 1909, native labor had increased from

70,608 to 156,065 and whites from 12,414 to 21,305. Significantly, working costs per ton dropped from 31s. 2d. in 1903 to 17s. 1d. in 1909. Nor had the departure of the Chinese caused disaster to the mining industry, for the value of the gold output was £24,579,987 in 1906, £27,403,738 in 1907, and £30,925,788 in 1908. The chief sour note struck came once again from the ranks of the Labour movement. The *Social Democrat* fulminated that the natives would continue to be the exploited class and, while working costs would go down, mineowners would pocket any additional profits.[94]

Perhaps it would not be inappropriate to offer a few comments on the later history of South African gold mining. Statistics show that instead of approaching exhaustion there seems to be no end to the productivity of the reefs. In 1959 the Rand yielded some 14,483,597 fine ounces of gold valued at £180,552,100, five-fold that of pre-World War I accomplishments. In addition, since 1946, the discovery of gold near Odendaalsrust in Orange Free State, ninety miles northeast of Bloemfontein, has contributed considerably to the gold output. The yield in 1959 was 5,581,881 ounces of fine gold valued at £69,583,567. For the Union of South Africa as a whole the computation in 1959 stood at 20,065,515 fine ounces of gold valued at £250,136,128. The total labor force in the gold mines was 368,164 including 40,227 whites. Allowing for a margin due to the increase of population, the two-fold bulge in native workers over pre-World War I days suggests that the Bantu are turning out in appreciable numbers.

4

Natal & the Zulu Disturbances

INITIAL INCIDENT

Zululand rises from a low coastal plain facing the Indian Ocean and reaches westward to the foothills of the Drakensberg range. Both Natal and the Transvaal have frontiers abutting the territory of Zululand. For many decades during the nineteenth century a state of war prevailed between white settlers and Zulu tribes over land disputes. After the defeat of Cetewayo, descendant of Chaka and Dingaan, in the campaign of 1879, the British government determined to end the periodic "washing of spears in blood." Cetewayo was sent to Capetown as a prisoner and the post of paramount chief was eliminated by dividing Zululand into thirteen parts and placing tribes under scions of houses which had ruled before the days of Chaka. A British resident was installed to be the "eyes and ears" of the Imperial State and to give advice to the thirteen "kinglets." But peace did not follow among the tribes and in 1882 Cetewayo was restored as king, although his royal powers were restricted, and a section of territory along the Natal border was set up as a native reserve to which those who did not like his rule could go. A restless ambition to extend his sway to the old limits soon involved Cetewayo in war with rival chieftains. He was defeated within a year and driven into the native reserve where he surrendered to British forces. He died in exile in February 1884.[1]

Dinizulu (also spelled Dinuzulu), son of Cetewayo, managed to revive royal authority over Zululand with the aid of a few Boer settlers living there and some Boer kinsmen from the Transvaal. But it was at the price of turning over to the infiltrating Boers a large block of land to the west and north known as the Vryheid district. In due time the territory was absorbed into the Transvaal (only to be ceded back to

Natal by the Treaty of Vereeniging in 1902). What remained of
Zululand was annexed in 1887 by Great Britain at Eshowe in the presence of 15,000 Zulus. The fortunes of Dinizulu turned for the worse
when he sought to crush Zibebu, a "kinglet" and leader of the opposition. The British government charged him with public violence and
high treason and deported him in 1890 to St. Helena. In 1897 the Imperial State transferred Zululand to Natal which had been pressing
for its incorporation, partly to assure the security of its frontiers and
partly to open up more land for sugar plantations. The arrangements
called for Natal to accept the repatriation of Dinizulu in 1898 as head
of the Usutu tribe but not as paramount chief. He was to be paid an
annual salary of £500 as government *induna* (adviser) to Natal on native matters. This salary could not be suspended without the concurrence of the Secretary of State for the Colonies in Great Britain.

Among other details of Dinizulu's repatriation was an order that he
live at Eshowe and be available for consultation with the resident
commissioner for native affairs in Zululand. Dinizulu was provided
with a house specially constructed and furnished for him at public
expense. But he found it difficult to control the affairs of his Usutu
tribe one hundred miles away and he was allowed to move there. If he
paid periodic visits to Eshowe for a while, he eventually discontinued
them and became more of a chief than government *induna*. Apparently without any preconceived intentions or purposes in mind, Dinizulu would seem to have accepted the veneration of natives in Natal
proper and Zululand for the descendant of the royal house. Indeed,
an aggrieved native population, confronted with alienation of their
land, payment of high rents to white farmers, and invasion of their
ancient habits and customs, looked upon Dinizulu as a natural champion. If Dinizulu was careful not to violate the conditions of his return and to avoid placing himself in a false position, he did not dis-
avow the pedestal upon which many natives would place him.

In the meanwhile the administration of the native people had become formally organized. According to the Census of 1904 the Zulus
numbered 900,000, including 200,000 in Zululand, compared to
97,000 whites. They pursued a pastoral economy and dwelled in kraals
or fenced compounds, their huts arranged in a circular formation. The
exterior of a hut resembled a beehive and was constructed of wattles,
thatched with grass, and supported inside by poles. The Zulus were

polygamists and each wife had her own hut. There was also a cattle pen or enclosure, oval in shape, and sheltered by the huts to guard their stock from beasts of prey. In Natal proper they lived on reservations and locations or squatted on Crown land or leased from white settlers on a rental plus labor-service basis. There were two hundred thirty-eight tribes, each ruled by a chief paid a small salary by the colony and assisted by headmen (also called *indunas*). The tribes were grouped together into thirty magistracies, each under a white officer. A corps of white troopers supplemented by native police performed the constabulary duties. A secretary for native affairs with cabinet rank in the colonial government determined policy. A separate administration was provided for Zululand, headed by a commissioner for native affairs. There were eighty-three tribes, each with its own chieftain, and grouped together into ten magistracies. The designation of the Crown-appointed Governor of Natal as paramount chief gave the British Colonial Office a locus in matters affecting the Zulus.

An economic depression in 1905 was responsible for a deepening cleavage in the relations between Natal and its native subjects. The dumping of surplus military stores on the local market would appear to have set in motion a stagnation in trade. George Morris Sutton, Prime Minister, presented to the Legislative Assembly in March 1905 a bleak picture of state finances. He estimated that for the current year there would be a deficiency of £583,000 on a total expenditure of £4,000,000. The public debt stood at £18,019,000, an increase of £2,000,000 over the previous year. The decision was made to impose a poll tax on every adult male over eighteen years of age.* A qualification was added that in the case of natives it would apply only to those not on the rolls for the hut tax of 14s. In essence, the unmarried adult native males were asked to share the burden of taxpayers. It was calculated that the poll tax would yield £165,000 of which the natives would pay about £100,000.[2]

The British Colonial Office staff exchanged views. Sir Henry McCallum, Governor of Natal, questioned requiring all adult males, rich and poor alike, to pay a poll tax. That was "a relic of medieval ages," unsuited to modern ideas of political economy. Lambert agreed that

---

*A dispute developed over proposals with regard to taxes on unoccupied land and houses, resulting in the resignation of Sutton on May 15, 1905 and his replacement by Charles John Smythe.

the poll tax seemed unfair and had been generally given up save in some American states (in the South to keep the Negro from voting). But he also felt that if Natal wanted to revert to anachronistic methods of taxation "I do not see that that is any business of ours." Lyttelton reasoned that the legal grounds for disallowance were not there. He could not very easily reserve the measure on the basis of legislation discriminating against natives because whites too had to pay. Accordingly, on May 22, 1905, Lyttelton informed McCallum that he would not withhold assent.[3]

When the Natal government dispatched agents in February 1906 to collect the poll tax, a crisis was precipitated. Although the effective date had been set for January 20, no legal proceedings of a compulsory nature were supposed to be instituted until after May 31. The Zulus, unhappy about the new tax burden, regarded the early attempt as pressing matters unnecessarily. On February 7, at Byrnetown, in the Richmond district, some twenty miles south of Pietermaritzburg, a group of warriors from the Mveli tribe reacted menacingly even though they had been disavowed by their chieftain. They waved their *assagais* (slender spears made of wood from the assagai tree and pointed with iron) at the revenue agents, who thought prudence the better wisdom and withdrew to report back to the resident magistrate of Umgeni. The next day Sidney Hunt, a subinspector, accompanied by eleven mounted police and four others, including two native constables, departed for the troubled area. The party had rounded up three natives and released one when beset by two score natives intent upon rescuing their comrades under arrest. Apparently hands were placed upon the bridle of Hunt's horse. A scuffle followed and two policemen, including Hunt, were murdered. The rest of the constabulary retreated in the face of superior Zulu numbers. They returned on February 9 with reinforcements to recover the bodies of their fallen comrades. The two slain were found at the spot of the attack covered with wounds inflicted by *assagais*.[4]

The Natal government responded quickly on the same day, February 9, with a proclamation of martial law, suspending normal civil rights and legal processes, and substituting peremptory trial by military officers. A force was assembled under Lieutenant-Colonels Leuchars and McKenzie to apprehend the culprits. McCallum moved a regiment of the Queen's Cameron Highlanders on February 12 from

Pretoria to Pietermaritzburg as a restraining influence upon natives while the Natal troopers moved into the disturbed area and applied punitive measures of destruction of kraals and confiscation of cattle and sheep. On February 14, two of the hunted natives were captured, tried by court-martial on the spot, and summarily shot after being declared guilty. Another two score, identified by the chieftain and his brothers as the disaffected, were arraigned on March 12 before a general court-martial and charged with complicity in the killing of law officers.[5] The findings brought convictions to seventeen on the count of public violence, to sixteen on the count of bearing arms against the state, and to twelve for murder and assault with intent to murder. For the first two groups, guilty of the less serious offenses, the sentences called for prison terms from two to twenty years of hard labor, twenty-five to fifty lashes, and confiscation of property. For the third group, numbering twelve, the death penalty was decreed.[6]

In London, friends of the condemned natives endeavored to take legal action. The leader was Frances Ernest Colenso, son of the late Rt. Rev. John William Colenso, Bishop of Natal and champion of Cetewayo. He had previously been a Natal barrister and now practiced in London. His source of information was two sisters living in Natal—Harriette Emily and Agnes Colenso. Closely identified was Edwin George Jellicoe, also a barrister and, like Colenso, a member of the Inner Temple. Alfred Mangena, a Zulu from Natal and a law student in Lincoln's Inn,* was the sponsor of the petition presented by Jellicoe to the Judicial Committee of the Privy Council, a high court of appeals for the British Empire. Mangena cited, as extenuating circumstances, the premature enforcement of the onerous poll tax and the panic which grew out of the dusk and fog hovering about the area. The general melee should be regarded as an unfortunate episode. The Privy Council answered that the appeal involved an act of the executive and was therefore beyond its purview.[7]

On March 28 Lord Elgin invoked the royal prerogative of mercy and requested McCallum to postpone the death sentences pending

---

*Mangena was the recipient of many harsh statements in the press, some of which prompted him to sue and win a verdict. The libelous charge was made that he had absconded with money collected from Cape natives to fight their forced eviction from a location. Mangena proved that the money had been given him for his defense in their behalf and to pay his transportation to London in furtherance of his legal training. P.P., 1906, LXXIX, Cd. 3027, pp. 95-97, 1908, LXXII, Cd. 4403, 130 pp.

assurance that a fair trial had been given the natives. British troops were being used to maintain order and so the Imperial State would be an accessory to the deed. And eventually the British Parliament would have to sanction a bill of indemnity covering acts committed under martial law. Smythe, Prime Minister of Natal, handed in the resignation of his cabinet as a protest against intervention in local affairs. However, when Lord Elgin expressed himself as satisfied with McCallum's response on March 29, that no injustice had been committed, Smythe resumed office. The executions before the firing squad took place on April 2 at Richmond in the presence of native kinfolk. The latter had been summoned to witness the event as a salutary reminder of the inexorable obligation of public order. Vicar Algernon J. Fryer, Anglican clergyman, performed the religious obsequies and sent his report to McCallum, who in turn passed it on to the British Colonial Office:

> The twelve men executed today all confess to guilt and justice of sentence. They died ignorant but penitent Christians fortified by their faith in God's Forgiveness to penitent sinners. All was done with utmost humanity.[8]

Lord Elgin would appear to have been influenced by his staff in temporarily suspending the death sentences. Keith observed that "we are morally responsible, for the Imperial forces are there on our order alone which renders possible the occurrence [court-martial trial of the natives]." Whether McCallum had failed to keep Lord Elgin fully posted is debatable. If he remained silent during the trial proceedings and in the days that immediately followed, there is on record a telegram of March 27 in which McCallum stated his satisfaction with the conduct of the trial. The reason why he had not previously given any details was because he did not think that His Majesty's government had any responsibility in court-martial cases. McCallum added that he had urged upon the Natal cabinet the use of civil tribunals but the latter felt to do so would be interpreted by the Zulus as a sign of weakness. McCallum assured Lord Elgin that he had personally checked the evidence against each native sentenced and no injustice had been done. Afterwards Lord Elgin wrote McCallum stating that no censure of him was intended but he would have liked daily reports. As for the peremptory resignation of the Natal cabinet, Lord Elgin thought the action unduly hasty but the less said the sooner relations with Natal would mend.[9]

The British Colonial Office staff could scarcely contain themselves over the naive description by the Vicar Algernon J. Fryer of the final moments before the executions. Keith observed that "this sort of thing is in very bad taste." Graham commented: "I am surprised that McCallum should have forwarded it." Just declared "that we cannot publish this." Churchill wasted few words: "Hallelujah! !" Later he dashed off a biting invective:

> The Rev. Algernon J. Fryer has evidently distinguished himself. I think the exertions which he made with the combined assistance of the Almighty and the interpreter to impress upon the prisoners the justice of their sentence and the abounding grace of the Church, should be brought to the attention of the Ecclesiastical Authorities in this country in order that some special mark of favour should be accorded him.[10]

Keith pursued the constitutional implications of Smythe's resignation, arguing that "ministers must carry on to remain part of the Empire, otherwise the veto is impossible." He continued:

> The prerogative of pardon is a royal one and the Governor has a clear duty. . . . All the Governor can do is not to exercise his power of pardon. . . . Natal desires with the aid of British troops to terrify by executions its native population and the threat of removing the battalion would be effective in reducing them to common sense.[11]

Cox took Keith to task for his strong words: "I consider this statement an outrage on a population which is quite as humane as Mr. Keith and has more knowledge of the circumstances." If Keith's views were to be put into action, they "would lose us not only South Africa but every Colony we possess." To his knowledge there was "no principle of constitutional law which prohibits ministers tendering their resignation." Lambert agreed that there was "no point to carrying on in office under a policy they [Natal cabinet] regard as ruinous." Perhaps resigna-

tion "is the only efficient way for ministers to make their point." At
any rate, "it is possible to be unpatriotic, even factious, and yet to remain well within the limits of constitutional action."[12]

McCallum supported the vigorous measures of Natal on the ground
of a possible native uprising. As early as January 5, 1906, he had written to the British Colonial Office that "the young men of the tribes
get more out of the control of kraal heads, and have indulged in much
irresponsible talk." Unless martial law and the use of a battalion of
British troops had been applied, bloodshed and outrages would have
followed. In a dispatch on February 16, he cited information which
seemed to him proof of the grave situation:

> [The] present native outbreak has been premature; . . . the unfathom-
> able unrest which has been observed amongst the natives of South Africa
> during the last two years was intended to culminate in simultaneous and
> concerted action; . . . the recent killing of pigs and white fowls was the
> outcome of instructions from Zululand to test whether the Natal tribes
> are to be depended on to obey further orders, and that these orders would
> be the simultaneous killing of everything else white, meaning the Eu-
> ropean population. Such orders were not to be issued until the mealies
> had been gathered in, and the present outbreak has been distinctly pre-
> mature, and upset calculations. . . .[13]

Moreover, after the executions had taken place, McCallum was
highly critical of the furor stirred up in Great Britain against the Natal
government. Writing on April 5, 1906, he commented:

> If a certain section of the public at home who appear to think that Bri-
> tons by coming to the Colonies divest themselves of feelings of human-
> ity, have an opportunity of reviewing documents . . . and also of the
> whole conduct of the Court Martial they will perhaps in the future be
> less inclined to characterize the proceedings as 'bloodthirsty murders.'
> Still less would they be inclined to do so were they resident with their
> wives and families in the veldt or bush surrounded by hordes of semi-
> savage blacks who are only kept in hand by firmness, integrity, and a sense
> of stern justice.[14]

Lord Selborne laid his views before the British Colonial Office after a visit to Natal. He gathered that the defiance of authority had been serious and that there apparently was a concerted movement for rebellion. The strategy called for the murder of as many whites as possible after the mealie crops had been harvested. The irritation of the poll tax provoked a premature and ineffectual explosion and rendered the whole plan abortive. The poll tax in itself was hardly objectionable and natives were lightly taxed in Natal. He placed stress upon Christian-secessionist native churches as a troublesome factor. Native clergymen, under the guise of religion, preached the doctrine of "Africa for the Africans." Lord Selborne did not seek to minimize the fact that local administration of the natives left something to be desired. The calibre of magistrates would seem to have deteriorated owing to low salaries, and the posts were now filled by persons about the career level of clerks.[15]

Liberal and Labour circles expressed extreme indignation at the conduct of the Natal government. The Zulus had a grievance against the poll tax, burdened as they were with a hut tax.* The high-handed step taken to collect it before May 31 increased native resentment. It was a rash if plucky undertaking for a small body of fourteen police to arrest several from a large gathering of armed natives. When Hunt found himself obliged to uphold the prestige of the state by emptying "his revolver into natives around him," some fatal issue was inevitable. The retaliatory vengeance wreaked upon native villages by the military could only be described as scandalous. Kraals were destroyed and fines of cattle, sheep, and goats were levied. This convenient doctrine of collective liability could drive the destitute natives to acts of desperation. Zulus as a whole had never shown any disposition to throw in their lot with lawbreakers and were entitled to the confidence of officials on the spot.[16]

The arrest and execution of two natives in the field by court-martial, with little pretense of a trial, must be condemned as a travesty upon justice. Access to civil tribunals had been available, leaving no excuse for a military court to be set up. A suspension of the death sentences to be meted out to another dozen natives, for an offense which had already forfeited two lives, was warranted. One could not be certain

*Churchill, as spokesman for the Liberal government, recognized that the native had justifiable complaints but he did not think the poll tax was excessive. *Commons*, Feb. 28, 1906, pp. 1239-43.

which natives actually took part in the murders and to randomly select some for execution was tyrannical. Military officers, bound by the nature of their profession to react belligerently against an enemy, could hardly be expected to maintain a judicial temper. Their conduct in the field, nourished by the specter of ten blacks to one white, reflected a determination to teach the natives a lesson. MacDonald sought to have the evidence laid before the House of Commons. The answer of Churchill was that Sir Henry McCallum did not think such a publication would serve any useful purpose in the unsettled circumstances.[17]

The Liberal government was taken to task for its lack of firmness. To be sure, when McCallum yielded to court-martial proceedings, he had somewhat bound the hand of Lord Elgin. But even at that Lord Elgin could have exercised the prerogative of mercy, which the Crown possessed throughout the Empire, and have forbidden the executions. If Natal had repudiated it, then the constitutional issue of British overlordship would have been joined once and for all. As it was, if but one single man among the accused emerged innocent, he too suffered because the Imperial State had abdicated the duty of judicial review. The claim that there should be no interference in the domestic affairs of a self-governing colony squared ill with the request for imperial troops. When citizens from the mother country were asked to shed blood for colonials, the home government had a right to see that unwise actions did not precipitate a native rebellion.[18]

The responsibility of the British Parliament to the Zulus was especially heavy, for lacking the vote they had no way to defend themselves politically. The barbarity with which the death sentences were carried out scarcely enhanced the image of imperial dignity. It was dreadful to compel attendance of natives at the death of their own kin. To govern by fear rather than by clemency would not dispose the Zulus to be more loyal. Great Britain owed backward subjects overseas assurance that its influence would not be on the brutalizing side. The *Tribune* hoped that these words of righteous anger in the public forum would make Natal "regret it as an ugly incident of their history as we with the Peterloo massacre [of 1819 in Manchester]." The *Manchester Guardian* traced sadly the unedifying psychology to date:

In Natal as in other places where a small minority are face to face with a vast majority of blacks, the lives of niggers are not generally regarded as the lives of men are regarded in England; on the outbreak or threat of a native disturbance there is usually a panic-stricken resort to severities which are afterwards found to have been impolitic but which are justified at the moment by cant phrases about 'fatal weakness' and 'the dangers of indecision'.[19]

MacDonald reviewed the basic principles of an imperial system. While Natal had been given self-government, that did not mean freedom to do as it wished. As a member of the Empire, Natal had inherited a tradition of liberty which frowned upon recourse to martial law. Surely a respect for law and the right to a fair trial were cherished parts of an imperial moral standard. Moreover, a more balanced judgment could be gotten at the center than in the outlying territories where passion and prejudice were apt to prevail. The mother country had the obligation to guide an offspring "away from raw frontiersman's views." The *Westminster Gazette* scored the brusque reception accorded the counsel of Whitehall as if it were nothing more than the catspaw of temporary political majorities:

> The great machine which governs the Empire is more than any cabinet and survives them all. It is a thing with a memory, with a great tradition behind it, with a vast store of experience gained on many a stricken field, with tried and trusty servants who are experts on all branches of Colonial administration to advise on matters of difficulty. To defer to men on the spot is to miss the true nature of the case of value of wisdom and experience which is of greatest service to settlers in new countries. The self-governing Colonies are not lowering their pride or sacrificing their rights if on occasion they defer to its advice.[20]

Conservative circles sympathized with the ordeal of the Natal government. Unless swift steps had been taken to avenge the wanton attack, whites would have lost face with natives. It was better not to underestimate the danger of a general rebellion remembering that Natal had 900,000 natives to 97,000 whites. Worse, overall figures for the lands south of the Zambesi River showed a lopsided margin of 5,000,000 natives to 1,000,000 whites. Fortunately, cooperation between the various tribes was lacking. Swazi had no dealings with

Basuto, nor Kaffir (Xosa) with Matabele, while tribes in the Transvaal were despised by the Zulus. Fortunate too that natives did not all have firearms and that much of their fighting skill was gone with the declining opportunities to hunt. Still, observed Stanley Portal Hyatt, soldier of fortune and onetime trader in Mashonaland, the risk of a conflagration remained present in the way that a native "goes into a struggle blindly, illogically, magnifying successes, disregarding defeats, never counting the cost." The native had no real conception of the white man's power and to that extent was capable of erupting and causing senseless bloodshed.[21]

Lord Elgin was strictured for suspending the death sentences. The condemned were murderers who slew in cold blood two white officers on a lawful mission. The court-martial proceedings were perfectly legal, for the offense related to a general state of affairs necessitating martial law. *The Times* pointed out that the evidence of as many as twelve whites and twenty-one natives was taken over a period of seven days. The decision was rendered by a properly-constituted court and approved by the ministry of a self-governing colony. Furthermore, the Privy Council to which the case had been submitted by friends of the natives in London, had refused to accept it, ruling that the facts did not warrant its intervention. As for the role of McCallum, there was nothing to prevent Lord Elgin from getting full details of the trial at any time he had so desired. Those who criticized McCallum were simply diverting attention from the weakness of their own position in order to discredit a highly respected servant of the Crown.[22]

The *Daily Telegraph* doubted the wisdom of the Imperial State in intervening in the domestic matters of a colony. Natal was a better judge of the danger threatening its people than any British government six thousand miles away. Admittedly, a native war would mean British troops and money. But the home government should appreciate colonial sensibility and limit itself to counselling a young people in a trying local situation. The rude inference was invited that the prejudices and sentimentalities of people in the British Isles had a higher moral value than the deliberate judgment of men in actual contact with the facts. The net result must be to increase the insecurity of the greatly outnumbered white population in Natal. The spectacle of Great Britain disputing with Natal must strike a blow at the prestige of the white man. Natives would come to regard lightly the authority of the colony and to believe that the governor sided with them. It was significant that both Australia and New Zealand condemned this manifestation of "Little Englandism."* The *Daily Mail* warned that the revolt of the American colonies "was due to their refusal to admit the authority . . . of the British House of Commons . . . to impose taxation" and a like meddling in Natal could bring a repetition.[23]

BAMBATA UPRISING

Expectations that the example of the twelve executed natives would restore order proved disappointing. Bambata, chieftain of the Zondi, a minor tribe dwelling in the Mpanza Valley, a dozen miles northwest of Greytown, was the new culprit. Two versions of his dereliction from duty are to be encountered. One source describes him as smarting from a decision of the Natal Native Affairs Department to relieve him of his authority because of despotic rule. Thus if he supported the reluctance of his warriors to pay the poll tax he might regain his popularity and keep his post. A second source describes him as in debt and harassed by creditors; the poll tax would mean draining even more money from his coffers. So he urged his young men to resist the payments. Be this as it may, when a special force of 100 troopers arrived during the second week of March to arrest him for refusing a summons to Pietermaritzburg, Bambata chose to flee. He crossed over into Zululand and sought the inner fastness of the Nkandhla forest. Many of his men accompanied him and efforts were made to win over other chieftains against the Natal government. A notable adherent was the aged Sigananda whose Amacube tribe was the largest in Zululand. He was a man of royal blood whose career dated back to the days of Cetewayo and the Zulu War of 1879 (and who, indeed, claimed to have participated actively in the massacre of Piet Retief and his party in 1838).[24]

A series of violent outrages followed. Bambata returned in a surprise

---

*The two Australasian states sought assurance that the constitutional powers of a self-governing colony were not vitiated by the prerogative of mercy. The British Colonial Office agreed that no precedent was intended but justified its right to precise information concerning acts under martial law because of the presence of British troops. P.P., 1906, LXXIX, Cd. 2905, pp. 32-35.

attack against his own tribe, captured his uncle, Magwababa, acting chief, and barely missed seizing his brother, Funizwe, due next year to become permanent chief. Magwababa was bound and carried off but escaped within a week to tell his story. The bodies of several white troopers were found badly mutilated. White families living in lonely places were escorted to safe retreats, often under fire from Bambata's men. The most publicized murder was that of Herbert M. Stainbank, Magistrate at Mahlabatini, on May 3, 1906, while carrying on his duties to collect taxes and to keep neighboring tribes in line. He was shot during the early evening by an unknown assailant while answering the telephone near a pitched camp site.[25]

Natal appealed to loyal native chieftains in Zululand for assistance. Rewards of £500 were dangled for the capture of Bambata dead or alive and £20 for each of his accomplices. Shortly, a complement of 5,000 troops were assembled to track down the fugitive chieftains, incidentally dispensing with the need for rewards. The Natal cabinet, still incensed over the intervention of Lord Elgin, refrained from asking for imperial military aid. However, an offer of the Transvaal to send five hundred fully equipped troops, expense free, was accepted with open arms. A similar gesture from Cape Colony elicited a grateful acknowledgement but was deferred for the time being and only a detachment of the Cape Mounted Rifles was ever called upon.[26]

Natal authorities were greatly concerned over the loyalty of several important chieftains whose defection might spark a general uprising of natives throughout the colony while troops were concentrated in Zululand. The kraals of Tilonko were located some thirty miles south of Pietermaritzburg in the area of Mid-Illovo. His followers had acted in an aggressive manner toward tax collectors and many had joined the rebellion. The kraals of Gobizembi were located some sixty miles northeast of Pietermaritzburg in the district of Mapumulo. His followers had shown disrespect toward tax collectors and Gobizembi had been able to deliver up only 20 of the accused 300 offenders. The kraals of Kula were located some eighty miles directly north of Pietermaritzburg. Kula was a grandson of Ngoza, once famous as Sir Theophilus Shepstone's principal *induna*, and held forth over a tribe estimated to number 18,000 of whom 2,500 were fighting men. Kula was accused of influencing his people against whole-hearted support of the poll tax as well as permitting acts of violence and failing to supply laborers for service on public works. The kraals of Messeni were located some forty miles northeast of Pietermaritzburg and some fifteen miles south of Mapumulo. Messeni was head of the Qwabe tribe, one of the most ancient in Natal. His men were charged with insolence toward the local magistrate and he with failure to deliver over the offenders and open military resistance. All four chieftains were rounded up to await trial while precautionary measures against further uprisings among their tribes included destruction of kraals and surrender of arms, cattle, and sheep.[27]

The major campaign took place in the Nkandhla forest where 2,000 rebels were estimated to be at large. Colonel McKenzie assumed command and the plan was to close in upon the enemy in a rough and precipitous terrain, much of it dense woods. Bambata and his allies fought craftily, confining themselves to night attacks and guerrilla warfare. Eventually the systematic destruction of kraals cut off food supplies and, combined with the superior weapons of Natal forces, brought victory to the colony. The climax came at Mome Gorge where, on June 10, Bambata was slain at the hands of loyal native scouts without awareness of their victim's identity. Four days later that fact was established. The head was severed from the badly decomposed body and carried to the Natal camp to be photographed for identification purposes. It was hoped that the pictures would combat the claim of witch doctors that Bambata was invulnerable and so convince his followers of the futility of their cause. Whether or not it had the desired effect, the rebellion came to an end in July, claiming a toll of 3,500 natives killed and a like number taken prisoners. Colonial losses were surprisingly small, 30 dead and 40 wounded, but the financial cost was heavy—£800,000.[28]

While the British Colonial Office in London simply initialed most of McCallum's dispatches posting the military events, the staff did what they could through the Governor of Natal to soften the worst vestiges of the bloodshed. Keith questioned resort to a reward for Bambata dead or alive. That was contrary to the whole spirit of *The Hague Convention of 1899* and would be intolerable in modern warfare. Furthermore, Bambata was "not exactly an ordinary murderer" but merely a rebel. If Lord Elgin too voiced his disapproval of the premium placed upon Bambata, he offered imperial troops whenever desired. Whether these expressions of disapproval influenced the withdrawal of the reward is a matter of conjecture. Reports of the decapitation prompted inquiries as to the propriety of such conduct. McCallum related the essential facts, adding that the tactful procedure was followed to cover the head with a cloth and afterwards to bury it with the rest of the body.[29]

Lord Elgin called attention to the charge that places of worship were being removed from locations. If true, it seemed rather unconnected with the suppression of a rebellion. McCallum explained that the action had been taken only against the cluster of Christian-secessionist native churches espousing the overthow of the white man's authority. The Natal Native Trust had a right to prevent its locations from being made a spawning ground for sedition. No less vigorous was McCallum's answer to the inquiry of Lord Elgin about accounts of excessive brutality. The fact that 2,000 (correctly, over 3,000) able-bodied and injured prisoners were in custody should give a lie to the propaganda of captured natives being murdered or maltreated. If kraals were destroyed, the reason was that cutting off supplies would hasten the end of war and save lives and money. For the rest, Lord Elgin welcomed the cessation of hostilities, informing McCallum of his satisfaction at the way "the emergency has been met and the conduct of the troops in the field and the restraint shown."[30]

Churchill followed closely the trials by court-martial of the many chieftains and headmen accused of rebellion, high treason, sedition, public violence, and murder. At the utmost he saw their crimes as failing to summon their young men to pay the poll tax or in wavering allegiance during the war. What he regarded as the utter ruthlessness of the Natal government exasperated him to the point of letting his staff know that he would merely read in the House of Commons the answers prepared on Natal matters. At the outset of the trial proceedings in May 1906, Churchill urged McCallum "to persevere in restraining his ministers from giving us a ferocious and belated encore." He termed still severe the commuted sentences meted out to twenty-five so-called "ringleaders" ranging from ten years to life imprisonment with hard labor, fines of hundreds of cattle, and lashes up to thirty.*

---

*Old age (put between 96 and 100 years) overtook Sigananda before the law could exact what apparently would have been a mild punishment considering his advanced years. Official reports describe his death on July 22, 1906 as "senile decay." P.P., 1906, LXXIX, Cd. 3247, pp. 37, 59-60.

Tilonko was given ten years' imprisonment and a fine of five hundred head of cattle and Messeni received life imprisonment. Churchill encouraged the appeal of Jellicoe to the Privy Council in behalf of Tilonko on the ground that since the Indemnity Bill went through the Natal Legislature on July 12, the subsequent trial of Tilonko on July 30 by court-martial was illegal. The Privy Council refused to entertain the case and Tilonko (along with Messeni and a score of chieftains) was sent to St. Helena. Gobizembi and Kula were removed to locations in Natal because they were regarded as politically less dangerous. On November 7, Churchill wrote a postscript, commenting that "Tilonko has been cruelly and harshly dealt with [;] a marked lack of justice and inhumanity is evident in the sentence imposed, upon a Chief who returned from parole to stand his trial, after restraining his tribe from joining the rebels."[31]

Liberals and Labourites did not deny the gravity of the situation in Natal. Whites were a mere handful among a horde of blacks and the martial spirit of the Zulus had apparently not yet subsided. Natives had witnessed the fight between whites for three long years during the Boer War and no doubt were emboldened to seek their independence again. Nor was the right of Natal contested to pursue Bambata into Zululand since it had been entrusted with this territory in 1897. What could be questioned was the political wisdom of making it a test of loyalty for chieftains in Zululand to help capture Bambata. If compelled to take sides, they might very well throw in their lot with beleaguered brethren. Sigananda had been thus forced into opposition when pressed by Natal to participate in rounding up Bambata. This maxim of "divide et imperii" was unworthy of civilized statesmanship. The Labour Leader condemned the very thought of offering a reward for Bambata dead or alive. Such vindictiveness could provoke a blood-curdling war of desperate resistance on the part of natives.[32]

No justification could be found, however, for the fury with which Natal pursued its military operations. Communications from colonials were revolting in their details of brutality against enemy natives. Rebels were hunted down like wild beasts. Kinsmen were expected to arrest suspect relatives or stand convicted as traitors. One read with horror the extent of the carnage. Kraals were systematically destroyed, crops burned, and cattle seized, leaving the innocent to suffer in the heartless determination to cut off sources of food for the rebels. It was disturbing to learn that wounded and captive prisoners were being slain.* MacDonald sought to intervene in the disposition of chieftains arrested for purported disloyalty—Kula, Gobizembi, Messeni, Tilonko. The crime, if so it were, had been failure to act with dispatch against the disaffected or to prevent their warriors from joining the disaffected.[33] After sentence was imposed, MacDonald concerned himself with their treatment as prisoners. A steady stream of inquiries were directed to the British Colonial Office about the health of those transported to St. Helena.[34]

Dr. Leslie Haden Guest, physician and socialist, penned a scorching condemnation of Natal barbarity:

> Tragic [was] the news of the cold-blooded massacre of 3,000 natives in Mome Valley. There should be no further talk of our power of intervention in a self-governing colony. . . . The same right which enables us to rescue a maltreated child from a savage and drunken parent must be invoked to rescue the miserable Zulus. . . . [There is need for] an enquiry . . . by a committee composed of representative Englishmen, impartial colonials, and one or more impartial coloured men.[35]

The *Westminster Gazette* dealt severely with Natal for the manner in which it rebuffed the mother country during the rebellion. Speeches of Natal ministers, attributing responsibility for the new outbreak to British suspension of the executions, were far from the truth. It would be closer to reality to say that Natal maladministration justified intervention by the Imperial State. Surely, Natal could pool experiences with the home government on so vital a matter as native policy. For a century the whole cost of Natal security had been borne by Great Britain. Natal should keep in mind too that a blunder on its part could endanger British rule of colored populations in other parts of Africa. In the House of Commons, MacDonald presented a conception of imperial relationship:

---

*The Rt. Rev. Wilmot Lushington Vyvyan (Bishop of Zululand) made the original complaint in July 1906. A court of enquiry was appointed by Natal to probe the charges of inhuman treatment of prisoners. After hearing the testimony of officers and soldiers, the allegations were stated to have no basis of support, P.P., 1906, LXXIX, Cd. 3247, p. 43 ff.

He did not hold the idea of a little corner of the Empire doing what it liked, without admitting that the rest of the Empire had any right to interfere or to advise. If we were to have an Empire, we must have something that corresponded to a political unity, . . . the parts . . . that shared in the glory, pretension, and honour of belonging to it must, as a quid pro quo, allow some central imperial authority to take charge of the traditions . . . and the reputation of the whole.[36]

Sinister motives were suggested as the cause for native unrest. Behind the poll tax lurked the evil design of forcing blacks to toil for whites. Obviously the need for cash to pay the revenue collector must compel the native to seek work on the terms of the white man. The facts belied the impression that the native did not bear his share of taxation. Besides customs duties, which often doubled the price of his necessities, the native was burdened with hut, land, and road taxes, as well as license fees for dogs and marriages.* No wonder that the native, lacking the franchise to air grievances, should complain bitterly. Englishmen, more than all other peoples, should appreciate the indignity of taxation without representation. A corollary aim could be to expropriate native lands and a native war gave the whites an excuse for breaking up the reservations. The way in which many of the chieftains convicted of rebellious conduct were punished (by withdrawal of jurisdiction over tribal lands) was very suspicious. The Imperial State should hold an inquiry into the evident strategy to reduce the native population to a proletariat bound in economic servitude to whites.[37]

Francis Ernest Colenso penned a vigorous defense of the native:

It is an ominous fact that speakers and writers on this side of the globe should continue in these days to harp upon the notion that the outlying districts of Natal are as dangerous as the Sioux-infested backwoods of Fenimore Cooper's novels, or as evil spots in England. . . . Journals of Natal may be searched in vain . . . for any instance of Native attacks

---

*Whatever allowances should be made for the value of their respective property holdings and professional skills, the absolute figures of taxation for 1904 are as follows (*Natal, Census of 1904*, pp. 912-14):

	POPULATION	TOTAL TAXES PAID	PER PERSON
whites	103,795	£3,584,148	£34 10s. 7d.
natives	904,041	£ 445,047	9s. 10d.

upon life or property, other than individual breaches of the law, such as occur in all communities. . . . The policy has all the appearance of a mad design, to force them into the position of 'rebels,' by compelling them to defend in despair all that our common humanity holds most dear. . . . Actually there is a 'White Peril' engendered by a combination between bureaucracy and panic, and not a little influenced by colour prejudice, from which the native needs protection.

Before the period of martial tyranny set in, Natal was for two or three years disturbed by 'rumours of Native unrest.' The governmental reports bear witness to what the responsible officials, after investigation, thought of these rumours.* There is no evidence that pains and penalties have been visited upon a single white miscreant for the sedulous propaganda of the present years. . . . What confidence can the Natives be invited to place in rulers who, for silly utterances, inflict the lash upon a multitude of irresponsible Black youths, but let White firebrands go scot free? . . . The present story of a Native conspiracy is on much the same footing of 'Dr. Titus Oates and his plot.'

And if allowance is claimed in the case of British combatants for brutality, think too of making allowance for the frenzy of Zulus who, with red ruin spreading over their peaceful homes, are driven to face the deadly Rexer, and to see their own kith and kin slaughtered by hundreds, . . . more especially if it be intensified by a hopeless sense of injustice, a horrible conviction of undeserved injury. . . .[38]

Conservatives had no doubt as to the rebellious intentions of Bambata. He had refused a summons to give an account of his resistance to the poll tax. He had fled to Zululand and persuaded other chieftains to join him against the Natal authorities. He had attacked a police force dispatched to rescue white women and children isolated in a disturbed district. His men had engaged in several running fights and troopers had been killed. Nothing could have been more audacious than kidnapping his uncle, Magwababa. The murder of Stainbank, leaving widowed and orphaned a wife and child, was outrageous.

---

*These rumors of unrest and disaffection which were described by the Natal Minister for Native Affairs on Dec. 28, 1905 as of no "concrete or tangible nature calculated to cause alarm" are not to be confused with the view expressed by McCallum to Lord Elgin on Jan. 5, 1906 of "young men of the tribes . . . [who] get more out of control of kraal heads." P.P., 1906, LXXIX, Cd. 2905, pp. 1-2.

George Wyndham, Conservative M.P. and Chief Secretary for Ireland in the Balfour government, likened the atmosphere to that depicted in novels dealing with the American West and the terror in which the Red Indian used to be held by the pioneer whites. The passion of the Zulus for fighting and shedding blood had been aroused. They possessed the heritage of a great military race even if the absence of wild game hampered their training and strong jealousies among the chieftains blunted the potency of their threat.[39]

Nor should the stern measures of Natal military forces be confused with brutality. In war those methods were often most humane which helped to terminate operations speedily. Seizure of cattle and goats and destruction of kraals reduced the staying powers of the enemy. If perchance Natal troops had killed wounded rebels, it should be remembered that men fighting in thick bush and rugged terrain could not distinguish easily between disabled and deployed opponents. This accusation of refusal to give quarter was ridiculous considering that Natal sustained almost 3,000 native prisoners at public expense. *The Times* had an answer for the account being circulated in the mother country that the decapitated head of Bambata had been flaunted as a trophy of victory. It referred to McCallum's recital of facts as giving the lie to such fabrications implying an arrogant white supremacy.[40]

While the fighting continued, Conservatives sought a reconciliation between Great Britain and Natal to assure a quick victory and a return to normalcy. The determination of the latter to do without imperial aid was understandable. Natal had a right to be resentful, for even if Lord Elgin did back down from his unwise suspension of the death sentences, the damage had been done. Natives had the impression that the Natal cabinet was no longer master in its own house. So they had decided to rebel, anticipating that an irate Crown would step in against the colony. The proffered military aid of the Transvaal and Cape Colony indicated that the rest of South Africa was equally resentful of British interference in colonial domestic affairs. Nevertheless, all this should now be water under the bridge and it behooved both parties to effect a rapprochement. The Imperial State ought to make a frank and straightforward offer of military assistance, and Natal should accept it for the sake of the safety of the white population. Together in arms, the insurrection could be set down in good time with a minimum of destruction and expense.[41]

The *National Review* termed preposterous the allegations that the poll tax was intended as a lever to force the native to work and to expropriate his land. It invited Lieutenant-Colonel Frederic Spence Tatham, a member of the Natal Legislature, to explain the facts to its readers. Colonel Tatham insisted that a trade depression and declining revenues were the reasons behind the search for more public income. He doubted that the poll tax would materially change the figures compiled in the *Census of 1904* showing that whites paid £30 11s. per head and natives only 9s. 6¾d., a ratio hardly suggestive of a Zulu population subject to fiscal oppression.[42] Nor had the incidence of the poll tax been flagrantly discriminating. The total amount received as of April 30, 1906 was £100,000 broken down thus: Europeans (£30,000), Indians and Cape Coloured (£24,000), Natives (£46,000).[43] Some £15,000 was still outstanding and mainly from natives. As for baiting the Zulus into rebellion and then taking their land, signs were not lacking that the Zulus harbored such thoughts themselves. The poll tax came at a most advantageous moment for the disaffected tribes with their grandiose aspirations of renewed Bantu supremacy. Natives were convinced that the Boer War had weakened the unity of whites in South Africa and opportunity for victory was now at hand.[44]

The frequent references in official circles to the diabolical influence of the Christian-secessionist native churches in promoting restlessness among Zulus was explained in the public forum. Liberals and Labourites accepted the challenge to interpret this religious movement. It had a perfectly honorable history, representing an effort to set up a Christian church confined exclusively to native people. Clergymen from the United States were sponsors of the African Methodist Episcopal Church which, in 1897, affiliated with the Negro Church of America. If it had excited large visions of freedom, that could be attributed to the inherent qualities of Christianity. If it preached the so-called heretical doctrine about the equality of white and black, that comported well with Christian ideals. If it taught that the Bible proclaimed one Supreme Being and only He need be respected and feared, that carried no more significance than a sober veneration of the Bible. The *Manchester Guardian* refused to believe that Christian precepts had made the Bantu conscious of an inveterate hostility between black and white. To say that Christianity had bred fanaticism among natives was to speak unworthily of its influence. Apparently, to whites in Natal, Christianity meant that while all men were brothers, some were born black and disinherited.[45]

Colonel Tatham extended his remarks to present the colonial viewpoint on the Christian-secessionist native churches. Whites in Natal had cherished the hope that the importation of American Negro ministers spreading the Gospel would be an elevating influence among the natives. Instead, unhappily, they had been filled with revolutionary ideas calling for the expulsion of the whites and the inauguration of a Negro republic. The itinerant Negro ministers from America had turned out to be half-civilized and quasi-Christian agitators, who should never have been allowed to set foot in a British colony. Ethiopianism, as the movement became known, was an expression of nascent nationalism and served as a catalyst to endow the spiritual eddies with a political goal. The kingdom of Ethiopia, triumphant in 1896 against Italian imperialism at the Battle of Adowa, was invoked as a living exemplar of an unconquered African people. If this interpretation were true, and there seemed no reason to doubt it, the *Pall Mall Gazette* favored energetic measures with the imperial stamp of approval to crush the treasonable propaganda of "Africa for the Africans." Perhaps a drastic aliens act to deport the American conspirators from South Africa was in order.[46]

Since the two schools of thought differed in their analyses of the Christian-secessionist native churches, the scholarly findings of Dr. Berndt G. M. Sundkler, Swedish Lutheran missionary, merit consideration. Most of the European churches (save Anglican and Roman Catholic) observed a policy of separate congregations for white and black because of colonial pressures. This trend, accentuated by harsh disabilities, economic peonage, and land expropriations, weakened the image of a universal Christ. Such was the background of the Bantu movement for independent Christian churches. The Ethiopian Church constituted an early forerunner, founded in 1892 among native "boys" on the Rand by malcontents seceding from Wesleyan church missions. Subsequently, in 1896, at a conference in Pretoria, native leaders of Ethiopian sectaries decided to seek affiliation with the African Methodist Episcopal Church of America which boasted over 800,000 communicants. A delegation was dispatched to the United States and their application received approval. The South African Republic granted corporate recognition and a period of expansion followed, over 10,000 members being weaned away from mission churches. Dr. Sundkler regards the thesis of conspiratorial overtones lightly, and sees the rapid appearance of independent Christian churches among the Bantu as a desire to come to grips with Christianity in a spiritual sense.[47]

ROLE OF DINIZULU

The conduct of Dinizulu, during the resistance to the poll tax and the Bambata rebellion, commanded close attention. He created a favorable impression of his loyalty by cooperating in the prompt payment of the poll tax and offering to send an *impi* (native troops) against the rebels in the Nkandhla forest. But the idea of using the prestige of his ancestry to hold other chieftains in line was dropped because an enhanced reputation might make him (as in the 1880's) a rallying point of opposition. Later, when rumors circulated of his harboring rebels and supplying them with rifles, McCallum summoned him to Pietermaritzburg. However, Dinizulu's ill health (attributed to dropsy) resulted in the interview of June 20-21, 1906 taking place with several of his headmen, including Mankulumana, principal *induna*. If McCallum expressed himself afterwards as satisfied with Dinizulu's behavior, he noted his failure to report the names of messengers to the Usutu kraal and the purpose of their visits. At the British Colonial Office a sigh of relief greeted the account, although Churchill would add that "it is a wonder . . . these constant suspicions do not drive Dinizulu mad."[48]

McCallum soon had reason to change his views as depositions from apprehended rebels implicated Dinizulu in the disturbances. But difficulties in the way of obtaining substantial evidence delayed any action. This was the status, in May 1907, when McCallum ended his tour of duty as Governor of Natal. As a last gesture of good will he decided to counsel Dinizulu again to watch his behavior. This time Dinizulu came to Pietermaritzburg and the interview took place on May 20-21 in the presence of cabinet members. Dinizulu availed himself of the occasion not only to protest his innocence and to air the grievances of the Zulu nation but also to complain that he was held responsible for all sins and yet ignored as government *induna*.

McCallum responded that he could certainly speak out against the rebellion and so avoid the innuendos of mysterious goings on at the Usutu kraal. McCallum made an unhappy choice of words in his final dispatch on June 1 when he wrote "that native matters were fairly flattened out." Churchill chose to have a Roman holiday with this phrase as "a good expression and does justice to the wisdom and humanity that have inspired, no less than to the beneficent results, that have attended the native policy of the Natal Government and Sir Henry McCallum."[49]

Events during the summer months of 1907 heightened suspicions of Dinizulu's disloyalty. Depositions from Siyekiwe, one of Bambata's wives, and from two of his children by other wives (a girl aged sixteen and a boy aged fourteen) were damaging. A messenger from Dinizulu arrived in March 1906 requesting Bambata to visit the Usutu kraal. Siyekiwe and the two children (plus a third who later died) followed Bambata. Siyekiwe explained that she feared to be left alone at her own desolate kraal away from other members of the tribe. The girl went as her companion and the boy happened to be herding goats at her kraal. Siyekiwe explained that she was pregnant at the time and so proceeded more slowly and the children accompanied her. It might be added that her child was born at the Usutu kraal in a hut where Dinizulu's wives previously had been confined.[50]

As Siyekiwe and the two children recounted their experiences at the Usutu kraal, they had overheard Mankulumana give a series of instructions to Bambata. The latter was to go back to Natal, commit an act of rebellion, and then flee to the Nkandhla forest and await the appearance of Dinizulu's men. Siyekiwe asserted that Bambata had several interviews with Dinizulu, Mankulumana, and Mgwaqo, second principal *induna*. Bambata was given a rifle and ammunition and left, accompanied by Cakijana, an agent of Dinizulu. It was on this trip back to Natal that Bambata kidnapped his uncle, Magwababa. During the subsequent fourteen months that Siyekiwe and the two children remained at the Usutu kraal, they testified to seeing messengers, warriors, and chieftains arriving and departing. Bambata returned once from the midst of the fighting in the Nkandhla forest for a three-day visit and Siyekiwe heard him complain to Dinizulu over the latter's failure to send promised troops into the battle area.

The decision of Siyekiwe to take the children and escape was a fear that Dinizulu intended to move them elsewhere and keep them under close surveillance because they knew too much. On July 3, 1907, after an all-night journey by foot, they showed up at the Mahlabatini magistracy and from there were conveyed to Pietermaritzburg. They gave their testimony at Central Gaol implicating Dinizulu in secret relations with Bambata, harboring rebels, and furnishing arms. It might be added that Siyekiwe and the two children (plus the one born at the Usutu kraal) were later returned to relatives in the Mpanza valley.

The regularity with which attacks upon loyal chieftains were occurring worried the Natal government. The most notable case was that of Sitshitshili, a Sibisi chieftain commended for the fact that not one of his men joined the rebels. Sitshitshili was shot to death on August 25 while in his hut by a young man described "as about 20 years of age and a perfect stranger to . . . his people." He had gained entrance by purporting to bring a message from another chieftain to the effect that all cattle seized from rebels during the disturbance were to be returned to them. In the circumstances the idea was entertained to have Dinizulu brought in for still another interview and to request Sir Matthew Nathan, new Governor of Natal, to summon two companies of imperial troops. Lord Elgin declined to authorize military patrols pending more detailed information. What prompted Natal to drop the idea was the conviction in October that the amnesty granted to many prisoners of the recent rebellion had had a pacifying effect. Since July some 500 to 600 of the 2,000 rebels had been released from prison.[51]

The British Colonial Office disliked the proposal that Dinizulu submit to a searching investigation. Hopwood felt that it would be "unfair to have him attend such a fishing inquiry, especially if he happens to know of the statements made by Bambata's wife." Lord Elgin was not impressed with the evidence of Bambata's wife, for "she had every inducement to make things worse for Dinizulu." Even if the charges were true, and he would certainly not condone them, they would appear to have come to an end voluntarily after Dinizulu's interview with McCallum. Moreover, the initial report of the Natal Native Affairs Commission (appointed in the fall of 1906 to review native administration) would indicate that the colony was not entirely blameless for the tension between blacks and whites.[52] Lord Elgin would accept an inquiry on Dinizulu's activities if it were not conducted by police be-

hind closed doors but by an impartial body in full public glare. Given
such a procedure and the promise of carrying out the reforms recommended by the above commission, Lord Elgin stood ready to move in
whatever imperial troops were deemed advisable.[53]

The murder of Mpumela, the loyal Ntuli chieftain, in the Nkandhla
district on November 20, 1907, shot to death in his hut by two fleeing
assailants, precipitated a crisis. The tragic fate of both Mpumela and
Sitshitshili was regarded as part of a developing pattern to put a
premium upon cooperation with the Natal government. Although the
Natal cabinet had no proof of his implication in these two instances, it
decided on November 28, 1907, with the concurrence of Nathan, to
wait no longer and to issue a warrant for Dinizulu's arrest on the
ground of high treason during the Bambata uprising. Nathan passed
on to Lord Elgin the pledge of the Natal cabinet to release all remaining rank-and-file prisoners of the late rebellion when the arrest had
been effected (which was done by April 1908) and to enact legislation
along the lines recommended by the Natal Native Affairs Commission.* A task force of 2,000 militia was sent to bring him into custody.
The further precaution was taken on December 3 of proclaiming
martial law in Zululand. Nathan questioned its use as premature since
no armed resistance to the ordinary processes of law had as yet occurred. After some uncertainty, because of his plea of ill health to
make the journey to Pietermaritzburg, Dinizulu (along with Mankulumana and Mgwaqo) surrendered on December 7 at Nongama.
He was escorted to the capital, reaching his destination the last week
of December and lodged in the Central Gaol to await trial.[54]

Since imperial troops were not used, the British Colonial Office
had to stay its hand. But sentiment among the staff was hostile to the
Natal government. Vernon observed that the Dinizulu proceedings looked like panic, "as if they wished to provoke the rebellion
which they profess to fear." When Nathan called attention to the
bitterly critical articles in the *Daily News* as encouraging natives to
think that the King had quarreled with Natal, Hopwood tartly com-

*A *Native Administration Act* was passed in 1908 to embody the idea of more personal contact with the Zulus. It included a reorganization of districts, apprenticeship of
children over ten years of age to promote habits of industry, the appointment of a
permanent secretary of native affairs subject to the Minister for Native Affairs, and a
council for native affairs to advise the Natal government on legislation. P.R.O., c.o.
179/247-48, 251-53.

mented that "we are not responsible for the *Daily News*." No less inhospitable was Hopwood to the wish of Nathan that the bad blood
stirred by the *Daily News* be counteracted with a telegram "making
clear that the Imperial Government views the recent murders in
Zululand with deep regret and fully sympathizes with the Colony in
its desire to restore order in that province." Hopwood answered that a
grave difference of policy existed between the home government and
Natal and "if we endeavour to bridge it by platitudes we shall fall between two stools." Lord Elgin commented that along with such a
telegram of approval as requested by Nathan "I might as well forward
my resignation." If his reply on December 9 did contain some words
of comfort for Natal, the emphasis was on the future hope that the
policy of amnesty and an improved administration of native affairs
would accompany the restoration of order.[55]

A preliminary examination of witnesses was held from December
23, 1907 to July 30, 1908, the lengthy period being explained by the
determination to investigate Dinizulu's role as far back as 1906.
Martial law remained in force from December 3, 1907 until August 11,
1908, on the ground that chieftains sympathetic to Dinizulu might
interfere with the collection of evidence in the locations. Dinizulu's
salary of £500 annually was suspended because as a prisoner he no
longer discharged the duties of his office. The defense brought over
from London the English barrister, Edwin George Jellicoe, previously
associated with the appeals of Mangena and Tilonko. Jellicoe arrived
on January 19, 1908, and stayed until February 17, when he abruptly
tendered his resignation and returned home. His complaint was that
Natal had placed impediments in his way to gather evidence in Zululand for the defense. William Philip Schreiner, past Prime Minister
of Cape Colony and an avowed champion of native rights, later took
his place. The findings formally committed Dinizulu for trial on
twenty-three counts, including high treason, incitement to public
violence, sedition and rebellion, accessory to murder, and illegal possession of firearms.[56]

The Imperial Factor had its tribulations during these several months
of the preliminary examination. A steady stream of questions was
raised in Parliament to assure that the British Colonial Office did
everything within its power to help Dinizulu. Francis Ernest Colenso

sent a daily epistle to Hopwood disclosing the latest injustices to Dinizulu as relayed by his sister, Harriette Emily Colenso. In turn, the staff directed regular dispatches to Nathan requesting information to satisfy critics. The treatment and health of Dinizulu in prison was a matter of constant concern. On one occasion the huge and corpulent man suffered a hemorrhage and had to spend a brief period in the hospital. The failure to assign Miss Colenso as interpreter to Dinizulu produced awkward exchanges. Truth was sought on her charges in February 1908 that natives were being flogged in Zululand to obtain evidence against Dinizulu. The crimes attributed to Dinizulu drew from Hopwood the caustic comment that "in this country no judicial officer would commit [him] for trial on any evidence we have seen [but] the colonial magistrates are not independent of the Government of the Natal and where would Moor* and his colleagues be if after martial law, troops, great expense, and bloodshed there was nothing to justify such drastic and unhappy action." Lord Crewe, successor to Lord Elgin as Secretary of State for the Colonies in April 1908, lamented wearily that "the cruel irony of the whole situation consists in the fact that this long-drawn preliminary enquiry, only excusable in its duration if carefully designed to protect the prisoner, can only result in his committal whatever the evidence."[57]

If the engagement of Jellicoe was not highly regarded by the British Colonial Office, it had to state that his credentials were in good order. Later this confirmation of his legal standing was compounded to imply status as a Whitehall appointee and Nathan called for a disavowal lest Jellicoe's denunciation of Natal after his resignation be interpreted as reflecting official opinion. Nathan objected to this English barrister because his connection with the Mangena and Tilonko cases could prejudice a Natal jury against Dinizulu. When Jellicoe threw up his brief, the personnel in the South African Department shed no tears, labeling it a blessing in disguise and "good riddance." However, an end to Jellicoe was not in sight, for upon his return to London he overwhelmed the British Colonial Office with letters describing the impossibility of

*Frederick Robert Moor had replaced Smythe as Prime Minister in November 1906. The issue was not the handling of native affairs upon which all parties were united but financial matters. Where Smythe proposed to tax unoccupied land and to increase the income tax, Moor favored retrenchment in expenditures to balance the budget.

justice in Natal and urging the transfer of the case to England. The
response to Jellicoe was that he should convey his indictments through
Dinizulu's counsel in Natal. Hopwood advised that

> we steer clear of handling Jellicoe as a scourge for the Natal Ministry. He
> may be in the right on many of his points but his methods and want of
> tact make him an undesirable agent and he certainly is not ours. The
> Natal Government may hang itself if we give it rope enough but I agree
> that the rope must not be long enough to hang Dinizulu as well.[58]

Finding a replacement for Jellicoe proved a protracted affair. The
legal staff assembled in Natal to defend Dinizulu did not command
much standing. Robert Charles Azariah Samuelson, a brother of
Samuel Olaf Samuelson, Under-Secretary for Natal Native Affairs, had
been an advocate of the Supreme Court since 1886; Eugene Renaud
since 1901. A well-known colonial lawyer should be procured, observed
Lambert, "so that he may be acquitted or hanged without misgiving."
If convicted, the Imperial State would have to face the issue of exercising the prerogative of mercy. After a lengthy correspondence, not concluded until the latter part of 1908, the British government agreed to
pay the fee of 2,000 guineas asked by Schreiner. Natal attached the
conditions that the fee not be paid nor the fact made public until the
trial was concluded. That would avoid having the natives interpret it
as British sympathy for the prisoner.[59]

Meanwhile, the British Colonial Office felt that Natal could promote a better climate of public opinion by answering Jellicoe's allegations. Lambert observed that the Natal government would make a
mistake in not refuting "Mr. Jellicoe *seriatim*—they [Natal cabinet]
are not so impeccable as to be able to assume a disdainful air of injured innocence, . . . a point abundantly made against them by that
paladium of licentiousness, the local press." While Nathan obtained
from his ministers a response to the specific points, the Natal government informed him that it had no jurisdiction over the preliminary
examination. In any case, assurance was given that 1) Dinizulu's advisers had full access to the evidence assembled by the prosecution, 2)
accusations of coercion of witnesses under martial law were baseless,
and 3) an opportunity would be afforded the defense to visit Zululand
in fitting time.[60]

The severest trial came in connection with the suspension of Dinizulu's salary. The British Colonial Office argued that he was not an ordinary civil servant and the agreement of 1898 stated that his salary could not be suspended without the consent of the Secretary of State for the Colonies. Moreover, to cut off his salary would prejudge the trial, a violation of the British law that the accused should be treated as innocent until proven guilty. What made the loss of his salary particularly serious was the need for funds to sustain his defense. Lord Crewe favored admitting joint responsibility and "if necessary declare ourselves liable without being asked." Acting upon the legal opinion of the Attorney General that Great Britain could be sued in court, Lord Crewe informed Natal that the home government intended to make up the arrears in Dinizulu's salary. Strong protests followed from Natal ministers who sought to avoid a humiliating blow to their dignity (in the eyes of natives) by announcing a payment of £500 toward Dinizulu's defense. Even though Natal did not acknowledge the legal right of Dinizulu to his salary, Lord Crewe accepted the offer of a sum "which we assume will be at least equal in amount to the salary and . . . we will suspend our own payment."[61]

Liberal and Labour circles came quickly to the fore in December 1907 when the warrant for Dinizulu's arrest was issued. The arraignment had all the earmarks of a campaign of persecution. Throughout the late "rebellion" he had been accused of complicity with Bambata, even being summoned to Pietermaritzburg for an extrajudicial cross-examination. The assassination of loyal chieftains were acts of renegades in the nature of revenge, an aftermath of vicious combat. If Dinizulu were really disloyal, he would have joined the fighting last year instead of waiting until the cause was hopelessly lost to commit himself. His tardiness to obey the summons was not a confession of self-guilt but ill health. Needless to say, a sigh of relief was breathed with the news that Dinizulu had come down from the Usutu kraal and given himself up to the military authorities. That should be prima facie proof of good faith and confidence in his own innocence.[62]

The suspicion was voiced that the proceedings against Dinizulu were part of a broader plot to deprive the native tribes of their land rights in Zululand. Even making allowance for the nervousness generated among a small white population outnumbered ten to one, it was difficult to believe that 2,000 troops had been mobilized just to round up one man. The circumstances pointed rather to a diabolical attempt to taunt Dinizulu into war and "establish white supremacy once for all with the new Rexer gun." What the white settlers wanted was to rid themselves of the reserves and parcel it out to "the salt of the earth." This sinister aim to reduce the Zulus to vassalage constituted but another accursed step of those forces still intent upon predatory imperialism. Mackarness saw fresh confirmation of this plot in the findings of the Natal Native Affairs Commission. As he read it, the report was a scathing indictment of the victimization of the Zulus. Their customs, legal rights, and educational needs were ignored and ridiculed.[63]

Julia Wedgwood, writer and descendant of the pottery family, acquainted the British nation with the shameful details of the preliminary examination. The use of a magistrate's court to determine if a case existed for committal was an implication of guilt and would put Dinizulu at a great disadvantage when he entered upon trial.* Refusal to permit the designation of Harriette Emily Colenso as Dinizulu's interpreter deprived him of a friend in fullest sympathy.** No doubt her offer to prove with names and circumstances instances of natives flogged for not giving state evidence prompted this vindictive action.[64] When the magistrate remanded Dinizulu for court trial, Miss Alice Werner, teacher of African languages at King's College, University of London, characterized many of the twenty-three counts as inherently improbable and some as mutually destructive of each other. A man described by his accusers as "constantly in a more or less drunken state unfitting him for the performance of his duties" could scarcely have the deliberate forethought necessary for the intrigues ascribed to him. The entire case had an overtone of malicious mischief attached to it.[65]

Jellicoe's complaint that under martial law Natal had assembled its evidence by intimidation and terrorism was instructive of the local

---

*Colonel Seely, Parliamentary Under-Secretary for the Colonies in the Asquith government (successor to the ailing Campbell-Bannerman as Prime Minister in 1908), regretted the existence of an ordinance dating back to 1845 which required such a preliminary examination. It did amount to two trials but there was little he could do in the face of the law. Commons, Apr. 29, 1908, p. 1240. For ready access to this ordinance see P.P., 1908, LXXII, Cd. 3998, p. 187.

**Colonel Seely explained Natal's refusal to assign Harriette Emily Colenso as interpreter because her activity as a molder of British public opinion in behalf of Dinizulu might prejudice the court against the accused. The appointment was given to Ncapai, a former secretary of Dinizulu. Commons, June 15, 1908, pp. 541-42.

milieu. The lash had been freely used and some natives were shot on the spot. Likely witnesses for Dinizulu were arrested and thrown into prison and their whereabouts kept secret.* In contrast he had been denied the right to enter kraals and to interrogate witnesses and even refused access to the affidavits of the prosecution upon which the case rested. The *Manchester Guardian* made much of Jellicoe's contention that Natal was after 4,000,000 acres of valuable native holdings in Zululand. The rumors of a conspiracy afoot to rob Zulus of their land by getting Dinizulu out of the way would appear to have substance. The announcement of a Delimitation Commission in 1904—that all Zululand worth having was needed for the native population and should be reserved for them—had been a blow to white land grabbers.** It was only since then that native scares had become endemic. If Natal were interested in rebutting these insinuations, then it should permit a proper brief to be prepared for Dinizulu's defense.[66]

A vigorous protest was lodged against the suspension of Dinizulu's salary. How could he be said to have been derelict in duty when his official position had been confined to that of a petty tribal chieftain and he had never been used in his capacity as government *induna*? What made the withdrawal of the stipend reprehensible at the moment was the need for money to finance his defense. Certainly, the home government had a right to make itself heard, for the agreement reached in 1898, when Dinizulu returned from St. Helena, stated that

*Colonel McKenzie, in charge of administering martial law in Zululand, answered that only whippings had been imposed and justified because of insolence in public, giving false information, contravening prison regulations, and withholding evidence. P.P., 1908, LXXII, Cd. 3998, pp. 79, 172-73, 184.

**Some confusion would appear to be present as to what the Zululand Lands Delimitation Commission did say and do. On the one hand, there is a statement favoring the whites: "It would be impossible to remove whole tribes from Districts they had occupied . . . and the only manner in which the Districts could be curtailed . . . was to group adjoining tribes into more limited areas. . . . We have acted on this principle . . . and thus able to recommend in the aggregate, . . . that a large proportion of the Province be thrown open for European occupation." On the other hand, when the preliminary report came out marking off 3,887,000 acres for native occupation and 2,808,000 acres for Europeans, the whites were dissatisfied and asked for a reconsideration of the allocations. A study of the pertinent material indicates that the whites were unhappy over the failure to get more of the inland and healthier parts of Zululand rather than the amount of their total acreage. The British Colonial Office denied the request, insisting that Natal abide by the recommendations of the Joint Imperial and Colonial Commission. *Zululand Lands Delimitation Commission, 1902-04*, pp. 45-46; P.R.O., c.o. 179/230-231, c.o. 879/86, No. 764.

his salary could not be terminated save with the consent of the Secretary of State for the Colonies. Natal should know that its treatment of the mother country bordered on that of "an unscrupulous suitor whom he hopes to browbeat out of a claim." Some modicum of satisfaction was derived from the apparent effect of the joint pressure of officialdom and public opinion to prod Natal into contributing the equivalent of his salary even though tied to the purpose of defraying trial costs.[67]

The continuation of martial law for several months after Dinizulu had given himself up drew stern words. Pleas to search for arms and to arrest persons suspected of hostile intentions were rather flimsy excuses. No impending paralysis of civic life threatened. Government by martial law in time of peace had been the way of the Stuart kings. Sir Charles Wentworth Dilke, Liberal M.P. and stern foe of colonialism, asked rhetorically "what was the use of Magna Carta—part of the law of Natal—if, when there was admittedly no armed rising, no rebellion, they were to have martial law of the kind set up by Natal?" The grant of self-government to a colony of 22,000 white electors had been a sad mistake, exposing 1,000,000 natives to a precarious life. There would be no peace unless the Imperial State restored Zululand to the status of a protectorate as it had done with Basutoland.[68]

Conservative circles commended the wisdom of Natal in arresting Dinizulu. The recent assassinations confirmed the existence of a conspiracy intent upon making loyalty to Natal a matter of life and death for chieftains. Dinizulu could not escape blame since, as a descendant of a great line of warriors, his influence could have prevented the disturbances from taking place. While the *Standard* held a low opinion of Dinizulu as a person, for he was said to have acquired all the vices of the Western world—drink, sensuousness, frivolity—still he claimed royal stock and his appearance at the head of an insurrection could stir dormant dreams of a native kingdom. The task force assembled to bring in Dinizulu prevented the situation from getting out of control and perhaps having to call on British imperial forces for aid. In the event that Dinizulu had taken it into his head to escape, assuming only a small party had been sent out, a very costly campaign might have followed. If the conviction was at all deep-rooted in native minds that the whites in South Africa could not hold their own, then a fiasco in Zululand would have been contagious. Englishmen at home would not have relished a daily newspaper diet of massacre and rapine as hordes of natives reverted to ancient savagery.[69]

Nothing wrong could be seen in a preliminary examination to determine the validity of the many depositions against Dinizulu. Although the period of inquiry might be considered unduly long, time was needed to reach witnesses in Zululand. Natal should be credited with great patience and forbearance in its repeated remonstrances with Dinizulu. McCallum had personally admonished him to abjure any course leading to suspicion. The series of murders perpetrated against faithful chieftains demanded that a painstaking investigation should be held once and for all. As for the suspension of Dinizulu's salary, that was inevitable and consistent with civil service practice after he had been removed from office. As soon as he proved his innocence any arrears would be made up. Lyttelton believed that tactful persuasion could bring Natal around to yield on the necessity of advancing money for the defense. Whether he regarded the grant of money by Natal for Dinizulu's legal costs as a vindication of this strategy is not on record. The retention of martial law was supported as a humane measure to keep peace while the inquiry went on. And it had been administered leniently with no known executions. Natal ought to be given the benefit of doubt for sincere motives in view of the large sum spent to send a military force into Zululand.[70]

The *Standard* scored the Liberal government for its one-sided position during the preliminary examination. From first to last the dispatches from Whitehall were couched in formal language. No words of sympathetic appreciation for the ordeal of Natal were included. It was treated as if incapable of appraising its own situation or meting out honest justice. The result could well be to drive into bitter antagonism a loyal British colony which had borne the brunt of the Boer War. Natal had been the very cornerstone of British supremacy in South Africa and if it were lost then everything was lost.* The intervention of the Crown in the salary dispute was especially mischievous. The notion that the want of money handicapped the defense could warp public opinion against Natal in the forthcoming trial. Natives would

---

*An interesting presentation of this point of view justifying the arrest and trial of Dinizulu and the need for greater understanding of the colonial predicament is contained in a letter, dated June 25, 1908, written by Lord Selborne to Balfour, now leader of His Majesty's Opposition. *Balfour Papers*, 49708, p. 165 ff.

have more proof that Great Britain took their side against Natal. The
effect was already visible in the difficulty with which Natal persuaded
natives to testify for the state. Naturally the assumption was that
Dinizulu would win and natives were reluctant to expose themselves
to his vengeance afterwards. Such meddling could undermine relations
between natives and the Natal government and throw the latter into a
less charitable frame of mind in dealing with native welfare in the
future.[71]

The special civil court set up to try Dinizulu consisted of three well-
known public figures. Sir William James Smith was a member of the
Transvaal Supreme Court. Henri Gillaume Boshoff was a Puisne Judge
of the Natal Native High Court. Henrique Charles Shepstone was an
ex-Secretary for Natal Native Affairs and son of the late Sir Theophilus
Shepstone, native administrator and well-known opponent of Cetewayo. Francis Ernest Colenso was not happy with the selections and
let Hopwood know it. He described Boshoff as "a Boer of the Boers
with little culture, and is quite certain to lean towards the 'down with
the nigger view'." His severest stricture, however, was reserved for
Shepstone: "I cannot imagine any step better calculated to convince
the Zulus that we desire the ruin of Dinizulu. To them this official, as
his father's son, represents the destruction of all Zulu hopes of justice
to the persecuted house of Cetshwayo [Cetewayo]." In Natal, at the
other end of the line, Harriette Emily Colenso protested to Nathan,
noting that Shepstone had issued the warrant in 1888 for the arrest
of Dinizulu. Nathan replied that since Shepstone had retired, his
record did not suggest any continued animus toward Dinizulu. While
Lord Crewe asked Nathan for information on Shepstone, he took the
position that the composition of the court met the dictates of a fair
trial.[72]

The trial was held in Greytown and commenced on November 10,
1908. Proceedings were conducted in English and Zulu and ninety-
five witnesses were examined for the prosecution and sixty-eight for
the defense over the seventy days of sittings. Dinizulu's two *indunas*—
Mankulumana and Mgwaqo—were tried as accomplices to the facts.
Judgment was delivered on March 3, 1909. Dinizulu drew conviction
on three of the twenty-three counts with which he had been charged.
The verdict of high treason came on the grounds of 1) harboring and
concealing one of Bambata's wives and two children, 2) harboring

and assisting Bambata during the progress of the rebellion, and 3) harboring and concealing one hundred twenty-five other rebels at various times between May 1906 and December 1907. On the first count he was given the option of a fine of £100 or twelve months in prison. On the second and third counts he was sentenced to four years' imprisonment. His term of confinement would be cumulative from the time of his surrender into custody on December 9, 1907. His positions as government *induna* and a chieftain were forfeited. His two headmen were found guilty on the same three counts. Mgwaqo was given fifteen months' imprisonment plus the option of a £50 fine or eight more months in jail. Mankulumana was given nine months' imprisonment plus the same option. Both their prison terms were likewise to be computed from the time of surrender in December 1907 which meant practical fulfillment of confinement.[73]

Little comment is to be encountered in the papers and dispatches of the British Colonial Office as to the equity of the sentences. Lord Crewe accepted the judgment of the court and acceded to the termination of Dinizulu's official status under the agreement of 1898. But "I wish to place it on record that I take it for granted that when the time comes [and he has served his sentence] suitable provision will be made for his maintenance."[74]

Nor did Conservatives have much to say beyond expressing satisfaction with the judgment of the court. Dinizulu had committed perjury in keeping silent when he had actually harbored rebels. As Sir John David Rees, colonial administrator and, after 1912, Conservative M.P., put it: his conduct had jeopardized the lives and goods of "a handful of fellow countrymen . . . amongst a vast African population."[75]

Not so Liberals and Labourites. Their indignation knew no bounds at the verdict of the court. To be sure, Dinizulu did break the law in concealing one of Bambata's wives and several children. But she was pregnant and could not be moved and that should be an extenuating circumstance. True, too, Dinizulu had kept silent on the visits of disaffected chiefs, including Bambata, and had given shelter and food "to some miserable starving hunted men of his own race." However, there was never any proof of Dinizulu's participation in the rebellion. Nothing more abominable had ever been perpetrated than this vindictive prosecution of a harmless chieftain for exercising no more than the Christian spirit of brotherhood. To succor destitute fugitives of one's own race might be illegal but it was to err on virtue's side. Certainly, the punishment meted out seemed excessive considering the nature of the crimes. A lengthy prison term and dismissal as government *induna* and chieftain would simply add to the impression that Natal wanted to get rid of a powerful leader whose prestige it feared. What a harvest of trouble local statesmen were storing up for South African whites. The memory of an injustice was no less long and rankling among natives "than Englishmen or elephants." [76]

The British Colonial Office had to swallow a bitter pill in the summer of 1909 when it was revealed that Miss Colenso's charges of natives being flogged to extract evidence against Dinizulu had some substance. When Lord Crewe sanctioned an *Indemnity Act* in August 1908, he had been assured by Natal ministers, as on previous occasions, that no basis existed for the charges. However, once the Dinizulu trial came to an end, an inquiry by police officers was ordered. The report, in July 1909, admitted that in northern Zululand some cases of rough handling and perhaps injustice did occur but the times were abnormal and the atmosphere that of sedition. Robinson dealt severely with the report, noting that one of the police officers was himself involved in the affair, and therefore apt to soften the incrimination. The situation must have been pretty bad to read descriptions of troops flailing women as they emerged from the tents in order to hustle them away for interrogation. Lambert observed that if the report were published "it would give the press the right to say one more proof of the unfitness of Natal to govern natives." Lord Crewe agreed to the suggestion of Colonel Seely "to send a dispatch regretting the floggings and the failure to appoint some impartial person with legal training to investigate." [77]

Subsequent remission of the sentence was welcome news to friends of Dinizulu. After the trial he had been transferred to Newcastle in northwest Natal pending selection of a permanent site of confinement. The imminent inauguration of the Union of South Africa in 1910 induced Natal to leave the final disposition of Dinizulu to the incoming Union government. General Botha, the first Prime Minister, proposed that the remainder of his sentence be commuted and his salary be restored on condition that he accept domicile in the Transvaal. Dinizulu agreed to the offer and in 1911 he and his family were settled on a farm at Rectfontein, eight miles from Middleburg in the central regions of the Transvaal.* Mankulumana was permitted to join him. The other chieftains still being held for their part in the rebellion, including the score on the island of St. Helena, were released and allowed to return to their locations.[78]

If British commentators evinced relief at the generous list of pardons, they hoped that this initial noble gesture on the part of the Union of South Africa presaged better things to come. This act of clemency would be meaningful if it led to amends for the errors of the past and a brighter future for the Bantu race.[79] For the rest, an effort was made to ease the financial burden falling upon Harriette Emily Colenso and her sister Agnes who had used their own modest capital to collect testimony for Dinizulu. An appeal to the British public was launched for funds and, according to Mrs. Elizabeth D. Schwann, secretary of the project and wife of Sir Charles Ernest Schwann, Liberal M.P., the donations reached £3,500. Natal refused to allow any subscriptions in the colony, claiming that the money would be turned to political purposes by the natives. The generosity of Schreiner merits notice, passing on the fee of 2,000 guineas to cover the services of his colleagues, as well as putting himself 1,600 guineas out of pocket by his own reckoning.[80]

*In a previous work, *J. Ramsay MacDonald in Thought and Action* (1952), p. 377, I made the erroneous statement that Dinizulu was sentenced to St. Helena. My authority was the *Cambridge History of the British Empire, South Africa* (1936), p. 628. The error is continued in the 1963, 2nd ed., p. 648. Perhaps the confusion is due to the earlier exile of Dinizulu to St. Helena in 1890.

5

The Native and Integration
Colonial Period

AN INVENTORY

The post-Boer War years witnessed a quickened interest in the native problem, occasioned by the intrusion of the Imperial Factor once again in the two conquered Dutch Republics. It seemed the height of wisdom to anticipate pressure from a British nation whose interest in South Africa had been reawakened by the war episode. When the Bloemfontein Conference convened in March 1903 to consider railway and tariff matters, a resolution was carried dealing with the native:

> That in view of the coming federation of the South African Colonies, it is desirable that a South African Commission be constituted to gather accurate information on affairs relating to the natives and native administration and to offer recommendations to the several governments concerned with the object of arriving at a common understanding on the question of native policy.[1]

In addition, the Bloemfontein Conference passed several resolutions of a more specific nature to serve as guideposts for the proposed commission. The native question was described as embracing the present and future status and condition of all aboriginal natives of South Africa and the relation in which they stood toward the European population. Advancement of the native should proceed under the direction and control of the state with the objects aimed at to be industrial training and moral and intellectual improvement. Total prohibition of the sale of intoxicating liquor to natives should be an avowed commitment. Recognition of the need to reserve land for the sole use and benefit of natives was coupled with an emphasis upon their obligation to provide a labor supply for the economic pursuits of the white community. In this connection the statement was made that the Bloemfontein Conference

deplores the misconception existing in certain quarters in the Mother Country . . . in the matter of obtaining native labour required for private enterprise and affirms that forced labour is not countenanced by any South African Government and is repugnant to civilized opinion throughout the country.

Lord Milner lost no time in taking advantage of what seemed like a favorable climate for a sympathetic consideration of native problems.* In September 1903 he appointed a South African Native Affairs Commission consisting of two members each from Cape Colony, Natal, Orange River Colony, and the Transvaal and one member each from Rhodesia and Basutoland. Sir Godfrey Lagden, Chief Native Commissioner for the Transvaal, served as chairman. The itinerary took the members all over South Africa. Hundreds of witnesses were contacted from different walks of life—public officials, employers of native labor, missionaries, traders, professional men. A special effort was made to seek out native personages and get their point of view. Visits were scheduled to native educational institutions, municipal locations, outlying reservations, and hospitals. The findings were published in the spring of 1905 as a Blue Book of ninety-seven pages.[2]

What seems most striking in the *South African Native Affairs Commission Report of 1905* is its adherence to the nineteenth-century philosophy that primitive peoples required paternal guidance. A native was defined "as an aboriginal inhabitant of Africa south of the Equator including half-castes and their descendants by natives." However, there was no intention to proceed along lines of uniformity, for the diverse conditions under which natives lived and their varying cultural stages made flexibility highly desirable. No realization seems

---

*The Transvaal Labour Commission of 1903 which investigated the labor shortage on the Rand, contributed valuable sociological data on the native peoples. P.P., 1904, XXXIX, Cd. 1896.

present that the industrial upheaval then in progress would make any controlled experiment in social evolution difficult. That the concentration of large native numbers in urban centers would introduce complex social conditions challenging tribal life had no prophets. The commission, unperturbed by the dynamic developments on the Rand and elsewhere, charted a conventional blueprint of enlightenment.

Major attention was paid to the economic structure of native society. The time had come for finality in landholding predicated upon the principle of segregation. Scheduled areas should be set aside for natives, to be held communally or individually. Squatting on Crown lands or those of white farmers, a precarious and wasteful system of agriculture, ought to be forbidden. Stress should be placed upon proper methods of animal husbandry, intensive cultivation of the soil, and control of erosion. Any calculations must provide native labor for the white man's enterprises. Thus far the results had been disappointing and a serious labor shortage prevailed. The native would not work continuously and preferred the indolence of a pastoral life. Nor should the bad conditions of work, especially in the mines, be overlooked as a contributing factor. As for indirect compulsion through a labor tax, the possibility of abuses was strong, particularly among those unequal to exhausting physical tasks. The better levers were to be found in increasing the desire to work and in the struggle for existence as population numbers mounted.

Several facets of native life were singled out for reference. Personal habits of hygiene and sanitation should be encouraged. While it was good to see natives donning European garb for both health and moral reasons, the corollary that clothes should be changed frequently and washed regularly need to be stressed. Perhaps if women went into domestic service in white homes a model of cleanliness could be fostered. Only Kaffir beer with a spirit content less than four per cent ought to be permitted and strictly for home consumption. The evidence was all too strong that an intoxicated native turned into a reckless savage. Christianity could do much to combat lax moral standards through its rites of marriage, exalting the sacredness of the monogamous union. Compulsory education was not favored and the initiative for formal schooling should be left to the individual native. When provided, the curriculum should feature vocational training and systematic religious and moral instruction. Great doubts were held as to native participation in the political life of white communities. The Cape Colony approach of a common roll for all who could meet property and literacy qualifications carried the danger of an ultimate native majority. A separate voting register for a limited number of legislative seats answered better the need to air grievances.

The *Natal Native Affairs Commission Report* of 1907 contained illumination on the status of the Zulus. It will be recalled that this body had been appointed in September 1906, after the suppression of the Bambata uprising, to get at the basic causes of the discontent. It comprised seven men regarded as being well acquainted with native affairs. The chairman was Henry Cooke Campbell, Judge President of the Natal Native High Court, and the panel included Maurice Smethurst Evans, a past member of the Natal Legislature and a well-known student of tribal life. How thorough the investigation was may be adduced from the list of thirty-four localities visited, three hundred one Europeans and nine hundred six natives examined personally or by deposition, and the collection of testimony from chiefs, headmen, and Christian natives. The findings were published in July 1907 in a condensed Blue Book of forty-one pages.[3]

If the report held fast to a conventional approach, it did contain a self-confession of past failure. Apart from the negative aim of preserving peace, the leading features had been curtailment of the powers of chieftains, detribalization, and dependence upon missionary societies. Contact had become impersonal through a bureaucratic administration. Family life was disintegrating and young men were growing up to be selfish and less disposed toward tribal authority. Young girls appeared indifferent to filial and marital restraints. While native women were often debauched by whites and no punitive action was taken, severe penalties were now applied to native men guilty of physical relations with white women. Relatively little had been done for native education, comparing the sum of £6 8s. 7¾d. spent for a European child and 17s. 11d. for a native child. The chasm between white and black had widened and distrust marked the attitude of the latter for the former. After sixty years of social evolution, the native question continued in an acute stage. Certainly, native fecundity precluded any possibility of the Bantu stock dying out as a solution to the problem.

An overhauling of native administration constituted the core recommendation. It must be more fatherly than official and stress personal contact. The seat of authority should be visible, permanent, and accessible at all times. Fluctuations in party politics, with attendant changes in the Department of Native Affairs, had been a source of confusion to natives. The Natal government should delegate powers to a council for native affairs, perhaps a seven-member body selected from individuals well acquainted with the Zulus. It should possess an autonomous character much like an army or a corporate municipality. Its function would be to advise the legislature and the executive on all native matters and maintain close liaison with the civil service. Magistrates should be freed from clerical details and encouraged to make the rounds of their districts often. Periodic meetings with chieftains and headmen would keep responsible authorities abreast of shifting social problems.

Concrete thoughts were offered on the everyday pursuits of the natives. The backward aboriginal should be set up as an agricultural laborer or a tenant and taught proper ways of manuring, deep ploughing, and systematic planting. An award of prizes might stimulate interest in truck gardening. Industrial schools should be set up to teach the arts and crafts. An apprenticeship system, contracting boys to responsible European employers, was worth an experiment. The more advanced native, qualifying by some education and conformity to civilized customs, merited different treatment. He should be exempt from native laws and pass regulations and not subject to a sort of corvée on public projects or to pin-pricking humiliations such as subservient salutations to the police. He should have the privilege to buy land outside native reservations. His children should have access to white schools providing a classical type of education. In short, for the time being the tribal system was needed to stabilize an uprooted native culture, but some kind of integration should be permitted for those capable of adjustment to the mores of the white community.

The South African Native Races Committee, formed in 1899 by persons in Great Britain interested in native welfare, contributed to the fund of knowledge.* Its announced aim was to collect accurate information with regard to their social and economic condition. Sir John

---

*The Times ran a series of articles by Dudley Kidd, student of primitive culture, author of several books on the Bantu, and active in the South African General Mission administering to British troops locally garrisoned. The Times, Dec. 27, 30, 31, 1902, Jan. 6, 1903.

MacDonnell, barrister and writer on legal subjects, was chairman and the thirty members on the committee were drawn from religious and lay circles. Correspondents from abroad and experts at home submitted reports. A first volume was published in 1901 and contained a wealth of data on native races—population, laws, customs, land tenure, administration, labor supply, occupations and wages, compound system, liquor control, education, taxation. A second volume was published in 1908 and discussed the developments that had taken place since 1901. No attempt was made to go over the same ground; attention centered upon a few topics and emphasized a spirit of progress.[4]

A greater awareness was revealed of the new ferment among a younger generation engaged for periods of work in the white man's community. An acquired sense of independence brought a critical reaction toward their ancient tribal ways. If channeled properly, the broadening vista could act as a catalyst upon retrogressive features of primitive society. Such schooling as had been offered would appear to have been too bookish and not enough thought paid to character training, hygiene, and the crafts. Facilities for advanced education need not be ignored, especially the preparation of teachers. An intercolonial native college warranted serious consideration. The Ethiopian movement was given an appreciative interpretation. Unfortunately some secessionist groups had injected a sense of national life through spiritual unity. But the remedy for healthy progress lay in supervision of native Christian churches by white missionaries. It was the rejection of this guidance by unfit native clergymen that had opened the door to racism. The immediate challenge was to overcome the uneven pace of reform owing to the different policies pursued by the several colonies.

British colonial administrators accepted the responsibility of joining in the discussion of the native question. Lord Milner presented the gist of his views in an address at the opening of a municipal congress, which met in Johannesburg on May 18, 1903. It is known as the Watch Tower speech, from the allegory he drew of himself as the "man on the watch tower [who] sees further than those on the veldt because of the mere accident of his topographical position." It was no use shouting that this was a white man's country, because the blacks outnumbered whites five to one. The justification for saying that the white man should rule did not rest on the ground of his superior civilization but because only through his assistance could the black man be raised to a higher level. The ascent would take centuries and for many the climb might never be possible. However, for those who reached the plateau of the white man, there should be privileges— exemption from native laws, cancellation of disabilities, endowment of municipal rights.[5]

In his last speech before a South African audience, in Johannesburg on March 31, 1905, prior to his departure for England, Lord Milner renewed his appeal for a sane approach:

> I believe as strongly as ever that we got off the right lines when we threw over Mr. Rhodes' principle of 'equal rights for every civilised man.'* At the same time, I am prepared to rely, for a return to what I believe to be the true path, upon a gradual change in opinion in this country itself. It is a South African question and nothing could be worse . . . than to attempt to influence the solution of it, even in a right direction, by external pressure. . . . There are far too many people who think that they can dispose of the Native Question by a few slapdash phrases. . . . The essence of wisdom in dealing with it is discrimination—not to throw all coloured people, from the highest to the lowest, into one indiscriminate heap, but to study closely the differences of race, of circumstance, of degrees of civilisation, and to adapt your policy intelligently and sympathetically to the social requirements of each.[6]

Sir Matthew Nathan, Governor of Natal and a colonial administrator with extensive experience of backward races throughout the British Empire, took a personal interest in the subject. In the library at Rhodes House, Oxford University, the Nathan Papers are housed, containing a wealth of information on native matters. However, a succinct presentation of his views are to be had in a foreword he wrote for Maurice Smethurst Evans' book, *Black and White in South East Africa*. Nathan suggested the appointment of an international commission to investigate the relations of black and white wherever they came into contact. This body would collect data from all sources—

---

*The complete statement of Cecil Rhodes is as follows: "Equal rights for every civilised man south of the Zambesi. What is a civilised man? A man, whether white or black, who has sufficient education to write his name, has some property or works, in fact is not a loafer." Millin (1933), p. 221.

experiences under the Union Jack, the story of the Negro in America, colonial policies of Portugal, France, Holland, and Germany. Trained observers could be dispatched on the spot to check actual results of varying types of administration. While it can only be conjectured, if this anticipation of functions later bestowed upon both the League of Nations and the United Nations had been taken in hand at this earlier date, perhaps the world would have been spared the agony of present-day African history.[7]

Lord Selborne was especially persistent in pressing forward a blueprint of native policy. His views are contained in any number of dispatches but two are especially notable. The first is a memorandum, written in 1907 for the benefit of the several colonies, on the merits of federation. Basil Williams, late Professor of History at Edinburgh University, regarded it as a state document comparable in significance to the Durham Report of 1839 urging responsible government for Canada. This memorandum was published in leaflet form and distributed by the thousands. The second is a lengthy letter of twenty-five pages, also written in 1907, stating his views to General Botha, then Prime Minister of the Transvaal. A copy was forwarded in January 1908 to Lord Elgin for review by the British Colonial Office staff. Both memorandums would seem to have had a common parentage in original notes set down by Lord Selborne.[8]

Lord Selborne made clear that he wanted "to avoid being thought of as a Negrophilist for it would weaken his influence." He wanted to guide the thinking of people so that they would realize there was no alternative to "equal rights for all civilised men." The white man need have no worry about the blacks becoming a serious rival, for the latter were quite incapable of that achievement. The accomplishments of Negroes in the United States since the Civil War had been small indeed despite an end to legal impediments [!]. Booker T. Washington, eminent American Negro educator, was the occasional exception and the publicity given this example of individual accomplishment by a Negro only proved the rule. Still there should be no statutory bars to personal advancement for the gifted native; any other course harbored the taint of servitude. Even the white man would profit from the theory of equality, guarding him against the narcotic of being pampered in the struggle for survival. The task of South Africa was clearly marked "to lead upwards in Christian civilisation the natives . . . who are in many stages of development—from the educated native whose aspirations must be regarded with wise sympathy to tribes still in the stage of barbarism."

TEMPO OF INTEGRATION

Conservative circles followed closely the inventory being taken of the native problem in South Africa. Their analysis mirrored a conviction that integration in the foreseeable future was out of the question. The native remained persistently unteachable and sooner or later reverted to his primitive environment. When he returned to the kraal after several months on the Rand and heard the drums beat and sniffed the blood of a freshly killed sacrificial bullock, he threw aside his European garments and the trappings of civilized society. Yet a do-nothing policy would leave the native to drop below the level of his environment year by year. The Bantu could not be permitted simply to swarm and multiply, sinking in hopeless sloth and ignorance around the growing centers of material progress. A scheme employing forbearance and discipline was imperative in order to help the native grow up to man's estate.[9]

An enlightened policy envisaged a native population settled in reserves with the able-bodied males making sojourns into the white community for tours of work. The *Morning Post* recalled that basically such a scheme had ensured lasting peace in Western Canada between Indian tribes and white settlers. Even in 1885, the firebrand Louis Riel, leading the métis once again in rebellion after a previous fiasco in Manitoba (1870), could persuade but two petty chiefs to join the uprising in Saskatchewan.* The reserves, of course, would have to be carefully protected against encroachment; otherwise the story could take on the tragedy of the American West where trespass by the whites had provoked a long series of Indian wars.[10] Likewise the bad example of the American South should be kept in mind, where industrialization had shunted the Negro into slums. Neither European nor Bantu should be allowed to acquire land held by the other.[11]

I. Dobbie, writing in the *Empire Review*, referred to the *Glen Grey*

*Indian embroilment on the side of Riel would seem to have been more than a token effort. Sir George E. F. Stanley *The Birth of Western Canada: A History of the Riel Rebellions* (London: 1936), pp. 332-79.

Act of 1894 in Cape Colony as holding promise for the future. Districts in the reserve areas were authorized to experiment along Western lines. When properly constituted such districts were empowered to levy a rate of not more than two pence on the pound on fixed property for construction of roads, dams, and bridges, the eradication of noxious weeds, and the establishment of schools. The exercise of these powers was in the hands of a council elected by native voters and so offered training in the ways of democratic government. The cultivation of the soil was laid out on the basis of individual tenure in the hope that the profit motive would spur the initiative. If implemented effectively elsewhere, these innovations could go a long way toward laying the groundwork for a sense of responsibility among natives and toward combating the impulse of primitivism. Natives would gain the feeling of a direct stake in the country and a chance to achieve self-respect like whites.[12]

(Sir) Lionel Phillips cautioned the British nation to go slow in espousing any ambitious program for native advancement:

> The attitude of the English people towards the native arises from its most honourable crusade against slavery, which has left behind it a tender feeling for all people who suffer from persecution or oppression; but it is nevertheless worthy of note that very few, if any, Englishmen, in reply to the question as to whether they would like to see their sisters married to black men, would answer in the affirmative; and the equality, therefore, upon which they are ready to place him is founded rather upon sympathy than reason.
>
> According to the present standards of measurement, the natives are in all respects, in strength, in stamina, in capacity, and in requirements, inferior beings, and, if that be acknowledged, the mission and the right of the white man lies in governing them with justice and firmness, in giving them a well-defined legal status, in promoting their intellectual and industrial training, in stimulating their power of self-control, and in inculcating the principles of morality. For the present they are separated from white men, not by colour, not by wealth, not even fundamentally by education, but by a gulf of profound mental dissimilarity.
>
> The native question is essentially a problem for South African statesmen, and should never be permitted to enter the sphere of party politics in England.[13]

A necessary preliminary to the emergence of the native from his primitive environment called for good work habits. The inability of Natal sugar planters to depend upon the Zulus had a familiar ring. The sugar crop was one which could be ruined by neglect in a very few hours and that disaster had been all too frequent with the unpredictable Zulus. Their savage instincts prompted them to leave work without "rhyme or reason" and had resulted since the 1860's in the importation of Indian coolies to do the job. Some form of compulsion seemed inevitable until increased wants stirred the native to greater industriousness.* And after all, the native had received many blessings from the rule of the white man. He had been given security of person, security against tribal wars, and security from famine. The black man needed to be purged of his indolence and stimulated to possess more material things. Nor was such prodding harsh, for experience showed that a native thrived best on discipline and that liberty was a boon he only abused. So it had been in America where the abolition of slavery soon had to be tempered with the passage of vagrancy laws.[14]

Direct taxation was a favorite suggestion to promote the dignity of labor. The native would have to seek work in order to obtain a source of cash income for meeting state impositions. The action of the Transvaal (in 1903) in amending its native tax laws was hailed as a step in the right direction. An added tax of £2 per annum for each wife beyond the first should compel those with several wives to hire out for wages.** Those who would term this a form of slavery might remember that the traditional purpose of polygamy was to acquire wives as farm hands. The native male should do something for the comfortable life now within his reach—mealie pap, cuts of mutton and roast beef, Kaffir beer, blankets, tobacco. Alexander Davis, writer and world traveler, described to his countrymen the need for pressures:

---

*(Sir) Lionel Phillips did not think that the day of increased desires was far off: "Until my recent visit to South Africa I had never seen a native on a bicycle; today dozens are met with on every road near the larger towns, and in the mine compounds they ride them for amusement. Formerly they took home chiefly umbrellas, and small travelling trunks; now they are beginning to take back finery for wives and sweethearts, after the Kaffir conception of good taste." Phillips (1905), pp. 102-03.

**The Transvaal abolished the tax of £2 per annum on each additional wife in 1906, substituting a £2 per annum aggregate tax which covered all wives beyond the first one.

Real, inculcated, and, if necessary, coercionary measures to induce labour among the natives [is] the first and most essential step to their ethical and mental advancement. . . . The proper solution is by a judicious application of laws tending to lead the native into an industrious from an idle life. . . . In years of plenty he revels in inordinate feeding and drunkenness; in years of famine he either dies or receives Government assistance. In either event he idles half the year. . . . It tends to mischief, crime, immorality. . . . He has a racial abhorrence to all hard and sustained labour. . . . If left to their own devices they will develop into a social danger. They must be induced to work.[15]

The *Pall Mall Gazette* opened its columns to Michael James Farrelly, Cape Colony barrister and writer, in order that the British public be acquainted with the importance of social restraints upon natives. Freedom of movement had to be curtailed for reasons of local security. It was hard to distinguish one native from another for identity purposes, a prime factor in curbing crime. This should explain pass laws and curfew hours. The ban against walking along footpaths constituted a precautionary measure for averting surprise attacks (and to avoid offensive odors and contagious diseases). The way in which a drunken native changed into a murderous savage justified stricter control of his liquor consumption. The death penalty for assaults upon white women was defended as the only deterrent to the unbridled sex passion of aboriginals. For the time being the sober mission of civilization had to be accompanied by a stern trusteeship.[16]

(Sir) Roderick Jones, news correspondent for Reuter's and later its owner, noted the anxiety manifested in the *South African Native Affairs Commission Report of 1905* over the threat which Ethiopianism posed to peace between whites and blacks.[17] He agreed with the appraisal in the colonies that this Christian-secessionist native church movement nurtured the political aim of "Africa for the Africans." The sad part was that it could so unsettle the mind of the native as to render useless all efforts at enlightenment in the coming period of organized tutelage. After the gullible native had dinned into him the grandiose idea of man's equality, he would be less willing to abide by the slower processes of evolution. *The Times* lamented any proposed unity of tribal peoples against the whites on the basis of a religio-political crusade.* It was a mischievous perversion of Christianity and courted disaster for all.[18]

Political enfranchisement of the native was discountenanced. His recognition as a voter should be proceeded with very cautiously, considering comparative statistics of population. Otherwise the white man would soon be overwhelmed at the polls and both the fruits of his own labor and his vital role in uplifting the native would be lost. One could scarcely say that the experience of America had been salutary. The sudden flood of Negro voters in the South after the Civil War had played havoc with security of person and property. Desperate and distraught whites were goaded to flout openly the law of the land and by fraud and force to disfranchise the blacks. The result was that forty years after his emancipation the Negro's civil rights were being steadily restricted.[19] Thus the application of the theory of human equality to the newly emancipated slave had been a blunder setting his advance back many decades. Dobbie quoted Booker T. Washington as affirming that he would prefer to guide his brethren along the paths of learning and industrial excellence.[20] This counsel to eschew superficial citizenship at the polls would appear to hold true even more for the aboriginals of South Africa.[21]

The right of qualified natives to vote in Cape Colony was termed a weak link in the progress of South Africa. If the mischief had not yet become unmanageable, the answer rested in the relative numbers on the register. For 1903 there were on the voting register 9,543 natives, 10,162 Cape Coloured, and 115,463 whites. But the figures of 250,000 adult native males compared to 200,000 adult white males in Cape Colony offered no comfort for the years ahead. The *Morning Post* gathered that in several precincts where Bond and Progressives were evenly matched it was humiliating to observe the sham Negrophilism of candidates on both sides anxious to command the "blanket vote."

*How far off the mark this analysis of Ethiopianism was may be seen in Dr. Sundkler's figures that, where in 1913 there were 30 native Christian churches, in 1948 the number rose to 800, and in 1960 to 2,200. What the Bantu sought was a sense of belonging which white Christian congregations denied them. Indeed, one might well draw the conclusion that the colonial whites did a disservice to Christianity by insisting upon separate churches for the two races. As practiced by the so-called Bantu prophets today, incorporating a blend of ancestor-worship, dreams, magic, and a modernized cult of "luck," Christianity often comes perilously close to the corruption of a higher form of spirituality. Sundkler (1961, 2nd ed.), pp. 302-03.

Apart from a day of reckoning for whites in Cape Colony, the example increased the difficulties of the other colonies to hold the line.[22] In Natal, where a non-European could have the vote on a property and educational basis, the administration of the law had been such as to allow only two natives and one hundred three Cape Coloured on the register.* In Orange Free State and the Transvaal prior to the Boer War public opinion would not have any kind of native franchise. As a compromise against the time when the franchise would be an issue at a convention for federation, the New Zealand model of special representation for the Maoris was favored.** Natives could be grouped as an electoral constituency and allowed a sufficient number of delegates to make known their needs but not enough to challenge white primacy.[23]

Liberal and Labour circles held a more abiding faith in the ability of natives to assimilate the culture of the white man. Dr. Guest pointed to the presence of physicians, lawyers, merchants, and skilled artisans among the colored population in Cape Colony as proof of their potentiality. Admittedly, many natives were still aboriginals but the rough edges could be smoothed out given the right kind of contacts with the whites. The native in his natural state was not the sanguinary brute so often depicted. Any excrescences of belligerency came from encroachments upon his person and dignity by predatory imperialism. What was fundamental and good in him the ages had wrought. What was aberrant and violent in him had been provoked by arrogant whites. Ethnology had advanced far enough to demolish the rationalization that inferior peoples could be left out of account and were fair game for extermination. All human beings must be embraced within the brotherhood of man. The responsibility of Great Britain was to inspire a new idealism for relations between white and black in South Africa.[24]

The native policy in vogue could not be described as progressive. The scene was that of a semiservile compound subject to onerous taxes, indignities, and disabilities. The Transvaal collected £650,000

---

*Official voting statistics for Natal in 1903 are as follows: 18,680 whites, 103 Cape Coloured, 7 Griquas, 2 natives, 154 Indians. P.P., 1905, LV, Cd. 2399, p. 67.

**An act in 1876 gave the Maoris the right to elect four representatives to the New Zealand Legislature. Horace Belshaw, ed., *New Zealand* (Berkeley: 1947), pp. 48-72 (I. L. G. Sutherland).

in revenue from natives whereas the whole cost of native administration did not exceed £200,000.[25] Natal collected £300,000 in revenue from natives and spent a meager £7,500 upon their education.[26] Sir Alfred Edward Pease, a resident magistrate in the Transvaal, onetime Liberal M.P., and active in the Aborigines Protection Society,* presented a distressing picture of the native's plight. When the native discarded his own garb for European raiment, he was sold the worse type of clothes—old bowlers, felt hats, filthy shirts, ill-fitting trousers. He had no conveniences for washing and bathing in the towns and his personal habits of cleanliness naturally deteriorated. No end seemed in sight for the accumulating "Jim Crow" regulations. He was forbidden the sidewalk, footpath, and public park. He traveled in railway boxcars used for cattle and was relegated on tramcars to the open backboard. If he got to associate with Europeans at all, it was with the least desirable class, those versed in evil and degenerate practices. As a descendant of Ham whose progeny propagated Africa, the native carried the curse of Noah on his son: "of a slave of slaves shall be his."[27]

A dignified future for the native should be charted, emphasizing integration but offering the option of a segregated life for those who preferred it temporarily or even permanently. Preliminary to any undertaking should be a real knowledge of what was valuable in native customs and worth preservation or adaptation in more modern form. In the interim MacDonald urged a sheltered environment of the Glen Grey type to introduce natives to the rudimentary elements of self-government, proper technique in soil cultivation, and the civic obligations attendant upon public services. The best catalyst for accelerating the tempo of acculturation was held to be vocational education, dispensing instruction in husbandry and the trades. Henry Richard Fox Bourne, secretary of the Aborigines Protection Society, stressed leaving the choice of worlds to the individual native. He could adapt himself to the standards of the white and ask for an equal share in the political, economic, and social life of an integrated society. Or he could retain his traditional mores in a territorial setting suffici-

---

*The Aborigines Protection Society was founded in 1836 to protect and promote the welfare of uncivilized tribes in the British Empire. This body is not to be confused with the British and Foreign Anti-Slavery Society which was founded in 1839 to combat the slave system wherever it appeared.

ent for his material needs and where he could identify himself with his ancestral heritage. In short, the ladder of human dignity could be erected to work both ways, horizontal as well as vertical.[28]

Compulsion in any form to make the native work for the white man was discountenanced. Granted that the native ought to do his part to develop the natural resources of South Africa, but as a British subject he should be free to choose the employer to whom he would sell his labor. Sir Sydney Olivier, socialist and veteran colonial administrator, defended the native against the charge that abundance of food in his natural habitat robbed him of all desire to labor. It was revealing to read in the *South African Native Affairs Commission Report of 1905* that of the estimated 900,000 able-bodied native males south of the Zambesi River over 450,000 were always at work.[29] Sir William Venables Harcourt found similar evidence of industriousness in the first volume published by the South African Native Races Committee. A statement favored leaving the matter of indolence to the laws of evolution in the confidence "that good wages, the growth of new wants, improved education, just treatment, and increased facilities for the movement of labour will . . . remove the chief difficulties experienced in the past."[30] Miss Violet Rosa Markham, sister of (Sir) Arthur Basil Markham, Liberal M.P., and an author and feminist leader in her own right, believed that forces were already operating to produce such a ferment, citing as a valuable ally of the white employer "the Kaffir bride arrayed in white satin and orange blossoms and attended by pages and bridesmaids."* Luxury tastes of this sort on the part of masculine admirers of feminity should mean sustained working engagements.[31]

Alterations in the fiscal laws of the Transvaal during 1903 were regarded suspiciously as an opening wedge for compulsory labor. True, the consolidated tax of £2 per annum for the adult native male did amount to a reduction for those with one wife (compared to a 10s. hut tax, a 2s. 6d. road tax, and a £2 poll tax). But the charge of £2 for each additional wife entailed an increase for practitioners of polygamy (subsequently reduced to an extra £2 whether one more or several wives). If the story were correct that a native aspired to possess several

---

*Miss Markham quoted from an observation made by Birchenough of what he saw at a local railway station while traveling through South Africa. *P.P.*, 1904, LXI, Cd. 1844, p. 13.

wives, this could mean working the year round and then some. Bourne answered those who parried his description of direct taxation as a form of slavery with aspersions upon the custom of wife purchase (*lobola*) as a sort of informal servitude indulged in by the native himself. The cattle paid over by the bridegroom to the bride's father did not imply that he could hold his wife as a slave. The cattle guaranteed good treatment, for if the wife were misused she could go back to her father and the cattle reverted to her possession.[32]

The *Tribune* warned that a fixed allocation of reserves could lend itself to compulsory labor. The recommendation in the *South African Native Affairs Commission Report of 1905* that the reserves be defined once and for all was disturbing to read.[33] Such an absolute delimitation struck at the very economic liberty of the native in view of his increasing numbers. Those unable to find roots in the soil would be forced to hire themselves out to the white farmer or to seek work in the mines. And if past performances were any criteria, the conditions imposed upon a native proletariat would approximate serfdom. That had been the history of landless unskilled laborers in England during the upheavals of the eighteenth century. The tragedy could come quicker and be even worse if the land settlement should further reduce native holdings. Percy Alport Molteno, Liberal M.P. and a son of Cape Colony's first Prime Minister, noted the legislative action of the Transvaal in 1907 which made legal the eviction of natives on Crown land without compensation.* The number could reach 180,000 and the uprooted natives would have no alternative but to make terms with the whites and pay extortionate rents instead of the token charges now levied by the Crown.[34]

Poor working conditions were singled out as a major factor in the reluctance of the native to staff the white man's enterprises. In Orange Free State the usual wage was 10s. per month and in terms of food it meant a diet of bread and coffee thrice daily. To make matters worse, his tax burden increased in 1904 from 10s. to 20s. per annum and if he lived in a village an extra 1s. per month for a domiciliary pass.[35] The

*The action of the Transvaal was based upon the *Squatters Law No. 21 of 1895* which forbade indiscriminate settlement on Crown land (more than five families per unit). The Transvaal gave three months' notice for removal of belongings but did grant the right to harvest growing crops. *Transvaal Native Affairs Department*, Annual Report, 1908-09, pp. 8-9.

low rate of wages in Natal and the Transvaal, compared to the cost of living, translated itself in visible poverty. The residence of the native was a miserable one-room hut, patched up with tin, straw grasses, and rubble. His leisure hours were spent amidst the pleasures of the *shebeen* (speakeasy) and the iniquitous dens of prostitution. A better response could be won from the native as a worker if his lot were improved. He should be allowed to live with his wife and children on the premises wherever possible. The Newcastle Colliery Company, operating coal mines in Natal, had erected cottages for miners and their families and given them good wages and these benefits had paid off in increased productivity. Sir William Butler scored the sharp practices in Natal where white owners of vast land aggregations induced Zulus to build kraals and to become tenants at nominal rents. Then, when the natives had improved the land, rents were raised and the fruits of toil siphoned off into the pockets of white landlords. Little wonder that natives shied away from European entrepreneurs and their shady business ethics.[36]

Dr. Guest submitted a socialist view of colored labor. The working class should recognize only grades of skill. The essence of competition should be between men with a relatively high calibre of competence. Natives who accepted low wages were as detrimental to the dignity of labor as cheaply bought Italians. If the colored man's work was as good as the white man's, he was entitled to the same wage. There should be a minimum capacity as well as a minimum standard of living and men who fell below this level ought to be separately handled as a backward class. Organized labor should insist on a serious "testing of the coloured peoples before the gates of their isolation were unbarred on the labour market." Pending, therefore, an evaluation of the Bantu, their recruitment should be strictly controlled. At the moment the colored man represented a blackleg, underselling and underbidding the white man. This situation, of course, was not of his own doing but that of international capitalism concerned with assembling a cheap robot supply by whatever methods possible. In contrast, organized labor was largely confined to individual state boundaries. However, the day would come when labor assumed an international identity and an emancipated colored race could take its place as a respectable member of the toiling legions.[37]

MacDonald stressed enfranchisement of the native as the keystone in any scheme of integration. Citizenship should be based not on race or caste but on the acknowledgement of the equality of men themselves. The black man should have before him only the admonition that he prove a worthy and industrious individual. To slam the door in his face was to introduce into the social fabric impulses that would only create turbulence and anarchy. Cape Colony deserved commendation for its generous policy in allowing the more progressive natives to share in the political life of the community. It was to be hoped that when federation came the Cape Colony example would lead the way to an enhanced status for natives throughout South Africa. As for the New Zealand plan, which grouped the Maoris into separate constituencies, Bourne could see merit only for the less civilized natives. However, from what he read, the result would appear to have made the Maoris more readily amenable to any laws imposed upon them. The Cape Colony franchise, open to all meeting the qualifications, offered the most in the long run for the advanced native.[38]

COLONIAL CONSTITUTIONS

A major moment in the destiny of the South African natives came with the proposal to grant constitutions to the Transvaal and Orange River Colony. Not that the home government had the welfare of the Bantu uppermost in its mind. What Great Britain aimed at was the treasured goal of federation with its military and economic potential for the British Empire. The fulfillment of self-government, pledged in the *Treaty of Vereeniging* as soon as circumstances permitted, could bring that event closer. Such a noble gesture should win gratitude from colonial Briton and Boer alike and go a long way toward their reconciliation under the Union Jack.

Lyttelton drafted a plan in 1905 for the Transvaal, delaying action on one for Orange River Colony until extremist views among Boers there subsided. What he had in mind was representative and not responsible government, explaining the partial instalment of democracy to await further signs of Boer loyalty. His constitution called for a unicameral legislature subject to the veto power of a Crown-appointed governor and a ministry answerable to him alone. The vote would be limited to adult white males based on wages and property qualifications. If a native franchise had to be bound over until after the grant

of responsible government, in accordance with the terms at Vereeniging, Lyttelton asserted that their interests were not forgotten. The
governor would be required by his instructions "to reserve any Bill
whereby persons not of European birth or descent may be subjected
to any disability or restriction to which persons of European birth are
not also subjected."[39]

Before the Lyttelton constitution could be promulgated, however,
a Liberal government took office and action was suspended. Not that
Campbell-Bannerman opposed the aim of reconciliation. What he
feared was that half a cup might invite colonial resentment and turn
Boer against Briton. His decision to press for responsible government
apparently stemmed from an interview on February 7, 1906, with
General Smuts. The latter had hurried to London when it was learned
that the pro-Boer Scotsman had become Prime Minister. The memorandum containing the arguments used by General Smuts may be
found both in the *Asquith Papers* at the Bodleian Library and in the
African (South) Confidential Prints at the Public Record Office. He
emphasized that the Boers had no wish to raise the question of the
recent annexations or the supremacy of the Union Jack. But the only
lasting security for the imperial connection was in the bond of affection forged out of trusting the people in South Africa. The grant of
responsible government would seal the partnership, particularly if the
electoral constituencies were based on population instead of registered
voters as proposed by Lyttelton and favoring the Rand plutocracy.
General Smuts expressed confidence that federation would come within five years after colonial self-government. As he recalled the talk,
Campbell-Bannerman said at its close: "Smuts, you have convinced
me."[40]

Campbell-Bannerman did not appear to have had an easy time con-
verting his cabinet. General Smuts reports that Churchill felt it was
asking too much to allow a conquered people so soon to govern themselves.* Morley told him that he would do what he could to help but

*An insight into the thinking of Churchill is contained in a minute addressed to Lord
Elgin on March 15, 1906. He regarded "the colonial British as our friends in the Transvaal and not the Boers." To delay a constitution "will alienate them and they took our
side in the struggle and ran great risks of life and property. . . . They only hear the
worst of us. . . . We are in danger of frittering the country away piecemeal. . . ." An
electoral constituency based on one vote one value and manhood suffrage for the whites
would assure the primacy of kinfolk in South Africa. P.R.O., co.o 879/106, No. 834.

both public opinion and the views of colleagues had to be considered. Lord Elgin remained noncommittal. Only Lloyd George gave any definite promise of assistance. Baron Riddle, newspaper proprietor, summarizes in his diary a chat he had with Lloyd George on April 27, 1913, as to what happened at the cabinet meeting on February 8, 1906. Lloyd George recalled that at the outset only John Burns and himself agreed with the Prime Minister's advocacy of responsible government. Then, in a dramatic ten-minute appeal, Campbell-Bannerman carried the cabinet with him in eliminating proposed safeguards. Lloyd George added that "it was the most impressive thing I ever saw" and "the speech moved one at least of the Cabinet to tears." Spender, in his biography of Campbell-Bannerman, includes two testimonial letters supporting Lloyd George's account. The first is from Lord Carrington, dated February 8, 1906, stating that "you must allow me to congratulate you on having so magnificently saved the South African situation today. . . . You pulled us through entirely and alone." The second is from Lloyd George, dated February 9, 1906, stating that "I hope you will not regard it as presumptuous of me if I congratulate you on the way you saved the Government from inevitable disaster."[41]

Accordingly, the Liberal government drafted its own constitution for the Transvaal, delaying action on one for Orange River Colony until a voters' list and electoral constituencies had been prepared. The traditional Anglo-Saxon machinery of government was prescribed, embracing a bicameral legislature, a prime minister and cabinet dependent upon a majority in the popular chamber, and a governor representing the Crown. A maximum grant of democracy was reflected in manhood suffrage for all whites, albeit the Boer population received a slight electoral advantage through an arbitrary allocation of seats. Where British influence prevailed in the thirty-four constituencies on the Rand, Boer influence dominated the nine constituencies in Pretoria and the twenty-nine constituencies in the rest of the Transvaal.* The hostility of the House of Lords, overwhelmingly Conservative in composition, to the probable restoration of Boer political control made

---

*A committee was dispatched under the chairmanship of Sir Joseph West Ridgeway to draw the boundaries of electoral constituencies. P.R.O., c.o 879/106, No. 853 (Transvaal), No. 854 (Orange Free State). Cf. Long (1941), pp. 75-80; Thompson (1960), pp. 25-26.

the parliamentary process inadvisable. Hence the necessity to circumvent a vote of rejection in the upper chamber by resort to an order-in-council. So, the constitution for the Transvaal was promulgated by executive decree on December 6, 1906 (and for Orange Free State on June 5, 1907).[42]

Campbell-Bannerman was confident that native interests were secured. Article 39(a) required the governor to reserve any bill subjecting non-Eupropeans to any disability or restriction to which Europeans were not subjected. Article 51 listed a number of safeguards. No assent would be given any law sanctioning conditions of a servile character, at the moment primarily directed against indentured Chinese coolies. The Crown would have two years of grace to assent to any bill which came under the reserved power, thus gaining the advantages of delay and time for the review of doubtful measures. No lands which had been or might hereafter be set aside for natives could be alienated or diverted from the purposes for which they were set apart save in accordance with legislative enactments. The governor was to hold the title of paramount chief with the power to summon an assembly of tribal chieftains and others to advise him on native matters. Swaziland would temporarily become a British protectorate, pending proof of good will by the Transvaal toward its own native population.[43]

It is illuminating to read British Colonial Office minutes recording staff comments on the native provisions. Graham observed that the number of Cape Coloured may be small indeed

> but the very white blood in their veins must incline their sympathies towards the black people of their national ancestry than towards their white paternal relations who are now so bitter against them, and our treatment of them may have great influence on the pure natives' view of the white man's administration.

Keith would draw a line between the Cape Coloured (and the civilized native) and the "blanket Kaffir" and allow for a generous policy of letters of exemption by the governor-in-council. He warned against the danger of doing nothing for those deserving cases who could become a rallying point for the malcontents. Lord Selborne put in a special plea for the Cape Coloured. Save for a recent arrangement to permit them to travel in first- and second-class carriages, albeit in separate compartments, their status remained much the same as that which had brought protests against the Kruger regime.[44]

Lord Selborne favored a nominated upper house with special jurisdiction in the field of native legislation. If the personnel were carefully selected by the governor (and not the governor-in-council), such a body could bring better minds and broader vistas to bear on the problem. No "Negrophilist" should be a member however much one might admire his moral courage, for his influence was apt to be discounted in advance. He credited the second chamber in Natal for getting the poll tax applied to whites as well as to natives and so preventing all the Zulus from joining in the recent disturbances. Keith argued against the proposal, feeling that the difference between two houses was a matter of degree rather than of principle. His preference would be for a reservation in the constitution of any measures discriminating against non-Europeans. As envisaged in the Lyttelton constitution, it would be referred to only in the instructions to the governor and thus likely to be overlooked. But if the reservation were inserted as a clause in the constitution (as Campbell-Bannerman did decree), then it became officially law and a valuable proof to natives of imperial concern for their welfare.[45]

Keith liked the idea of reserving a sum of money for native services. When Western Australia received responsible government in 1890, it was required to budget £5,000 annually for the education and relief of the aborigines. When Natal received responsible government in 1893, it was required to budget £10,000 annually for the improvement of the native population. Lambert doubted the efficacy of any stipulations affording the right of the Imperial State to intervene. Their mere existence had been obnoxious to colonies and a continual object of attack. Their enforcement was difficult when executive authority rested in colonial hands. Even the designation of the governor as paramount chief had its limitations, provoking endless friction.* The

---

*Subsequent upon the grant of responsible government to the Transvaal, an exchange of views took place on the role of the governor as paramount chief. The British Colonial Office held to the position that the everyday administration of native affairs should be in the hands of responsible ministers but that the governor must have final jurisdiction. The locus given the governor was intended to let natives know of his accessibility and

power must either be dormant as in Natal or when exercised excite the most violent opposition.[46]

Lord Selborne would seem to have arrived at a point of frustration after failing to get his ideas across. In reply to an eleventh-hour request of Lord Elgin for comments on the draft of the Letters Patent, Lord Selborne penned a rather dispirited answer:

[I favor] a clause prohibiting alienation of all locations in Crown lands which has been set aside for the occupation of aboriginal natives except by an Act of the Transvaal Parliament and providing for their being vested in an officer of the Government or in a Board. Beyond this I have nothing to recommend except that the Royal Instructions dealing with the reservation of legislation affecting native races should be embodied . . . as they were in those of March 31, 1905 [Lyttelton]. I am against reserving any other land for natives since local people have had no voice [in drawing up the constitution] and it would be resented by whites to the ultimate detriment of the natives. With regard to reserving sums for the benefit of aboriginals as in Natal and Western Australia, I would prefer it be voluntarily and would hope that a Transvaal Responsible Government [be left to meet the obligation].[47]

That the Liberal government had made up its mind to seek an alliance with the colonial whites is evident from the reception given the African Political (People's) Organization, founded in 1902 at Capetown to champion the rights of Cape Coloured in South Africa. A deputation headed by Dr. Abdullah Abdurahman, a medical practitioner of Malay descent, arrived in July 1906 to present their case. The discussion centered about the correct translation of the words used in the Dutch text of the *Treaty of Vereeniging.* According to the authorities consulted, the word "naturellen" employed in the official document was commonly applied to African aboriginals. On the other hand, colored persons neither white nor pure black but of mixed blood went by the terminology of "kleuringen." Lord Elgin answered that he must be guided by the view of the local white population lumping

friendly concern for them. In any case, in the final analysis, the smooth management of native matters depended upon the tact and diplomacy practiced by both sides. P.R.O., c.o. 291/119, 126, 128-29.

together both colored elements as natives. Nor was there any more heart-warming answer to a petition in October 1906 for a guarantee that a franchise would be granted to the Cape Coloured (and the more advanced natives) within a year after the issuance of the Letters Patent. The formal reply sent back by Lord Elgin stated that "having regard to the interpretation generally placed upon the Vereeniging terms, His Majesty's Government are precluded from prejudging the views of the future Government of the Transvaal by any reservation in the constitution such as is proposed in the resolution." [48]

Liberals and Labourites were prepared grudgingly to abide by the *Treaty of Vereeniging.* But they gave both the Conservative and Liberal governments in turn to understand that the status quo could not be maintained indefinitely. Dilke sounded the tocsin of alarm, proclaiming that an imperial moral standard was at stake. A small congeries of whites, motivated by greed for riches, must not be left to hold in their hands the destiny of several million blacks. The Imperial State might win over the colonial whites in the Transvaal and Orange Free State by assuring their political supremacy but the movement for federation might well receive a deathblow in the detachment of Cape Colony. The latter would probably not enter any union which compelled a surrender of its non-European voters. More importantly, the mother country should weigh the serious consequences of formally condoning a color bar. This ill-considered action could encompass the collapse of the British Empire, alienating native peoples everywhere under the Union Jack. [49]

Sir Charles Bruce, a retired colonial administrator, lamented the interpretation by British statesmen of Article 8 in the *Treaty of Vereeniging* to mean a sweeping disfranchisement of all save whites. Admittedly, there would be some awkwardness to establish a distinction between native and Cape Coloured at the present time. Nor would amendments to the constitution along this line be easier to effect since Lyttelton incorporated (and Campbell-Bannerman followed suit) a further limitation upon the Crown by reserving bills which discriminated against natives. By sharply emphasizing the mutually exclusive worlds of black and white, no margin had been left for exceptions. It was not wise to lump all colored people, from the highest cultural level to the lowest, into one indiscriminate heap. Rather the approach should be "to study closely the differences of race, of circumstances, of degrees of civilisation, and to adapt the policy of the State intelligently and sympathetically to the several requirements of each." Bruce warned that the dignity of colored races was of supreme importance to the Empire. The sentiment of loyalty so zealously and successfully cultivated among them represented an imperial asset and should be preserved at full value.[50]

Universal native suffrage had few adherents, to be ruled out by the many gradations of culture among the Bantu. Even Cape Colony excluded semiwild aborigines by a substantial property qualification. Liberals and Labourites agreed with Conservatives that the sad experience in the American South during the reconstruction period was proof enough against a wholesale enfranchisement. White ingenuity had been quickened to devise means of nullifying political equality and the onslaught of an unchecked Negro electorate. The *Friend* would be satisfied with the doctrine of Cecil Rhodes: "of equal rights for all civilised men south of the Zambesi." If the opportunity were present for a few to get the franchise, it would act as a stimulant for others to improve themselves. MacDonald disliked the grant of the franchise to all adult white males regardless of property or educational qualifications. His dissent was directed not so much toward the democratic nature of the suffrage clause as toward the difficulty it would pose for even a limited native franchise in the future. The colored people would sense the indignity of having to meet higher requirements than white voters and it could stir a hornet's nest, possibly discouraging any concessions.[51]

Lacking a right to vote, safeguards for the native population were sought in the constitution. Dilke placed little trust in the bare designation of the governor as paramount chief. Clarification was needed on whether the native could freely approach this symbol of the Crown or only with the consent of his ministers. If it were the latter and more likely proposition, then it was no approach at all. Bruce hoped that no loopholes would be permitted in the right to reserve discriminatory legislation; if not, the whites would be certain to use them. In particular, all matters relating to native reserves should be unequivocally marked out as within the province of the Imperial State. Byles would go even further and formally proclaim the prerogative of the Crown as supreme guardian of native interests. If the mother country could not intervene on the franchise issue because of the *Treaty of*

Vereeniging, there was nothing to prevent primacy in other areas. Otherwise, weighing the unhappy record (compiled by Orange Free State and the Transvaal) of heavy taxation, alienation of lands, harsh pass laws, and no social services, the future of the South African black would be very bleak indeed.[52]

Academic as the point might be, Bruce wondered if the Lyttelton constitution did not contain the better guarantee of protection for the natives. The proposal had been to grant the Transvaal only representative government, thereby leaving administrative control over enforcement of the reserved power in the hands of the British Colonial Office. Under responsible government as granted by Campbell-Bannerman, however, the transfer of the executive to the control of the colonial legislature weakened the significance of the reserved power. Measures insisted upon by the Imperial State for the welfare of natives could not possibly be administered fairly by officials equally hostile to the letter and the spirit of such laws. One of the main causes of the Boer War was the difference between the English principle of equal civil rights for white and black and the fundamental conception of white supremacy in the South African Republic. A Boer cabinet in the Transvaal would pose a definite threat to the exercise of the reserved power. To pretend not to see this fact was "to play the ostrich."[53]

Conservatives accepted as necessary the exclusion of the native from the suffrage. The consequences would be dire if the home government insisted upon absolute equality between white and black. The application of finely spun theories to hard facts would bring a "reign of terror" worse than that perpetrated by the architects of the French Revolution. Considering how the doctrine of liberty had run amok in the more sophisticated society of France, it must have little chance when applied to the aborigines of South Africa. As it was, the security of the few whites remained perilous amidst a swarming mass of blacks. The methods of the Boer were commended as the best example to handle the natives effectively. The Boer displayed admirable ability in the management of natives, blending severity with kindness. Natives were made to feel almost as members of the family and responded with respect and obedience.[54] The Briton might express more beautifully exalted ideals of justice but accompanied them with social aloofness.[55]

Lord Milner registered a strong plea for the Cape Coloured. As he had seen them during his stay in South Africa, a number resembled whites in physiognomy more than they did natives. In personal habits of hygiene and social finesse they were the equal of whites. It had not been in his mind at Vereeniging to include the Cape Coloured along with the native in the provision deferring native suffrage until after the grant of responsible government. Like Dr. Abdurahman, he noted that the word "naturellen" had been used in the Dutch text of the treaty whereas the accepted word in the Dutch language for the Cape Coloured was "kleuringen." In his opinion, therefore, the British government need not feel itself precluded from incorporating in the constitution the right of the Cape Coloured to qualify for the vote.[56]

The *Spectator* agreed that physically the Cape Coloured were more than half white. It warned that to bar them would eventually require a complicated definition of blood admixture. Many Boers who were offspring of marriages between Dutch and half-castes might lose the franchise. Revision courts could well be choked with pedigree cases. Was it not preferable to adopt the definition in the *South African Native Affairs Commission Report of 1905* and confine the term native to mean an aboriginal inhabitant of Africa south of the Equator? If the yardstick were education, character, and property, many Cape Coloured were fit candidates for full citizenship. And the fact should be weighed soberly that unless given a partnership in the life of South Africa, the Cape Coloured might be driven into the native camp, there to become the vengeful leaders of vast numbers of disaffected natives.[57]

A few more words would seem in order regarding the position of Lord Milner. Already in 1905, when the Conservative government was drafting its constitution for the Transvaal, he had second thoughts over the wisdom in yielding to the Boer entreaty at Vereeniging on the native franchise. Writing to Lyttelton, dated March 18, 1905, he regretted his failure to be more explicit about the Cape Coloured whom he regarded as "the class of all British subjects which is most hardly dealt with and yet are more deserving in every way." Again, writing to Lord Selborne, dated May 10, 1905, in an even more bitter vein, he declared that

if I had known . . . the extravagance of the prejudice on the part of al- most all the whites—not the Boers alone—against any concession to any coloured man, however civilised, I should never have agreed to so absolute an exclusion, not only of the raw native but of the whole coloured population from any rights of citizenship, even in municipal affairs.

Lord Milner confessed frankly that his optimistic belief in the good will of the colonial white to do right by the native was the greatest mistake he had ever made.[58]

Liberal government spokesmen refused to budge from the letter of the Treaty of Vereeniging. Any exceptions would reflect upon the honor of the Imperial State. To demand alterations now would be taken as a sign of distrust toward the colonial whites. The better thought was to hope that the Transvaal would take its cue from Cape Colony and develop a progressive native policy. Lord Elgin sympathized with the special plea by Lord Milner in behalf of the Cape Coloured. To be sure, he himself had seen such persons possessing a noticeable complement of the white man's physical features. Many were men of intelligence and education whose case for the vote had validity. But he could only say that in this instance he saw no evidence in official correspondence to warrant any claim that the peace terms opened the door to citizenship for the Cape Coloured. Public opinion in the two colonies was definitely against the vote for non-Europeans and that fact could not be ignored.[59]

More positively, Lord Ripon, Lord Privy Seal, insisted that the constitution took every precaution for the protection of the native consistent with the dignity of self-governing colonies. Swaziland had been reserved for direct administration under the High Commissioner and thus secured from the unhappy plight of Zululand. Designation of the governor as paramount chief should provide ample opportunity to exert influence on behalf of the native. The ban against alienation of lands set apart for native occupation should go some way to ward off economic servitude. What must be avoided was opening up avenues of intervention that brought prolonged conflicts with an offspring.[60]

6

The Native and Integration
Union Period

DRAFT CONSTITUTION

An unparalleled opportunity to fashion a sound native policy came with the movement for federation. The initiative had been taken by Cape Colony in November 1906 when, with the endorsement of the other colonies, it urged Lord Selborne to review publicly the manifest benefits of political union. The Selborne memorandum discussed the derivative values of economic prosperity, military security, and a common native policy.[1] A national convention was held behind locked doors at Durban, from October 12 to November 5, 1908, with delegates on hand from Cape Colony, Natal, Orange Free State, and the Transvaal. A second session was held in Cape Town, from November 23, 1908 to February 3, 1909, following which a draft constitution was released on February 9 for public consumption. The several colonial legislatures held sessions in March to consider the scheme. It was approved without alteration in the Transvaal and with only minor changes in Orange Free State. A severe struggle took place in Cape Colony where the Boers insisted upon more favorable representation of rural constituencies. The fiercest battle was fought in Natal for terms more advantageous to its economic interests and a referendum had to be held in June 1909 before agreement could be procured (11,121 to 3,701). In the meanwhile a third session of the national convention was held in Bloemfontein during May to put the finishing touches on the constitution.[2]

The British government followed closely the constitutional developments in South Africa. That its concern would be chiefly with the native provisions was made known at an early stage. Conversations were held with Sir Henry de Villiers, Chief Justice of Cape Colony and a lifelong advocate of federation and a brother of Melius de Villiers, Chief Justice of Orange Free State, when he stopped over in London in July 1908 on his way to attend the tercentenary celebrations in Canada. Both Asquith and Lord Crewe gave him to understand that the Imperial State would allow the colonies a free hand in everything except the native question and the disposition of the three protectorates—Basutoland, Bechuanaland, Swaziland. In fact, Lord Crewe urged Asquith to get a South African delegation over to London to impress them with the strong parliamentary feeling on the subject. But apparently some of the Liberals, notably Churchill, "regarded this with terror as do others although not clear why [perhaps the fear of stirring public agitation over the native question]."[3]

During the sessions of the national convention, Lord Selborne served as an intermediary for the Imperial State. He was supplied with copies of the proceedings and held frequent discussions with de Villiers, named chairman of the national convention. At the outset Lord Selborne submitted the views communicated to him by the British Colonial Office and his statement was read to the members of the national convention. Emphasis was placed upon the point that the time had come to frame a native franchise provision. Article 8 of the *Treaty of Vereeniging* implied that such would be done after self-government had been received. But recognition was accorded the need to distinguish between cultural levels, and the home government would be prepared to accept a more formidable qualification for the native. Perhaps a certificate of civilization could be issued to a native at the age of thirty (by a judge or some other person nominated by the Supreme Court) upon satisfactory evidence of education, industriousness, and decent social habits. Only after the third generation of a continuous civilized existence would the test be dispensed with for descendants. In the case of the Cape Coloured, the age of consideration could be less and sons could be recognized upon maturity without further proof.[4]

When the national convention, meeting at Durban, balked on a native franchise, Lord Selborne would appear to have been instructed to retreat. He was amenable to the status quo—that is, continuing the suffrage laws currently in vogue in the several colonies. The offer of special protection to Cape Colony by requiring a large majority in the Union Parliament for the repeal of its franchise seemed adequate. Nor did he persevere in an effort to get more favored treatment for the Cape Coloured. When he was sounded out as to a proposed clause declaring non-Europeans ineligible for membership in the legislative houses, Lord Selborne interposed only the vague condition—"if it were part of an otherwise satisfactory settlement of the native franchise question." Apparently, de Villiers was encouraged to tell the national convention that the British government would probably concur in the enactment of a constitution even if it contained a color bar.[5]

The national convention interpreted liberally the extent to which it could go in differentiating between European and non-European. For the time being each province would retain its own franchise laws with the ultimate determination vested in the Union Parliament. The only qualification related to Cape Colony, requiring a two-thirds majority of the combined membership in the two houses for cancellation. European adult males would constitute the basis for the apportionment of representatives in the lower chamber. A color bar was imposed for membership in both the House of Assembly and the Senate by the stipulation that seats would be confined to those of European descent. However, the governor-general-in-council would name four of the eight nominated senators from persons conversant with the needs and wants of the native. This specific clause supplemented the transfer of native affairs from the four provinces to the Union government.[6]

The Imperial State was more exacting as to the disposition of the three protectorates. Basutoland and Bechuanaland had placed themselves voluntarily under British authority and Swaziland had come willingly and all three had been loyal to the Crown ever since.* Each was administered by a resident official responsible to the high commissioner. Each was governed by indirect rule, bestowing extensive powers upon chieftains and entrenching native customs. Lord Selborne explained to de Villiers that Great Britain regarded itself as trustee and felt honor bound to insist upon requisite conditions before transfer. No specific date should be set for handing them over to the Union.

*Their populations in round numbers were Basutoland (350,000), Bechuanaland (120,000), and Swaziland (85,000). For literature on the protectorates see Perham and Curtis (1935).

The schedule should provide for no alienation of native lands, no sale of liquor, a proper share of customs duties, and preservation of tribal assemblies. De Villiers agreed to proceed on this basis in drafting the clauses pertinent to the protectorates. It is interesting to note that in March 1909 Lord Selborne visited the protectorates to assure the chieftains of British concern for their interests, particularly that they would be consulted prior to incorporation into the Union.[7]

Imperial insistence that the schedule specify the participation of the governor-general in naming the special commission to administer the protectorates after the transfer took place proved a bone of contention. De Villiers argued that this proposed arrangement implied a distrust of South Africa, intended as it was to bring in British officials and to attach the power of disallowance. Lord Crewe felt himself caught between two fires as he explained negotiations to Asquith. On the one hand, Lord Selborne required careful handling lest he resign on the ground "that he was not being backed up in his endeavours to secure the natives their rights—a by no means inconceivable event." On the other hand, the crisis with the national convention had reached a point "where we have to walk warily in order to get what we want—or most of it—without seeming to interfere too directly." The schedule as finally set forth allowed direct transfer to the Union with the executive organ to be the supreme authority. The special commission of not less than three would be a purely advisory body appointed for ten years by the governor-general-in-council with the right to present its reasons on any matter before the Union Parliament.[8]

Presentation of the constitution to the British Parliament was set for the summer of 1909. Lord Selborne asked that the South African delegation reach London by July 17 "to give time for the Secretary of State to discuss with it any modifications . . . which appear to His Majesty's Government to be necessary or any points of drafting which may have been raised." However, at the final session in Bloemfontein, de Villiers moved a resolution that delegates be precluded from consenting to any substantial amendment. While approved, a further suggestion was turned down to debar the delegation from the slightest departure in the words of the constitution. It was better to leave the door open for alterations if the situation dictated such strategy. Sir Walter Francis Hely-Hutchinson, Governor of Cape Colony, told Lord Crewe that he hoped there would be no changes in the native provisions. For Great Britain to insist upon amendments might boomerang against the native vote in Cape Colony as well as jeopardize native interests throughout South Africa. A climate of public opinion was growing up solicitous about native welfare and intervention by the Imperial State could strangle it.[9]

The South African official delegation headed by Sir Henry de Villiers arrived in June 1909. King Edward VII had General Botha dine with him on July 22 and a state banquet was held at Buckingham Palace on July 24 for all delegates. Formal conversations between Lord Crewe and the overseas spokesmen commenced on July 20, a day after de Villiers had been handed a copy of amendments desired by the British Colonial Office. Most of them were of a nominal character intended to clarify the meaning of clauses. The only serious trouble related to amendments forbidding differential railway rates on produce from the protectorates entering other ports of the Union, strengthening the clause on salaries and pension rights of the special commission, and stipulating that curbs on the sale of intoxicating liquors be stringent. De Villiers persuaded Lord Crewe to drop the proposals, "fully relying on the Union Parliament to deal with these matters in a reasonable and liberal manner." When the discussions were concluded on July 21, Lord Crewe warned that the native provisions would probably receive rough sledding in the House of Commons, but he assured the delegates that the British government would see the draft constitution through as it stood.[10]

Deputations were dispatched by non-European organizations to present their views to the Imperial State. A Bantu delegation was led by Schreiner, whose defense of Dinizulu had further enhanced his stature as a champion of native interests. Accompanying him were John Tengo Jabavu, a pure Fingo and editor of a native newspaper, and Rev. Walter P. Rubusana, a native Congregational clergyman (and, after Union, the first full-blooded Bantu to serve as a member of the Cape Colony provincial council). The Cape Coloured were represented by Dr. Abdullah Abdurahman, D. J. Lenders, and M. J. Fredericks. Both deputations were welcomed by an array of friends from the British and Foreign Anti-Slavery Society, the Aborigines Protection Society, the London Missionary Society, and the South African Native Races Committee.[11]

Even before the delegates representing the natives sailed for London their case was in preparation by their British supporters. In March 1909 Dilke sought out Colonel Seely and discussed the draft constitution first published in February. Dilke told him that one point in particular needed to be reviewed, namely, the exclusion from both houses "of any and every coloured member who might otherwise be elected." In May 1909 Dilke led a group of Liberal and Labour M.P.'s to meet with Lord Crewe, drawing from him a promise to do what he could for the natives. When the Bantu and Cape Coloured deputations arrived in London, an interview was obtained for them on July 22 with Lord Crewe. Schreiner wrote to Dilke that the meeting "did not advance matters beyond the facts of great courtesy, real sympathy and earnest attention." MacDonald arranged a reception for them on July 29 with a group of forty members of the British Parliament. *The Times* opened its columns to lengthy letters from Schreiner, Jabavu, and Dr. Abdurahman, all of whom predicted a bleak future for non-Europeans under the proposed constitution unless the Imperial State altered the document.[12]

Whether or not its counsel was of any moment, the British Colonial Office staff had its say upon suitable native provisions in the scheme of federation. A native franchise in the Transvaal and Orange Free State held the greatest promise of a progressive common denominator for all colonies. Since responsible government had now been granted them, Great Britain was no longer bound by the *Treaty of Vereeniging* to keep silent on the political rights of the natives. It was agreed that universal male suffrage was out of the question, for nothing would make a black man the equal of a white man in South Africa. Indeed, observed Lambert, no white population would ever appear to have given up willingly this hard-and-fast line in the history of mixed communities. The Southern states of America were coerced by arms and the Cape constitution of 1853 had been more a manifestation of Downing Street pressure than a gesture of magnanimity on the part of the colonial whites. Certainly, it could be said of the Cape suffrage, however few the proportion of natives to whites on the voting register, that it was a "safety valve for the better class of native and Coloured and prevents Parliament from being the organ of a white oligarchy as in Natal and will be in the Transvaal." At least by the Cape method "you do something real to obliterate the distinction and remove the injustice and stigma of hopeless inequality."[13]

Liberal statesmen put on a bold front publicly in defending the draft constitution.[14] Both Lord Crewe, in the House of Lords on July 27, and Colonel Seely, in the House of Commons on August 16, argued the merits of the native provisions. The Cape Colony franchise, symbol of hope to non-Europeans, was in no danger, buttressed as it was by the prohibitive hurdle of a two-thirds majority to overthrow it. Surely, the Union would not care to set the unenviable precedent in democratic times of disfranchising a great body of inhabitants. Nor was the exclusion of non-Europeans from membership in the legislature so reactionary a measure upon closer examination. It was only in the Cape that they had the vote and it seemed stretching the point to grant a right which had no practical application in the greater part of the Union. Moreover, neither Cape Coloured nor Bantu had ever been elected to the Cape Assembly and the grievance really seemed an academic one. As for the protectorates, their welfare was secured by a schedule of safeguards and prior negotiations for their transfer.[15]

Colonel Seely stated frankly that the official delegation was quite adamant against amendments and read a letter from de Villiers to that effect in the House of Commons.* Nevertheless, he would put faith in these men "to want to do right and justice to . . . all races and creeds in South Africa." A national government with the best brains in the country at its disposal and dedicated to righteousness would mean a happier life for native peoples. Lord Crewe placed reliance upon the right of Great Britain to reserve bills relating to natives under the provisions of Clause 147. That should guarantee against any worsening of their condition until South Africa grasped the political and moral significance of the issue. Asquith confidently predicted that

*The letter of de Villiers dated August 17, 1909, summarized the sentiments of the official delegation against alteration of the native provisions: "1) The Delegation has no authority, expressed or implied, to accept any Amendment of the nature referred to which would destroy a compromise that was arrived at after prolonged discussion. 2) Any Amendment affecting important principles would have to be remitted to the Legislatures in several of which the acceptance of the alteration proposed would be more than doubtful. 3) As you are aware, the Act was submitted to a referendum in Natal, and any alteration would have to undergo a similar ordeal. It is probable that in a matter affecting the very foundations of social relations in South Africa other Parliaments would insist on a similar course of procedure. 4) Under the most favourable conditions great delay would ensue and the accomplishment of union would be postponed for a very considerable time if not entirely ended." Commons, Aug. 19, 1909, p. 1601.

the heritage of humanitarianism in British history would yet triumph in this newest of dominions:

> How you are to adapt and to evolve free institutions in a community where two different races in totally different stages of civilization find themselves sitting side by side and intermixed is essentially a modern problem. . . . The experience in Cape Colony itself shows that [it] can yield . . . to judicious treatment and to wise and humane arrangements. . . . You ought to allow the community itself with whom the responsibility lies, which will benefit by improvement, which will suffer by deterioration, to determine how from time to time . . . its representative and parliamentary institutions shall be adjusted to the existing state of circumstances.[16]

PUBLIC FORUM

Liberal and Labour circles made plain their disappointment with the franchise provisions. The decision to preserve the prevailing suffrage laws meant that in the Transvaal and Orange Free State (as well as in Natal) the natives would not be voters. Surely the agreement made at Vereeniging should not be allowed to remain forever a millstone against the advance of the native. The chance to become first-class citizens in Cape Colony had stimulated many natives to win distinction in professional careers. Molteno granted that the American experience with the Negro vote had not been an edifying one but the parallel was not the same. Negroes in the United States were "an amorphous mass just liberated from slavery" whereas in South Africa the native social order remained cohesive and the transition could be more properly directed. Edward Carpenter, socialist and author, gathered that the hostility of whites in the Southern States was rooted in the apprehension that a vast number of black voters would open the door to political demagoguery as in the nightmarish period of reconstruction. In South Africa, no one, least of all the native population, wanted universal suffrage overnight. Negro voters in the Cape had exercised their vote most discreetly and their brethren in the other colonies should be accorded the same privilege subject to property and educational qualifications.[17]

MacDonald wondered whether the native franchise in Cape Colony could be sustained. The allocation of seats in the House of Assembly gave fifty-one to Cape Colony, thirty-six to the Transvaal, and seventeen each to Natal and Orange Free State. Every province possessed eight seats in the Senate, with eight additional seats to be filled by nomination. A calculation would show that one hundred eight out of the one hundred sixty-one total combined membership comprised a two-thirds majority. Those provinces bitterly opposed to a native franchise—Natal, Orange Free State, the Transvaal—held ninety-four seats. One could assume that the eight senators nominated by the governor-general-in-council would be in the camp of the opposition including even the four named for their supposed acquaintance with the wants of the natives. Thus only a switch of six votes in the Cape contingent was needed to repeal the native franchise in that colony. Hardie believed that the very existence of a mathematical formula to protect the Cape franchise suggested a conspiracy afoot to wipe it out. He referred to a speech of General Botha on February 24 to the effect that Cape Colony had been forced by the British Colonial Office to include in its constitution of 1853 a franchise with no color bar and "the only possible course for us to follow in the draft constitution . . . was to create machinery which would enable the people of South Africa to settle this question."[18] Unless a stronger anchor was found for the Cape franchise, Great Britain would be placed in the discreditable position of committing a breach of faith to loyal native subjects.[19]

The color bar set up for membership in the Union Parliament made that body an inner citadel behind which colonial whites could carry on the struggle for supremacy if need be. Baron Courtney of Penwith, a writer on government, decried this restriction of candidacy to men of European descent as bound to further stifle native aspirations, for the vote was simply a first step in the true exercise of citizenship. He recalled the same kind of a barrier against Roman Catholics sitting in the House of Commons (until 1829) and how much bitterness it generated even though the opportunity to qualify as a voter was there. Dilke referred to the case of Dr. Abdurahman who spoke both Dutch and English and who thrice had been elected chairman of the Cape Town Health Committee, a body of importance in the municipality. Despite four generations of Cape descent, as a member of a dark-skinned race which came from Malay shores, he would be excluded from the Union Parliament. If no native had ever sat in the Cape legislature, the answer probably was a sense of extreme modesty. But the image of eligibility held something dignified for mankind. The argument that none had ever been elected should not be used to justify a formal prohibition.[20]

The vaunted safeguards in behalf of the protectorates were not highly esteemed. The ultimate concentration of administration in the hands of the Union Prime Minister had the appearance of a bureaucracy unresponsive to public opinion. The special commission to be nominated by the Prime Minister for a ten-year period would have little independence in an advisory capacity. Amendments were in order before the subject of transfer could be raised. The schedule ought to include a stronger guarantee of tribal land and consultation on tax proposals. The right of appeal to the Union Parliament against executive decisions should be inserted. Specific recognition of the *pitso* would provide ready at hand the nucleus of democratic training.* In any case, a referendum should be held in each protectorate prior to negotiations for transfer. The *New Age* was intransigent in its views, stating bluntly that no South African could be trusted in dealing with blacks. The only equitable settlement was permanent trusteeship by the mother country.[21]

Liberals and Labourites joined in a grim epitaph decrying the moral abyss into which the Asquith government had allowed itself to fall. The Union constitution marked a retrogressive step in the annals of the British Empire. History would have to record the dismal fact that a handful of assorted whites in South Africa had enlisted the aid of the Imperial State to enslave native subjects. Henceforth the military might of Great Britain, entailing lives and money, would be at the beck and call of an unbridled white community riding roughshod over a helpless helotry. The mother country should not have allowed itself to be meekly shunted aside with the admonition neither to touch the document nor to tack on to it. The approval of the Union constitution

---

*A *pitso* originally meant a gathering of the tribe or clan but in 1875 the Basuto held one on a national level. In 1903, at the suggestion of British authorities, they formed a national council of one hundred representatives on a permanent basis. The presiding officer was the resident commissioner and the membership comprised ninety-four chiefs and five nominated natives. The *pitso* had no binding legislative powers and acted only in an advisory capacity. Raymond L. Buell *The Native Problem in Africa* (New York: 1928), I, pp. 180-82.

would represent the first color bar ever formally enacted by the British Parliament. It should be recalled that the constitutions of Orange Free State and the Transvaal had been issued as orders-in-council by the executive branch.[22]

Hobson penned an especially harsh commentary:

Both parties appear to regard the sanction of the Imperial Parliament as an act destitute of real responsibility. It is indeed understood that the Colonial Office procured some minor modifications. . . . But all effective criticism or amendment was denied to the House of Commons by a bold and very simple form of bluff. South African delegates were aware of Liberal objections to the denial of native political rights . . . and aware that any free exercise of Imperial legislative power would amend their Act . . . to secure the standard of equality formulated by Mr. Rhodes' [of] 'equal rights for all civilised men south of the Zambesi,' and [so] agreed upon the terse formula that any such amendments would 'wreck the Union.' And it worked although South African States would probably have accepted amendments. . . . To describe as a self-governing nation the white oligarchy that has, with our connivance, fenced itself against admission of the ablest and most progressive members of races living in their midst and by general admission capable of a civilisation at least as high as that of the ordinary wage-earner, is an outrage to political terminology. . . . There can be no enduring peace, no steady progress and prosperity in a South Africa where the vast bulk of the work of industry is done by men who are denied all opportunity to participate, proportionately to their proved capacity, in the government of the country which is morally theirs, in the sense that they are genuinely interested in it, and have put their personal effort into the development.

At best the South African Union will be a close replica . . . of the Southern States of the American Commonwealth, where the races subsist side by side in the same land in no organic spiritual contact with one another, each race suffering the moral, intellectual, and industrial penalty of this disunion. . . . But the black population grows at least as fast as the whites and it cannot be expelled or put into reserves because it is required for the white man's wants and it will gain in knowledge and demand rights.[23]

Conservative circles accepted the status quo in the suffrage laws as a realistic recognition of the varying conditions in the four provinces. The *Morning Post* saw in the makeshift arrangement the hope that no discouraging pattern had been set. Moreover, where the Cape franchise could not be repealed except by a two-thirds vote, a bare majority could give the native the voting privilege in the other colonies. Undoubtedly, the two former republics would find it difficult to maintain side by side a universal suffrage for whites and a restricted suffrage for natives. But the Liberal government was to blame for this dilemma. It had refused to accept Lyttelton's restricted suffrage for whites based on property qualifications and substituted a sweeping grant to all whites. The native voter in the Cape would be a beneficiary, for the protection of a two-thirds majority marked an improvement over the bare majority sufficient to reverse it in the old Cape legislature. Only Lord Lansdowne was disturbed about the formula of a two-thirds majority. The margin of comfort seemed very narrow when one considered the widespread prejudice in the other colonies. And he did not rate highly the power of reservation as a supplementary barrier in the light of British hesitancy to use it against the several dominions.[24]

The *Daily Telegraph* repeated anew the lessons to be learned from the evolutionary processes of acculturation. The British working class had received the franchise less than fifty years ago (1867). It appeared extravagant, therefore, to say that natives, who were a thousand years behind Anglo-Saxons on the ladder of civilization, could bridge the gap overnight. The doctrine of equality before the law was as much respected in South Africa as in Europe but that did not mean all men were entitled to the full privileges of citizenship. Such an inheritance did not go to "minors" in England and whites quite correctly regarded the natives as "minors" to whom the greatest solicitude should be given but not political equality. The tragic experience of America with Negro voting rights was an ever present reminder. That ill-conceived and partisan stroke, at the moment a strategy to swamp the white vote in the Confederate States, had been the one blot upon President Lincoln's career.* The wild orgy of terror and bankruptcy

*American historians describe Abraham Lincoln as preferring to restrict the colored vote to the very intelligent and to those who had fought gallantly as soldiers. James Ford Rhodes *History of the United States* (New York: 1910), IV, p. 485; James Garfield Randall and David Donald *The Civil War and Reconstruction* (Boston: 1961, 2nd ed.), p. 556.

visited upon the South by irresponsible "carpetbaggers" was a lesson
never to be forgotten. The Negro now found himself exposed to worse
treatment than he had ever met with in his slave days. And this from
men who had been hitherto the most kindly and humane.[25]

No criticism was voiced against the restriction of membership in
the Union Parliament to persons of European descent. The action
reflected the unanimous opinion of white South Africa and for the Imperial State to have resisted in any way would have brought a collapse
of the federation movement. Every consideration which could be
urged against the extension of the "blanket vote" applied a fortiori to
the presence of native deputies in the Union Parliament. No native
had ever stood for election in Cape Colony during the fifty years in
which the door had been open and it seemed a waste of effort to quarrel over something so little prized. More bluntly, the *Edinburgh Review* averred that if one native had ever been elected to the Cape
legislature a law to prevent the recurrence would have been forthcoming. Natives were aware of its impracticality and so refrained from
putting up any candidates. For that matter, the Union was a new
creation and the theoretical right in Cape Colony did not establish a
precedent to be imposed upon the other three provinces as well. However, neither native nor Cape Coloured would lose anything substantial, for they would find in the Union Parliament many representatives
who had been lifelong friends of their cause.[26]

The blueprint for the three protectorates raised no objections.
Criticism of the administrative system could be held over until a transfer had been actually proposed. It was enough that an integrated life
with the Union could be envisaged and a constructive set of guideposts outlined. Their lands were secured to them. They would be
protected from the liquor trade. Their share in customs duties would
be generous. What the Imperial State could do as trustee during the
transitory period ahead was to help the native population over the
worst aspects of its primitive culture. However, Lord Curzon saw a
potentially aggravating situation if the settlement produced one type
of stewardship for the 4,500,000 natives inside the Union and another
for the 600,000 natives under British jurisdiction. It would be unplea-
sant to have the Union complain that the native policy of the Imperial
State was undermining the effectiveness of its own program. The
sooner the transfer took place the better it would be for all concerned.[27]

Whatever might be the shortcomings of the constitution, Conservatives expressed a sturdy faith in the future of the native in South Africa.* The document reflected the uneven development among the provinces at the moment but it was susceptible to alteration and the color bar could not possibly be a permanent feature. The example of Cape Colony should have an elevating influence upon its neighbors. Then, too, the advent of the Union should eliminate the mischievous tendency to hysteria of individual colonies lacking the resources to cope with a major native rebellion. The greater sense of security and freedom from panic conferred by federation should win a more charitable reception for the native. Still again, the psychology of earning the plaudits of world opinion and the desire to add the three protectorates would be effective spurs to assure fair treatment.[28]

The *Spectator* urged the Liberal government not to permit amendments. Such a course would be fatal and would force the Union delegation into an ugly mood. The local people were the ones who lived side by side with the natives and were best fitted to deal with them. An improvement in the lot of the Bantu must come from their own efforts and from an enlightened opinion in South Africa. For Downing Street to insist upon new provisions in the constitution was within its power but hardly an intelligent thing to do. William Robert Wellesley Peel, Conservative M.P. and later possessor of a distinguished career in India as Viscount (and Earl) Peel, recalled the case of the American colonies when the Grenvilles (George and faction) were arguing the right of Great Britain to tax them. While Edmund Burke and the elder Pitt (Earl of Chatham) did not dispute this right, their retort was: "Yes, . . . but is it wise?"[29]

Balfour offered a keen analysis of the Conservative point of view. The problem of relations between Europeans and Africans was new and extremely complex and no conclusive solution had yet been found. The United States had not solved it. After starting with "a very crude a priori statement of the equality of mankind and a brutal application of the most rigid principles of slavery," America had extricated itself

---

*If the Archbishop of Canterbury voiced qualms over the native's eclipse in the constitution, he assumed that it was temporary and based on the conviction that the white man constituted the racial adult and the black man the racial child. When the latter grew up and demonstrated his fitness, he would be given all the rights at present withheld from him. *Commons*, July 27, 1909, pp. 789-91.

from the unhappy contradiction by abolishing slavery. But then it came face to face with "the immutable principles of their constitution which laid down in true eighteenth-century language that men were equal." All men might be equal on some counts but to suppose that natives in Africa were the equal of men of European descent in higher cultural pursuits was an absurdity. There were very fundamental differences between black and white which had been hardening since the dawn of history. To concede equal rights, without the corresponding ability to meet the tests of maturity, could imperil the fabric of Western civilization. The best way to find the correct solution was to give full control to the Union of South Africa. The people on the spot must bear the responsibilities, rewards, and penalties of their conduct.[30]

Liberal whips informed party members during the committee stage that no amendments would be welcomed. While some thirty Radicals ignored the admonition and joined with Labour members in proposing fifty-three amendments, only one was pressed to a division. George Nicoll Barnes, Labour M.P., moved to allow non-Europeans from Cape Colony and Natal to sit in the Senate. It was defeated by a vote of one hundred fifty-five to fifty-five but the sparse attendance in the House of Commons would not appear to be so much an indication of indifference to the native problem as perhaps a discouraging realization of the impossibility of doing anything. Among the amendments proposed and then withdrawn may be mentioned 1) apportionment of seats in the House of Assembly on the basis of all registered voters and not just adult white males (advantageous to Cape Colony), 2) substitution of a two-thirds vote of members only from Cape Colony to alter its franchise, and 3) a minimum of ten years before negotiations could take place on the transfer of the protectorates.[31]

Labour party members agreed not to divide the House of Commons on the third reading lest it diminish Asquith's plea for unity. But they were fervid in their hopes that amendments bearing upon native welfare would be enacted at the earliest opportunity by the Union Parliament. So, on August 4 in the House of Lords and on August 19 in the House of Commons, the constitution achieved third readings. Royal assent was given on September 20 to the creation of the Union of South Africa.[32]

AFTERMATH

Viscount Herbert Gladstone, fourth son of William Ewart Gladstone, became the first Governor-General of South Africa. A congratulatory letter from James Bryce (Viscount), scholar, statesman, and diplomat, counseled

> that one of your most important and difficult functions is to secure the rights of the Natives. It is a delicate matter, but . . . is the really important question for South Africa. That was borne in on me in 1895 [while visiting there] and it is not less true now.

Lord Gladstone urged General Botha to take the office of Minister of Native Affairs along with the premiership. The possibility of Swaziland being brought into the Union made that a logical combination of portfolios.* Since the schedule called for direct administration by the Prime Minister, unity could thus be best maintained. However, General Botha pleaded inability to do justice to both posts and appointed Henry Burton, previously Attorney-General of Cape Colony, as Minister of Native Affairs.** Lord Gladstone expressed himself as satisfied, for Burton came from the Cape where the treatment of the native was most progressive.[33]

Lord Crewe manifested special interest in the four senators to be nominated for their acquaintance with the reasonable wants and wishes of the native people. He stressed "that we can not of course interfere but they should know we are interested and regard it as important to select men of undoubted sympathies and experiences." Lord Gladstone reported General Botha as saying that "the British Government had done so much for South Africa that he wished to meet their views as far as possible." Lord Gladstone approved of the

---

*The failure to have Swaziland incorporated in the Transvaal at the time of the grant of responsible government had been a matter of disappointment to General Botha. The British Colonial Office lent some encouragement to his wish that Swaziland might be the first protectorate to be transferred. *Viscount Gladstone Papers,* 45996, Crewe to Gladstone, June 17, 1910, pp. 51-52; P.R.O., c.o. 879/102, No. 933.

**Lord Gladstone voiced pleasure when General Botha took over in 1913 as Minister of Native Affairs. The office had changed hands four times and perhaps now "it will stay in his hands where it should." To interpolate, the sequence of ministers included Henry Burton (1910), James Barrie Munnik Hertzog (1912), Jacobus Wilhemus Sauer (1912), Louis Botha (1913). P.R.O., c.o. 551/58.

calibre of the four senators nominated in October 1910. There was no need to dwell upon the merits of Schreiner as an avowed champion of the Bantu all his life. Nor could there be any debate over the solicitude of Colonel Walter Ernest Mortimer Stanford, a past secretary of the Department of Native Affairs in Cape Colony. As for the other two nominated senators, their careers had been identified with native matters. Johannes Christoffel Krogh was a former resident magistrate of Nylstroom in the Transvaal and a member of the South African Native Affairs Commission of 1905. Frederick Robert Moor had been Premier of Natal during the Zulu disturbances and he also had service as a Minister for Native Affairs.[34]

Lord Gladstone had warm words of encouragement when native deputations appeared before him. In October 1910, just before the actual selection of the four senators to represent native interests, he was visited by a contingent from the Transvaal bearing a list of sixteen suitable candidates including both Schreiner and Stanford. While he responded that the decision rested with his ministers, he had the highest hopes for their just treatment. Again, in July 1911, he was visited at Durban by a Natal Native Congress deputation expressing anxiety at the omission of recognition of a fair share of life for them in the Union constitution. Lord Gladstone answered with optimism, noting provisions which ought to meet their aspirations. Natives should not overlook the axiom that the Union would see the native question in a broader perspective than the harried provincial administrators. The status of the protectorates should act as a lever for the Union to develop a model native program. So forces for good were present to promise early dividends to the Bantu.[35]

Lord Gladstone accompanied action with words in the instance of the so-called Black Peril. The background was a reprieve given to a native condemned for rape in Southern Rhodesia. An outcry followed this exercise of the royal prerogative of mercy and dire prophecies poured in of the dangers which would now confront white women in South Africa. Lord Gladstone discussed the subject frankly with Burton in a letter dated June 28, 1911. There seemed to be no adequate statistics kept on the number of rape cases or the best deterrent measures (death, corporal punishment, long term imprisonment). But more than this, there appeared to be a White Peril perhaps exceeding in gravity the Native Peril. No one spoke for the black woman

ruined by the white man and reports had thousands of such cases
carefully concealed by the press. The reprehensibility of the white man
was worse when one considered the temptations thrown in the path
of blacks little better than savages. Objectionable literature of the
most obscene kind was allowed to reach the natives. Black servants had
constant access to white women in their bedrooms and helped to dress
and undress them. Lord Gladstone had the satisfaction of getting a
commission appointed in June 1912 to study the matter. To interpolate, its report in 1913 disclosed shortcomings on both sides and a
series of recommendations were made.[36]

Those in British circles attached to the cause of the native did not
find much to cheer about in the years between 1910 and the outbreak
of World War I. Dr. Guest deplored the *Mines and Works Act of
1911* entrenching the economic primacy of white workers through
reservation of a list of jobs paying high wages. Natives continued to be
regarded as mere robots, herded in compounds and separated from
their families. Mining companies failed to tackle the technical problem of silicic rock dust and the scourge of pthisis ran riot. A medical
commission, appointed by the Union government, found in 1912
that 27 per cent of 1,100 natives examined were suffering from phthisis. Nothing yet had been done to improve native living accommodations in Johannesburg which could only be described as "a slum called
the location, built of old boards and tin cans, the foulest, filthiest spot
imaginable." A series of native villages connected by electric railways
to the gold mines and providing separate huts and gardening plots
suitable to family life would be an invaluable boon.[37]

The status of the native remained that of a second-class citizen.* He
still traveled in separate third-class accommodations. He could not
purchase a postage stamp at the regular counter but had to go down
to a dismal basement room. He could not venture into most parks or
watch sports contests on athletic grounds frequented by whites. Colored people without a pass must observe curfew after dark. Native
evidence against a white man was not permissible in the courts. Children of black parents were not admitted to schools attended by white
children. A black man, whatever his professional standing, had no entry to a white man's home on social occasions. The excuse that the

*Even a Conservative organ, the *Morning Post* (April 15, 1913), was moved to describe the native policy of the Union government as "dark, uncertain, and ominous."

black man lacked self-discipline, and was especially prone to uncontrollable sex passions, was quite specious. Miss Markham pleaded for an end to these distressing humiliations:

> Teach the Kafir to despise himself, overwhelm him with the sense of his inferiority, and you open the door to all the racial vices which spring from a lack of self-respect. Courtesy, forbearance, strict justice—these the white man can give to the black without the smallest encroachment on the intimacies of life. He must be given some sense of his worth as a man and a citizen. The policy of repression was one of despair. The growing self-consciousness of the native mind must be recognized and guided by the European or distrust and suspicion will be gangrened.[38]

S. H. Halford, writing in the *Socialist Review*, prophesied that the white man would yet rue the day he set out to degrade the native. The association of manual work with the despised Bantu nourished the poisonous thesis that toil was unworthy of whites. It was assumed that providence had created the Caucasian race to dominate the colored race as overseers and governors. An aristocracy of white men, served by a mass of ignorant and maltreated automatons, spelled its own doom. Such a patriciate, furthermore, would be able to draw only upon highly positioned women for marriage, since the adornments of decorativeness would be expected in the female species of a self-constituted elite. Naturally, women conscious of the importance of preserving their charm would not care for a life of reproduction and the birthrate would be as abnormally low as in Jamaica. The British aristocracy at home would have disappeared long ago but for the persistence of some upper-class women to raise large families (and the steady creation of new peers and the occasional intermarriage with commoners). But the play of these factors would not be present in the tenser atmosphere of the subcontinent. The consequence would be a growing disproportion between whites and blacks and the initiation of desperate measures by the former to preserve the status quo. What a colossus of clay the white man was building for himself in South Africa.[39]

From all circles came expressions of concern for the future of the colonial whites. *The Times* was frankly worried by the trend to abandon unskilled labor to the natives. Steady elimination in the areas of physical toil had brought the immigration of Europeans to a standstill. Children of the white artisan class would find themselves cut off from the only school of experience by which they could acquire apprentice- ship for skilled trades. The white man's efficiency must decline, for labor which qualified at the top could never be so good as that which had worked through all the lower grades. Miss Markham referred to the *Report of the Transvaal Indigency Commission of 1908* on the growth of the poor-white class as a first instalment of retribution. This impoverished segment of the European community was the peculiar product of a bicolored state where manual labor had been vested en- tirely in the hands of the black race.* This was the identical experi- ence of the Southern States before 1861, illuminated by Bryce's description of the depressed whites as a "shiftless ignorant improvi- dent class of poor white trash, economically superfluous, disliked by the planters, and despised by the slaves."[40] Unless something were done quickly, the white population, lacking outlets for its natural energy, would shrink and South Africa would wind up as a settlement lost to the European side of the ledger.[41]

Sir Henry Mortimer Durand, whose busy career was distinguished by a mastery of Oriental languages, diplomatic service on three conti- nents (including service in Washington, D.C.), and an unsuccessful candidacy as a Conservative in 1910, wrote a discerning and sym- pathetic analysis of the white man's dilemma in South Africa:

> What strikes a traveller in South Africa most forcibly is the attitude taken up by the white man that manual labour of every kind is 'Kafir's work' and he will not touch it. . . . Friends in South Africa told him that if they import English grooms for their stables the experiment is rarely successful. After a short time the men become infected with the local feeling and say that 'grooming horses is a Kafir's work'. . . . Rather than do Kafir's work or accept a Kafir's wage, the white man will be content to do nothing and live on charity. . . . In the Southern States

---

*While this report marked out the baleful influence of race prejudice as the greatest factor, reference was also made to the high cost of living, unprogressive farming, lack of education, and the Dutch law of intestacy requiring equal division of property among all sons and thus rendering the farm unit too small and uneconomical. *Transvaal Indigency Commission, Report 1906-08*, 411 pp.

of the American Union slavery produced what the negroes used to call 'po white trash,' and in South Africa the so-called caste system is doing the same. It would almost seem as if a curse were upon the white man who tries to make his home in a country occupied by the black. . . . Unless these toils be broken . . . South Africa can never become a great population of white men. She will be at best a nation of black men, with a comparatively small number of white rulers and overseers—an aristocracy of colour.

Great Britian is not free from responsibility in the matter . . . and should look on with sympathy and give some help. It is earnestly hoped that she will not let her strong and generous feelings toward the black races lead her into the course of action which has done so much in the past to complicate the position.

The American 'abolitionist' was not always fair to his brethren in the Southern States . . . and led him into acts . . . now generally regarded by Americans as mistaken. So with us. . . . Some of us see in brethren outside England . . . only narrow-minded oppressors brutally ill-treating the 'niggers.' But the responsible white man who has to live with and manage the black population is a wholly different type. . . . Maybe some measure of 'segregation' may be found practicable though American experience does not point that way. . . . And this would not be a hardship in itself if protected native states and native reserves on a large scale were maintained. . . .[42]

Liberals and Labourites entered a strong plea for integration as the only enduring settlement. Statistics showed that natives were multiplying four times as fast as whites, thereby rendering definitive territorial limits for each impractical. Whereas in 1904 there were 1,120,485 Europeans and 4,137,309 natives, in 1911 the census figures read 1,278,125 Europeans and 4,680,474 natives. *Justice* argued that the nature of the South African economy precluded a policy of separateness. There was no other labor supply available for the white man. So long, therefore, as the native had to leave his reserve periodically to work in the white community a segregation scheme was unreal. Surely, if a native discarded his primitive mode of life and fitted himself for the white man's competitive system, he should have a chance for equal rights. Bryce declared that if nothing were done to impede the course of human events, one could "only begin to conjecture the forms it [possible solutions] is likely to take when the Kafirs become more civilised."[43]

Miss Markham submitted a well-thought-out plan for assimilating natives into an integrated community. Her basic premise was the oft repeated one that whites could not afford to follow a genuine segregation policy because of the need for labor in their industrial and agricultural enterprises. It followed that the native who made possible the wealth of the white community should have an opportunity to rise above the level of helotry and fit himself for a civilized existence. She would not, however, apply one rule of ascent for all. The raw savage required personal government during the interim period of tutelage. The native with some human sensibilities could be provided with the type of environment set up by Cape Colony under the *Glen Grey Act of 1894.* The completely Westernized native, who was capable of conforming in all respects to European standards, should be given full civic and political privileges. The test for reaching this final rung in the ladder could be along the lines suggested by Lord Selborne—of appearance before a judicial tribunal to make good a claim of maturity.[44] If this evolutionary process were applied with careful screening, whites need not have nightmares of an inundation of black voters lacking the disciplined intelligence to exercise the franchise.[45]

Miss Markham was acutely aware of the danger of going too fast even if one accorded the principle of equality in theory. She too found the American scene rich with sociological data:

> [One should take warning] of the example in the United States of the application of the doctrines of political equality and equal franchise rights to white and black alike. The Southern States have peace only because of virtual suppression among the negroes of political rights to which theoretically they are entitled by the constitution. . . .
>
> It seems incredible that the politicians of the North should have thrust manhood suffrage and full political rights without discrimination of any kind on a mass of emancipated savages. . . . Experiments in government so suicidal were bound to issue in the violences and injustices which unhappily have been too common in the later history of the Southern States. The South felt bitterly that it had been sold—not in pursuance of doc-

trines of natural rights, but in order to gratify a spirit of personal revenge on the part of hostile Northern statesmen. . . .

The racial antipathies of the present are the product less of the emancipation of the slaves and the sufferings of the war than of the orgy of misgovernment which followed the peace. The South applied its mind . . . and by one device after another the American negro has been practically stripped of all his theoretical political privileges. Bryce estimated that only 10 per cent of qualified negro voters exercise that privilege today. . . .[46] Those who have suffered the most . . . are of course the negroes themselves. The bitter spirit created . . . has made the evolution of a sound and wise policy infinitely more difficult—the due rights of the negro as man and as citizen.[47]

Only a few commentators are to be encountered insisting that a genuine segregation policy of mutual exclusiveness was the better approach. Liddell Geddie (possibly John Liddell Geddie, editor of Chambers' encyclopaedias and biographical dictionaries), predicated his thinking on the conviction that the faster multiplication of natives and the growing number being educated would lead to a crisis in the relations between the two races. The white man would find it increasingly difficult to arrive at a balance of power with the native either under integration or a modified type of convenient segregation. The only solution was to set up two entirely separate and independent worlds. Within his own territorial enclave the native would be free to rise on the ladder of life, both as a skilled artisan and a professional man. Elsewhere the white man would be free to begin as low as he liked on his ladder of life, even to become an unskilled laborer without losing caste as a European. Thus the dignity of toil and the dictates of humanitarianism would be affirmed in South Africa. Presumably the phenomenon of the industrial revolution could be ignored or adjusted to suit a pressing racial problem.[48]

A last chapter in the Bantu story prior to World War I related to the Natives Land Act passed in June 1913. The purpose was to implement an announced policy of modified segregation by demarcating the areas to be reserved for active occupation by blacks and whites respectively. Neither would hold or lease land in those areas assigned to the other by a commission of inquiry (later known as the Beaumont Commission). Lord Gladstone saw no objection to the measure and informed the British Colonial Office that unless he received instructions to the contrary he would not reserve it. Even in Cape Colony, where the franchise provision afforded natives the chance to acquire land anywhere, they would be better off under the new proposal. The competition of whites had been too much for most natives and alienation of locations went unchecked. Lord Gladstone discounted the protests of squatters on white farms that their elimination would be a hardship on them. He understood only a small number would be involved.[49]

The British Colonial Office accepted the fact that the Union of South Africa should settle its own native policy. Nor did it object to the general principle of the bill which would assure the natives at least of a portion of the land. But to deny natives any further acquisitions of land until the completion of the allocation plan and simultaneously to allow white farmers to end squatting on their property bothered staff members. That was to put an economic squeeze on the native, perhaps to get his labor. However, despite numerous telegrams of protest from native societies in South Africa, the measure received assent. Moreover, when native leaders announced their intention of sending a deputation to England, no encouragement was given. Lewis Harcourt, successor to Lord Crewe as Secretary of State for the Colonies and a younger son of the late Sir William Venables Harcourt, regarded such a move as most unfortunate. It could not be productive of any good in matters properly within the competence of Union ministers. Harcourt sought (vainly) to have Lord Gladstone dissuade them from their mission. It might be added that the Botha government voiced stern displeasure at the bypassing of Union channels by the native proposal.[50]

The deputation from the South African Native National Congress arrived in London in June 1914. The group comprised Rev. John L. Dube, president, Solomon Plaatje, secretary, Saul Msane (Transvaal), Thomas M. Mapikela (Orange Free State), and Rev. Walter Rubusana (Cape Colony). The Aborigines Protection Society and the British and Foreign Anti-Slavery Society gave them a reception, arranged a hearing with members of the British Parliament, and obtained an interview with Harcourt.[51] Their story was a pathetic one of natives being evicted from tenancies before any new reserved areas had been provided for them. To make matters worse, a freeze had been put on any interim acquisitions of land by natives anywhere. And the hope of an equitable settlement for the future seemed dim because of the denial of native representation on the Beaumont Commission.[52]

Somewhat disheartening to the supplicants must have been the reply of Harcourt. Apart from the lack of evidence that injustice was really being done the natives, the latter should make their appeal to the Union government as the responsible authority. The suggestion that Harcourt extract a guarantee of good faith from General Botha brought the response that dominion status made such an approach unconstitutional. Ill-success likewise met the forlorn request for an audience with King George V, whatever might have been the publicity value of such a strategy. Lord Gladstone, having completed his term as Governor-General, had returned to London and was present at the time of the visit of the native deputation. He defended the *Natives Land Act of 1913* as an honest attempt to improve relations between blacks and whites. It showed a want of judgment on the part of native leaders to complain before the commission had submitted its recommendations.[53]

Friends of the native in British circles made themselves heard. Sir Alfred Spicer, Liberal M.P., charged that the termination of occupancy, when the native had as yet no alternative, was intended to reduce him to a state of servitude. The option to retain his lease for the time being on condition of fulfilling a labor service let the "cat out of the bag." That had all the earmarks of a throwback to medieval serfdom. It was the old feudal arrangement of working for the lord in return for the usufruct of land which had been theirs for decades on a tenancy basis. Those natives who refused the harsh terms of white farmers were being turned off the soil to wander about with their families and stock like nomads. The *Westminster Gazette* confessed sadly that royal assent could not be easily withheld in the current spirit of the imperial relationship. It was becoming more and more difficult for the mother country to interfere with self-governing offspring. One must tremble for the destiny of non-Europeans in South Africa.[54]

The *Daily News* focused attention upon the proposed allocation of land. According to a statement of the native deputation, at the moment 1,500,000 whites possessed 132,000,000 morgen (a morgen equals 2.12 acres) and 4,500,000 blacks possessed 9,952,000 morgen.

If the Beaumont Commission followed the present disposition (and its recommendation was 10,500,000 morgen for the natives), then the allocation would be frozen at a figure detrimental to a rapidly growing Bantu population. Granted the unhappy prospect of segregation, the least that should be done was to have the reserved areas bear some relation to the needs of the natives. The Union ought to foot the bill and buy up some of the white man's disproportionately large holdings. Miss Markham interpreted the act as reflecting a stern and calloused treatment ahead for natives. A program of avaricious self-interest with no thought of human dignity ought not to be condoned under the Union Jack. The sooner Great Britain divested itself of the responsibility for such immorality the better it would be. The true glory of an empire should rest on a code of ethics. Only when viewed thus could it bring a gift worth having and stand forth as an instrument of righteousness.[55]

Recent historical research places the blame for British hesitancy to force the issue of native welfare upon the desire for a federation of the four colonies. To be sure, both Liberal and Conservative statesmen professed confidence that the Union would do right by the natives. But Nicholas Mansergh, Smuts Professor of the History of the British Commonwealth, Cambridge University, observes somewhat severely "that the harsh facts of non-European exclusion from all effective participation in the political life of the Union [being] glossed over with philosophic generalities" reflected a rationalization process concealing less worthy aims.[56]

Geoffrey Barker Pyrah, University College, Leicester, is equally critical of imperial motives:

> Yet Union was not attained without cost—the cost, which the non-European had to pay, of racial discrimination. . . . Because of conflicting obligations, unavoidable, the shortcoming of Liberal as also of Unionist, policy lay in the fact that, though its consciousness of trusteeship was sufficiently sharp to protect the natives of the Protectorates, it secured no rights for the non-Europeans of the Colonies, with the result that self-government was awarded to a dominant white minority for the most part inimical to the interests of the other races.[57]

Leonard Monteath Thompson, formerly Professor of History at

the University of Cape Town and more recently at the University of California at Los Angeles, bluntly discusses the point that the Imperial State regarded itself as having a choice between the loyalty of the colonial whites and the interests of the Bantu. The British government could have insisted that the *Treaty of Vereeniging* did not include the Cape Coloured and that qualified natives should be given the vote within a tolerable period. Neither was done because of the fear, "and with reason," that reconciliation with the Boers would be lost if it departed "one iota from an absolute political colour-bar." What dominated the thinking of the British government was that "in time of war the Suez Canal might be closed to the shipping of Great Britain in which case the Cape route would reassume its former commercial and strategic importance and a friendly united South Africa would be a vital asset."[58] To interpolate, the growing estrangement with Germany added the further vital fact of the Union's proximity to German South-West Africa and German East Africa.

That such was the thinking of British statesmen is to be gleaned from scattered observations. In the course of his chat with Lord Riddle in April 1913, Lloyd George commented that "if we had a war to-morrow, Botha and 50,000 Boers would march with us side by side. He would, if necessary, drive the Germans out of South Africa." General Seely, writing in 1930, recalled his days as Parliamentary Under-Secretary for the Colonies: "I had been forced to the conclusion that war with Germany must come in the near future. If war came with a hostile population in South Africa, . . . the Empire would be confronted with immense strategical difficulties [and so regarded Union as urgent]." Viscount Samuel, writing in 1945, saw no incongruity in commending the Liberals for a policy of wisdom in South Africa compared to the heavy price paid during World War II for failing to fulfill Irish aspirations in the form of a neutral Eire denying its ports to Great Britain and America in their campaign against German submarines and the spying opportunities afforded German and Italian legations in Dublin: "If, after the Boer War, the same policy of negation and procrastination had been pursued in South Africa, can anyone doubt that similar consequences would have followed there?"[59]

Evidence of like thinking is also to be encountered among Conservative leaders. If Lyttelton, in the House of Commons on July 31, 1906, declared "that a particularly inappropriate moment had been chosen to grant self-government to the Boers because they might well, in an Anglo-German war, join forces with the enemy in German South-West Africa," the point is that his concern too was for a loyal South Africa but leaning heavily on the Anglo-Saxon element and relegating native interests to a place of secondary importance. Sir Austen Chamberlain, eldest son of Joseph Chamberlain and a member of several Conservative cabinets, reminisced in October 1921 and confessed that there were only one or two votes he would change over his parliamentary career of thirty years. One was his vote against granting self-government to the Transvaal and Orange Free State. As he saw it now, that action had not turned out "a rash and wicked thing to do," destroying imperial security, "but its completion and its fulfillment." For that bold venture had "led directly to the reconciliation of the races in South Africa; it led to the Union of South Africa; it brought South Africa into the war with us; added German East Africa and German South-West Africa to British territory."[60]

The Imperial State must, then, share some of the culpability for entrusting the destiny of the native to South African whites. In extenuation, given the trend to rely upon the bonds of affection and loyalty of white offspring for identification of economic and military purposes, the time would appear past to dictate policies on any matters. That is not to say that the reserved powers could be ignored and that consultation was not actively pursued. The evidence would indicate that British statesmen utilized persuasion and counsel to blunt some of the worst vestiges of colonial rigidity in native affairs. Perhaps most cherished was the hope that the Anglo-Saxon heritage of fair play would eventually win over South Africa to a better appreciation of its obligation to non-Europeans.

7

The British Indian & Integration
Colonial Period

THE PATTERN

The British Indian in South Africa did not find the post-Boer War years a period of brighter promise. The Transvaal provided the locale for the pattern of events. Colonial whites reemphasized the threat which this non-European element posed to the economic and social well-being of the community. The familiar arguments were repeated of unfair competition, obnoxious customs, and unsanitary habits. Two immediate demands were made of Lord Milner. First, an influx of Indians far beyond the numbers resident before 1899 must be halted. Second, *Law No. 3 of 1885* should be implemented requiring separate trading and residential locations for Asiatics. The British Indians countered with petitions demanding equal rights as subjects of the Crown. The assumption of political power by Great Britain should provide a *tabula rasa* from which to start anew.[1]

Lord Milner yielded to the pressure of the whites for legislation but sought to alleviate the worst aspects of racial humiliation. He agreed to *Ordinance No. 5 of 1903* to amend the *Peace Preservation Ordinance of 1902* (intended to keep out persons of seditious character in the aftermath of the Boer War) to include illegal Indian entrants. But he promised that the new permits requiring thumb impressions and a registration fee of £3 would establish once and for all the right of Indian residents previously domiciled to remain. He agreed to *Government Notice 356 of 1903* enforcing *Law No. 3 of 1885* for a segregated Indian community. But he promised that the locations would be healthful residential sites and accessible for trade. Lord Mil-

ner stressed the exemption to be accorded Asiatics of good social habits
and substantial wealth to reside elsewhere and an assurance to those
who held licenses before 1899 to trade outside the proposed bazaar
areas. For the rest, an Asiatic Department would be created to deal
with matters pertaining to the British Indians.[2]

However, Lord Milner defended the principle of segregation for
the lower classes of British Indians on sanitary grounds, citing the
testimony of Dr. Charles Porter, Medical Officer of Health for
Johannesburg:

> It [Indian dwellings] consists of a congeries of narrow courtyards, con-
> taining dilapidated and dirty tin huts, without adequate means of lighting,
> and ventilation, and constructed without any regard to sanitary conditions
> of any kind. In the middle of each slop-sodden and filth-bestrewn yard
> there is a well from which the people get their water supply, and, as in
> other places, they choose this well for washing purposes, the urinals and
> closets in one of the places being in the immediate vicinity. . . . It
> [location] is densely populated and its existence and continuance is
> fraught with danger to Johannesburg, and it surpasses all insanitary spots
> I have ever seen. . . . Both the general mortality and the occurrence of
> infectious disease within the area are excessive in comparison with the
> figures of the rest of the town.[3]

The British Colonial Office was early made aware of the fact that
the British Indian problem in South Africa could not be shunted aside.
A petition was received in October 1902 from the British Committee
of the Indian National Congress recalling the disabilities of the British
Indians under the late Kruger regime and the opportunity for Great
Britain now to make amends. Staff discussion focused attention on
the several reasons why the Imperial State could not stand by idly and
acquiesce in their maltreatment. Great Britain had consistently denounced the two Dutch Republics before 1899 for their anti-Asiatic
measures; it had an obligation to secure for the British Indian the
human dignity which twentieth-century idealism heralded as the
rightful inheritance of all mankind; and the mother country had a
vital stake in the homeland of these transplanted Asiatics. India was
the jewel of the Empire, contributing riches and military assistance to

the island people. British rule in India could be made suspect and the difficulties of administration multiplied if prejudice were allowed to run riot in South Africa.[4]

In connection with Lord Milner's sanction of the measures in 1903, Sir Mancherjee Bhownaggree, Conservative M.P. with antecedents as a Parsee merchant, dispatched to Lyttelton a lengthy exposition of the Indian case, dated September 15, 1903. Lord Milner was accused of attaching undue weight to the anti-Asiatic feeling in the Transvaal and by doing so had greatly stimulated its growth. Bhownaggree recalled that British Indian grievances had been made a casus belli of the Boer War and yet the Transvaal Crown colony bid fair to worsen their lot. He would not condone unsanitary conditions but the answer was that some guilt rested with the municipality for allowing the deterioration. Nor could letters of exemption for some to trade and live elsewhere be anything less than offensive to the mass of low-class Hindus. It was a slur upon the dignity of Oriental peoples to set up a separate Asiatic Department to handle domiciliary rights for returning Indians. He described an ordinance to suppress immorality which bracketed Indians, Chinese coolies, and natives together with severe penalties attached as another in the long category of insults. The Indian people were civilized and not to be linked with semisavage and backward tribes.[5]

Sir Arthur Lawley, Lieutenant-Governor of the Transvaal, took cognizance of Bhownaggree's criticism and answered it in a letter to Lord Milner, dated April 13, 1904:

In all towns of the Transvaal the Asiatic question overshadows all others. . . . [Their sentiments] cannot be ignored. They have got to be reckoned with. It is true that the British Government have laid down:— 'that there shall not be in the eye of the law any distinction of qualification whatever founded on mere distinction of colour, origin, language or creed. . . .' Pledges such as those contained in the proclamation of Sir Charles Napier [correctly, Sir George Thomas Napier] were made at a time [1843] when large sections of the British nation had not come into touch with coloured races as they have today. . . .* It was commonly

*Sir George Thomas Napier, Governor of Cape Colony, issued the proclamation in May 1843 as a preliminary to the annexation of Natal.

supposed that all . . . were capable of the same civilization. . . . Today the Government cannot fail to perceive the effects of such a doctrine
[racial equality] on the social composition. . . .

[Take] the remote community of Pietersburg in the Transvaal. Almost
the entire retail trade is in the hands of Indians. There are a few large
stores belonging to European merchants which are the retail depots of
wholesale establishments. . . . The town from a commercial point of
view has a hybrid appearance, the Indian element being rather more
prominent than the European. But the most serious feature is the increasing predominance of the Indians. The total white population is
estimated at 1,684. The registers of the Asiatic Department show no less
than 135 Indians, almost entirely adult males, and practically all engaged
in the business of storekeeping.

To come now to Natal. . . . So prevalent is the Indian element . . .
that the moment one crosses the Transvaal border he loses the impression
that he is travelling in a European country at all. [European] traders have
vanished and their business is now entirely in the hands of Asiatics. . . .

Maybe the introduction of unskilled Asiatic labour develops the country but not the admission of Asiatics of the second class. It closes a sphere
for white men in a temperate zone where they can live. If South Africa is
to be a sphere for the development of an English population, then Asiatic
traders will have to be restricted. The outbreak of bubonic plague in the
Johannesburg quarter has further increased the determination of whites.*

A *modus vivendi* is possible to restrict future Asiatic immigration . . .
but to treat fairly those already allowed to come into the country. . . .
At the present time the market is glutted with farms for sale and if . . .
restrictions . . . were removed, thousands of acres would at once pass
into the hands of British Indians.⁶

Lord Milner sought to clarify his position in a letter to Lyttelton,
dated April 18, 1904. An indiscriminate influx of Asiatics into the
Transvaal was a danger to plans for an immediate increase in the white

*This bubonic plague took place in March 1904 in the Indian section of Johannes-
burg. Mahatma Gandhi claimed that natives working in mines were responsible for
passing it on to the few Indians also working there. The latter brought it back to Johannesburg where an estimated one hundred Indians quickly succumbed. Gandhi was in-
strumental in moving the entire Indian population out to an open plain thirteen miles
distant and then setting fire to the location. *P.P.*, 1904, LXI, Cd. 2140, pp. 84-87, 1905,
LV, Cd. 2401, p. 107; Gandhi, *Autobiography* (1948), pp. 354-62.

population. The latter were most apt to be townsmen seeking business opportunities and Moslem traders would be too great a competition, as they were in Natal. Furthermore, British policy was to deal with the Transvaal as if it were self-governing and the vast majority of Europeans there disliked Asiatics. Admittedly, Great Britain would be placed in a position of embarrassment by the fact that the affected were British subjects from India. But he hoped that giving Asiatics of a superior class a special status and treating them virtually like Europeans might temper the edge of racism. Perhaps such a concession would induce the India Office to acquiesce in the virtual exclusion of the petty-trader class. Lord Milner proposed two measures to stabilize the situation: 1) an immigration law along the lines of an education test, as in Cape Colony and Natal, applying generally to all immigrants but administered to keep out Asiatics and 2) an ordinance assuring the status and privileges of legally domiciled Asiatics.[7]

The India Office manifested a sympathetic appreciation of the difficulties confronting Lyttelton and its views of a settlement were quite moderate. In the case of the proposed immigration law, an ability to read and write Indian languages should be placed on the same plane as European languages. No objection was voiced to the removal of lower-class Indians to locations on sanitary grounds save that the sites ought to be selected with care and not be too far removed from the designated bazaar area. Stress was laid on the desirability of having a central authority, rather than the more biased municipalities, exercise jurisdiction in selection of sites. But for the better class of Asiatic merchants both residences and businesses should be allowed outside the locations. An option should also be given Indian servants of the well-to-do to live with their masters. Finally, respectable Asiatic traders and shopkeepers should be exempt from the disabilities set up under municipal regulations which restricted access to footpaths, tramcars, and railway accommodations.[8]

During 1904, agitation flared up anew among colonial whites for additional anti-Asiatic legislation. For one thing, *Ordinance No. 5 of 1903* gave no authority to deport illegal Indian entrants. For a second thing, a decision of the Supreme Court in May 1904 affirmed that *Law No. 3 of 1885* applied only to restrictions on residence, thus allowing all Asiatic traders to conduct business in white shopping areas. Lord Milner informed the British Colonial Office that he was being subject to great pressure lest these weaknesses open the door to un-restricted Asiatic penetration. Lyttelton replied in two letters, on July 8 and July 20, stating his position. The British attitude had been to accept the arbitral award of 1895 that the South African Republic was within its right to treat the influx of British Indians as a domestic matter. At the same time friendly representations could be made in specific cases. If Great Britain would not withhold sanction to a measure curbing immigration (and a European language test should do the job), then it would insist upon the right of those legally domiciled to obtain licenses and to trade outside the bazaar. Again, if Indian locations for residence would be agreed to on sanitary grounds, the upper class should be free to dwell anywhere. Above all, legislation lumping natives and Asiatics together should cease.[9]

The suggestion of Lord Milner (and pursued by his successor, Lord Selborne) that a commission be appointed to study the troublesome matter of trading licenses was reviewed by the British Colonial Office staff. The stumbling blocks related to its composition, the suspension of new trading licenses in the interim, and the limited terms of reference. Influential personages from England and representatives from India, as well as men from the Transvaal, should be members. The objection to a temporary halt in receiving applications from Asiatic shopkeepers was that it surrendered the principle of no more disabil-ities for those legally domiciled. Just hoped that the scope of the commission would be widened to include all the aspects of the Indian problem. However, he was ready to grant that a settlement of the trading license controversy "might ease the situation of British Indians with regard to the rest of their disabilities." Ommanney saw a possible value in a commission as an instrument "to dispel ignorance and pre-judice in South Africa[;] our only hope seems to be to try and educate South African opinion not to legislate in a manner against the public sense of justice here." Lambert doubted the merit of a commission now: it "would have been better before we set our policy last year and it would have strengthened our hands." Perhaps the increase in Asiatic trading licenses had come to an end and matters could be left to "drift until the population forces our hands as it will no doubt do."[10]

Lyttelton weighed the possibility of safeguarding Indians through provisions in the proposed constitution for the Transvaal. He in-formed Lord Milner in a dispatch, dated March 15, 1905, that he had in mind extending the franchise "to such coloured British not of African birth who on grounds of education, profession, or trade are exempted from laws relating to passes." Lyttelton actually went so far as to include it in an early draft of the Transvaal constitution under section III (1). Lord Milner did not respond encouragingly, observing that it would be "a fresh slap in the face of the Cape Coloured people" who would, of course, be regarded as "natives" under the *Treaty of Vereeniging.* They were a class most deserving in every way and more likely to be of political use to South Africa. It would be better to include a statement in the Letters Patent leaving the door open for an ordinance by a future Transvaal legislature on behalf of both groups. What changed Lyttelton's mind was a talk in the meantime with Sir Richard Solomon, agent for the Transvaal in London. Thus, on March 21, 1905, Lyttelton announced his decision to omit any reference to the franchise for "coloured British not of African birth." It was not "desirable to incur the charge, however ill-founded, of an infraction of the Terms of Surrender, without securing to the persons in question any real benefit."[11]

Lord Selborne presented the case of the colonial whites most forcibly in a series of letters beginning in 1905 and climaxed by a lengthy one of twenty-three pages, dated May 21, 1906. What the British public should realize was that the Imperial State had a new set of responsibilities toward Europeans in the Transvaal. Previously they had been subjects of a foreign state and their sensibilities mattered little, but now they were British subjects and their views merited equal consideration with those of the British Indians. The charge, therefore, that Great Britain was going back on its pledges did not hold water. The fact that Asiatic immigrants were from the most unwarlike elements of the Indian nation would add to the military obligations of the home government. British troops would have to be imported to replace the dwindling numbers of colonial whites unable to meet the strangling competition of Asiatics. But if the aspirations of a white community were intended, then he would propose new certificates of registration not easily tampered with, an immigration act excluding Asiatics, and fair treatment along moderate lines for those legally domiciled.[12]

The British Colonial Office favorably received the recommendations of Lord Selborne. Perhaps the best analysis is that of Lambert:

Half a loaf is better than no bread. . . . To do nothing will mean worse measures later with an Elected Legislature. If we go beyond what we can do, we will find ourselves in conflict with practically the whole white population. Lyttelton asked for more than what is now advocated. He gave up the claim for the entry of Indians and this has to be done under any possible circumstances. But for those [domiciled] in the country [Lyttelton] claimed new legislation in place of the *Law of 1885*, preserving the right to trade outside locations, exemption to the superior class from residence in locations, and [the right] to acquire business premises and [relief] from municipal regulations. . . . Lyttelton's measure could never have been carried out—a howl already when proposed— and Selborne advises a similar measure in the interest of the Indians.

Churchill dissented, observing that "these South Africans wish only to exploit the other races of mankind, black, brown, or yellow." However, Lord Elgin agreed to let the proposals of Lord Selborne go before the Transvaal Legislative Council.[13]

The Transvaal government wasted no time, enacting in September the *Asiatic Law Amendment Ordinance No. 29 of 1906*. It called for a new registration procedure to stem the flow of illegal entrants. Henceforth the certificate of identification would include a photograph and a ten-digit fingerprint. In addition, particulars were to be given for children under eight and applications made out for future registration at sixteen of those over eight years of age. Only women were to be exempt from the measure. Legal domicile was defined as 1) possession of a permit taken out under *Ordinance No. 5 of 1903* or 2) proof of residence as of May 31, 1902. Lord Selborne strongly supported the measure, convinced that once the incubus of an overwhelming Indian population was erased, the white community would be prepared to review the disabilities of those legally domiciled. Reproaches upon the Imperial State for indulging a Crown colony in discriminatory legislation lacked perspective. While the moral obligation to British Indian subjects remained, the home government had no right to make any changes, such as free entry of Asiatics would constitute, until the white community became self-governing. To let the bars down now would be to present the Transvaal with a fait accompli.[14]

The British Indian population in the Transvaal denounced in no uncertain terms a measure imposing a fingerprint impression (usually reserved for criminals) and threatening their domiciliary rights. Mahatma Gandhi and H. O. Ally, a wealthy Moslem merchant, were dispatched to London to ask that assent be withheld. Lord Selborne forwarded petitions from Indian groups satisfied with the security afforded by the measure and stating that Gandhi did not represent a majority of their community. If Lord Elgin replied, assuring the High Commissioner that he saw no useful purpose likely to be served by the deputation, he felt bound to grant them an interview when they arrived. On the other hand, Ommanney urged that the ordinance should be disallowed and the matter left over for the new legislature. True, the Asiatic would "gain little by the postponement of the question," but at all events the Transvaal would not be able to argue the legislation of the Crown colony as a justification for an anti-Indian policy. Then, if a self-governing Transvaal re-enacted a measure disallowed by His Majesty's government, "we can at least say that we have a clear and unquestionable expression of the wishes of the Transvaal community and have not acted merely on the interested representations of the white shopkeepers." Churchill frowned upon the mission of the deputation, for it "will certainly stir up difficulties in the House of Commons." It would be better to leave an elected legislature to "shoulder the burden. . . . Dawdle or disallow—preferably the former."[15]

An interview took place on November 8, 1906, attended by several friends of the British Indians, with career backgrounds as Indian civil servants and members of Parliament.* Gandhi protested that the "Black Act" not only constituted a breach of Lord Milner's pledge in 1903 (of no more registration formalities) but imposed humiliating conditions upon British Indians. Undoubtedly, the unfavorable sentiment among the British Colonial Office staff and the cogency of his visitors' case had some influence in Lord Elgin's belated decision to disallow the measure. However, he explained his change of mind to Lord Selborne on November 29 on the ground that the ordinance

---

*Those present were Lord Stanley of Alderley, Dadabhai Naoroji, Sir Mancherjee Bhownaggree, Sir George Birdwood, Sir John David Rees, Harold Cox, Amir Ali, Thomas H. Thornton, Sir Lepel Griffin, and Sir Henry John Cotton. The deputation was also received by Lord Morley, Secretary of State for India, on November 22, 1906. For an account of the latter interview see *Journal of East India Association*, Apr. 1907, pp. 35-50.

differed considerably from the earlier drafts sent to him.[16] For one thing, the registration of Asiatics was altered from optional to compulsory and enforceable by severe penalties for refusal (£100 or three months' imprisonment). For a second thing, the magistrate had the power to expel persons, who were refused registration as unlawful residents, without right of appeal to the Supreme Court. Lord Selborne regretted the disallowance, observing that on the strength of his promise to get the measure sanctioned, he had persuaded "the Europeans to forego further agitation."[17]

The white community in the Transvaal were not to be denied, however, and awaited only the advent of responsible government to renew their intentions. Within the short space of twenty-four hours, on March 21, 1907, the opening day of the legislative session, the *Asiatic Amendment Act No. 2 of 1907*, carrying the same provisions as its predecessor, was passed through all the parliamentary stages by an unanimous vote in both houses. Lord Selborne asked for a quick approval by the British Colonial Office so that the alarming rate at which the illegal influx of Asiatics was proceeding could be halted. He cited a long list of specific cases uncovered and brought to trial, testifying to the traffic in the sale and forgery of permits, even to the point of bribing and corrupting the police. Lord Elgin reluctantly accepted the ordinance as the evident will of a self-governing colony.* But he put on record his view that the measure had not satisfactorily settled the position of British Indians. And he would expect that the disabilities to which legally domiciled Indians were subject would now be relaxed.[18]

A difference of opinion arose between the Secretary of State for the Colonies and the colonial governor over the fingerprint provision. Lord Selborne defended the device, quoting Edward Richard Henry, London Commissioner of Police, as to its use not only to apprehend criminals but also to prevent impersonations for collection of pensions and as a substitute for illiteracy in the courts.[19] Lord Elgin disagreed, pointing out that the type of fingerprint taken in India varied in the

---

*Gandhi accused Lord Elgin of deceit in disallowing the previous measure of 1906 and at the same time assuring Sir Richard Solomon that if an identical bill were introduced after the grant of responsible government the royal assent would not be refused. Gandhi does not state where he got his information and there is no mention of it in British Colonial Office dispatches. Gandhi (1954), pp. 124-26.

several instances. Both in the army and for pensioners it was an impression of the right-hand thumb and four fingers of the left hand. For registration of documents it was an impression of the left-hand thumb. The full ten-digit fingerprint was confined to criminals and this distinction carried some weight in India. When General Botha visited in London during May 1907, Lord Elgin urged upon him the adoption of other methods of identification which could not be regarded as degrading. It would go a long way to remove the impression that the Transvaal government was disposed to act harshly toward the domiciled Asiatics.[20]

The *Immigrant Restriction Act No. 15 of 1907* was a companion measure, designed to keep out future Asiatic immigrants. A European language dictation test constituted the principal instrument. At the same time, the definition of a prohibited immigrant (section 2, clause 4) was extended to include those failing to take out registration certificates and those previously refused permits. More protracted were the negotiations between the British Colonial Office and Lord Selborne over this bill, drawn up in August but not significated until December. The principal reason for the delay was a referral of the bill to the India Office for its views. Lord Morley gathered that the education test would be applied against Asiatics and that all British Indians, including even graduates of European universities and members of the learned professions, would be debarred. Equally grave were the possible injustices in store for British Indians previously domiciled but presently out of the country and hence unable to register. An unsympathetic administration of the definition of a prohibited immigrant could mean many cases of hardship.[21]

Despite the qualms of Lord Morley, the British Colonial Office could see no alternative but to accept the measure. The Imperial State had acknowledged the competence of the Transvaal by the grant of self-government and immigration legislation had been enacted in other self-governing colonies. His Majesty's government, having approved *Act No. 2 of 1907*, could hardly resist a provision in *Act No. 15 of 1907*, the object of which was to enforce the deportation of illegal entrants. True, it was not pleasant to envisage imprisonment or expulsion meted out to those coming under the definition of a prohibited immigrant. But Vernon argued that there could be no picking or choosing among the clauses of the bill. To ask for amendments would provoke a bitter controversy. And it did seem reasonable to assume that all bona fide prewar Asiatic residents ought to have returned by this time. The proper defense for sanctioning this measure should be to say that efforts henceforth would be to ameliorate the lot of those legally domiciled. What served to reconcile an unhappy India Office to this statement of policy was an assurance that distinguished Indian visitors would be granted temporary permits.[22]

The British Colonial Office did not ignore a similar pattern of anti-Asiatic legislation in Cape Colony. The passage of *Immigration Act No. 47 of 1902* brought further protests of discrimination. The emphasis upon a European language test but with an express exemption for illiterate Europeans able to produce a certificate of engagement as agricultural or domestic servants rubbed salt into the wound. Assent was given only on the understanding that the measure would be liberally interpreted with regard to the better class of Asiatics and that amendments would be enacted to make it less offensive to Asiatics. Not until 1906, after frequent proddings, did Cape Colony pass an amended measure but hardly meeting the spirit of its pledge. The word European remained in the dictation test, Yiddish was added as an acceptable European language, and a period of three years' residence specified for proof of domicile. All it conceded was an opportunity for Asiatics to obtain a permit to be temporarily absent from the country without being subject to an education test upon their return. What prompted Lord Elgin to acquiesce again was the realization that the agitated mood of the white inhabitants would brook no retreat. The Cape ministry actually had had to resist an amendment to exclude all Asiatic immigrants.[23]

Particularly worrisome was the effort in the Cape to reduce the number of Asiatic trading licenses. In March 1905 a general dealers' license bill had been read for a second time, specifying as a factor for renewal an ability to keep accounts in a European language. The justification advanced was that in cases of insolvency the absence of such legible data made a trying situation for courts. On this occasion the British Colonial Office obtained the withdrawal of the bill even though the Cape would have agreed to consider the employment of a clerk versed in English as fulfilling the requirement of proper business records. Less objectionable was *Act No. 35 of 1906*, guaranteeing a vested interest in existing licenses, reserving only the grant of new licenses to municipal officers, and requiring a two-thirds vote for a rejection. The subsequent administration of the act left much to be desired. Complaints were noted of specious reasons being entered to militate against the grant of licenses to Asiatics. Their shops lacked ventilation. The drainage was bad. Sleeping quarters were too close to the business area. But no interference was possible "with the discretion of the Cape town councils, however much the abuse of withholding licenses."[24]

The story in Natal consisted of tightening up laws against an Indian population already equal in numbers to the whites. Act No. 30 of 1903 established a more stringent European language test, required a continuous residence of three years for domicile (exclusive of any indentured period), and imposed a ceiling of sixteen years of age for those seeking to join their families. Act No. 3 of 1906 set limits to the rights of those previously domiciled and their families returning from a visit abroad to enter without an education test. Hostile municipal officials put all kinds of obstacles in the way of renewing trading licenses and awarding new ones to Asiatics. Increased pressure was put upon the ex-indentured to depart through a measure in 1903 extending the £3 annual residence tax to their wives, sons over sixteen years of age, and daughters over thirteen years of age. Negotiations were attempted with the Indian government to have the indentured coolies automatically repatriated to India at the termination of their contracts. These plans collapsed because Natal refused to concede unlimited rights of admission to free immigrants and a sweeping grant of trading licenses. Natal ministers explained that the prospect of ten thousand "Arab" traders would be a matter of grave import and too great a price to pay.[25]

The British Colonial Office made its stand on the issue of trading licenses. Lambert averred that "Natal should know we have our backs up to the wall." If it were argued that the Cape got its way, the grievance there "is not as yet of long standing and [its] Government is at least sympathetic." If it were argued that the Transvaal got its way, the British Indians "have no case and must be thrown over in their fresh difficulties—the sooner the better so they know they have to come to an agreement with Smuts." Admittedly, the statistics on trading licenses showed that the Asiatics were pressing uncomfortably on the Europeans. In 1906 it was 1,226 Asiatic traders (plus a horde of

hawkers) against 2,252 European traders. However, the threat to take
away their licenses would leave them without the means of a livelihood. An effort to salvage the situation was made when Natal sought
permission to disfranchise Indian taxpayers not on the municipal voting rolls and to reduce the number of women accompanying the
indentured coolies from 40 per cent to 33 per cent. Lord Elgin attached, as conditions, a recognition of existing licenses and the right
of appeal to the Supreme Court. Not only did Natal refuse the *quid
pro quo* offer but proposed legislation 1) to end the grant of new
trading licenses to Asiatics after December 31, 1908 and 2) to revoke
all existing licenses to Asiatics after December 31, 1918. As a grim
epitaph in denying assent, Lambert wrote that "they must learn to
tolerate the scruples of Downing Street as long as they legislate on the
present lines."[26]

Lord Morley suggested in December 1908 that further shipments of
indentured coolies to Natal be terminated. That would eliminate the
constant demand for free immigrants from India to provide the necessary professional services and perhaps lessen the antipathy to those
domiciled. The current humiliations visited upon British Indians in
South Africa gave agitators in India ammunition to preach sedition
and to multiply the difficulties of the Viceroy's government. What
worried Lord Crewe, now Secretary of State for the Colonies, was the
possible effect such an announcement would have upon the prospects
of the federation movement in Natal if the latter resented the threat
to its sugar industry. The passage of two measures in 1909, granting
the right of appeal to the Supreme Court in the case of existing
licenses and relaxing the payment of the £3 annual residence tax for
women on grounds of ill health or old age, eased the situation. Lord
Morley announced that the Indian government would postpone its
proposed action, first set for June 30, 1909, until the close of 1910,
pending an appraisal of the intentions of the Union of South Africa.
However, with the concurrence of Lord Crewe, the India Office sanctioned a resolution adopted on February 25, 1910, by the Viceroy's
Legislative Council to the effect "that the Governor-in-council should
be empowered to prohibit the recruitment of indentured labour in
British India for the colony of Natal."[27] That should put meaning
into the determination of the Indian government to apply pressure
upon South Africa.[28]

STALEMATE

The Transvaal provided the locale for a concentrated effort by the British Indians to seek an equitable settlement just as it had for the pattern of anti-Asiatic legislation. The prospective enactment of an objectionable immigration law and the approaching date of November 30, 1907, fixed for the humiliating registration procedure, brought matters to a head. In September Gandhi launched the strategy which he called *satyagraha* or soul-force and which later was to become the chief feature of the nationalist movement in India. He would have his followers rely upon noncooperation and nonviolence to establish the righteousness of their case. They were to refuse the compulsory ten-digit impression and to accept arrest and imprisonment without rancor or resistance. Only five hundred British Indians took out certificates and an overflowing prison population faced the Transvaal government. Gandhi himself invited arrest and was sentenced to a two months' term of imprisonment. General Smuts hastened to assure the British Colonial Office that he would exercise the power of expulsion with the greatest caution. However, there would be no further concessions which might be interpreted as a sign of weakness. Already Gandhi was emboldened to demand the repeal of *Act No. 2 of 1907* in its entirety.[29]

Lord Elgin believed that the substitution of a thumb impression for the more offensive ten-digit requirement could be the basis of a compromise. Lord Selborne explained the objection of his ministers on the ground that the courts often rejected it as insufficient proof. Thumb marks could be rendered illegible by tricks of superimposition of other imprints. Such had been the experience under *Ordinance No. 5 of 1903.* In the meanwhile every effort was being made to avoid deportations, although the ringleaders had to be prosecuted as an example. Nor should the fact be overlooked that the natives watched closely to see if a small number of Asiatics could defy the Transvaal government. In the end, relief came from a realization on the part of General Smuts that the passive resistance campaign drew the support of most British Indians. He had sent every leader and hundreds more to prison. It was a physical impossibility to contemplate an estimated 10,000 Asiatics locked up. Furthermore, the damage to the reputation and prestige of the Transvaal would be highly undesirable.[30]

Accordingly, General Smuts sought out Gandhi and effected a modus vivendi with him on January 29, 1908. The ten-digit impression with the option of a two-thumb mark would be retained but on the basis of voluntary registration plus an opportunity for those educated, owning property, or possessed of public character to substitute a signature. These several alternatives would also be applicable for those entitled to enter the Transvaal by reason of previous residence and who had not yet returned. Nor would any information be demanded regarding relatives and wives, a subject which Indian social mores looked upon as a matter of privacy. Gandhi did not avail himself of the concessions to amour propre, announcing that he would submit to the fingerprint impression along with lower-class Indians as an act of brotherhood. This seemingly noble gesture infuriated the conscious-proud Parsees (descendants of Persian refugees and followers of the Zoroastrian religion who settled in Bombay) and they assailed him severely enough on February 10 to require hospitalization. But the passive resistance campaign was terminated and the statistics showed 7,010 fingerprinted, 1,960 given a two-thumb impression, and 70 registered by signature.[31]

If Lord Elgin heaved a great sigh of relief over the apparent break in the stalemate, he believed that the trying situation need not have happened.The Transvaal should have better informed itself on the insulting nature of a ten-digit impression to British Indians. There was no reason why the several alternatives included in the compromise could not have been offered at the beginning. Lord Morley informed him of his satisfaction at the registration issue having been settled but emphasized that such episodes provoked great agitation in India and made British administration there unpopular. The Transvaal should be persuaded to recognize the importance of removing the conception in India that their countrymen in South Africa were exposed to harsh treatment and that His Majesty's government was unable to protect them. In this instance Lord Elgin defended the Transvaal "as showing every desire to do justice to the difficult position in which Great Britain was placed." Nor was the British Colonial Office indifferent to the disabilities of Asiatics, but the governing factor must necessarily be the state of public opinion in the colony. And at the present time it would be useless to press for further concessions to resident British Indians.[32]

An end to the conflict was not, however, in sight. Recriminations were exchanged between General Smuts and Gandhi over the nature of the legislation to accompany the validation of the voluntary registration. In February 1908, Gandhi prepared a series of suggestions which he claimed were implied on the occasion of the compromise. The repeal of *Act No. 2 of 1907* would follow the completion of voluntary registration. An indefinite time extension would be accorded British Indians previously resident but not yet returned to enter without an education test. For free Asiatic immigrants there would be an unlimited right of admission on the basis of the education test. General Smuts rejected these demands and denied that he had ever made such promises. *Act No. 2 of 1907* was needed to check the continued influx of illegal Indian entrants who sought to establish domicile by all sorts of flimsy proofs. To extend the three months' period of grace beyond May 1908 for voluntary registration would confront the colony with a perpetual succession of domiciliary cases. As for opening the door to all Asiatic immigrants who could pass the education test, that would defeat the aspiration of the Transvaal for a white community. Where truth lies in the conflicting versions of the two men is a matter of conjecture. Perhaps neither was untruthful, each stretching the realms of wishful thinking as to what should be the state of finality.[33]

General Smuts proceeded to legislate unilaterally. He pushed through *Act No. 36 of 1908* in August to validate the voluntary registration undertaken by over 9,000 British Indians. He included a number of concessions in the hope that Gandhi might yet be reconciled. He added one year of grace for previously domiciled Indians not yet back from abroad on proof of continuous residence for three years prior to 1899. He provided a right of appeal to the Supreme Court for those denied domicile. He promised that temporary permits by executive action would be granted for a few educated Asiatics to enter. The British Colonial Office regarded these provisions as a very generous settlement and would give public approval in order to convince the British Indians of the futility of further agitation. While the India Office declared itself prepared to do likewise, it feared that insistence on continuous residence for three years prior to 1899 and adherence to the policy of no more Asiatic immigration would not quiet the resentment in India.[34]

Gandhi pronounced the new measure to fall short of justice for British Indians in the Transvaal. He called upon his followers to destroy the certificates taken out under voluntary registration. At a gathering convened on the grounds of the Hamidia Mosque in Johannesburg, on August 16, 1908, over two thousand threw their guarantees of domicile into blazing fires lit in two immense cauldrons. Once more *satyagraha* was invoked and acts of nonviolence were committed. Gandhi personally led a group across the Natal border into the Transvaal to invite arrest for illegal entry. The entire band of seventy-five were taken into custody and given sentences for failing to produce identification papers and contravening *Act No. 36 of 1908*. Gandhi served his second sentence at Pretoria Gaol, on this occasion for three months. Breaches of law mounted and large numbers of British Indians were thrown into prison and required to do hard labor. Those who could not establish domicile were deported, ultimately an estimated three hundred.[35]

Lord Crewe was sorely distressed by the new turn of events. He believed that General Smuts had acted in good faith. All those meriting domicile had been covered and for others an opportunity afforded to appeal. He refused to admit the validity of Gandhi's claim that the repeal of *Act No. 2 of 1907* and unlimited entry for educated Indians had been implied. The position of the Imperial State was to acquiesce in no more immigration but to seek fair treatment for resident Indians. Any other course had no chance of acceptance until public opinion in the Transvaal had undergone a change. However, Lord Crewe, after consultation with the India Office, agreed to urge a compromise upon General Botha. Two concessions were sought: 1) considerate treatment of those possessed of prewar domiciliary rights but not in the Transvaal continuously for three years and 2) the annual admission of six educated Asiatics to replenish the needed professional services. Such an arrangement would strengthen the hands of Great Britain in dealing with public opinion at home and in India. General Botha was agreeable provided that the six educated Asiatics came in on temporary permits and that a strict immigration exclusion policy be accepted. Gandhi rejected the terms as inconsistent with human dignity.[36]

The British Colonial Office did what it could to ameliorate the condition of those imprisoned for defiance of the registration and immigration laws. The aversion of Indians to nakedness in the presence of others should be recognized while being fitted for prison clothes or subject to medical inspection. A protest was registered against the unsuitability of mealie meal for a people accustomed to a rice diet. It showed a callous indifference toward Moslem religious scruples to mix porridge with animal fat. Lord Crewe commented that "if the Chief Rabbi had to go to Holloway [London prison] we should not diet him on ham sandwiches." The supply of ghee (clarified buffalo milk) was regarded as unsatisfactory, being served only to those in prison more than three months and then thrice weekly. Lord Crewe was quite incensed over high-caste Hindus being put to work cleaning water closets and carrying out slop. That was religious defilement and surely disciplinary measures in the jails did not have to go to that length. He assured the India Office that he "has no patience with the crass stupidity of the Transvaal Government in these matters and a formal complaint should be made every time they transgress so that they may at any rate know what we think of them."[37]

Lord Morley disclosed the obstacles put in the way of Moslem prisoners to observe the fast of Ramadan. This was the ninth month in the Moslem year and required rigid adherence for thirty days during the hours between dawn and dusk. But the Transvaal prison authorities refused to provide night meals, asserting that they did not have the staff for this extra burden. Lord Crewe gathered that practices in Indian jails varied, Punjab alone acknowledging an obligation to meet the needs of Moslem prisoners during Ramadan. Cape Colony had many more Moslems and made no special arrangements. Indeed, he understood it was possible for a prisoner to delay compliance with Ramadan until his sentence had been served. Lord Morley advised that no alternative existed and the resentment of Moslems in India was intense. However, before Lord Crewe could pursue the subject further the month of Ramadan had passed and the question ceased to be a practical one.[38]

Accounts of harsh treatment were checked closely.* The testimony

---

*Only the reputed indignities to Mahatma Gandhi drew doubts coupled with the charge that the purpose was to arouse public sympathy. Lambert commented that "it is his friends and not he who makes the claims." The image of Gandhi being taken on foot to prison (even though his habits would suggest a preference for walking) and put to hard labor on the streets would serve that end. P.R.O., c.o. 291/129, 136.

of Parsee Rustomjee, wealthy philanthropist, was revolting. He had
been handcuffed and his leg heavily bound to that of another prisoner. His physical ailments were ignored and he suffered much when
compelled to work. The cells were reported to be filthy and lacked
facilities for washing and for privacy to change clothes. No effort was
made to separate young from old, or *satyagrahis* from hardened criminals. Manilal Gandhi, seventeen years of age and a son of the leader,
had been kept with the worst Chinese criminals during his term of ten
days. The language of the jailers was rough and insulting. Indians
were addressed as coolies or "sammies" in derision of the many Indian
names ending thus, for example, Veerasammy. Apparently the aim
was to break the spirit and resolution of the passive resisters.[39]

Most troublesome of all was the resort to deportation by the Transvaal. An arrangement with the Portuguese East African authorities
had the latter seize those expelled as the trains crossed the frontier
and place them on ships bound for India. There was little the British Colonial Office could do to halt the practice. The Portuguese governor had issued a decree on July 15, 1909, declaring "that
all Asiatics entering by land without a permit to reside there or in
neighboring colonies must leave by the first boat." Further inquiry
disclosed that the negotiations had been completed by Arthur Tilney
Long, agent for the Transvaal at Lourenço Marques, in the absence
of Reginald Charles Fulke Maugham, British Consul-General. This
led Lambert to observe that "a British colony has therefore in fact
successfully arranged with a foreign colony, in part through a consular
officer, for the expulsion of British subjects." The Foreign Office was
acquainted with the facts and dispatched a note to the Union government through the British Colonial Office, stating curtly that the
British Consul-General at Lourenço Marques "is always to be kept informed by Transvaal Agents of any question touching the interests of
British subjects beyond the Transvaal so that Imperial interests are
sufficiently safeguarded."[40]

What opened the door to representations were charges by the India
Office that domiciled British Indians were being deported with no
right of appeal allowed. Nor did the accounts of their families being
left destitute go unnoticed in India where public demonstrations of
protest were growing in intensity. The British Colonial Office had
Lord Selborne inform his ministers that those domiciled in the Trans-

vaal could not be expelled and those domiciled in other South African colonies could only be sent back to their residence of origin. Specific cases of deportees who had voluntarily registered for certificates in the Transvaal were cited as proof. Similarly, the fact that the Portuguese bylaw of July 15, 1909 violated a decree of December 1907 assuring British subjects of thirty days to appeal an expulsion should have been respected by the Transvaal. Hopwood advised "a grumbling dispatch. We ought always to put on record our complaints. The self-governing Dominions never spare us." Lord Crewe agreed.[41]

PUBLIC FORUM

While Liberals and Labourites were in the van of those defending the rights of British Indian subjects in South Africa, the array of champions tended to cross party lines. Many Indian civil servants with no particular political affiliations cooperated closely. In the House of Lords, the second Baron Ampthill, a former Governor of Madras, and other peers dropped their Conservative predilections on the issue. Apart from respect for the principal of human dignity and distress over man's inhumanity to man, the retention of India and the very existence of the Empire were involved. All these assorted bedfellows joined hands to form the South African British Indian Committee. This body was organized in 1906 as a result of the visit of Gandhi and Ally in November to protest *Ordinance No. 29 of 1906* and its fingerprinting procedures. Lord Ampthill was named president and Lewis Walter Ritch, once articled to Gandhi for professional services but now in London studying for the bar, became its secretary.[42]

The Imperial State merited reproach for failing to take a strong stand. As a conquered territory the Transvaal should not have been allowed to continue the harassment of British subjects. The *New Age* saw no reason to commend even the exemptions bestowed upon the more affluent Asiatics to trade and reside elsewhere than in locations. If that meant humbler folk were to remain as pariahs, then there could be no gratitude for a generosity coupled with the invidious distinction of class legislation. The revival of *Law No. 3 of 1885* squared ill with the complaints lodged against the Kruger regime. It was now history that the latter's anti-Indian measures were an important factor in the casus belli against the Boers. One need only recall the famous

speech of Lord Lansdowne at Sheffield on November 2, 1899, when
he said that "amongst the many misdeeds of the South African Republic, I do not know that any fills me with more indignation than its
treatment of these Indians." Yet whereas Kruger had never enforced
his laws to the point of aggravation, the Transvaal Crown colony pursued a heartless course. If Kruger were said to have chastised them
with a whip, Lord Milner used a scorpion. Great Britain must speak
out on this shameful episode transpiring under the Union Jack.[43]

Ritch, who described himself as an Englishman, a Jew, and a South
African colonist of seventeen years, was in the forefront of those
denouncing the two retrogressive measures of 1907. The British
nation needed to be fully apprised of the mortifying details of *Act No.
2 of 1907.* The registration procedure called for an impression of all
ten digits and the possession of a certificate carrying this and other
information on one's person to be produced on the demand of a
constable. It should be remembered that in India a ten-digit impression was applied only to criminals. *Act No. 15 of 1907* had equal
humiliation in store, specifying an education test in European languages with the frank intent to exclude Asiatics. And such as were admitted by reason of previous domicile would have to comply with the
registration procedure involving a fingerprint impression. It was most
enlightening to note that all other Asiatics were lumped together with
illiterates, paupers, and criminals as prohibited immigrants.[44]

Sir Charles Bruce, whose service as Governor of Mauritius had
given him an appreciation of the Indian coolie as a worker, joined
Lord Ampthill and Ritch to offer a sympathetic interpretation of the
events of 1908. As they sifted the accounts of the negotiations between General Smuts and Gandhi during January, the inference of a
repeal of *Act No. 2 of 1907* did seem warranted. Gandhi had fulfilled
his part of the bargain, persuading over 9,000 to register voluntarily.
Nor was the concession (under *Act No. 36 of 1908*) of an additional
year of grace for previously domiciled Indians not yet returned devoid
of embarrassment. A definite time limit for voluntary registration
meant a compulsory procedure after that date with strict adherence to
fingerprinting. As for the grant of temporary permits to six professional men, that qualification suggested the likelihood at any moment
of a sudden withdrawal of the right to replenish the technical skills

necessary to the existence of resident Indians—priests, doctors, teachers, clerks.[45]

What British Indians asked above all was the symbol of brotherhood and being stamped as undesirables rankled deeply. Their community in South Africa would even accept no more Asiatic immigration if it were done administratively and with the understanding that a few educated Indians would be allowed in on a permanent basis. But the indispensable condition must be an end to disabilities for those domiciled. General Smuts was guilty of sharp dealing if the report of an interview with a *Johannesburg Star* correspondent on February 5, 1908 were true.[46] The statement attributed to him was that once the voluntary registration took place he would be in a position to prevent any further Asiatic immigration. And since few Indians had their wives in the country, their population would decrease and in twenty years there would be no Asiatic question. Evidently the corollary strategy was to accelerate the process by a squeeze on the availability of professional people and by making life intolerable for those domiciled. To interpolate, if this were General Smuts' intention, he would appear to have been overly optimistic; for, according to the *Census of 1904*, if the female population in the Transvaal amounted to only 1,522, the number in Natal was an impressive 37,421.[47]

While the passive resistance campaign was disliked, the British Indians could do little else, lacking legitimate channels for protest. It was the only course open to a self-respecting minority desirous of defending themselves on ethical lines. To suffer in one's own person until the conscience of the tormentor awakened to a proper sense of duty constituted a dignified answer. In the light of such genteel conduct the severe sentences of imprisonment with hard labor and expulsion seemed excessive. These were vindictive actions against fellow subjects who possessed a legal right of domicile and whose only offense had been not to take out "ticket-of-leave" passes by which the law branded them as pariahs. Before the derogatory certification procedures were invoked they had been exemplary law-abiding residents. Men of the highest cultural attainment were included in those condemned. Some had served on military fronts in the defense of British interests.[48] They had been garrisoned to Malta and Cyprus. They had fought in Egypt and the Sudan. Yet today neither the King's coat nor war medals could save these ex-soldiers from being treated as felons.[49]

Lord Ampthill denounced the trickery connected with the deportations. He described how Indians were beguiled out of the Transvaal by administrative manipulation. Registration papers were asked to be shown although the constabulary knew that they had been destroyed. Then the deportees were put on board a train and dumped across the border forty miles away in Portuguese territory. "Liberation" consisted of being taken into custody by the Portuguese authorities as undesirable aliens and shipped across the ocean to India at the expense of the Transvaal. It was "unprecedented in the annals of the Empire that British subjects should be handed over for punishment to a Foreign Government." Many of the three hundred deported (perhaps one-third) were born in South Africa, attested to by the fact that shipping companies could not land them elsewhere. Ritch noted the havoc wrought by the persecution, reducing the Asiatic population in the Transvaal from 13,000 to 7,000.* The repressive measures were slowly but surely achieving the sinister goal of eliminating all Indians.[50]

Great Britain had a moral responsibility to make its influence felt. It had sanctioned the importation of indentured Indian coolies into Natal, inviting one race to be cheapened in the eyes of another. President Theodore Roosevelt had minced no words in declaring his intention to employ all the forces of the United States to secure justice for resident Japanese in San Francisco where their businesses were being boycotted and their children excluded from schools.** Lord Ampthill lamented the refusal of the home government to raise the issue of citizenship in the British Empire at the Imperial Conference held in 1907. Despite the risk of arousing colonial sensibilities, the stake of racial harmony should have made the effort worth it. Lord Elgin replied that the uncompromising debate between (Sir) William Lyne,

---

*The British Colonial Office challenged Ritch's figure of 7,000 left, obtaining a different set of calculations from Lord Selborne. There were over 8,000 (correctly, 9,158) British Indians registered under the acts of 1907 and 1908. Then there should be added at least 4,000 minors whose registration could not be effected until they were sixteen years of age. Finally, there could be reckoned 2,000 more adult Indians unaccounted for and who had no claim to registration. P.P., 1908, LXXIII, Cd. 4327, p. 35, 1910 LXVI, Cd. 5363, p. 65; P.R.O., c.o. 291/141, 145, c.o. 551/2.

**Roosevelt uttered his statement in a message to Congress on December 18, 1906. Fifty-Ninth Congress, 2nd Session, Document No. 142, Senate, p. 2.

Australian delegate, and Sir James Mackay of the India Office over the relative wages paid Australian and Indian sailors should be a sufficient answer.[51] It was playing with fire to invite a debate on racial matters at an imperial conference.[52]

Lord Elgin was taken to task for his failure to implement Article 39(a) of the Transvaal constitution requiring the governor to reserve any bill subjecting non-Europeans to any disability or restriction to which Europeans were not subjected. Surely, declared Bruce, this power of veto had been inserted with an eye to what had happened in the past and was meant to be used. How could Lord Elgin excuse his inaction on the ground that the Transvaal had received self-government? Harold Cox, Liberal M.P. and onetime mathematics instructor at an Indian college, gathered that registration was quite unnecessary for purposes of identification in the case of a very large number of Indian residents. Many had lived in the Transvaal for fifteen years or more and were known to everybody. Their signature or word of mouth was worth thousands of pounds. Yet they must have their fingers imprinted on official paper and keep a permit on their persons "as a dog in England is compelled to carry a collar." Lord Elgin knew that the British Indians had solemnly declared to accept imprisonment and ruin rather than to submit to such degradation. He was "under the constitution of the Transvaal framed by himself, their sole protector, and yet he sanctioned this Act, and . . . at a moment when the Transvaal Government, so far from being able to resist our legitimate demands, was begging for our bounty in the shape of a guaranteed loan."[53]

Dr. Vickerman Henzell Rutherford, Liberal M.P. and practising physician, joined Lord Ampthill and Ritch to focus attention upon the equally reprehensible conduct of Natal. That colony appeared to have been emboldened in its arrogant course by the spectacle of the Transvaal whites riding roughshod under the status of a Crown colony. The list of disabilities mounted by the year. Separate compartments in lower-class accommodations was their lot on the railways. No matter what the weather, in tramcars they had to stand on the open backboard. The *Immigration Act No. 30 of 1903*, emphasizing a dictation test in a European language, was administered to keep out Asiatic applicants. The period of residence required for domiciliary certificates had been lengthened from two to three years. The age at which children had the right to join their parents was reduced from twenty-one to sixteen, proof being required afterwards. Most recently a proposal had been made to deny Asiatics the municipal franchise. While to withhold the vote for colonial elections might be defended on the specious ground that Indians did not possess comparable representative institutions, the same could not be said of municipalities in India.[54]

The attack upon Indian trading licenses had become particularly vexing. Asiatic shopkeepers of twenty and thirty years standing were denied permits on the flimsiest pretexts. One of the cheapest tricks was to trap an Indian dealer into breaking the law against Sunday sales by planting a customer "desperately" in need of a few items to tide him over the Sabbath. Most perilous to their existence were measures proposed to entirely eliminate the Asiatics as traders. One bill called for no more new trading licenses to Asiatics. A second bill called for an end to all licenses held by Asiatics on December 31, 1918, albeit some compensation would be awarded. It was a great relief to know that in this instance Lord Elgin had put his foot down. Moreover, comfort could be taken for the future from his explanation given in the House of Lords for refusing assent. The statement included the sentiment that

> the imposition of such disabilities on a class which owes its presence in the Colony to the Colony's own necessities and whose numbers have been augmented by the voluntary action, and indeed the continuous action, of successive Colonial Governments over a period of fifteen years since the advent of self-government [1893], would appear to constitute a hardship of a particularly grievous character.[55]

Sir William Wedderburn, Judge of the High Court of Bombay and a past Liberal M.P., along with Cox and Ritch, identified the white shopkeeper as the evil genius behind the oppression of the British Indian. This narrow-minded and parochial European possessor of the vote used the political lever to crush an inconvenient rival. In diabolical fashion he brought into play the fires of racial prejudice, already glowing brightly against the black man. The heinous crime of the Asiatic hawker was to keep prices down and treat his customers with courtesy. Nor did the Indian achieve his advantage by living in foul surroundings. Ritch recalled his visits to the homes of Indian and Moslem merchants and their high standards of comfort and hospitality. There was nothing to warrant the accusation that "they live on the smell of an oil-rag." Certainly, data in the *Census of 1904* for the Transvaal did not justify the complaint that Asiatics were crowding fields of employment normally performed by whites. A sampling of Europeans and non-Europeans (Asiatics and natives) respectively in trades would show that fact: masons (2,192 and 105); carpenters (5,197 and 180); painters (2,659 and 98); tailors (950 and 150); market gardeners and florists (717 and 185); shoemakers (498 and 63).[56] The only possible test in the survival of a business was the classical yardsticks of price and service.[57]

Harold Cox reviewed the significance of the Asiatic as an economic factor in the Transvaal. With the exception of a few skilled white miners virtually the whole of the working-class population was black or Asiatic. Instead of competing with the white earner as in Australia, the British Indian assisted him as an unskilled worker. In the case of trade, the willingness of the Asiatic shopkeeper to accept a narrower margin of profit meant that the hard-pressed laborers could buy their everyday necessities at prices within the range of their limited wages. For that matter, South African whites could not reserve forever a part of the earth's surface where the tropical climate militated against European settlement. Cox quoted a letter from an Englishman, who had for twenty years adopted Australia as his home, on the disastrous effect of such a policy there:

In the northern territory of South Australia—comprising 523,000 square miles and containing enormous potential resources within the tropical area—there are only about 800 whites, who are being slowly killed off by a climate for which they are not dermically equipped by nature. For about half a century ignorant white adventurers, who fail to distinguish latitudes suitable for whites from those which are unsuitable, have essayed to live and work in the open field in the tropics, with the invariable result that they have grown anaemic, and fallen a prey to tropical diseases. The result of this dog-in-the-manger policy—of being unable as whites to withstand the evil climatic influence of the tropics while banging the door in the face of coloured labour—is that nearly three-fourths of Australia, one of the most magnificent countries in the world, remains a waste howling wilderness.[58]

The contributions of Indian subjects to the Empire were recalled. The initial impetus to the economic life of Natal could be attributed to the work of indentured Indian coolies. They made possible the vast array of sugar plantations in a heat-belt zone where whites could not work and Zulus would not work. Later, as ex-indentured cultivators, they had given Natal its current distinction as a "garden city." Both during the Boer War and the Bambata uprising, British Indians had organized a hospital and stretcher-bearer corps to succor the suffering.[59] Over two score of the thousand who signed up to follow the British forces in the Boer War were awarded war medals.* Over two score were engaged in nursing wounded Zulus whom the whites would not touch during the Natal campaign against Bambata. After the abolition of slavery in the West Indies (1833), Indian coolie labor had prevented many of the islands from going out of cultivation and perhaps being ceded to the United States. If that had happened, the Caribbean would have become a sphere of American influence. A similar role had been enacted in Mauritius where Indians had saved the sugar plantations and perhaps forestalled the entire island from reverting to French control. If that had happened, the Indian Ocean would have become a sphere of French influence. The saga of Indian subjects in the British Empire had been an honorable one.[60]

A plea was entered to consider the disastrous effect which the maltreatment of British Indians in South Africa produced in India. References were frequent to a great demonstration held at Bombay decrying the plight of passive resisters. Agha Khan, Moslem religious leader, presided at the gathering and the participants included Hindus, Moslems, and Parsees.[61] It would be the beginning of the end for the Empire if India should become an unwilling and refractory partner. An intransigent India could properly ask whether imperial responsibilities begot imperial rights when its military forces were summoned to

*An obelisk has been erected by public subscription gratefully acknowledging the role of British Indians in the Boer War. It is located on a lofty eminence looking toward Pretoria to the north and the Bezuidenhout Valley to the south.

serve in the protection of the several dominions overseas. Was it not worth confirming in the minds of the people of India the noble sentiment of an empire established by their aid and to be preserved by their loyalty? Bruce recalled the proclamation of Queen Victoria in 1858 on the assumption by Great Britain of political control from the hands of the East India Company.[62] The Indian people were promised relief from all disabilities by reason of creed and race, an acknowledgment that theirs was not a barbarous but an honorable and venerable civilization.[63]

Membership in the Empire implied a common citizenship. Allegiance to the Union Jack should confer upon all the right to emigrate and to trade on equal terms in every part. Imperial comradeship ought not to be doled out in proportion to the whiteness of skin. If one segment of the King's subjects could not freely enter, work, vote, or acquire land in territories over which the symbol of the Crown prevailed, then the great Roman example of a uniform status which overrode other distinctions would be cast aside. The *Tribune* reproached Canada and Australia as well as South Africa for their indifference to the sensibilities of fellow British Indian subjects. All enjoyed an armed protection absorbing two-thirds of the annual imperial budget and the least they could do was to make an effort to conduct their affairs so as not to endanger the imperial fabric. It behooved the home government to collect facts and opinions and to hold an ad hoc conference on the subject of racial discrimination. Unless the question were given immediate attention, it would become insoluble and the Empire would be rent asunder.[64]

Conservatives gave the case against the British Indians a sympathetic hearing in home circles. The *Pall Mall Gazette* presented the measured views of two men on the spot as to the challenge posed by Asiatics. Douglas Blackburn, an expert in cipher codes, noted that in Natal the cost of living was 6s. per day for a white and 1s. per day for an Asiatic. An Asiatic trader's place of business was usually a shoddy corrugated-metal building just off the refined shopping area and open at all hours. Naturally, with less overhead and a lower standard of living, he could afford to sell his wares cheaper. No intelligent community could carry the fetish of low prices so far as to allow an inferior to replace a superior civilization. Lawrence Elwin Neame, Johannesburg journalist, traced the extent of the havoc already wrought. The score in Natal for agriculture stood at 32,436 Indians engaged as against 7,346 Europeans.[65] The score in Johannesburg for Asiatic general dealers' licenses in 1903 stood at 397 out of 3,418 or 11.61 per cent and in 1904 at 535 out of 3,799 or 14.13 per cent.[66] If this trend continued the stake of a white South Africa would be in the balance.[67]

An interesting analysis of the economic aspect is offered by Mrs. Mabel Anne St. Clair Stobart who described herself as having spent three years in the Transvaal. After the Boer War, Lord Milner had granted her husband six thousand acres of land on the veldt. In addition to farming they had run a store catering to natives. If this new offspring, she wrote, was ever to be a sound British colony, it must be possessed of the basic population elements. The third-class layer of unskilled whites had been checked by the use of Chinese coolies on the Rand. Whether a middle class too would be frustrated depended on the containment of the Indian shopkeeper. The rural white trade usually meant Boer customers and that involved long-term credit and often payments in kind. It was the native patronage that provided a cash income. The Indian undersold the white merchant in competition for the native trade and so deprived the latter of a ready source of cash. Whites accepted the obligation of a community life as embracing schools, churches, and roads whereas Asiatics got along on a minimum of these adjuncts of a civilization. The more compelling aim at this embryonic stage of the young colony was to collect the best human material for empire building. The primary concern, in a land with the advantages of climate and bountiful natural resources such as the Transvaal boasted, should be to preserve it as a nursery for Anglo-Saxon stock.[68]

A white community with Western ideals remained the issue. British Indians were too deeply rooted in Oriental ways to be assimilated. A people who said they were forbidden by a religion older than Christianity to tell civil officers the names of relatives could hardly be desirable material for citizenry. If Asiatic immigration were unchecked the end must be a very regrettable type of white aristocracy dominating a polyglot helotry. Respectable whites of lower-class background would not emigrate to places where an honorable spot in the social body was not to be theirs. Neame pointed out that the population figures in Natal were sufficiently alarming to suggest a crisis. Whereas in 1891 there were 41,142 Indians and 46,749 whites, the *Census of*

1904 showed 100,749 Indians and 94,226 whites (correctly, 97,109). This reflected an increase of 144.88 per cent for the former against 101.38 per cent for the latter. The choice was between rapid acquisition of wealth and a homogeneous white stock. Nor should it be forgotten that Asiatic immigration posed a greater danger than the natives to an advanced concept of colonization. The Oriental was higher up in the scale of ability and his presence would be a hindrance in seeking a partnership with other white dominions.[69]

Since an aroused Transvaal chose to secure its territory for a white community, concrete measures were in order to stem the tide of illegal entrants. The permits authorized by Lord Milner with the best of intentions had proved inadequate owing to the collusion among members of the Indian colony. The permits had been treated as marketable property and sold to newcomers. Richard Jebb, exponent of imperialism, was not unduly surprised at the ingenuity of the Indians to slip by the immigration officers through studied impersonation. The registration of domiciled Asiatics to forestall an unlimited influx had a history of evasion everywhere. In the early days of Australia, the strategy of Victoria aimed to keep them out by the imposition of a high fee (£10) at the port of debarkation. What happened during the 1850's was that Asiatics entered South Australia and then went overland to the goldfields of Victoria.[70] In North America the lengthy frontier with Canada multiplied the difficulties of the United States in enforcing a restrictive Asiatic policy.[71] The Transvaal registration procedure should be commended as the only way to check the crafty Asiatic.[72]

Ridgeway gave short shrift to the passive resistance movement. *Act No. 36 of 1908* had redressed the main grievance of a humiliating registration procedure. A generous offer of permitting a number of educated Asiatics to come in had been made. The tactics of Gandhi seemed to be that of constantly demanding new concessions. General Botha had stated it accurately when he complained to the British Colonial Office that Gandhi was always raising new issues in order to keep alive the image of a persecuted minority.[73] Gandhi should cease his campaign of noncooperation and reconcile himself to some disabilities for his countrymen. Nor was it the height of wisdom for Lord Ampthill and his associates to encourage the British Indians in the belief that imprisonment and deportation would enlist the sympathy

of the British public. The Transvaal would resent this attempt to force
its hand and the result could well be wholesale exclusions including
those legally domiciled. It was indeed a pity that the race problem
had ever been permitted to fester in South Africa. But first principles
could no longer be realized and a self-governing colony had the right
to consider its own survival as a white community.[74]

Conservatives spun their theory of citizenship in the British Empire.
The imperial purpose was not to integrate all subjects into one mold
but rather to enable a number of different cultures to develop along
their own lines. It would be impossible to frame one set of laws applicable to Europeans, Orientals, and Africans. A wide variety of communities paid allegiance to the Crown. There were democracies as
advanced as Australia and Canada, colonies as disparate as those in
South Africa, and an India with a conglomeration of elements ranging
from the exalted society of the Parsee to the barbaric tribesmen along
the North-West frontier. The secret of the Empire had been that the
mother country assumed the role of all things to all offspring. The
essence of constitutional monarchy was applied in Australia and
Canada. The essence of "capricious personal rule" was applied in the
West Indies and Malta. If Great Britain once sought a standardiza-
tion of the parts, an epitaph for the Empire would not be far off. So
too had the Roman Empire observed a marked distinction in the
treatment of the western and eastern provinces. A ruthless policy of
Romanization had been imposed upon the younger peoples of Gaul
and Spain. A large degree of autonomy had been permitted in the
Near East where older cultures existed. In this way Rome averted for
a long time what seemed the inevitable day of collapse. The British
Empire should take heed and adapt itself to an environment lacking
racial homogeneity.[75]

The Times did not see fit to echo Conservative views, dedicated as
it was to the great destiny of the British Empire in India.* Maltreatment of Asiatics in South Africa would leave an indelible imprint on

---

The Times was put out by Australian encouragement of the anti-Asiatic policy of
the Transvaal. Australians should remember that India had been the halfway house
enabling Great Britain to colonize their continent. Moreover, British supremacy in
India was a factor in Far Eastern politics and Australia should be vitally concerned in
this aspect. *The Times*, Sept. 5, 1908, 13b.

the various strata of Indian society. Those educated in European ways and traditions would find difficulty reconciling such conduct with the vaunted liberties so often extolled to them under the Union Jack. Those uneducated save in their indigenous customs, and comprising the bulk of the population, would be exposed to professional agitators. The latter would exploit the persecution of their brethren across the seas to justify sedition against British rule in India. Only upon the occasion of the renewal of passive resistance in the fall of 1908 did *The Times* have sharp words for the South African Indians. It was hard to see where the Transvaal had trespassed upon the essential points sought—assurances to previously domiciled Indians, permits for distinguished Indians as visitors, entry to a small number of educated Indians required for professional services. One could not thrust aside the uncomfortable suspicion that Gandhi was sowing a fresh crop of conditions in the hope of reaping further support from the Imperial State.[76]

Several Conservative peers added their jeremiads over the possible effect upon British prestige in India. Earl Roberts, whose military career included distinguished service in India, prefaced his observations with an appreciative recognition of South Africa's desire to remain a white community. But it was a grievous error to demand a fingerprint impression for a certificate of registration and bound to cause offense in India where amour propre counted for much. Insistence upon the names of female relatives being put on the registration forms was tactless, for in India, even among the most intimate friends, such allusions were never made. Lord Curzon spared no words in denouncing the state of affairs in South Africa. The British Indian was penalized not for his vices but for his virtues—sobriety, industry, frugality. While Lord Lansdowne admitted the right of self-governing colonies to decide the substance of their own population, resident British Indians merited respectful consideration. It was disheartening to read of people herded into locations like cattle, forbidden to acquire property, and queued like criminals for a fingerprint impression. As these peers saw it, a fair settlement should provide decent conditions for the Indian coolies and exemption from disabilities for the better class of Asiatics.[77]

The *Morning Post* broached the possibility of transplanting South

African Indians elsewhere.* The mother country could offer a substantial pecuniary inducement to those accepting voluntary transfer.
A monetary sacrifice of this kind by Great Britain would betoken a
more realistic acknowledgment of the facts than to berate the Transvaal whites as guilty of moral delinquency and imperial indifference.
A precedent existed in the way that slavery had been abolished in
1833 with compensation for their owners. A variety of suggestions
were advanced as to the availability of land. The tropical conditions in
West Africa approximated those in India. There were opportunities
for cotton plantations in the Sudan. British Central and East Africa
contained large tracts of undeveloped land. The mention of these last
two territories brought a quick dissent from the third Baron Hindlip,
a member of the Allsopp brewing family and himself a noted explorer
and director of several African enterprises. He feared that the attach-
ment of the African hinterland as a sort of annex to India would
spell the deathknell for the aspirations of a small but growing white
settlement.[78]

Jebb was not overly optimistic that the British Indians would accept
settlement in virgin territories. Asiatics had never shown themselves to
be pioneers. Through the centuries they had made no attempt to oc-
cupy neighboring Australia. The attraction to them of the populous
British colonial communities was the high scale of profit possible in
their economic life. Where others had sown, Indians sought to reap.
Still, Jebb would go for transplanting them if it could be effected
without compulsion or hardship. Nor would he object to a generous
financial inducement on the part of the home government, considering its initial responsibility for the mistaken advice to Natal that indentured Indian coolies be tried on the sugar plantations. His own
long-range thought was, however, that India be made a more self-
sustained economic unit. This would not only eliminate the constant
need for emigration but also show that the imperial intent to promote
nation-states was not formulated for the exclusive benefit of European
stock.[79]

*Liberal dailies would support the proposal as second best if South Africa would not
have the British Indians. The population of India was expanding rapidly and other parts
of the Empire might be opened freely to them. Daily Chronicle, Jan. 29, 1908; Westminster Gazette, Feb. 5, 1908.

8

The British Indian & Integration Union Period

OFFICIALDOM

A chance to break the deadlock came during the summer of 1909 when the British Parliament reviewed the South African draft constitution. A British Indian delegation was dispatched to seek the friendly intervention of Lord Crewe with General Smuts. Four were selected but only two went, the other two having been arrested and sentenced in connection with the passive resistance movement. The two who arrived in London in July were Gandhi, his term of imprisonment having been served, and Hajée Habib, a Moslem merchant from Pretoria. Consultations were held with responsible officials and a major change in the constitution was effected (Clause 147), transferring jurisdiction over Asiatics from the four provinces to the Union. Perhaps a more generous status might be achieved by thus removing consideration of their grievances from the narrow and prejudicial outlook of the individual colonies to the national level. Furthermore, the Asiatics were given a "locus" with the Imperial State in the instructions handed Lord Gladstone "that those Bills . . . which affect Indians towards whom His Majesty's Government as responsible for the government of the Indian Empire must always have special responsibilities [were to be reviewed]."[1]

Since the Union of South Africa would not come into existence for another year, an effort was made by all concerned while still in London to arrive at a settlement. Separate interviews were held by Lord Crewe with General Smuts and Gandhi, supplemented by an exchange of letters. Gandhi listed his essential conditions: 1) repeal of

Act No. 2 of 1907, 2) admission of six educated Asiatics each year on certificates of permanent residence, 3) use of a uniform education test omitting the word European and excluding Asiatics by differential administration. In addition, he reserved for the future the right to raise the subject of the disabilities under which his countrymen labored in the several provinces. General Smuts was prepared to accept the first two conditions but not the third. He would be honest and candid and say that the Transvaal could not recognize in its legislation the equality of races. If exclusion remained purely administrative, he believed that there would be perpetual agitation to increase the number admitted. Under the circumstances General Smuts preferred to let the matter be held over until the advent of the Union government.[2]

Lord Crewe submitted, on October 7, 1910, prior to exchanging his post as Secretary of State for the Colonies for that of Secretary of State for India, his measured views on the subject of the British Indians. He regarded Gandhi's conditions as eminently fair, particularly his insistence on theoretical equality in any immigration law. He called to mind that the *Australia Act of 1901* had been amended in 1905 to substitute for the test in a European language one "in any prescribed language" and it had effectively removed the social affront to Asiatics. That conformed to the traditional policy of the Empire, numbering as it did millions of non-Europeans, to obviate distinctions of race and color. One accepted the right of a self-governing community to choose the elements of which it should be constituted and asked only that it not be done with humiliation to others. The Union of South Africa could be even more helpful if it were set up as one immigration area and invidious restrictions on Indian transient movement eliminated. In the event a fresh registration were undertaken to start matters off anew, a fingerprint impression should be required only of uneducated persons and solely of the thumb on the left hand. As for those domiciled, Lord Crewe urged an end to their disabilities and a closer integration into the life of the community.[3]

When General Botha replied on December 20, 1910, Lewis Harcourt had been installed as Secretary of State for the Colonies. General Botha regarded the views of Lord Crewe as reasonable and legislation could be drawn up along the lines suggested. He would repeal *Act No. 2 of 1907*. He would adopt a dictation test modeled on the

Australian law with differential administration to exclude Asiatic immigrants. He would not even fix the number of educated Indians to be allowed in at six but would leave it more flexible, perhaps twelve per year. Currently, as a sign of a new spirit abroad, he stressed how a patient administration of *Act No. 36 of 1908* had reduced the passive resistance campaign to a nominal character. A fingerprint impression was resorted to only in the case of uneducated Indians. Where Asiatics were able by reason of education or social standing to make use of other means of identification, options were freely accorded. General Botha was likewise confident that given time a more charitable treatment of those domiciled would be possible. But on the right of transient movement from one province to another he confessed himself unable to budge the Transvaal. Harcourt welcomed the conciliatory tone of General Botha, questioning only the limit of twelve permits annually as possibly too small. Natal alone in 1909 had allowed in thirty to supply the professional skills required by the Indian community.[4]

During 1910 the British Colonial Office staff discussed the strategy to pursue. Lambert would have the India Office specify what reforms were necessary or threaten to cut off the supply of indentured labor. But the India Office should wait until the Union government requested coolies, otherwise the anti-Asiatic party would press General Botha not to initiate negotiations. The fact was quite obvious that "gentle appeal . . . has produced about all that it ever will." Colonel Seely was of a different opinion as to the course of events. From conversations he had with both General Smuts and Sir Richard Solomon, he gathered that the Union could not care less for indentured coolies. The fewer Indians around the easier to deal with the problem. If the India Office should raise the subject of closing the lid on the supply of coolies, that would be to pull the chestnuts out of the fire for them "and save the Union from the bother of overruling Natal." This threat, therefore, offered no real lever to get better terms. Indeed the exact opposite was true; concessions for domiciled Indians could best be achieved if the India Office terminated the recruitment of indentured coolies for South Africa.[5]

The India Office in September 1910 expressed its views as to a satisfactory settlement. It was not keen on the Australian education test even though it omitted any reference to European languages. If an immigration officer should capriciously require the test in Swedish or modern Greek, the publicity growing out of it would provoke unhappy repercussions in India. The *Canadian Immigration Act of 1910* was to be preferred, empowering authorities to prohibit applicants belonging to any race deemed unsuited to the climate or requirements of Canada. The limited number of cultured Asiatics to be admitted annually should be given the education test in the English language in which they were usually well prepared. The opportunity for temporary travel passports to Indian visitors of distinction should be spelled out. Registration procedures for domiciled Indians should be established on the basis of signatures for educated Indians of good standing and an impression of the left thumb in the case of others. On January 3, 1911, the Viceroy of India announced that the stoppage of indentured coolies would go into effect the following July. The decision was explained on the formal grounds that no guarantee had been forthcoming of ex-indentured Indians being accepted as permanent citizens. Thus the pressure of resentful sugar planters was taken off the back of the Union government.[6]

When the *Immigrants Restriction Bill of 1911* was published in February, the British Colonial Office had words both of praise and criticism. The adoption of the Australian education test permitting any prescribed language had merit. True it would be administered to keep out Asiatics but, given sincere officials, any offense to the dignity of Orientals could be avoided. It was all to the good too that the several laws enacted by the Transvaal, notably Act No. 2 of 1907, would be repealed. However, as a measure seeking to encompass a national immigration policy, several points wanted clarification. The right of children to join their parents should be stated. All persons born or domiciled in the Union should be guaranteed automatic entry after being outside the country. Disappointment was registered at the replacement of the less rigorous education tests of Cape Colony and Natal by the stiffer Union measure to restrict interprovincial movement. As proposed, the limit of twelve educated Asiatics annually would be too few, considering that only six would be earmarked for Cape Colony and Natal. Still the lesser of two evils would be to go along with the measure if it meant that the Union government would be in a better position to remove the disabilities of the resident Indian population.[7]

The bill was withdrawn in March 1911. Orange Free State objected to the possibility that the twelve educated Asiatics to be admitted into the Union might wish to enter its territory. That might mean the invalidation of its declaratory statement required of all Asiatics entering that they acquiesce in certain disabilities—no permits to trade, no farming, no ownership of fixed property. General Smuts confessed to Lord Gladstone that he had not been able to budge Orange Free State. Nor for that matter could he get the Transvaal to exempt the twelve educated Asiatics from the registration procedure even though only a signature was required. General Smuts promised that he would bring in a more acceptable bill the following year. Lord Gladstone expressed himself as vexed at Orange Free State, for the professional services of the twelve educated Asiatics would not be needed there with its fewness of Asiatic numbers. The India Office shed no tears, feeling that the proposal was designed to remedy the situation in the Transvaal and in doing so had worsened the prospects for Indians in Cape Colony and Natal.[8]

The specter of a reinvigorated passive resistance campaign spurred a temporary agreement in April 1911 between General Botha and Gandhi. General Botha promised to maintain existing British Indian rights, to permit six of the educated passive resisters not eligible for domicile under the present laws of the Transvaal to remain, and to declare an amnesty for those in prison. Gandhi pledged to end the strategy of noncooperation,* to advise his compatriots to register under Act No. 36 of 1908, and to drop his demand for unrestricted entry of Indians into South Africa. At the same time Gandhi frankly listed matters which would continue to be the subject of memorials. Demands against Cape Colony included the need for more clerical help than the quota proposed, elimination of the £1 fee for each re-entry after travel to another province, a halt to curtailment of dealers' licenses, and the extension of the time limit for visits to India from the current one year to a new maximum of three years. Demands against Natal included repeal of the onerous £3 annual residence tax on ex-indentured Indians and their families, a halt to curtailment of dealers' licenses, acceptance of an aggregate three-year period of resi-

*A study of the documentary evidence would indicate that when the passive resistance was terminated in the spring of 1911 over 3,000 Indians had passed through the jails and all but 150 had served with hard labor.

dence (but not continuous) to establish domiciliary rights for re-entry, and a guarantee of automatic admission to wives and minors of domiciled Indians returning after a visit abroad.[9]

A new bill was drafted in the fall of 1911, scheduled for introduction in the next session the following year. Robinson analyzed the proposal for the consideration of his fellow staff members in the British Colonial Office. The rights of domiciled Indians and their families seemed to be fully safeguarded from the education test upon returning from visits abroad. The positive criterion for domicile could have been made clearer instead of clothed in all kinds of legal phraseology. But it would be unwise to multiply contentious points and it did lay down the right of appeal to the courts. The grievance of Cape Indians to extend temporary permits for continuous absence to three years had been met. The grievance of the Transvaal Indians to relax the registration procedure under Act No. 36 of 1908 for the educated Asiatics admitted had been met. The Australian education test in any prescribed language was retained even though the automatic exemption of white persons with proof of service engagements as agricultural and domestic servants and the like revived the color bar. The most objectionable features continued to be 1) the application of the Union education test to interprovincial movement and 2) the declaratory statement of accepted disabilities for entrance into Orange Free State.[10]

An exchange of views followed between the British Colonial Office and the India Office. The latter was disappointed that the Union would persist in barring interprovincial movement, thus ending a privilege previously enjoyed by Cape merchants to recruit a supply of clerks from Natal. Perhaps the Union would be willing to offset this sealed avenue by increasing beyond twelve the number of educated Indians to be admitted annually. The desirability was raised of an appeal to the Supreme Court against the harsh administration of trading licenses in Natal and Cape Colony. Lambert questioned the propriety of putting forward these varied complaints. They were neither new nor of vital substance and it would be better "to let them take their course" for the time being. General Smuts should certainly be aware of these and "further representations will irritate . . . and prejudice an Immigration Bill in the present temper of the Union Government." While Robinson readily agreed that the bill was "no better and even worse than the old bill, . . . it is impossible to devise a solution which will satisfy everybody." The governing factors that ought to be considered were

> 1) that we cannot ignore the [white] Cape feeling in favor of excluding the Natal Indian, especially as we allowed the Transvaal before the Union to do that very thing, and 2) that the claim of the Indians [for the twelve educated Indians] to have free entrance into the Orange Free State is absolutely unreasonable, . . . those Indians are to cater for the religious and professional needs of the resident population and in Orange Free State there is no resident population and exclusion is no real grievance. . . . If we get the bill, we shall at all events get a settlement of one of the main problems of difficulty on lines generally acceptable and can then tackle the question of the treatment of resident Indians with more freedom.[11]

Lord Gladstone pressed General Smuts to proceed with his bill. Writing to him on May 29, 1912, he observed that "the present uncertainty and condition of law is a chronic source of danger and of far greater trouble in India." This placed "a burden on the Indian Government and the British Government out of all proportion to what after all is a limited area of difficulty here." But General Smuts found the opposition too strong in the Union Parliament, especially against the theoretical equality implied in the Australian education test, and the session ended still with no immigration bill. Harcourt expressed his disappointment, observing irritably "that the Union Government got what they wanted out of us—no more indentured coolies to Natal." The bill would have been of great value to the Imperial State as a tangible evidence of an effort to meet Indian complaints. Actually "the grievance to be removed is purely sentimental [theoretical equality] and does not therefore really cost the Union anything to give." As for the indifference of the Indian government to the loss of the bill, "they are very foolish, because they are really hankering after free entry for the Indian and the removal of a lot of practical disabilities . . . which they will never get as long as South Africa has free institutions, . . . half a loaf is better than no bread."[12]

A new figure entered the picture in the fall of 1912. Gopal Krishna Gokhale, a past president of the Indian National Congress and the

sponsor of the motion in the Viceroy's Legislative Council to terminate indentured coolies, visited South Africa during October and
November. He came at the invitation of British Indians to study at
firsthand their precarious plight. Many demonstrations were held by
the Indian community in his honor. The Union government was
surprisingly cooperative and allowed the principal railway stations to
be decorated for his welcome. Furthermore, during his stay at Pretoria,
it put him up at the Transvaal Hotel and placed a railway saloon car
at his disposal for trips. Gandhi provides us with an account of the
two-hour talk which Gokhale had alone with Generals Botha and
Smuts. Gokhale told Gandhi afterwards that the main points of contention had been settled. Both Act No. 2 of 1907 in the Transvaal
and the £3 annual residence tax on ex-indentured Indians in Natal
would be repealed and the color bar would be entirely removed from
the immigration laws. Gandhi recalls his own reply to Gokhale, expressing skepticism that these promises would be quickly fulfilled.[13]

ORDEAL

While officialdom struggled to resolve broad issues, the
British Indians suffered new reverses in the Transvaal. The most important related to the Vrededorp Stands Act No. 3 of 1906 and the
Gold Law Act of 1908. In past years land had been leased in mining
areas to indigent persons for open stands. The passage of time had
witnessed a number of these leases transferred to Indians with the
result that mixed residential areas had grown up and trading rivalry
was keen. To circumvent these land laws, which prohibited such vested
rights by any but Europeans, the registration of the fixed property was
put in the names of trusted whites and recognized by the courts as
legal. Both Ritch and Henry Salomon Polak, practising solicitor, editor
of the Natal Indian Opinion, and a lieutenant of Gandhi, entered into
many such transactions leasing the property back to Indian merchant
friends. But in 1910 new ordinances were introduced to eliminate the
subterfuges and to enforce in essence the principle of segregation.
Henceforth registered owners of fixed property occupied by non-
Europeans would be prosecuted and their holdings forfeited. While a
period of grace would be granted, the laws stated that this property
in trust could be attached by creditors of the European owners.[14]

A second alarming prospect related to the proposal before the Union Parliament to confirm jurisdiction over trading licenses in the hands of the municipalities. The India Office feared that in the Transvaal this power would probably be used to expel Indian shopkeepers from the province. Such had been the history of trading licenses in Natal, where harsh and capricious rejection of renewals had gone on for years and a similar trend could be discerned in Cape Colony. Harcourt sought the views of "Union Ministers as to what considerations should guide those vested with the discretion" and urged that if action were taken the power "be vested in a judicial officer, than in a body on which the Indian traders' rivals may usually expect to be strongly represented." The proposal as finally drafted in 1912 and (actually passed in April 1913) was included in the *Financial Relations Act*. It provided for the unconditional delegation of the power to issue general dealers' licenses to the provinces alone. The British Colonial Office hoped that General Smuts would add amendments to permit the grant of new licenses to Asiatics and a right of appeal to the courts. Nothing was effected, however, save a security for existing holders of licenses, and this was about all that could be expected—for any more would "only be batting our heads against a stone wall, not a very dignified operation."[15]

British Indian resentment deepened with the passage in June 1913 of an *Immigrants Regulation Act*.[16] Gandhi refused to accept it on the grounds that the concessions were weakened by sins of both commission and omission. Orange Free State was accorded the right to continue its requirement that entering Asiatics make a formal declaration of acquiescence in their disabilities. Cape Indian merchants would be hard put to obtain an adequate supply of clerks gifted in both English and Indian tongues. Their quota from the dozen educated Asiatics to be admitted annually would be small and the application of the stiff Union education test at provincial frontiers would curtail transient movement. Natal Indians would be keenly disappointed in the failure to abolish the £3 annual residence tax on ex-indentured coolies and their families. A precise statement to assure ex-indentured Indians in Natal who had arrived after 1895 of the right to reestablish domicile upon return from India (even though they had not fulfilled the continuous three-year period of residence) was also lacking. Most regrettable of all was the revival of the color bar in the restoration of

European languages (including Yiddish) for the education test and the automatic exemption from the education test of persons of European descent who could show proof of service engagements as agricultural and domestic servants and the like.[17]

An accompanying threat to Indian marriage customs added a further woe. On March 4, 1913 Justice Malcolm William Searle of the Cape Supreme Court gave judgment in a case to the effect that any marriages save those celebrated according to Christian rites were outside the pale of legality in South Africa. Then, in October 1913, in the wake of the *Immigrants Regulation Act*, Justice John Carnegie Dove Wilson of the Natal Supreme Court handed down a decision which placed an alarming interpretation upon the new law. One Kulsam Bibi was denied the right to enter South Africa despite the fact that she was the lawful living wife of Mahboob Khan and that the marriage was contracted by the latter as a widower. The judgment stated that the marriage had been celebrated under a law which allowed four wives and that made it an illegal union. Polygamous marriages were recognized by Moslems, while Hindu religious practice allowed a second wife if there was no male issue and then only with the consent of the first wife. As the British Indian community assessed the situation, families were confronted with separation of loved ones and all kinds of heartrending scenes.[18]

The British Colonial Office approved of the *Immigrants Regulation Act*. The new Immigration Boards of Appeal, consisting of three or more members, ought to do much to obviate hardships caused by any autocratic decisions of immigration officers. And on questions of law there would still be access to the courts. The categories of those not to be challenged on seeking re-entry would be broadened to include Indians possessing earlier types of permits and education test certificates. It was warming to note that the Union government promised in some years to let more than twelve educated Asiatics enter and to invite the participation of the Indian government in the selection of those allowed to come in.* If no provisions were incorporated to validate Indian marriages, Union ministers pledged that Indians would be allowed, as heretofore, to introduce one wife into the country. True,

---

*Lord Gladstone reported that in 1912 Natal admitted twenty-nine and Cape Colony seventeen Asiatic males, all by virtue of their education tests which were still in force pending Union legislation. P.R.O., c.o. 551/39.

it was regrettable that the color bar should be revived in the education test adopted. But the more significant point was that Indians would be excluded on the basis of a new clause modeled along the lines of the Canadian approach, namely, on grounds of poverty or standards and habits of life unsuited to the requirements of the Union.[19]

Lord Crewe, now Secretary of State for India, expressed unhappiness over the retention of several grievances of long standing: 1) the declaratory statement of disabilities to enter Orange Free State, 2) the reinsertion of European languages for the education test, 3) the prohibition against interprovincial movement. While Harcourt saw no reason to exercise the power of disallowance, he made a special effort to conciliate the India Office in the matter of the Natal £3 annual residence tax on ex-indentured coolies and their families. Lord Gladstone should impress upon his ministers that the collection of the tax was so imperfect, compared to the irritation produced, as to make its existence illogical. As of December 31, 1912, the figures showed that 8,612 men out of the 10,206 liable and 5,048 women out of the 5,089 liable were in arrears. However, not even an eleventh-hour attempt to get Indian women exempted was successful. Somewhat wrathfully, Lord Gladstone wrote to Harcourt that the blame must fall on the "truculent and minatory attitude of the Indian community and of Gandhi in particular." Union ministers had felt that the exemption of women "would not allay unrest and so why bother."[20]

In September 1913 Gandhi announced the renewal for a third time of passive resistance. An early incident related to a group of "sisters" living on Tolstoy Farm, twenty miles out of Johannesburg. Through the beneficence of Herman Kallenbach, an architect of German extraction and a devoted lieutenant of Gandhi, Tolstoy Farm had been founded as a haven for families of *satyagrahis* languishing in prison. As Dr. Mabel Palmer, onetime lecturer in Economic History at Natal University College and organizer of its non-European branch, describes the incident, these "sisters" crossed the frontier from the Transvaal into Natal while a group of women volunteers simultaneously crossed from Natal into the Transvaal. The contingent from the Transvaal proceeded to the colliery at Newcastle and persuaded Indian miners to go on strike. Arrests and sentences of three months' imprisonment followed.[21]

A second incident transpired on November 1, 1913, when Gandhi led 2,500 British Indians and their wives and children in a march from the Newcastle mines in Natal past Laing's Nek and Majuba Hill toward Volksrust in the Transvaal, a distance of approximately thirty-five miles. The journey was undertaken on foot, the passive resisters camping out in the open and eating sparsely. The physical discomforts of a mass exodus were suffered stoically. A constabulary unit awaited them near Volksrust. They were arrested and deported back to Natal by train. They were prosecuted for breaches of the *Immigrants Regulation Act*, convicted, and punished with prison terms or assignment to mining compounds as a labor force. Gandhi and his two lieutenants, Kallenbach and Polak, received sentences of three months with hard labor for incitement to strikes and inducement to illegal crossing of frontiers.[22]

A third incident took place the last week of November 1913 on the sugar plantations in Natal. On November 24, at the Beneva Sugar Estates, near Esperanza, over two hundred Indians defied a dozen European mounted police. On November 27, at the Natal Estates Limited, near Mount Edgecombe, over seventeen hundred Indians defied a force of two hundred European mounted police supported by a small number of native foot constables. In both instances, when arrests were ordered, the Indians brandished cane sticks, knives, stones, and bricks. Scuffles followed and a number of policemen were thrown off their horses and suffered injuries. Acts of incendiarism were committed. Time and again the policemen were surrounded and threatened by the emotionally excited Indians. In self-defense the policemen drew their revolvers and fired into the hostile mob of attackers. More than a score were wounded, a few slain, and many taken prisoners.[23]

The British Colonial Office tried to maintain a balanced position. On the one hand, close vigil was exercised to assure a sympathetic operation of the *Immigrants Regulation Act*. Lord Gladstone was instructed to check closely the work of the Immigration Boards of Appeal, especially to discountenance the appointment of immigration officers to these boards; otherwise the boards reviewed their own decisions. Between the representations of Lord Ampthill and the South African British Indian Committee, referrals to the Union government were endless. Complaints covered denial of entry, expense of hotels and legal suits, and high-handed conduct of immigration officers. Unfavorable reports of the exclusion of Indians on grounds of poverty and standards of life unsuited to the requirements of the Union brought demands for a review of this provision. The publicity given such cases when appealed had turned out to be more of an indignity than the European language test, their racial background "rubbed in on every occasion." The admission of a single bona fide wife seemed quite often to be made needlessly difficult because of lack of proofs; marriages in India were often contracted at a tender age and without issuance of any certificate.[24]

On the other hand, the Union should not be condemned in its desire for a Western social system. There was nothing wrong in an insistence upon the monogamous principle as the foundation for the family. It would be preposterous to let a small community of 150,000 Indians force an alien and lower view of marriage (as Christians saw it) upon South Africa. In regard to the contention that General Smuts had promised Gokhale to repeal the £3 annual residence tax in Natal, the documents showed his words to be: "if he can get the consent of Natal men which he did not." The ex-indentured Indians did not really have a legitimate complaint, for the £3 tax was rarely collected from women and only irregularly from men. Somewhat chary, however, was the British Colonial Office staff to the request of General Smuts that the India Office be asked to allow repatriation of currently employed indentured Indian coolies at the end of their contracts, thereby reducing their numbers and the attendant pressure for professional men. Just observed that "we pulled chestnuts out of the fire for him once in getting India to end indentured labor." It would be a confession that the position was hopeless and would give "a handle to those in South Africa who want to get rid of the Indians born in South Africa including the Indian trader."[25]

Nevertheless, the several incidents provoked an imperial crisis. Baron Hardinge of Penshurst, Viceroy of India, protested vehemently 1) the omissions in the *Immigrants Regulation Act*, 2) the court decision against Indian marriages, and 3) the brutal treatment of Indian sugar plantation strikers. General Botha, after a sharp exchange of notes with Lord Hardinge, agreed on December 10, 1913, to set up a commission of enquiry. The personnel comprised Sir William Solomon, Judge of the Union Supreme Court and brother of Sir Richard Solomon, Ewald Esselen, Judge of the old Transvaal Republic Court, and Lieutenant-Colonel James Scott Wylie, a Durban lawyer. The sessions were held in Durban from January 26 to February 7, 1914. Lord Hardinge sent Sir Benjamin Robertson, Chief Commissioner of the Central Provinces, as an observer in the interests of an aroused Indian nation. The three leaders of the passive resistance campaign—Gandhi, Kallenbach, Polak—were released from prison on December 18, 1913, in the hope that they would persuade the strikers on the sugar plantations to testify. But Gandhi and his associates refused to do so because no representative of the British Indians was named to the commission. This action rendered useless any investigation of the allegations of brutality during the strike.[26]

The commission of enquiry decided, therefore, to concentrate upon the catalogue of grievances. In March 1914 a list of recommendations was submitted to the Union government. Briefly, they were as follows:

1) admission of one wife and minor children borne by her to a domiciled Indian irrespective of the fact that the marriage was solemnized according to tenets recognizing polygamy, 2) compilation of a register of the few marriages polygamous in fact and accord such wives and children the same rights of re-entry so long as the husband continued to reside in South Africa, 3) provision for the appointment of marriage officers from among Indian priests of different denominations, 4) legislation to validate *de facto* monogamous marriages, 5) repeal of the £3 poll tax in Natal, 6) grant of temporary permits to Indians desiring to travel in other provinces, 7) facilitate certification of women and children proceeding from India to South Africa for reunion with husbands and parents, 8) recognition of Natal certificates bearing thumb impressions as conclusive evidence of the right to enter the Union as soon as identity was established, 9) expedite application procedures of Cape Indians traveling to and from Cape Colony, 10) elimination of the declaratory statement for entry into Orange Free State.[27]

The British Colonial Office pooled its thoughts with Lord Gladstone as to the counsel which might be passed on to the Botha government. Lord Hardinge's public censure of South Africa was to be deplored. It played into the hands of anti-imperialists to stigmatize Union legislation as unjust, to imply sympathy with organized resistance to the law, and to impute uncivilized methods of repression. While Harcourt was not keen on the selection of Colonel Wylie, who represented the white Natalian view and had a record of opposition to the Indians, he accepted Lord Gladstone's recommendation that all three nominees were "good and fair." Disapproval was voiced of Gandhi's demand that the commission be composed of Sir William Solomon, a second selected by the planters, and a third by the Indian community. Harcourt advised that to do "this would be sheer madness," for it would destroy the judicial character of the commission and turn it into an arbitration board. The India Office should be asked to deprecate this proposal of Gandhi and if the latter persisted in abstaining from cooperation, then General Smuts should persevere rather than enhance Gandhi's prestige. When the commission handed in its recommendations in March 1914, the verdict was that "if the Union legislates in accordance with these recommendations they will have conceded as much as possible."[28]

The Union government accepted in the main the recommendations of the commission. The *Indians Relief Act No. 22*, enacted in July 1914, repealed the £3 annual residence tax paid by ex-indentured Indians in Natal and clarified the legality of Indian marriages as monogamous (if so in fact) even though celebrated according to the tenets of a religion recognizing polygamy. The other issues were the subject of administrative negotiations with the several provinces. A liberal interpretation was obtained on domiciliary rights for ex-indentured Indians who had arrived after 1895 in Natal. The Orange Free State agreed to a less objectionable way of establishing the Asiatic disabilities. A declaratory statement would be printed on the back of the general sheet filed at the coastal port of entry and acceptance assumed. Plural wives and their children, in an existing polygamous marriage, would be allowed to join a domiciled Indian if an inquiry confirmed that their numbers were very limited. Cape Colony was assured more flexibility to recruit clerks in adjoining provinces by extending the right of South African-born Indians to enter subject to the older Cape Colony education test. In short, the exclusion of Asiatic immigration would be enforced but with honorable treatment for domiciled Indians and their families.[29]

While Gandhi expressed his satisfaction with the concessions granted, he stressed, in his letter of thanks to General Smuts, the desirability of conceding full civic rights to resident Indians. It was to be hoped that the modus vivendi marked a change in the policy of the

Union government toward British Indians and substantiated their right to be consulted on matters affecting them. Indeed, he would like to think that the settlement might come to be regarded as the Magna Charta of Indian liberty in South Africa. Again, it could re-affirm the theory of British constitutional development and the heritage of the British Empire that there should be no legal inequality between different groups of the Crown's subjects. He appealed to the colonial whites to take a humanitarian view in future relations with Asiatics and to the British Indians to win for themselves a role of respectability. Gandhi declared the passive resistance campaign at an end and on July 18, 1914, left for India where an even greater challenge would soon await him.[30]

The British Colonial Office was happy to close its books on the ordeal of the British Indian in South Africa. It was remarkable that the Union government, after an originally intransigent attitude, could be so amenable later. No doubt the recent industrial strikes, on the Rand in July 1913 and on the railways in January 1914, had a sobering effect. A defiant British Indian community, along with discontented skilled white miners and the ever-present native peril, would have created a dangerous political situation. Both General Smuts and Gandhi were commended for their yeoman's work in bringing their respective camps into line with a compromise not entirely satisfactory to either. Lord Gladstone recorded, in his farewell letter to Harcourt on July 11, 1914, the value of letting the Union handle the problem of its own non-Europeans:

> What has the Empire gained from the four years of Union? To speak of racialism as dead would be foolish. . . . But the one hope of establishing the Imperial idea was through and on a South African ideal . . . of a responsible State, free to work out its own destinies in its own way as an integral part of a great whole, giving in its growing strength a true return for what it received from the British Crown and the British flag.[31]

PUBLIC FORUM

Liberal and Labour circles, working closely with the South African British Indian Committee, interpreted sympathetically the ordeal of Asiatics in the Union. Memorials to remove humiliating disabilities contained no arrogant demands.* Trading licenses and residential quarters were vital to their material existence. "Jim Crow" regulations in post offices and on the railways, tramcars, and footpaths were matters of crushing mortification. The cornerstone for emancipation from disabilities and stigmas centered in the achievement of theoretical equality in immigration laws. The British Indian recognized only too well the strength of existing prejudices among the white community. He squarely faced the distinction between the ideal and the practical. But South African immigration laws had taken the inhuman step to single out Asiatics, classifying 300,000,000 people in India in the same category as paupers, criminals, lepers, and procurers. At least Australia and Canada had closed their doors to Orientals through tests which formally drew no invidious distinctions.[32]

It was not surprising that the British Indians should refuse to accept the *Immigrants Regulation Act*. Despite three years of drafting one bill after another, the final product retained the crucial weaknesses. The annual £3 residence tax for ex-indentured Indians remained on the statute books in Natal. The declaratory statement required of Asiatics accepting disabilities remained on the statute books of Orange Free State. Cape Colony was closed to transient Indians from other provinces. The Indian family unit was placed in jeopardy by the omission of any clause to offset court decisions denying entry to wives and children of marriages contracted under Hindu and Moslem religious rites. The adoption of a European language test ignored the dictum of theoretical equality. As Lord Ampthill compared the provisional settlement in 1911 and the measure in 1913, the latter violated two essential conditions: 1) removal of the racial bar and 2) maintenance of existing rights. The new legislation would worsen the lot of the British Indian.[33]

Regrettable as the resumption of passive resistance in September 1913 might be, no other course seemed possible in the face of oppression and the continued absence of political articulation. Excessive harshness on the part of the Union government in combating acts of noncooperation drew criticism. Highly questionable was the return of the coal miners, who had followed Gandhi into the Transvaal, back to their Natal collieries which were then transformed into penal colonies.

---

*The British Indian Association of South Africa furnished Harcourt with a complete list of disabilities. *P.P.*, 1912-13, LIX, Cd. 6087, pp. 9-12.

Admittedly, under the *Prisons Act of 1911*, employment of convicts by private collieries could be arranged. But it appeared unreasonable to pretend that the clauses providing for such an engagement could be made to cover passive resisters who had left the mines to participate in a demonstration. No less reprehensible was the imprisonment of Gandhi, thus removing the key restraining influence against the forces of disorder. The *Manchester Guardian* described the repression connected with the sugar plantation strikes as ruthless if the reports were accurate. Strikers were thrown into prison and flogged as though they were runaway slaves. Particularly unwise had been the use of native policemen, for that introduced the added peril of racial strife.[34]

The Imperial State was reminded of the many opportunities it had lost for the exercise of more effective pressure than mere persuasion. When the Transvaal and Orange Free State became Crown colonies in 1902, the anti-Asiatic legislation of the Kruger regime could have been wiped out. A stronger statement could have been inserted in their constitutions as self-governing colonies in order to salvage minimum rights for the British Indians. The guarantee of a £5,000,000 loan to the Transvaal in the spring of 1907 could have been made contingent on the alleviation of Indian grievances. Ratification of the Union constitution could have been coupled with an insistence upon the removal of Indian disabilities. The unsatisfactory *Immigrants Regulation Act* could have been dealt with by the power of reservation. When imperial issues were at stake there was no reason why Great Britain should hesitate to intervene in the affairs affecting the dominion. The fact should never be forgotten that British troops were garrisoned in South Africa and the navy hovered about as an instrument of protection.[35]

Lord Ampthill invited the British nation to weigh again the evil fruit which the South African scene was bearing in India. A meeting of the Indian National Congress in December 1909 at Lahore produced generous subscriptions for the relief of harassed brethren in the Transvaal. Polak, attending as a delegate of the South African British Indian community, reported that the sum of £5,000 had been raised.[36] Nothing could be more disturbing than the action of the Viceroy to terminate the supply of indentured coolies for Natal. Although the measure had been taken against Natal as the most convenient means of retaliation, one should be aware that the conduct of the Transvaal was no less abhorred. The *New Statesman* referred to the intensity of Indian national feeling as accounts poured in during 1913 of the clashing incidents between British Indians and the Union government. Demonstrations were organized everywhere in the subcontinent to protest the harsh sentences meted out to passive resisters and strikers in South Africa.[37] The refusal of the Union courts to recognize polygamous marriages provoked seditious overtones against British rule. All this could mean that a crisis was brewing in India and that the Oriental quest for human dignity had moved to the center of the stage.[38]

The *Manchester Guardian* pleaded the destiny of a lofty imperial moral standard. The identification of British citizenship as one of honor or servitude was in abeyance. If equal rights for all peoples under the Union Jack were abandoned in South Africa, then the British Empire became a fiction. It could be broken in two, white and black, a division as grave as that of Rome into Eastern and Western Empires during the reign of Diocletian. Indians were proud of their imperial membership and had taken at face value the boast of Lord Palmerston (third Viscount), nineteenth-century Liberal statesman and Prime Minister, that the ancient adage of *Civis Romanus sum* held true for British subjects everywhere. The *Daily News* spoke gloomily, lamenting that British allegiance was now a thing of gradations and territorial lines. A white man could go where he pleased and be a citizen. A colored man could be excluded or, if allowed in, treated as a pariah. Whether the Empire could hold together proclaiming that there need be no affinity between white and colored subjects was to be doubted. The unanimous refusal of dominions to accord British colored subjects a free access to their shores or civil rights to those resident introduced a fatal rift within the Empire.[39]

Conservatives contented themselves with reaffirming the right of South Africa to contain the Asiatic element. Already in Natal the Indians preempted many trades and their cutthroat competition foreshadowed restricted avenues of livelihood for the rising generation of whites. The *Daily Mail* saw this specter of economic suicide well mirrored in a statement of Lafcadio Hearn, English-born American journalist who married a Japanese woman and became a Japanese citizen, to the effect "that the East can underlive the West."[40] The willingness of the Indian to accommodate himself to slum conditions, a sparse diet, and few broadening interests was evident to the naked eye. If the population trend continued the Indian would soon overtake the white in South Africa. By 1913, for Natal, the figures read 120,000 Asiatics (correctly, 135,000) to 97,000 whites (correctly 99,000). Sir Francis Younghusband, explorer and diplomat, counseled that pioneer white communities, in the initial stage of their development, must protect themselves from an overwhelming influx of alien peoples. The white man had adventured in South Africa and so earned the right to give his imprint to the cultural pattern.[41]

Younghusband insisted that the plight of the domiciled British Indians was not as desperate as their leaders made out. They were not being massacred and their lot was far superior to that visited upon Armenians by the Turks. He personally would vouchsafe from his travels through South Africa that the British Indian, with all his disabilities, appeared far better off than kinfolk in India. The Asiatic would do well to remember the advantages he enjoyed as the result of the white man's resourcefulness. One should look for a reasonable attitude toward those upon whom his own prosperity depended. After all, India was geographically closer to South Africa than Great Britain and for many centuries had an unchallenged opportunity to colonize "the dark continent." The Indian people lacked the enterprizing zeal of Europeans and must expect that the rewards would go to those who risked their lives in a colonial undertaking.[42]

Ridgeway had no patience with the resort to passive resistance. Defiance of the law must be met by energetic measures. One should bear in mind that the native population might emulate the Asiatics if the latter were successful in humbling the Union government. He discounted the emphasis placed upon South African events for the unrest in India. English-educated malcontents in India were on the alert for any cause célèbre to whip up their followers. Any incident in their hands was bound to be ballooned out of all proportion. British Indians in South Africa should realize that, by permitting themselves to be a pawn in the game of Indian agitators, they only jeopardized their own chances for an equitable settlement with the governing whites.[43]

The Times continued to be conditioned in its thinking by the risk to British rule in India. The announcement of the Indian government to prohibit further importation of indentured coolies to Natal had an ominous ring. It was obviously a reprisal for what went on in

South Africa and a gesture to still the rising anger in India itself. Where the catalyst was racial antagonism, the feud could be extremely dangerous. Valentine Chirol, *The Times* correspondent in India, has an interesting account of the Viceroy's Legislative Council session on February 25, 1910, at which Gokhale moved his resolution to end indentured coolie labor for Natal. Every Indian member endorsed his sentiment and had a vote been taken it would have had the unanimous support of all and the sympathy of every British member. Lord Hardinge wisely averted an open condemnation by accepting the resolution.[44] No less portentous were the demonstrations during 1913 at which resolutions of sympathy were passed and contributions offered to the beleaguered Indians abroad. This spectacle of criminations and recriminations exercised by one member against another in the British Empire had gone beyond the mere bounds of an exchange of hard words.[45]

The Times lent vigorous support to the proposal of Lord Hardinge for a thorough and impartial inquiry into the disorders. The Viceroy had advanced the idea in a speech at Madras on November 26, 1913, after reading official telegrams while entrained for that city. Reports of strikers being flogged and of prisoners at forced labor in coal mines were not to be treated in silence. *The Times* urged Lord Hardinge to speed up the process of a truce by sending his own agent to discuss the matter at firsthand with General Botha. The Imperial State should be invited to participate, perhaps as an arbitrator, to help extremists on both sides see the problem in better perspective.[46]

An interesting postscript is to be found in Lord Hardinge's account of his viceroyalty in India. He understood that the first impulse of General Botha upon hearing of the speech at Madras was to press for his recall on the ground of interference in the affairs of South Africa. Later, at the Paris Peace Conference in 1919, the two men met and Lord Hardinge asked General Botha what he would have done in the face of a provocation which was making the task of the Viceroy in India twice as difficult. General Botha admitted that his reaction would probably have been the same and perhaps his protest would have been couched in stronger language.[47]

Jebb offered alternative solutions to resolve the impasse. The possibility of transplanting British Indians elsewhere should be further reviewed. British Guiana possessed a vast hinterland suitable for settlement. If the emigration were spread over a period of years and carefully organized, perhaps a community of eighty thousand Indians might be located there. He calculated that a grant of £100 per family and liberal land allotments should be attractive inducements. Failing this, Jebb recalled the plan proposed in 1895 of making the indentured contracts expire in India, thereby ensuring repatriation. Gladstone had sanctioned such a law in 1884 for the Crown colony of Western Australia.[48] Actually, to interpolate, the idea had been broached for Natal in 1894 when a deputation of two were sent to India to press the proposal.[49] But the Indian government did not take kindly to the suggestion that Natal be supplied with cheap labor later to be washed ashore on the Indian coast. Among the British Colonial Office staff this approach was referred to as "the sucked orange policy." The Indian government rejected it and this had been the background to the adoption in 1895 of the annual £3 poll tax for ex-indentured Indians seeking residence in Natal. It is surprising that Jebb should suggest the plan again after one failure but perhaps he thought a second time might be the charm.[50]

Whatever the solutions advanced might be, the *Daily Mail* warned against British embroilment in the domestic affairs of South Africa. The final decision on the status of the British Indians should be left to the men on the spot. Lord Hardinge deserved censure for his attack upon the Union government as out of place and more likely to harden its statesmen against any compromise. The imperial relationship ought to be that of a family in which persuasion alone could be exercised. For the mother country to intervene was to risk a resignation of the Botha cabinet. That certainly would not help the British Indian and it might instigate a movement for secession of South Africa from the Empire. All that the Imperial State could do was "to advise, exhort, scold, and abuse." Ridgeway pleaded for the acceptance of a flexible constitutional structure:

> Within the fortified *enceinte* of the British Empire there are many houses, each inhabited by its own family. These households have common interests but each manages its own affairs without interference from the others. . . . The British public [would be well advised] not to interfere with South Africa [and] any attempt will be resented by self-governing dominions.[51]

Conservatives were blunt in discussing the relationship between Europeans and Asiatics in the British Empire. Henry Hamilton Fyfe, journalist on the staff of the *Daily Mail*, observed that "it is easy to declare rhetorically that Indians are our fellow countrymen; it is not true, but the words have a plausible sound." Indians were not in any sense fellow countrymen and not even fellow subjects. While both Anglo-Saxons and British Indians acknowledged the sovereignty of the Crown, the former were members of a free monarchy and the latter were subjects by virtue of the sword. Indians in the British Empire simply could not be tolerated as competitors, for their methods were meaner and their living standards lower. They were brought in as laborers to do work which whites would not do and their status should remain such. Rees called for an end to glib mouthings of visionary utopians:

> It is evident that no step more fatal to the Empire can be taken than to attempt to force on colonists a code of conduct, such as could never be made applicable to inhabitants of other non-European countries, whether or not such are fellow-subjects of the Crown.
>
> South Africa has the right to decide for itself of what material the future nation shall be built. . . . The theory that all subjects of British Imperial rule are entitled to equal treatment in every part of the Empire must break down wherever it is exposed to a working test. Carry this theory to its logical conclusion and it will be necessary to reserve the tropical possessions of Great Britain for the Indian and the temperate zones for the European colonists, and any attempt to coerce the self-governing colonies in this behalf can only result in their ceasing to be integral parts of the Empire.[52]

The Times did not differ radically from other Conservative organs on the nature of the Empire. The question of the British Indian in South Africa was not a test case of what it should be. Perhaps British citizenship had been conceived of as conferring an equal status in all parts of the King-Emperor's domains in the same way as had Roman citizenship. But this principle, if it had been put fully to the test in Roman times, would most certainly have failed had the lower classes tended to migrate. In any event, it was impractical now, for young and expanding states insisted upon the right to choose the human material to build their communities. The Imperial State should strive to have Indian fellow subjects realize that inequality in South Africa was not owing to any theory of racial superiority but to the wish for social homogeneity. Already confronted by a Bantu population of overwhelming numbers, the addition of an appreciable Asiatic element would swamp the white community.[53]

Jebb submitted a finely spun theory distinguishing between subject-hood and citizenship in the British Empire. Common to all who satisfied the citizenship requirements of each political component was the status of subjecthood under the symbol of the Crown. Subject-hood carried the twin rights of protection against any foreign state and from oppression in territories of the Crown. Citizenship implied a right to take part in the government of the Empire, exerting influ-ence through the parliament of one's own state. But this "Britannic Alliance . . . accepts . . . the existing condition whereby each State determines by its local statutes the qualifications of citizenship." A necessary corollary was control of entry from one country to another within the Empire. In the case of the British Indian, the Imperial State could intervene in his behalf against the Transvaal when it was the South African Republic. However, when the Transvaal became part of the Empire, the colonial whites there had a right to be heard on the question of citizenship.[54]

Comments from all circles were favorable toward the *Indians Relief Act No. 22*. There was an advantage in a settlement, whatever the convictions on the day-to-day struggle or on the contemporary con-cepts of imperialism. The *New Statesman* congratulated Gandhi and his associates for having won recognition after a prolonged and painful struggle. Granted that a strict limit on the numbers admitted had to be conceded. But there was also something encouraging in the way Natal had been overruled on the matter of the £3 annual residence tax. Narrow provincialism was susceptible to nobler impulses in the greater aggregate. The *World's Work*, edited by Sir Henry Norman, Liberal M.P., welcomed the measure as embodying the bare duty of the Union toward its Indian community. The mutual spirit of give and take was to be commended, as if the new legislation were saying "that Asiatics shall not become a part of this population, but as much hospitality as we can safely show them we will offer with a good grace." *The Times* praised the Union government for its deeper appreciation of imperial interests and its readiness to swallow a compromise on that altar. The concessions were as generous as could be consistent with safeguarding its own future as a white community and it did conclude a controversy that had put strain upon the imperial banner.[55]

9

A Survey of Events since 1914

This chapter is intended for the layman and not the scholar or expert. History cherishes as one of its merits the element of continuity essential to appraise developments of today in fair balance. To stay with the documentary record of the years from 1902 to 1914 and cut the story at the latter date would certainly serve the purposes of the professional man. But for others, especially since the subject of non-Europeans in South Africa has become the major issue in that country, some glimpse into happenings since World War I would seem desirable. To be sure, what is given here can only constitute a capsule summary and each highly compressed paragraph could well be expanded into many more. However, it is hoped that the attempt at the total picture will give the reader a sense of intellectual satisfaction in following events of his own times.*

The political scene from the inception of the Union in 1910 until 1948 was dominated by three heroes of the Boer War—Botha, Smuts, Hertzog. All had the ultimate ideal of a united South Africa. Where they differed was in the nature of the acculturation process between Briton and Boer. Botha (who died in 1919) and Smuts, his successor, wanted to merge the two racial streams of Briton and Boer into one nation culturally but bilingual in tongue (English and Afrikaans which had replaced High Dutch among the Boers). Hertzog wanted a nation evolving along the lines of two distinct cultures, each preserving its own inherited tongue and accorded proper dignity. Neither Smuts nor Hertzog ever succeeded in establishing their concepts.

*For literature see the section in the bibliography entitled, *Suggested Readings on Apartheid and Related Issues.*

After World War II the electorate cast them aside to follow another ideological approach. South Africa should be one nation assuredly but based upon the Afrikaans culture.

This new scheme of things is the program of the Nationalist party which has held power since 1948 under the successive leadership of Dr. Daniel François Malan, Johannes Gerhardus Strydom, and Dr. Hendrik Frensch Verwoerd. Its majority has increased steadily in successive general elections and today occupies a seemingly well-entrenched position. However, critics are quick to point out that these triumphs came through advantageous features in the electoral process. Enfranchisement of white women in 1930 had greater significance for the Boer population which constitutes the backbone of the Nationalist party. Extension of universal suffrage to all whites in Cape Colony and Natal, as in Orange Free State and the Transvaal, brought the poorer classes of Boers on the voting register. Retention of rural constituencies with a preponderance of Boer farmers, despite declining population, favored the Nationalist party.

A new conception in imperial relationship ran concomitant with the radical developments on the South African political scene. The *Statute of Westminster* in 1931 set forth the formula of "autonomous communities, . . . equal in status, in no way subordinate one to another in any aspect of their domestic or external affairs, though united by a common allegiance to the Crown and freely associated as members of the British Commonwealth of Nations." South Africa has been in the vanguard of dominions implementing constitutional maturity. The traditional British powers of disallowance and reservation were eliminated. An appeal to the Privy Council in London by citizens or provinces against decisions of the South African Supreme Court was ended. The position of governor-general has been filled by personages from political circles in South Africa itself instead of from the British peerage. The Union flag came to fly over public buildings and *Die Stem van Suid-Afrika* became the official anthem. A Union diplomatic corps was formed to take over the conduct of foreign affairs. In short, the Imperial Factor disappeared from the everyday life of South Africa.

The Nationalist party went even further than vitiating the British connection. An aggressive campaign was inaugurated to promote the Afrikaans culture among Anglo-Saxon stock. The achievement of republicanism in 1960 by a popular vote of 849,598 to 775,978 harbored the hope that cutting ties with the Crown might orient Anglo-Saxons toward South Africa as their homeland. Resistance to assimilation invited sterner measures, notably an emphasis upon Afrikaans as the language for civil service employment. The *Citizenship Act of 1949*, extending the period of residence from two to five years and requiring satisfactory evidence of being a worthy citizen, would appear to have been aimed against British-born immigrants. It is labeled a throwback to the tribulations of the Uitlanders and an attempt to avoid any appreciable numbers from the British Isles that might alter the political complexion. Whether the outcome will mean second-class citizenship for the stubborn core of British stock remains to be seen.

The fortunes of the non-Europeans were profoundly affected by the political developments. Not that there was any fundamental difference in practice among the white population toward a policy of segregation. But the Nationalist party would go to the extreme and spin a final theory of separateness. Apartheid is the formal name given its plan and it stresses each race being an entity unto itself. The intent is a series of vertical communities, the individual being free within his grouping to find his level of professional and social life. The goal must be the development of the Bantu as Bantu and the Europeans as Europeans wherever they may be in the country. The alternative proposal of an integrated community must wind up with certain domination by the overwhelming native population and perhaps even expulsion of the whites. The challenge has been how to relate theory to reality. Some kind of territorial division setting up several autonomous regions would seem necessary. Yet there is also the hard fact that the economic life of the white community depends upon native labor. The nearest presentation of a concrete scheme is the report submitted in 1954 by a Commission for the Socio-Economic Development of the Bantu Areas under the auspices of the Union of South Africa. It is known as the *Tomlinson Report*, after Professor Frederick Rothman Tomlinson, its chairman and an expert in agricultural economics.

The *Tomlinson Report* concerned itself only with the Bantu. The central premise was that reserves should constitute the national home of natives within which they could develop their own latent faculties.

But outside the reserves, that is, in the territory of the white man, native workers would be sojourners and shorn of any political rights. A total of seven major reserves including the three protectorates, the addition of which was calculated to double the land at the disposal of the natives, were envisaged as sufficient to settle 14,000,000 out of 21,000,000 natives estimated as the population by A.D. 2000. Extensive soil conservation projects and establishment of industries were counted upon as the means to provide those in the reserves with a livelihood. The other 7,000,000 natives would be transient workers in the community of the white man, living in special urban locations. An expenditure of £100,000,000 over the first ten years was suggested as the minimum to get a scheme of industrialization underway in the reserves.

The Nationalist party did not go along with many features of the *Tomlinson Report*. The points of difference were so marked as to place the apartheid scheme in an embarrassing perspective. The proposed initial outlay of £100,000,000 was held to be out of line with budgetary considerations. A meager water supply in many reserves would make the introduction of industrial enterprises difficult and expensive. An answer would have to be found to the question of raw materials. The effect of mushrooming native manufactures upon the economy of the white man would have to be weighed. It could endanger the latter's labor supply and the sale of his own manufactures. As it was, Union secondary industries were experiencing keen foreign competition in the home market. Fortunately the debit balance brought on by importation of raw materials in these new ventures was made up by credits earned by the gold mines. The immediate need was to increase sales, and competition by native factories would wreck that hope. Most of all, the *Tomlinson Report* was incompatible with an avowed policy to strengthen tribalism, authority of chieftains, and communal tenure of land. A modern industrial economy would inevitably break down the ancient institutions of native peoples.

Actually, the initial steps along the road to apartheid were taken during the 1930's under General Hertzog. The *Native Trust and Land Act of 1936* almost doubled the amount of land set aside from 10,410,290 morgen (in 1913) to 17,660,290 or from 7.3 per cent to 12.3 per cent for 8,000,000 natives against 125,000,000 morgen for 2,000,000 Europeans. The expectation was that besides 3,000,000 natives already living in the reserves, another 3,000,000 currently employed also could be settled there. As for the 2,000,000 living in urban centers and engaged industrially by white employers, they would be housed in locations. The *Natives Representation Act of 1936* removed native voters in Cape Colony and Natal from the common roll. A vote of one hundred sixty-nine to eleven fulfilled the constitutional requirement of a two-thirds majority of the combined two houses. Henceforth, natives meeting property and educational qualifications were to have a separate voting roll to elect three whites to the House of Assembly and four whites to the Senate. In addition, a native representative council with the function of an advisory body on native affairs was set up, consisting of twelve elected and four nominated members plus the five chief native commissioners. The *Native Laws Amendment Act of 1937* required a rigorous enforcement of the pass system to control native movement from rural and reserve areas to urban labor centers. Powers were bestowed to determine what towns the natives could enter and even to send them home.

However, after 1948, a flurry of legislation spelled out the scheme of apartheid. The *Population Registration Act of 1950* was the cornerstone, decreeing that the racial identity of all males over sixteen years of age be registered under the headings of Bantu, Cape Coloured, Asiatic, and White. Thereafter, amending acts fixed more rigidly a life of separateness between European and Bantu. Severe penalties were enacted against mixed marriages and illicit physical relations. An elaborate system of permits and passes was contained in a so-called reference book which was to be kept on the person of the Bantu at all times. An amenities act called for separate facilities in public buildings, railways stations, and recreational areas. The Union government could declare an area reserved for residence by a particular race and remove others to new sites. An education act prescribed the tribal tradition as the basis of Bantu schooling, to be taught in the mother tongues and suited to the needs of unskilled workers. A separate Bantu university was contemplated for whatever professional skills should be provided. An industrial act gave the Ministry of Labour authority to define the range of jobs for the Bantu. Even the separate representation given them in the Union Parliament by General Hertzog was abolished. An elaborate hierarchy of chieftains, headmen, and councillors serving tribal and regional echelons was planned. The crowning feature was the creation of the Department of Bantu Administration and Development to replace the Department of Native Affairs. It would be responsible for administration of reserves, recruitment of labor, and the municipal locations. In this connection the *Bantu Laws Amendment Act of 1964* set up a state-controlled system of labor bureaus empowered to determine the admission of natives into white areas for work and permission could be withheld on such varied grounds as undesirable or a labor surplus.

The Cape Coloured, numbering 1,000,000 in Cape Colony, 100,000 in the Transvaal, 30,000 in Natal, and 15,000 in Orange Free State have fared badly in the new scheme of things. They have been designated non-Europeans and their destiny lumped with natives in the color distinction of black and white. Their previous history had been one titanic effort to link themselves with the white community. Many possess the physiognomy and pigmentation of whites. Most of them speak both English and Afrikaans. Those who could pass the test of a white person (in appearance and by general repute and acceptance) had to make a heartrending decision to sever bonds with Negroid relatives or else risk detection and transfer to a non-European register. The literature of South Africa offers a number of novels dealing with this tragic theme of parents and children going their separate ways so that the latter might enjoy the advantages of white society. There is no more agonizing account of man's inhumanity to man than the novel of Sarah Gertrude Millin, *God's Step-Children*.

For the larger number of the Cape Coloured riveted in the classification of non-European, life came to assume a grim outlook. The Nationalist party refused to honor the promise of General Hertzog that they would have political rights, residential areas, and educational and job opportunities detached from the environment of the Bantu. Legislation on amenities have cast them with the Bantu and they can no longer share the same space with whites in tramcars and railroads or attend the same cultural events. There has been discrimination in wage scales for teachers and nurses and social-service benefits have been less. They have not received equal treatment in the courts of justice; sentences are severer and prison-cell conditions are appalling. They are losing out in civil-service jobs and are excluded from serving in the army in a combatant capacity. Their children have parallel organizations in the Boy Scouts and the YMCA. A crushing blow was dealt in 1956 when they were removed from the common voting roll after a struggle in which the Nationalist party clashed with the Supreme Court and had to increase Senate membership before a two-thirds majority could be achieved. The Cape Coloured now constitute a separate electorate to name four Europeans to represent them in the House of Assembly. The governor-in-council nominates one European for the Senate on the basis of being acquainted with the wants of the Cape Coloured.

Nor has the British Indian fared any better under the scheme of apartheid. Gandhi's hope that acquiescence in the prohibition of Indian immigration would make the Union more receptive to end disabilities imposed upon domiciled Indians has not been realized. What intensified the hostility of whites was the phenomenal birthrate of the resident British Indian community. From a prewar figure of 150,000 the Asiatic population jumped to 280,000 in 1946 and 400,000 in 1960. This fact of tremendous fecundity has been accentuated by the broader implication of Indian increases in neighboring British African possessions. Indians outnumber Europeans three to one in Kenya and twelve to one in Uganda while Indian settlements are sprouting in Tanganyika, Nyasaland, and the Rhodesias.* During the 1920's and 1930's round-table conferences were held and one suggestion revived the idea of colonization elsewhere under the political aegis of India. The Union government sought a repatriation scheme with generous financial assistance but only 20,000 accepted and it was abandoned in the 1940's. Signs are not lacking that a sterner effort along these lines will be resumed in the future.

In the meanwhile, British Indians have had applied to them the principle of apartheid and their disabilities have been accentuated severalfold. They are classified as non-Europeans and required to utilize facilities set aside for Bantu and Cape Coloured. Further limitations have been placed upon property ownership and occupancy

---

*Statistics from the latest available sources are as follows:

	EUROPEAN	ASIATIC
Southern Rhodesia	176,300	13,206 (including coloured)
Northern Rhodesia	72,000	6,000
Nyasaland	6,700	8,150
Kenya	29,660	97,687
Tanganyika	20,598	76,536
Uganda	3,448	33,767

in areas reserved for whites where many Indians had been previously allowed to reside. A separate voters' roll was assigned for Indians to elect three Europeans to the House of Assembly and one European to the Senate. The Indians refused to avail themselves of this offer and in 1948 their representation was canceled. The situation became tense in 1949 when a riot broke out in Durban pitting Bantu against Indians. It started as a result of an apparently unfounded rumor that an Indian shopkeeper had brutally beaten a Zulu boy to death. In retaliation a crowd of Zulus broke into Indian stores and looted them. Then Indian quarters were invaded and many homes were set on fire. When order was restored the toll stood at over three hundred killed, one thousand wounded, £300,000 property damage, and several thousand Indians homeless. Critics attributed the holocaust to the preaching of intolerance and hatred in high places. Some commentators insisted that the Nationalist party was not unhappy at the possibility of exploiting Bantu animosity to rid the country of Indians.

The Nationalist party argues that apartheid is the only means of maintaining the identity and existence of a European stock whose courageous pioneering made South Africa an habitable land. To accept political equality as the principle of white and black relationship must yield supremacy to the latter. Events in the Belgian Congo are pointed to as a warning against relaxation of white overlordship. Afrikaners describe themselves as having no other home but South Africa and if a like attempt to drive out whites is made it could be only into the sea. Their roots are not in Holland and their fortunes are irrevocably wedded to the land of the veldt. Nor can there be any halfway station of formal contacts in a quasi-integrated society. Intimate social intercourse would follow any appreciable amount of mixing in professional and civic life. The consequence of miscegenation is depicted as a progeny of degenerate hybrids. The oft-encountered rhetorical phrase, "Would you want your daughter (or sister) to marry a black?", is their way of assessing the horrors of integration.

Granted even that these Afrikaner jeremiads against an integrated society have some relevance. The pertinent question then is the degree of earnest intent that apartheid will be of mutual benefit. Will the Bantu get sufficient land and of a quality good enough for them to have a thriving agriculture? Will the whites provide the technical knowledge necessary to enable several millions of Bantu to possess an industrial structure beyond their own modest state of intelligence? Will those Bantu brought into the white man's territory be given adequate living and working conditions? Will their separate facilities and amenities be of a standard equal to those of whites?

Statistics thus far are not such as to dispel the accusation that apartheid is merely segregation at the convenience of white interests. Where a minimum standard of living for a native family in urban centers has been set at £23 10s. per month, the average earning is £15 18s. per month. Where the Union government spent £65,000,000 over a ten-year period from 1943 to 1953 for white housing, it was £31,000,000 for native housing. Where the Union government spent £23,872,000 for the education of whites or £43 17s. per year per child, it was £7,884,775 for natives or £7 per year per child. One may appreciate the brief of the Nationalist party that the goal cannot be achieved overnight and grant that more has been done for the native in the last few years than in all previous decades together. But the proof of genuineness in the final analysis must be a sympathetic approach that recognizes the fundamental ideal of human dignity. If apartheid becomes basically neighborliness between black and white, it would deserve a respectable hearing.

What casts an element of doubt upon apartheid as a positive program is the repression and terrorism to which non-Europeans have been subjected. The Nationalist government has passed a series of measures practically eliminating civil rights. Policemen have wide discretion to enter homes without warrants and to make arrests for conduct interpreted as stirring up agitation against the state or designed to strengthen the forces of communism. This could and has meant anything—criticism of the government, an industrial strike, a demonstration protesting legislative enactments. Parades and meetings arranged to register protests have been answered by wholesale arrests and imprisonments. Reports of police assaults and rough treatment of those taken into custody seem to be endless. Pass laws are described as being administered with heartlessness. Most ominous is the *General Law Amendment Act of 1963* which empowers police to detain suspects without access to courts, legal advisers, or kinfolk, for periods of ninety days for "interrogation." It will no longer be necessary for the government to hold treason trials and undergo the embarrassing possibility of acquittals. Guilt and innocence could become irrelevant legal niceties and the state emerge with total power over the individual.

Such harsh treatment and disregard of civil rights cannot make for a spirit of good will and the faith which should attend voluble protestations in behalf of apartheid. It is an historical truism that only righteous means can bring a righteous end. If the Bantu have reacted hostilely to apartheid, the only answer can be patience in a trying situation and not physical brutality. After all, a century of anarchy in native policy is not calculated to dissolve the instinct of suspicion that the separateness of two worlds is merely a subtler form of predatory imperialism. Apart from probably losing the cooperation of the Bantu for any kind of segregation scheme, the tactics of the Nationalist government may wind up in a drift toward a totalitarian state. An atmosphere of fear and the animal instincts that go with it could stalk the land. What South Africa might come up with is not a reasonable facsimile of Western civilization but a narrowly conceived and arrogant white civilization.

Even though the Imperial Factor had disappeared, apartheid provoked friction with Great Britain. The Nationalist government has called upon the Imperial State to make good the promise in the constitution to transfer the three protectorates. The British government has refused on the ground that the Bantu distrust the color prejudice of the Union. Nationalist leaders contest the allegation, pointing to the fact that over one-half of the 200,000 able-bodied natives in the protectorates flock annually to the Union for work in mines and factories. The protectorates are furnished with post and telegraph facilities and access to roads, railways, and air services. The Union is the principal source of their imports and the principal market for their exports. Indeed, comparing the relatively more efficient educational and health services which the Union provides for its own native population to those which an overextended Imperial State is able to supply the protectorates, the Bantu stand to benefit immeasurably by incorporation in the Union.* The idea of consulting native opinion is

*The amount spent annually per native for education and health is as follows (Spooner (1960), p. 190):

	EDUCATION		HEALTH		
	s.	d.	£	s.	d.
South Africa	15	9	1	6	11
Bechuanaland	4	10		5	0
Swaziland	5	7		5	11
Basutoland	5	6		4	4

ridiculous, for the advantages of transfer are beyond comprehension by aborigines.

The situation has been further exacerbated by Union charges that the protectorates are being used by Bantu leaders to direct their campaign against apartheid. The Chief of the South African Security Police has accused Great Britain of allowing Bechuanaland to become "not only a haven for . . . political refugees, but a base for sabotage against South Africa." Retaliatory measures have been undertaken by the Union. Only entry for work would be allowed, attended by the most rigid travel and living restrictions. Particularly vulnerable to discrimination is Basutoland which, at any given moment, has over 100,000 natives working in the Union. Already a dozen and more police control posts are being constructed to patrol the frontier along the border between the two states. The Union threatens to revise the customs agreement apportioning railway revenues and to secure the repatriation of "foreign natives." Recently, in September 1963, Dr. Verwoerd put out a feeler, offering to administer the protectorates as Bantustans or self-governing black areas and to set up an economic common market.

The resignation of South Africa on March 15, 1961, from the Commonwealth is a product of apartheid. At a meeting of Commonwealth Prime Ministers in London, if an affirmative answer was given South Africa's request to continue membership under republican status (as had been allowed India), the Union government came in for criticism because of its racial policies. The senior members—Canada, Australia, New Zealand—expressed their disapproval. But it was the Afro-Asian bloc which provided the most blunt criticism. India, already at sword's point and having withdrawn its High Commissioner from the Union and broken off trade relations in 1946, had sharp words for the treatment of Indians. Malaya presented a fourteen-page indictment. Nigeria pressed for a strong resolution against the indifference to human rights in the Union. Tanganyika went so far as to say that it would not seek membership in the Commonwealth if South Africa stayed.

This was the background to the decision of Dr. Verwoerd to withdraw his country from the Commonwealth. He commented that otherwise Great Britain would be placed in the position of having to choose between South Africa and the Afro-Asian members. He recalled grimly that South Africa had not joined the chorus of critics against Ghana, India, Malaya, and Ceylon when these states were accused of flouting the principles of democratic government and practising oppression and discrimination. As Dr. Verwoerd saw it, the Commonwealth was forsaking the tradition of variety and insisting upon ideological conformity. Harold Macmillan, Prime Minister of the United Kingdom, expressed deep regret at the severing of ties and hoped it would be possible some day for South Africa again to play its part in the Commonwealth.

Apartheid has pursued the Union of South Africa to the broader stage of the United Nations. Resolutions have been passed from 1946 on by the Assembly condemning the racial policy of the Union. India has raised persistently the violation of human rights as enshrined in the United Nations Charter. The new African states fashioned out of the French, Belgian, and British colonies have placed on the agenda statements scoring apartheid as a euphemism of neighborly separateness and describing it as a threat to world peace. A United Nations Commission of Inquiry Report in 1955 formally indicted apartheid. While Great Britain abstained from casting a vote on these occasions, accepting the Union's contention that it constituted a matter of domestic jurisdiction, the loyalty was to the links of the past. Union delegates in the United Nations have reacted bitterly to the criticism heaped upon their country. India should remember the caste system and the millions of untouchables. The United States should remember segregation practices in the South. The answers of India and the United States stressed that they had at least proclaimed their intention to end abuses of human rights. Their outlook was forward and not static.

The status of South-West Africa has added to the difficulties of the Union government in the United Nations. This German territory was received as a mandate after World War I. When the League of Nations collapsed at the outbreak of World War II, South Africa regarded the obligation of trusteeship as no longer binding and in 1949 incorporated it as a province in the Union. The United Nations refused to accept this unilateral action and insisted that all mandates pass into its custody. South Africa had the responsibility to turn in annual reports and to allow commissions to investigate complaints of maladministration. Behind the niceties of international law the issue is the charge that the natives (370,000) are finding apartheid as strangling as their counterpart in the older provinces of the Union. The International Court of Justice at The Hague, to whom the question had been referred, ruled in 1950 that the mandate was still in effect. The emergent independent African states have pressed that the Assembly impose sanctions 1) denying capital, 2) cutting off supplies of essential commodities, and 3) boycotting South African exports.

The Sharpeville incident on March 21, 1960, disclosed the full force of the disrepute which South Africa has stored up for itself. The South African Native National Congress had decreed the day as one of protest against the pass laws, to take the form of peaceful demonstrations in front of police stations. At Sharpeville, a small community near Vereeniging in the Transvaal, the constabulary equipped with armored cars opened fire and killed several score natives and wounded another two hundred. The news was front page all over the world and nations hastened to express their sympathy for the victims, their comments ranging from a sense of shame to outraged humanitarianism.

In Norway, on the day of the funeral, flags were flown at half-mast on public buildings. Brazil recalled its ambassador from Pretoria and canceled a football match in Rio de Janeiro against a South African team. Walter Nash, Prime Minister of New Zealand, asked an audience to stand in silent memory of the dead. John George Diefenbaker, Prime Minister of Canada, deplored the loss of life and the policy of racial discrimination which had been responsible for it. Christian Herter, American Secretary of State, regretted the tragic loss of life and hoped native peoples could get redress for their legitimate grievances by peaceful means. The British government recorded its deep condolence but shelved a motion of the Labour party censuring the Union government. In Asia the reaction was to provoke antiwhite feeling. Pandit Jawaharlal Nehru, Prime Minister of India, moved a resolution in the India Parliament likening the Nationalist party to the Nazis. Malaya condemned the inhuman brutality of South African police as a travesty upon justice and decency. In the Security Council of the United Nations, after a debate of three days in which communist states led the attack, a resolution was passed lamenting the episode and calling upon the Union to abandon apartheid and bring about racial harmony on the basis of equality.

The ramifications of apartheid may even be followed in the cold war between the West and Soviet Russia. Both sides are keenly conscious of the value accruing in the good will of over one hundred millions of colored people in Africa, at the moment in the throes of catapulting from primitivism to political independence. Their numbers and resources could well tip the scales in the ideological struggle between capitalism and communism. Both sides are making strong bids for their friendship, dangling technical aid and diplomatic support to erase colonialism. Great Britain has made a contribution by assisting its possessions to reach self-government. Macmillan, on a visit to South Africa in February 1960, frankly informed the Union Parliament at Capetown that there was a "wind of change" in Africa and that Great Britain would line up against racial discrimination in the event of trouble. The moral arsenal of the Western world would be immeasurably strengthened by a South Africa committed to an enlightened non-European policy, be it a reasonable scheme of apartheid or the concept of integration.

It is of interest to compare the story of South Africa and current developments in Southern Rhodesia. The Federation of the Rhodesias and Nyasaland, founded in 1953, was dissolved by the British government in 1963 at the behest of the native population. The latter claimed that the federation was a move on the part of the white settlers to establish European domination. In overriding the objection of the white settlers, the British government insisted further that the evolution of the three component parts toward self-government must include political rights for the natives. In Northern Rhodesia (now Zambia), where there were 75,000 Europeans and 2,510,000 Africans, the result has been to establish an African majority. In Nyasaland (now Malawi), where there were 9,000 Europeans, and 3,000,000 Africans, the result has been the same. In Southern Rhodesia, however, the white population of 220,000 resisted any political domination by 4,000,000 Africans. The British government refused to grant independence on the basis of the constitution of 1961 which, in its complicated franchise qualifications embracing annual income earnings, property ownership, and educational achievements, provided at best for an African opposition of fifteen in a legislative assembly of sixty-five.

What will be the outcome of the unilateral declaration of independence by Southern Rhodesia in November 1965 remains to be seen. But the announcement of Great Britain to stand by the principle of the paramountcy of native interests is certainly in strange contrast to its dealings with the Union of South Africa prior to World War I. Perhaps it is the determination not to repeat the sad aftermath in South Africa relative to the interests of the non-Europeans. Perhaps it is the changing character of the Commonwealth producing an Afro-Asian majority bloc. Perhaps it is the fear of communism exploiting the situation in Africa if the West falters as a champion of native interests. At any rate, Great Britain no longer apparently places any stock in the hope that the Anglo-Saxon heritage of fair play would win over the Southern Rhodesian whites to a full appreciation of their obligations to the natives.

In retrospect, for the period from 1902 to 1914, South Africa constituted a major baptism for Great Britain in the complexities of a multiracial colonial community. In the case of the Chinese, the British nation was united in opposing their permanent residence on the Rand. Debate centered on whether to ban their advent in the first instance or to permit a temporary entry under an indentured status. While an assured destiny for the white stock through a stimulated economy, especially an augmentation of Anglo-Saxon immigrants, was a vital goal, a searching review ensued over the possible rearing once again of the ugly head of enslavement. In the case of the British Indians, it is true that Great Britain shared responsibility for their initial introduction on the sugar plantations of Natal. But an effort was made to blunt the worst vestiges of the humiliations heaped upon them subsequently. If an assured destiny for the white stock must take priority against the threat of substandard competition, some degree of human dignity should be accorded those British Indians who had come to make South Africa their home. Debate centered on the extent to which disabilities should be imposed, views ranging from acquiescence in a modest complement of such restrictions to a demand for recognition of their right to first-class citizenship.

Turning to the non-European elements more indigenous to South Africa, the British nation would make a distinction between the Cape Coloured and the Bantu. The Cape Coloured merited an opportunity to integrate with the white community on the basis of a demonstrated ability to assimilate Western culture. Many had coped with formal education, acquired property, pursued professions, and were on the common voting roll. The Bantu, of course, constituted the hard core problem, for they were vastly superior in numbers to the white population. Debate centered on the potential of the native to assimilate Western culture, views ranging from optimism as to its achievement in the near future to doubts that it could come off before many generations. What made the discussion seem an empty one was the determination of the colonial white population to entrench itself as the dominant political and economic class.

Great Britain did not achieve appreciable success in pressing its views upon South Africa. Save for playing an active part in the termination of the Chinese experiment, the Imperial Factor could effect little for the other non-European elements. The blunt fact was that constitutional developments had left the British government with no more than the role to advise and to cajole its autonomous offspring. It might be true that there were clauses in the colonial constitutions permitting formal intervention. But the mother country was reluctant to join the issue of human dignity, preferring the hope that Anglo-Saxon ideals would yet permeate South African society. This is not to say that Great Britain was indifferent to imperial considerations. The desire for a loyal Union of South Africa in the face of a growing German threat is granted. The desire to placate an Indian nationalist movement indignant over the treatment of their countrymen in South Africa spurred efforts at mediation. The desire to share in the profits of trade and the diamond and gold mines can not be discounted. Still, the British nation—officialdom and public opinion—held aloft doggedly the vision that an imperial moral standard must govern the conduct of member states.

NOTES

NOTES TO CHAPTER ONE

1. For secondary literature dealing with the material in this chapter see *Cambridge History of the British Empire: South Africa* (1936), VIII; Cory (1910-30), 6 vols.; Eybers (1918); Marais (1957); Theal (1927, 4th ed., rev. and enl.), 5 vols.; Walker (1957).

2. Hofmeyr (1952, 2nd ed., rev.), p. 66.

3. Walker (1957), p. 199.

4. R. I. Lovell (1934), p. 8.

5. Macmillan (1927), pp. 267-68.

6. DeKieweit (1937), pp. 201-02.

7. DeKieweit (1937), p. 89.

8. DeKieweit (1937), p. 69.

9. C. R. Lovell, *American Historical Rev.*, Jan. 1956, p. 308 ff.

10. For secondary literature dealing with British Indians in South Africa see Calpin (1949); Gandhi (1954); Kondapi (1951); Palmer (1957); Polak (1909); Younghusband (1899).

11. *P.P.*, 1895, LXXI, Cd. 7911.

12. Headlam (1931), I, p. 304.

13. *P.R.O.*, c.o. 879/59, No. 600.

14. *The Times*, Nov. 3, 1899, 7b (Lansdowne).

15. *Annual Register*, 1900, p. 165.

16. *Trades Union Congress, Annual Reports*, 1900, pp. 54-55, 1901, pp. 80-81.

17. *Labour Representation Committee, Annual Report*, 1901, p. 20.

18. Sacks (1952), pp. 362-66.

19. For an account of the Fabian Society's position see Edward R. Pease *The History of the Fabian Society* (New York: 1926, new and rev. ed.), pp. 128-38.

20. George Bernard Shaw *Fabianism and the Empire* (London: 1900), 101 pp.

21. Sacks (1952), pp. 362-63.

22. *P.R.O.*, c.o. 879/73, No. 650, p. 74, Chamberlain to Milner, Feb. 27, 1901.

23. *P.R.O.*, c.o. 879/73, No. 650, pp. 77-79, c.o. 879/71, No. 665, p. 178.

24. *P.P.*, 1902, LXVII, Cd. 1163, p. 10. Cf. Cana (1909), pp. 210-11; Pyrah (1955), p. 90; Worsfold (1906), pp. 489-90, 546, 549-50.

25. *The Times*, Oct. 13, 1897, 10e.

26. Headlam (1931), I, pp. 177-78. Cf. Pyrah (1955), p. 87 ff.

27. *Campbell-Bannerman Papers*, 41210, pp. 187-89, Asquith to Campbell-Bannerman, June 3, 1900.

28. *Ibid.*, 41224, p. 159, Ripon to Campbell-Bannerman, Jan. 19, 1901.

29. *Ibid.*, 41243A, p. 64, Notes [ca. Jan. 1901].

30. DeKieweit (1937), pp. 71-72.

31. For literature on the British Colonial Office see Sir George Fiddes *The Dominions and Colonial Offices* (London: 1926); Henry L. Hall *The Colonial Office* (London: 1937); Charles Jeffries *The Colonial Empire and Its Civil Service* (Cambridge: 1938).

NOTES TO CHAPTER TWO

1. For literature on South African gold mining operations see Bleloch (1902, 2nd ed., rev.); Emden (1935); Goodfellow (1931); Van Der Horst (1942).

2. *P.R.O.*, c.o. 291/53, 62.

3. Amery (1951), VI, pp. 332-34; *P.P.*, 1903, XLV, Cd. 1683, p. 4.

4. *P.P.*, 1903, XLV, Cd. 1640, p. 12.

5. *P.P.*, 1904, XXXIX, Cds. 1894, 1896, 1897; *P.R.O.*, c.o. 291/58.

6. *P.P.*, 1904, XXXIX, Cds. 1894, 1896, 1897.

7. *P.P.*, 1904, XXXIX, Cd. 1896, pp. 1-43.

8. *P.P.*, 1904, XXXIX, Cd. 1897, pp. 404-05.

9. *P.P.*, 1904, XXXIX, Cd. 1896, pp. 45-77.

10. Headlam (1933), II, p. 458 ff.; *P.P.*, 1904, LXI, Cd. 1895, pp. 76-88.

11. Headlam (1933), II, pp. 476-77.

12. Headlam (1933), II, pp. 476-77.

13. Headlam (1933), II, p. 481 ff.; *P.P.*, 1904, LXI, Cds. 1895, 1899, 1941; *P.R.O.*, c.o. 879/80, Nos. 721, 747.

14. *The Times*, Aug. 24, 1903, 4a (Botha).

15. Headlam (1933), II, p. 481 ff.; *P.P.*, 1904, LXI, Cd. 1899, pp. 6-11; *P.R.O.*, 879/80, No. 721, 879/81, No. 728. Cf. Millin (1937), I, pp. 200-01; Pyrah (1955), pp. 193-94.

16. *P.R.O.*, c.o. 291/59, c.o. 879/84, No. 744.

17. *P.R.O.*, c.o. 291/53, 65, 68.

18. *P.R.O.*, c.o. 48/572-73, 575-77.

19. *P.P.*, 1904, LXII, Cd. 2028; *P.R.O.*, c.o. 879/84, No. 744.

20. *P.P.*, 1904, LXI, Cd. 1941, pp. 28-29, Cd. 1895, pp. 231, 237; *The Times*, Jan. 12, 1904, 3d, Jan. 20, 1904, 6a and Jan. 29, 1904, 4a (news items).

21. *Commons*, Feb. 17, 1904, p. 29 (Malcolm), Mar. 21, 1904, pp. 303-04, 309 (Parker); *Lords*, Feb. 11, 1904, p. 987 (Marlborough); Parker (1904), pp. 10-12. Cf. *P.P.*, 1903, XLV, Cd. 1586.

22. *Commons*, Feb. 17, 1904, pp. 48-49 (Rolleston); *Empire Rev.*, Apr. 1904, pp. 229-30 (Kinloch-Cooke); *Lords*, Feb. 12, 1904, pp. 1146-47 (Earl Grey); *Morning Post*, Dec. 29, 1903, Feb. 17, 1904; Parker (1904), p. 5. Cf. *P.P.*, 1904, LXI, Cd. 1844.

23. *Empire Rev.*, Apr. 1903, pp. 233-34 (Goldmann); *Journal of the Society of Arts*, Apr. 29, 1904, p. 501 (Earl Grey); *Lords*, Mar. 21, 1904, pp. 201-02 (Lytton); *Morning Post*, July 5, 1902.

24. *Empire Rev.*, Apr. 1904, p. 218 (Kinloch-Cooke); *Lords*, Feb. 12, 1904, pp. 1149-50 (Earl Grey), Mar. 18, 1904, p. 30 and June 20, 1904, pp. 443-46 (Marlborough). Cf. *P.P.*, 1904, XXXIX, Cd. 1897, pp. 385, 389, LXI, No. 205, pp. 11-13, 1905, LV, Cd. 2401, p. 16.

25. *Commons*, Feb. 17, 1904, pp. 32-34 (Malcolm), p. 64 (Meysey-Thompson); *The Times*, Feb. 26, 1904, 10a-b and Mar. 21, 1904, 10a-b (Swettenham); Davis (1903), p. 139; Kinloch-Cooke (1904), p. 2.

26. *Commons*, Feb. 17, 1904, p. 33 (Malcolm); *Morning Post*, Dec. 1, 1903; *National Rev.*, Jan. 1904, pp. 835-36; *Pall Mall Gazette*, Mar. 21, 1904; *Spectator*, Mar. 26, 1904; Kinloch-Cooke (1904), p. 2; Van Laun and Wills (1904), p. 11. For official correspondence on the negotiations for Indian coolies to work on the Transvaal railways see *P.P.*, 1903, LXV, Cd. 1683; *P.R.O.*, c.o. 879/80, No. 721.

27. *Morning Post*, May 5, 1904; *Spectator*, Mar. 5, 1904 (Vachell); *The Times*, Feb. 26, 1904, 10a-b (Swettenham).

28. *The Times*, Nov. 26, 1903, 5f (Wortley).

29. *P.P.*, 1904, LXI, Cd. 1895, pp. 177, 246 ff.

30. *Transvaal, Legislative Council*, Second Session, 1903-04, pp. 378-79.

31. *The Times*, Mar. 7, 1904, 5f (news item).

32. *The Times*, Mar. 12, 1904, 7c (news item).

33. *Commons*, Feb. 16, 1904, pp. 1540, 1545 (Lyttelton); *Lords*, Mar. 18, 1904, p. 32 (Marlborough), Mar. 21, 1904, p. 170 (Windsor); Kinloch-Cooke (1904), pp. 11, 28-29.

34. *P.P.*, 1904, LXI, Cd. 1899, p. 6; *The Times*, Jan. 22, 1904, 3d (news item).

35. *Commons*, Feb. 16, 1904, pp. 1540-41 (Lyttelton); *Daily Telegraph*, Feb. 12, 1904; *Lords*, Feb. 11, 1904, pp. 998-1001 (Marlborough), Feb. 12, 1904, p. 1149 (Earl Grey).

36. Willard (1913), pp. 135-86.

37. *Ibid.*, pp. 92-93.

38. *Commons*, Feb. 16, 1904, pp. 1547-48 and Mar. 21, 1904, pp. 278, 284 (Lyttelton); *Empire Rev.*, Feb. 1904, pp. 24-26 (Kinloch-Cooke); *Lords*, June 20, 1904, p. 432 (Harris); Jebb (1905), pp. 129-31.

39. *Commons*, July 21, 1904, p. 779 (Fowler); *Nineteenth Century and After*, Nov. 1902, pp. 724-27 (Johnson); *The Times*, Dec. 22, 1902, 12a-e (Johnston), Feb. 16, 1904, 13c (Pethick-Lawrence).

40. *Daily Chronicle*, Jan. 12, 1904; *Lords*, Mar. 18, 1904, pp. 41-42 (Spencer), June 20, 1904, p. 414 (Coleridge); New Reform Club (1904), p. 17. For Lord Milner's statement see *P.P.*, 1904, LXI Cd. 1895, p. 41.

41. *Commons*, Mar. 21, 1904, pp. 318-20 (Bryce); *Labour Leader*, Mar. 26, 1904; *Truth*, Nov. 24, 1904; *Westminster Gazette*, Feb. 17, 1904. For the correspondence relating to the £10,000,000 to be underwritten by the mineowners see *P.P.*, 1904, LXI, Cd. 1895, pp. 1-8.

42. *Campbell-Bannerman Papers*, 41211, pp. 263-64, Campbell-Bannerman to Bryce, Dec. 31, 1903; *Commons*, Mar. 24, 1903, pp. 92-93 (W. V. Harcourt); *Daily Chronicle*, Feb. 1, 1904; *Labour Leader*, Apr. 23, 1904 (Muggeridge).

43. *Commons*, Feb. 17, 1904, p. 97 (Burns); *Manchester Guardian*, Mar. 25, 1904; *Speaker*, Jan. 31, 1903, Feb. 20, 1904; Buxton (1904), p. 20.

44. *P.P.*, 1904, LII, Cd. 2025, pp. 1-41.

45. *P.P.*, 1904, XXXIX, Cd. 1897, p. 385, LXI, No. 205, pp. 4, 8.

46. *Independent Rev.*, May 1904, pp. 599-600 (Burns); *Manchester Guardian*, Mar. 25, 1904; *Speaker*, May 28, 1904; *Westminster Gazette*, Jan. 28, 1903.

47. *Commons*, Feb. 16, 1904, p. 1518 (Samuel); *Daily Chronicle*, May 16, 26, 1904; *Westminster Gazette*, Mar. 22, 1904.

48. *Commons*, Feb. 17, 1904, p. 59 (McArthur), Mar. 21, 1904, pp. 317-18 (Bryce); *Daily News*, Jan. 20, 1904; *Manchester Guardian*, Feb. 17, Mar. 25, 1904.

49. *Daily News*, May 22, 1903; *Ethics*, Dec. 12, 1903 (Sanders).

50. *Church Times*, Dec. 18, 1903.

51. *Clarion*, Oct. 9, 1903; *Commons*, Feb. 16, 1904, pp. 1517-18 (Samuel); *Daily News*, Dec. 31, 1903; *Speaker*, Jan. 2, 1904.

52. *The Times*, Dec. 21, 1903, 15f (news item).

53. *Aborigines' Friend*, Jan. 1904 (Bourne); *British Weekly*, Mar. 10, 1904; *Fortnightly Rev.*, July 1904, pp. 113-15 (Hales); *Lords*, Mar. 18, 1904, pp. 17-18 (Coleridge), Mar. 21, 1904, pp. 166-67 (Alderley).

54. *Commons*, Mar. 21, 1904, p. 264 (Campbell-Bannerman), p. 312 (Bryce); *Daily News*, Feb. 18, 1904; *Lords*, Feb. 11, 1904, pp. 984-85 (Ripon), Feb. 12, 1904, pp. 1156-57 (Carrington).

55. For literature on the New South Wales episode see Willard (1923), pp. 84-85.

56. For literature on the Chinese problem in British Columbia see Charles James Woodsworth *Canada and the Orient* (Toronto: 1941), p. 45.

57. *Daily News*, Feb. 18, 1904; *Lords*, Feb. 12, 1904, pp. 1157-58 (Carrington), Mar. 21, 1904, p. 187 (Tweedmouth); *Pilot*, Mar. 26, 1904.

58. *Commons*, Feb. 22, 1904, p. 639 (Malcolm); *Empire Rev.*, Apr. 1903, pp. 235-36 (Goldmann), Apr. 1904, pp. 219, 222 (Kinloch-Cooke); Kinloch-Cooke (1904), p. 25.

59. For the story of the English navvies see *P.P.*, 1904, LXI, Cd. 1895, pp. 117-18, 159-60.

60. *Transvaal Mines Department, Detailed Statistics, June 1902-07*, p. 7.

61. Sir George Farrar had his staff undertake this comparison. *P.P.*, 1904, LXI, Cd. 1895, p. 258.

62. *Commons*, Feb. 16, 1904, pp. 1548-50 (Lyttelton), p. 1571 (Duke); *Empire Rev.*, Apr. 1904, pp. 219-20 (Kinloch-Cooke); Kinloch-Cooke (1904), pp. 22-24.

63. *Commons*, Feb. 16, 1904, pp. 1590-91 (Cust), pp. 1548-49 (Lyttelton); *Daily Telegraph*, Dec. 26, 1903; *Lords*, Mar. 21, 1904, pp. 151-52 (Selborne); *The Times*, Feb. 17, 1904, 4d-e (Lovat).

64. *Commons*, Mar. 21, 1904, p. 279 (Lyttelton); *Empire Rev.*, Nov. 1903, pp. 367-68 (Kinloch-Cooke); *Lords*, Feb. 12, 1904, pp. 1142-45 (Grey); *Morning Post*, Mar. 11, 1904; *Ninteenth Century And After*, May 1904, p. 861 (Goldmann).

65. *Investors' Rev.*, Feb. 20, 1904; *Manchester Guardian*, Aug. 5, 1902, Apr. 1, 1903, Jan. 12, 1904; *New Liberal Rev.*, Apr. 1904, pp. 278-80; MacDonald (1902), p. 73.

66. *Daily Chronicle*, Nov. 18, 1902; *Investors' Rev.*, Feb. 7, 1903; *Lords*, Mar. 21, 1904, p. 141 (Carrington); *Manchester Guardian*, Dec. 2, 1903.

67. *Clarion*, Jan. 30, 1903; *Commons*, Mar. 24, 1903, p. 84 (Samuel); *Manchester Guardian*, Jan. 12, 1904; *The Times*, Mar. 28, 1904, 7e (Johnston); MacDonald (1902), p. 73.

68. For Creswell's own account from which Samuel drew his facts see *The Times*, Feb. 1, 1904, 3e-f.

69. Cf. *P.P.*, 1904, LXI, Cd. 1895, p. 159.

70. *Commons*, Feb. 16, 1904, pp. 1510-12 (Samuel); *Daily News*, Dec. 7, 1903; *Manchester Guardian*, Feb. 15, 1904.

71. For literature on the Chinese in America see Mary Roberts Coolidge *Chinese Immigration* (New York: 1909); Elmer Clarence Sandmeyer *The Anti-Chinese Movement in California* (Urbana: 1939); George F. Seward *Chinese Immigration* (San Francisco: 1881).

72. *Daily Chronicle*, Jan. 16, 1903; *Fortnightly Rev.*, Mar. 1903, pp. 506-11 (Maxim); *Labour Leader*, Sept. 26, 1903; *Westminster Gazette*, May 20, 1904.

73. *The Times*, Feb. 9, 1903, 8c (news item).

74. *The Times*, Feb. 10, 1903, 12e-f (news item).

75. P.P., 1904, XXXIX, Cd. 1896, pp. 65-66.

76. *Justice*, Jan. 9, 1904; *Lords*, Feb. 11, 1904, p. 970 (Portsmouth), Feb. 12, 1904, p. 1160 (Carrington); *Manchester Guardian*, Feb. 10, 1903; *Westminster Gazette*, Feb. 11, 1903.

77. P.P., 1904, LXI, Cds. 1895, 1898, 1941, 2026. Cf. Campbell (1923), p. 176 ff.

78. P.P., 1904, LXI, Cd. 2026, pp. 3-4, 53-56, LXII, Cd. 1956, 5 pp.; P.R.O., c.o. 291/68-70, 75-76, 79.

79. *Commons*, Feb. 17, 1904, pp. 49-50 (Rolleston), Feb. 22, 1904, pp. 653-54 (Lyttelton); *Lords*, Feb. 12, 1904, p. 1152 (Earl Grey), Mar. 18, 1904, pp. 37-38 (Marlborough); *Pall Mall Gazette*, Mar. 22, 1904; *The Times*, Feb. 25, 1904, 8b (Lyttelton). For the views of the Archbishop of Canterbury see *Lords*, Feb. 11, 1904, pp. 1002-05, Mar. 4, 1904, pp. 187-90, Mar. 21, 1904, p. 58.

80. *Laws of British Guiana* (1895, new and rev. ed.), IV, pp. 1-93, Ordinance No. 18 of 1891, Incorporating Amendments, Ordinance No. 16 of 1894.

81. *Lords*, Mar. 21, 1904, p. 150 (Selborne); *Morning Post*, July 22, 1904; *Pall Mall Gazette*, Feb. 12, 1904; Kinloch-Cooke (1904), pp. 10-13.

82. *Commons*, Feb. 17, 1904, p. 109 (Brodrick), Mar. 21, 1904, p. 307 (Parker), pp. 349-50 (Balfour); *Daily Telegraph*, Feb. 18, 1904; Kinloch-Cooke (1904), p. 13.

83. *Commons*, Feb. 16, 1904, p. 1593 (Cust), Mar. 21, 1904, p. 333 (Seton-Karr); *Lords*, Mar. 21, 1904, p. 154 (Selborne); *The Times*, Jan. 29, 1904, 7d, Mar. 5, 1904, 11d-e.

84. *Commons*, Feb. 22, 1904, pp. 662-65 (Asquith), Mar. 21, 1904, pp. 266, 270 (Campbell-Bannerman); *Manchester Guardian*, Mar. 12, 1904 (Samuel); *Reformer*, Mar. 15, 1904, p. 143 (Robertson); *Westminster Gazette*, May 20, 1904.

85. *Commons*, Feb. 16, 1904, pp. 1525-26 (Seely); *Lords*, Feb. 12, 1904, p. 1161 (Carrington), Mar. 4, 1904, pp. 169-70 (Stanmore); *The Times*, Mar. 12, 1904, 6d (Wray); Seeley (1930), pp. 105-08.

86. *Commons*, Feb. 17, 1904, p. 94 (Burns), Mar. 21, 1904, p. 366 (Asquith); *Daily News*, Feb. 17, 1904; *Labour Leader*, May 6, 1904 (Muggeridge); *Manchester Guardian*, Feb. 18, 1904; *New Age*, Feb. 18, 1904.

87. *Catholic Times*, Feb. 26, 1904; *Examiner*, Feb. 25, 1904; *Guardian*,

Feb. 10, 1904; *Methodist Times*, Feb. 11, 1904; *Pilot*, Jan. 30, Mar. 12, 1904.

88. A parliamentary return tabulated the conditions under which coolies labored in the British Empire. *P.P.*, 1906, LXXVII, No. 357, 48 pp.

89. *Commons*, July 21, 1904, pp. 789-98 (Fowler); *Daily Chronicle*, Jan. 7, 1904; *Lords*, Mar. 4, 1904, pp. 171-76 (Stanmore), Mar. 21, 1904, pp. 192-93 (Tweedmouth); Buxton (1904), pp. 12-23.

90. For the Kanaka affair see Willard (1923), pp. 135-86.

91. For the Peruvian affair see Watt Stewart *Chinese Bondage in Peru: A History of the Chinese Coolie in Peru, 1849-1874* (Durham: 1951).

92. For the Portuguese affair see Campbell (1923), pp. 152-58.

93. *Commons*, Mar. 21, 1904, pp. 267-69 (Campbell-Bannerman); *Daily Chronicle*, Mar. 28, 1904; *The Times*, Feb. 25, 1904, 8b (Ellis); *Truth*, Jan. 28, 1904; *Westminster Gazette*, Mar. 21, 1904.

94. *Commons*, Feb. 16, 1904, p. 1505 (Samuel); *Daily Chronicle*, Mar. 22, 1904; *New Liberal Rev.*, Mar. 1904, p. 143 (ed.), pp. 148-49, 155 (Thomson).

NOTES TO CHAPTER THREE

1. *P.P.*, 1904, LXII, Cd. 2183, pp. 26-27, 1905, LV, Cd. 2401, pp. 68, 80-86, 1906, LXXX, Cd. 3025, p. 151; *The Times*, June 13, 1904, 7e (news item).

2. *P.P.*, 1904, LXI, Cd. 2026, pp. 22-52, LXII, Cd. 2183, pp. 2-3, 9-13.

3. *P.R.O.*, c.o. 291/80-81, 83-85, 87.

4. *P.P.*, 1906, LXXX, Cd. 3025, pp. 167-68; *P.R.O.*, c.o. 291/91.

5. *P.R.O.*, c.o. 291/91, 93.

6. *P.R.O.*, c.o. 291/78, 84, 90.

7. *P.R.O.*, c.o. 291/84-86, 93.

8. *P.P.*, 1906, LXXX, Cd. 2786, pp. 57-60.

9. *P.R.O.*, c.o. 291/83-85, 90.

10. *P.P.*, 1906, LXXX, Cd. 2786, pp. 83-86; *P.R.O.*, c.o. 291/85-86.

11. *P.R.O.*, c.o. 291/86.

12. *P.P.*, 1906, LXXX, Cd. 2786, pp. 26-27; *P.R.O.*, c.o. 291/83-85, 91.

13. Foster (ca. 1904), 4 pp.

14. *Commons*, Feb. 17, 1905, pp. 515-16 (Worsley-Taylor), pp. 525-27 (Lyttelton); *Lords*, May 16, 1905, pp. 424-25 (Marlborough).

15. Burt (1905), pp. 53, 59.

16. *Commons*, Feb. 17, 1905, p. 505 (Parker), pp. 514-15, 519 (Worsley-Taylor); *Lords*, May 16, 1905, pp. 427-28 (Marlborough); *Imperial South African Association* (1905), p. 17.

17. Phillips (1905), pp. 103, 108-10.

18. Commons, Feb. 17, 1905, pp. 505-06 (Parker), p. 515 (Worsley-Taylor), pp. 524-27 (Lyttelton); Lords, May 16, 1905, pp. 440-42 (Archbishop of Canterbury); Cf. P.R.O., c.o. 291/74.

19. P.P., 1905, LV, Cd. 2401, pp. 70-71.

20. Lords, May 16, 1905, pp. 425-27 (Marlborough); Standard, Sept. 22, 1905; The Times, Sept. 9, 1905, 11f (F. Milner), Nov. 24, 1905, 8a-b (Balfour).

21. Commons, Mar. 30, 1905, pp. 1779-80 (Parker), pp. 1772-73 (Lyttelton); Lords, Feb. 27, 1905, pp. 1282-83 (Marlborough), pp. 1286-88 (Harris); National Rev., Dec. 1905, pp. 754-56.

22. Commons, Feb. 17, 1905, p. 503 (Parker), July 27, 1905, pp. 691-93 (Lyttelton); Standard, Oct. 2, 1905; The Times, Nov. 14, 1905, 3b (Duncan); Westminster Gazette, Jan. 9, 1906, (Schumacher); Parker (1905), 16 pp. For the statistics on food and recruitment costs see P.R.O., c.o. 291/80.

23. Lords, Feb. 27, 1905, pp. 1283-84 (Marlborough); National Rev., Feb. 1905, pp. 1000-01 (Chaplin); The Times, Oct. 31, 1905, 15d (Blyth), Jan. 9, 1906, 4d (Pearson).

24. Liberal Magazine, Aug. 1904, pp. 437-38 (Buxton); Manchester Guardian, Dec. 26, 1904; Methodist Times, June 30, 1904; "English Witness" (1905), pp. 49-50.

25. Lords, May 16, 1905, pp. 445-46 (Stanmore); The Times, July 17, 1905, 12e-f (Burt); Burt (1905), p. 62; Hobson (1905, rev. ed.), p. 243.

26. For the complete statement of Boland see P.P., 1906, LXXX, Cd. 2819, p. 2.

27. Daily Chronicle, July 31, 1905; The Times, July 17, 1905, 12e-f (Burt); Westminster Rev., Oct. 1905, p. 457; Burt (1905), pp. 60-63; "English Witness" (1905), pp. 64-75.

28. P.P., 1906, LXXX, Cd. 2786, pp. 9-10.

29. Daily Chronicle, Nov. 25, 1905; Daily News, Dec. 8, 1905; Manchester Guardian, Sept. 1, 1905; Westminster Gazette, Sept. 5, 1905; "English Witness" (1905), p. 82ff.

30. Commons, Feb. 17, 1905, pp. 482-83 (Macnamara); Daily Chronicle, Sept. 8, 25, 1903; Daily News, Sept. 1, 1905; Lords, May 16, 1905, pp. 455-60 (Ripon); Speaker, Dec. 17, 1904; "English Witness" (1905), pp. 99-103; Naylor (1904), p. 6.

31. Naylor (1904), pp. 3-5. Cf. The Memoirs of Herbert Hoover: Years of Adventure (London: 1952), p. 87.

32. Commons, Feb. 17, 1905, pp. 496-97 and July 27, 1905, pp. 667-68 (Samuel); Manchester Guardian, Sept. 10, 1904; Westminster Rev., Feb. 1906, p. 219. Cf. Creswell, 1905.

33. *P.P.*, 1906, LXXVII, Cd. 2976, p. 6.

34. *P.P.*, 1905, XCVIII, No. 137, p. 22.

35. *Commons*, Feb. 17, 1905, pp. 496-97 and July 17, 1905, pp. 667-68 (Samuel); *Manchester Guardian*, Jan. 16, 1905; *Westminster Gazette*, Mar. 2, 1905; Hobson (1905, rev. ed.), pp. 243-44.

36. *Liberal Publication Department, Pamphlets and Leaflets*, 1905-06; *National Liberal Federation, Proceedings*, 1904, pp. 78-81; Campbell-Bannerman in W. T. Stead (1905), p. 23.

37. *Campbell-Bannerman Papers*, 41238, pp. 55-63, Ltrs., Campbell-Bannerman and Mackarness, July 28, 1905. Cf. *Commons*, July 27, 1905, pp. 702-04 (Campbell-Bannerman).

38. *Commons*, July 21, 1904, pp. 827-35 (Markham); *The Times*, March 21, 1904, 10f-11a and Apr. 5, 1904, 8e (Markham), Feb. 28, 1906, 4f (Fiennes), Mar. 6, 1906, 10f (Kincaid-Smith).

39. *P.R.O.*, c.o. 879/85, No. 761, pp. 224-25, Lyttelton to Selborne, Oct. 27, 1905.

40. *Commons*, Feb. 22, 1906, pp. 558-59 (Churchill); *P.P.*, 1906, LXXX, Cd. 2788, pp. 1-5; *P.R.O.*, c.o. 291/88.

41. *Campbell-Bannerman Papers*, 41210, pp. 256-57, Asquith to Campbell-Bannerman, Dec. 27, 1905; *Commons*, Feb. 22, 1906, p. 559 (Churchill); *P.P.*, 1906, LXXX, Cd. 2788, pp. 5-10; *P.R.O.*, c.o. 291/88, 96, c.o. 879/89, No. 798, c.o. 879/106, No. 807.

42. *P.R.O.*, c.o. 291/95, c.o. 879/89, No. 797.

43. *P.R.O.*, c.o. 291/97-98, co. 879/106, No. 807.

44. For the initial draft notice see *P.P.*, 1906, LXXX, Cd. 3025, p. 147.

45. *P.P.*, 1906, LXXX, Cd. 3025; *P.R.O.*, c.o. 291/99-100, c.o. 879/106, No. 807.

46. For the redrafted notice see *P.P.*, 1906, LXXX, Cd. 3025, p. 190.

47. *Commons*, Feb. 26, 1907, pp. 1427-28 (Churchill); *P.R.O.*, c.o. 291/100-102, 116, c.o. 879/106, No. 807.

48. *P.R.O.*, c.o. 291/88, 95, 97-98, c.o. 879/106, No. 807.

49. *P.R.O.*, c.o. 291/88, 95.

50. *P.P.*, 1906, LXXX, Cds. 2819, 3025, 1907, LVII, Cd. 3528; *P.R.O.*, c.o. 291/93, 95-96, 98-100, 110. Cf. *Transvaal Labour Importation Ordinance Handbook* (1906), pp. 29, 68-74.

51. *P.R.O.*, c.o. 291/105-106, c.o. 879/106, No. 807.

52. *P.R.O.*, c.o. 291/98-99, 112, 114.

53. *P.R.O.*, c.o. 291/99-100, 105-06, 114.

54. *Commons*, July 31, 1906, pp. 748-49 and Dec. 17, 1906, p. 1136 (Churchill); *Lords*, July 27, 1906, p. 12 and Nov. 26, 1906, pp. 1184-87 (Elgin); *P.R.O.*, c.o. 291/99-100, 103-06, 109, 114, 116.

55. *Daily Chronicle*, Jan. 10, 1906; *Manchester Guardian*, Jan. 10, 11,

1906; *Westminster Gazette*, Jan. 10, 1906. For the figures of licenses issued see *P.P.*, 1906, LXXX, Cd. 2788, pp. 7-8.

56. *Daily News*, Feb. 20, Aug. 16, 1906; *Manchester Guardian*, June 15, July 6, 1906; *Westminster Gazette*, Feb. 20, 1906.

57. *Commons*, Mar. 21, 1906, p. 464 (Byles), pp. 471-72 (Mackarness), pp. 488-93 (Churchill); *Manchester Guardian*, Feb. 21, Apr. 27, 1906; *Tribune*, Mar. 21, 1906; *Westminster Gazette*, Feb. 24, 1906.

58. *British Weekly*, Nov. 8, 1906; *Commons*, Nov. 15, 1906, pp. 199-206 (Churchill); *Daily Chronicle*, Nov. 16, 1906; *Daily News*, Nov. 5, 1906; *New Age*, Nov. 15, 1906; *The Times*, Nov. 19, 1906, 17e (Hereford).

59. *Daily News*, July 2, Oct. 29, 1906; *Manchester Guardian*, May 10, 1906; *Westminster Gazette*, Mar. 5, 27, 1906.

60. *Commons*, June 8, 1906, p. 657 (Walsh); *Economist*, Aug. 4, 1906; *Westminster Rev.*, Sept. 1906, pp. 244-45; Butler (1907, 2nd ed.), pp. 219-20.

61. Dugdale (1937), I, pp. 322-23; *It Is Slavery?* (1906), 15 pp. Conservative Central Office pamphlet.

62. *Lords*, Feb. 26, 1906, pp. 729-30 (Harris), Feb. 27, 1906, p. 935 (Londonderry); *Morning Post*, Jan. 5, 1906; *The Times*, Mar. 6, 1906, 9e, June 9, 1906, 11d.

63. *Empire Rev.*, Apr. 1906, pp. 204-05 (Kinloch-Cooke); *Lords*, Feb. 26, 1906, p. 733 (Harris), p. 965 (Winchester), Mar. 5, 1906, p. 6 (Marlborough), pp. 21-22 (Harris); *Pall Mall Gazette*, June 9, 1906; *Standard*, Feb. 28, 1907.

64. For the memorandum prepared at the request of Lord Selborne to present the case of the mineowners see *P.P.*, 1906, LXXX, Cd. 2819, pp. 67, 102.

65. *Daily Mail*, June 9, 1906; *Daily Telegraph*, Jan. 10, 1906; *Fortnightly Rev.*, Apr. 1906, p. 648 (Mills); *Lords*, Mar. 5, 1906, p. 16 (Ridley); *Saturday Rev.*, Mar. 17, 1906; *The Times*, Feb. 21, 1906, 6c-d.

66. *Fortnightly Rev.*, Apr. 1906, pp. 648-49 (Mills); *Morning Post*, Nov. 7, 1906; *The Times*, Feb. 21, 1906, 9c-d.

67. Robert Raine *Transvaal Labour, Unskilled Whites—Manager of Village Main Reef on Mr. Creswell* (London: 1906), 15 pp. Cf. Raymond W. Schumacher *A Transvaal View of the Chinese Labour Question* (London: 1906), 60 pp. Both are Imperial South African Association pamphlets.

68. *Fortnightly Rev.*, Apr. 1906, p. 651 (Mills); *The Times*, Aug. 15, 1906, 10c (Hunter); *Westminster Gazette*, Jan. 9, 1906 (Schumacher).

69. *Lords*, Nov. 26, 1906, pp. 1179-83 (Harris).

70. *Commons*, Feb. 22, 1906, pp. 550-51 (Parker), Mar. 21, 1906, pp. 478-79 (Chamberlain); *Lords*, Feb. 27, 1906, pp. 930-31 (Milner).

71. *Commons*, Nov. 15, 1906, pp. 209-13 (Lyttelton); *Lords*, Nov. 15,

1906, pp. 39-42 (Davidson); *Pall Mall Gazette*, Nov. 16, 1906. For the original statement of the Archbishop of Canterbury see *Lords*, Mar. 4, 1904, p. 190.

72. *P.P.*, 1906, LXXX, Cd. 3250.

73. *Manchester Guardian*, Aug. 1, 1960; *Speaker*, May 19, 1906; *Tribune*, July 16, 1906; *Westminster Gazette*, Feb. 9, 1906.

74. *Empire Rev.*, Mar. 1906, pp. 105, 109 (Kinloch-Cooke); *Fortnightly Rev.*, Apr. 1906, pp. 658-59 (Mills); *The Times*, Aug. 2, 1906. For the joint statement of the Het Volk and the Responsible Government Association see *P.P.*, LV, Cd. 2563, p. 8.

75. *P.P.*, 1907, LVII, Cd. 3528, pp. 160-61, 1908, LXXIII, Cd. 3994, 10 pp.; *The Times*, Mar. 22, 1907, 5a and June 15, 1907, 7a (news items).

76. *Annual Register*, 1907, pp. 223-24, 406-07, 1908, pp. 402-03, 1909, p. 407, 1910, p. 6.

77. *P.R.O.*, c.o. 291/107, 116-20, 123, 138-39, 144.

78. *P.R.O.*, c.o. 291/115-16, 121, 124.

79. *P.R.O.*, c.o. 291/116, 119.

80. *Lords*, June 27, 1907, pp. 57-60 (Harris); *Morning Post*, Nov. 8, 1907; *National Rev.*, June 1907, pp. 575-77 (Griffith-Boscawen); *The Times*, June 15, 1907, 13c-d.

81. *P.P.*, 1908, LXXIII, Cd. 4120, pp. 3, 10-11.

82. *Commons*, Mar. 11, 1907, pp. 1280-83 (Lyttelton); *Morning Post*, Jan. 28, 1907; *National Rev.*, June 1907, pp. 547-80 (Griffith-Boscawen); *The Times*, Apr. 16, 1908, 4e-f (Parker).

83. For the official story of the £5,000,000 guaranteed loan see *P.P.*, 1907, LVII, Cd. 3621, 28 pp.

84. *Commons*, June 20, 1907, pp. 715-16 (Lyttelton); *Daily Telegraph*, Aug. 20, 1907; *Morning Post*, May 29, 1907; *Pall Mall Gazette*, May 29, 1907; *The Times*, Aug. 20, 1907, 7e-f.

85. *P.P.*, 1908, LXXIII, Cd. 3993, 120 pp. (Nyasaland), Cd. 4357, 8 pp. (Madagascar).

86. *P.P.*, 1908, LXXIII, Cd. 4120, pp. 3, 9-15.

87. *Commons*, July 28, 1908, pp. 1250-53 (Lyttelton); *Daily Telegraph*, Mar. 7, 1908; *Morning Post*, Mar. 3, June 16, 1908; *Pall Mall Gazette*, Mar. 30, 1908; *The Times*, Apr. 16, 1908, 4e-f (Parker).

88. *The Times*, Apr. 16, 1908, 4e-f and May 1, 1908, 21e (Parker).

89. *Daily News*, Mar. 22, 1907; *Manchester Guardian*, Feb. 22, Mar. 16, 1907; *Tribune*, Mar. 22, 1907.

90. *Daily Chronicle*, June 15, 1907; *Nation*, June 29, 1907; *Review of Reviews*, July 1907.

91. *Daily Chronicle*, Aug. 20, 1907; *Daily News*, June 1, Aug. 20, 1907;

Manchester Guardian, June 22, 1907; *Tribune,* Aug. 20, 1907; *Westminster Gazette,* Aug. 20, 1907.

92. *Clarion,* Aug. 23, 1907 (Jowett); *Justice,* June 22, 1907; *New Age,* May 9, 1907.

93. *British Weekly,* Mar. 3, 1910; *Daily Chronicle,* Aug. 17, 1909; *Manchester Guardian,* Mar. 24, 1908; *Methodist Times,* Feb. 20, 1908; *New Age,* Mar. 10 and Apr. 28, 1910 (Stanhope of Chester); *Social Democrat,* Mar. 15, 1910, p. 122.

94. *British Weekly,* Mar. 3, 1910; *Daily Chronicle,* Mar. 1, 1910; *Daily News,* Mar. 1, 1910; *Social Democrat,* Mar. 15, 1910, p. 122.

NOTES TO CHAPTER FOUR

1. *P.P.,* 1898, LX, Cd. 8782, 42 pp.; Stuart (1913), p. 28ff.

2. *Natal Legislative Assembly,* May 4, 1905, pp. 246-55; *P.P.,* 1906, LXXIX, Cd. 2905, pp. 59-60. Cf. Stuart (1913), pp. 98-100.

3. *P.R.O.,* c.o. 179/231.

4. *P.P.,* 1906, LXXIX, Cd. 2905, pp. 2-8. Cf. Bosman (1907), pp. 1-2; Holt (1913), pp. 183-86; Stuart (1913), pp. 119-26.

5. For an account of the full testimony given during the trial see *P.R.O.,* c.o. 179/234.

6. *P.P.,* 1906, LXXIX, Cd. 2905, pp. 2-26. Cf. Bosman (1907), pp. 2-13; Holt (1913), pp. 186-89; Stuart (1913), pp. 130-51.

7. *P.P.,* 1906, LXXIX, Cd. 2905, p. 33, Cd. 2927, 9 pp., Cd. 3027, p. 18.

8. *P.P.,* 1906, LXXIX, Cd. 2905, pp. 26-34; *P.R.O.,* c.o. 179/234. Cf. Bosman (1907), pp. 13-15; Stuart (1913), pp. 151-54.

9. *P.P.,* 1906, LXXIX, Cd. 2905, pp. 26-34; *P.R.O.,* c.o. 179/233-234, c.o. 879/106, No. 807.

10. *P.R.O.,* c.o. 179/234.

11. *P.R.O.,* c.o. 179/233.

12. *Ibid.*

13. *P.P.,* 1906, LXXIX, Cd. 2905, pp. 1-5; *P.R.O.,* c.o. 179/233.

14. *P.P.,* 1906, LXXIX, Cd. 2905, p. 48; *P.R.O.,* c.o. 179/234.

15. *P.R.O.,* c.o. 879/89, No. 800.

16. *Clarion,* June 15, 1906 (MacDonald); *Independent Rev.,* Sept. 1906, pp. 137-39 (Mackarness); *Labour Leader,* Apr. 6, 1906 (Hardie); *Manchester Guardian,* Feb. 13, 1906; *Tribune,* Mar. 14, 1906.

17. *Commons,* Apr. 2, 1906, pp. 188-89, 247-49 (MacDonald); *Daily News,* Mar. 30, 1906; *Manchester Guardian,* Mar. 30, 1906; *New Age,* Apr. 5, 1906. For Churchill's reply see *Commons,* June 25, 1906, p. 634.

18. Commons, Apr. 2, 1906, p. 250 (MacDonald); Daily Chronicle, Apr. 3, 1906; Manchester Guardian, Mar. 31, 1906; Tribune, Mar. 31, 1906.

19. Labour Leader, Apr. 6, 1906; Manchester Guardian, Apr. 3, 1906; Speaker, Apr. 7, 1906; Tribune, Apr. 3, 1906.

20. Commons, Apr. 2, 1906, pp. 249-50 (MacDonald); Tribune, Apr. 2, 1906; Westminster Gazette, Mar. 31, 1906.

21. Commons, Apr. 2, 1906, p. 280 (Fell); Morning Post, Feb. 13, 1906; Pall Mall Gazette, Feb. 21, 1906 (Hyatt); Spectator, Feb. 17, 1906.

22. Commons, Apr. 2, 1906, p. 263 (Parker); Daily Mail, Mar. 31, 1906; Morning Post, Mar. 31, 1906; Standard, Mar. 30, 1906; The Times, Apr. 3, 1909, 9d-e.

23. Daily Mail, Apr. 3, 1906; Daily Telegraph, Mar. 30, 1906; Standard, Mar. 30, 1906; The Times, Mar. 30, 1906, 10b-c, Apr. 3, 1906, 9d-e.

24. Bosman (1907), p. 18ff.; Holt (1913), pp. 189-91; Stuart (1913), p. 155ff.

25. Bosman (1907), p. 20ff.; Holt (1913), pp. 191-98; Stuart (1913), p. 167ff.

26. P.P., 1906, LXXIX, Cd. 2905, pp. 43-46; P.R.O., c.o. 179/236-37. Cf. Bosman (1907), p. 25ff.; Stuart (1913), p. 211ff.

27. P.P., 1906, LXXIX, Cd. 2905, passim, Cd. 3027, passim; Stuart (1913), passim.

28. P.P., 1906, LXXIX, Cd. 3027. Cf. Bosman (1907), p. 29ff.; Holt (1913), pp. 199-218; Stuart (1913), p. 222ff.

29. P.P., 1906, LXXIX, Cd. 2905, passim, Cd. 3027, passim, Cd. 3247, pp. 39-40; P.R.O., c.o. 179/234-236.

30. Ibid.

31. P.R.O., c.o. 179/235, 239.

32. Daily Chronicle, Apr. 19, 1906; Daily News, Apr. 6, 1906; Labour Leader, Apr. 20, 1906; Manchester Guardian, Apr. 19, 1906; Tribune, July 25, 1906.

33. Commons, June 8, 1906, pp. 671-73, July 19, 1906, p. 389, July 31, 1906, pp. 701-03, and Aug. 4, 1906, pp. 1815-17 (MacDonald); Daily News, July 19, 1906; Labour Leader, Aug. 24, 1906 (Hardie).

34. For a sampling of MacDonald's queries see Commons, June 5, 1907, pp. 667-68, June 10, 1907, p. 1074, July 18, 1907, pp. 897-98, 911-12. Cf. P.P., 1907, LVII, Cd. 3563.

35. Labour Leader, July 20, 1906 (Guest).

36. Commons, Aug. 4, 1906, pp. 1814-15 (MacDonald); Daily Chronicle, Apr. 23, 1906; Tribune, Apr. 25, 1906; Westminster Gazette, Apr. 23, 1906.

37. Manchester Guardian, Feb. 13, and July 19, 1906 (ed.), Apr. 21,

1906 (Pethick-Lawrence); *New Age*, Apr. 5, 1906; *Tribune*, Mar. 14, 1906; *Westminster Rev.*, May 1906, p. 574; Butler (1906), p. 136.

38. Colenso (pseud. Gebuza) (1906), pp. 6, 10-11, 29. See also *The Times*, Feb. 14, 1906, 10f (Colenso).

39. *Commons*, Apr. 5, 1906 (Wyndham); *Daily Telegraph*, May 5, 1906; *Spectator*, Apr. 21, 1906; *Standard*, Apr. 5, 1906; *The Times*, Apr. 6, 1906, 9d.

40. *Gentleman's Magazine*, Aug. 16, 1906, p. 214; *Pall Mall Gazette*, July 18, 1906; *Spectator*, July 21, 1906; *Standard*, July 18, 1906; *The Times*, July 19, 1906, 9d-e.

41. *Daily Mail*, June 6, 9, 1906; *National Rev.*, May 1906, pp. 519-22, June 1906, p. 702; *Standard*, June 6, July 6, 1906.

42. See editorial note on p. 182.

43. *P.P.*, 1906, LXXIX, Cd. 3027, p. 42.

44. *Daily Telegraph*, July 5, 1906; *National Rev.*, June 1906, pp. 581-83 (Tatham); *The Times*, Feb. 12, 1906, 9c.

45. *Daily News*, Mar. 30, 1906; *Manchester Guardian*, Feb. 13, 1906; *New Age*, May 3, 1906; *Tribune*, Apr. 12, 1906.

46. *Daily Mail*, Mar. 31, 1906; *National Rev.*, June 1906, p. 582 (Tatham); *Pall Mall Gazette*, June 18, 1906; *Standard*, Feb. 13, Apr. 3, 1906.

47. Sundkler (1961, 2nd ed.), pp. 38-43, 68-70.

48. *P.P.*, 1906, LXXIX, Cd. 2905, pp. 1-16, Cd. 3027, *passim*; P.R.O., c.o. 179/237.

49. *P.P.*, 1908, LXXII, Cd. 3888, pp. 1-88; P.R.O., c.o. 179/238, 241.

50. *P.P.*, 1908, LXXII, Cd. 3888, pp. 113-27, Cd. 3998, pp. 19-23. Cf. Stuart (1913), pp. 423-35.

51. *P.P.*, 1908, LXXII, Cd. 3888, pp. 141-42; P.R.O., c.o. 179/241-42, c.o. 879/96, No. 887. Cf. Stuart (1913), pp. 430, 442, 459.

52. For the Report of the Natal Native Affairs Commission see *P.P.*, 1908, LXXII, Cd. 3889.

53. P.R.O., c.o. 179/241, c.o. 879/96, No. 887.

54. *P.P.*, 1908, LXXII, Cd. 3888, pp. 109, 174, 199-200; P.R.O., c.o. 179/242. Cf. Stuart (1913), p. 430ff.

55. P.R.O., c.o. 179/242.

56. *P.P.*, 1908, LXXII, Cds. 3998, 4001, 4194, 4195, 4328. Cf. Stuart (1913), pp. 460-67; Walker (1937), pp. 277-303.

57. *P.P.*, 1908, LXXII, Cds. 3888, 3998, 4194, 4328, 4404; P.R.O., c.o. 179/243-44, 251.

58. *P.P.*, 1908, LXXII, Cd. 3998, pp. 78-100, 103-05, 139-40, 143-44, 160; P.R.O., c.o. 179/244, 248, 251.

59. P.P., 1908, LXXII, Cd. 3998, pp. 66, 106, 108-09; P.R.O., c.o. 179/244, 248, 251-52.

60. Ibid.

61. P.P., 1908, LXXII, Cds. 3998, 4001, 4194, 4328; P.R.O., c.o. 179/244-46, 251.

62. Albany Rev., Jan. 1908, p. 478; Daily Chronicle, Dec. 10, 1907; Daily News, Dec. 5, 7, 10, 1907; Nation, Dec. 7, 14, 1907; Manchester Guardian, Dec. 3, 1907.

63. Daily News, Dec. 5, 1907, Jan. 16, 30, 1908; Labour Leader, Dec. 6, 1907; Nation, Dec. 7, 1914; Review of Reviews, Jan. 1908; The Times, Dec. 9, 1907, 10e (Mackarness).

64. For the list of flogging instances cited by Harriette Emily Colenso on July 23, 1908 see P.P., 1908, LXXII, Cd. 4328, pp. 45-47, 95-98.

65. Albany Rev., Sept. 1908, p. 669 (Werner); Commons, June 15, 1908, pp. 541-42 and July 28, 1908, pp. 1280-81 (MacDonald); Daily News, May 12, 1908; Manchester Guardian, Jan. 30, 1908; Spectator, Mar. 14, 1908 (Wedgwood).

66. Daily News, Feb. 10, 1908; Labour Leader, Feb. 14, 1908; Manchester Guardian, Mar. 6, 1908; Nation, May 16, 1908.

67. Albany Rev., Sept. 1908, p. 669 (Werner); Commons, June 3, 1908, pp. 102-05 (Mackarness); Daily Chronicle, June 4, 1908; Manchester Guardian, July 28, 1908; Nation, May 16, 1908.

68. Commons, June 3, 1908, p. 115 (Dilke), July 28, 1908, p. 1299 (G. G. Greenwood); Daily News, May 12, 1908; Manchester Guardian, Aug. 20, 1908; Nation, Mar. 28, 1908.

69. Daily Telegraph, Dec. 3, 1907; Morning Post, Dec. 9, 1907; Pall Mall Gazette, Dec. 3, 1907; Standard, Dec. 11, 1907; The Times, Dec. 3, 1907, 9c-d.

70. Commons, July 28, 1908, pp. 1257-59 (Lyttelton); Pall Mall Gazette, June 2, 1908; Standard, Feb. 10, 1908.

71. Morning Post, July 29-30, 1908; Pall Mall Gazette, Aug. 7, 1908 (Haigh); Standard, Feb. 10, June 16, 1908.

72. P.P., 1908, LXXII, Cd. 4195, 6 pp., Cd. 4328, pp. 103-04, 109-10; P.R.O., c.o. 179/245-47, 251.

73. P.P., 1909, LX, Cd. 4585.

74. P.P., 1909, LX, Cd. 4585, p. 49; P.R.O., c.o. 179/252.

75 Morning Post, July 7, 1909; Pall Mall Gazette, Mar. 4, 1909; Rees (1921), pp. 182-83.

76. Commons, Mar. 4, 1909, p. 1577 (MacDonald); Daily News, Mar. 4, 1909; Justice, Mar. 13, 1909; Labour Leader, Mar. 12, 1909; Manchester Guardian, Mar. 4, Apr. 16, 1909; New Age, Apr. 1, 1909.

77. P.P., 1908, LXXII, Cd. 3998, pp. 40, 65, Cd. 4194, p. 3, Cd. 4328, pp. 10-12, 95-98; P.R.O., c.o. 179/248, 251, 253.

78. P.R.O., c.o. 551/1-2; Union of South Africa, Native Affairs Report, 1910, p. 45.

79. Anti-Slavery Reporter, Oct. 1910; Commons, June 20, 1910, pp. 5-6 (MacDonald); Daily News, June 2, 1910; Manchester Guardian, June 2, 1910.

80. Anti-Slavery Reporter, July 1910; Manchester Guardian, Apr. 2, 1909 and Jan. 1, 1910 (Schwann); Walker (1937), p. 302. Cf. P.R.O., c.o. 179/248, 252-53.

NOTES TO CHAPTER FIVE

1. P.P., 1903, XLV, Cd. 1640.

2. P.P., 1905, LV, Cd. 2399.

3. P.P., 1908, LXXII, Cd. 3889.

4. South African Native Races Committee The Natives of South Africa (1901), 360 pp., and The South African Natives (1908), 247 pp.

5. Milner (1913), pp. 89-90.

6. Ibid.

7. Evans (1911), vii-x.

8. P.P., 1907, LVII, Cd. 3564, pp. 5-9, 12-61; P.R.O., c.o. 291/84, 125; The Selborne Memorandum (1925), pp. 108-17.

9. Daily Telegraph, Feb. 6, Apr. 16, 1903; Macmillan's Magazine, Mar. 1906, pp. 392-400 (Hyatt); Quarterly Rev., July 1905, p. 288; Standard, Aug. 23, 1905; The Times, Mar. 25, 1903, 9e-f.

10. Helen Hunt Jackson A Century of Dishonor: A Sketch of the United States Government's Dealings with Some of the Indian Tribes (Boston: 1886), 514 pp.

11. Morning Post, Oct. 20, 1904, Feb. 20, 1905; The Times, May 11, 1905, 5d-e.

12. Empire Rev., July 1903, p. 585 (Dobbie).

13. Phillips (1905), pp. 120, 137-38.

14. Daily Telegraph, Apr. 18, 1906; Morning Post, Sept. 1, 1902, Apr. 11, 1913; The Times, Mar. 25, 1903, 9e-f; Balfour-Browne (1905), pp. 85, 99-100; Kinloch-Cooke (1904), pp. 16-17.

15. Commons, Mar. 14, 1903, pp. 106, 110-12 (Chamberlain); Morning Post, Sept. 1, 1902; The Times, Mar. 25, 1903, 9e-f; Balfour-Browne (1905), pp. 99-100; Davis (1903), p. 71ff.

16. Pall Mall Gazette, July 22, 1902 (Farrelly).

17. *P.P.*, 1905, LV, Cd. 2399, p. 47.

18. *Morning Post*, Dec. 7, 1904; *Nineteenth Century and After*, May 1905, pp. 771-73 (Jones); *The Times*, May 23, 1904, 7c-d.

19. For literature on Negro emancipation in the United States see Paul Lewinson *Race, Class, and Party: A History of Negro Suffrage and White Politics in the South* (Oxford: 1932); John Hope Franklin *From Slavery to Freedom: A History of American Negroes* (New York: 1956, 2nd ed., rev. and enl.); E. Franklin Frazier *The Negro in the United States* (New York: 1957, rev. ed.).

20. Booker T. Washington *The Future of the American Negro* (Boston: 1899), pp. 132, 142.

21. *Daily Telegraph*, Jan. 13, 1908; *Empire Rev.*, July 1903, p. 585 (Dobbie); *Nineteenth Century and After*, May 1905, pp. 769-70 (Jones); *Standard*, Mar. 21, 1905.

22. For the facts on the franchise in the several colonies see *P.P.*, 1905, LV, Cd. 2399, pp. 66-67.

23. *Morning Post*, Oct. 20, 1904, Apr. 6, 1905, Mar. 29, 1907; *Nineteenth Century and After*, May 1905, pp. 763-66 (Jones); *Standard*, Mar. 21, May 8, 1905; *The Times*, Apr. 21, 1908, 7e-f.

24. *Clarion*, July 29, 1904 (Guest); *International*, Feb. 1908, pp. 191, 194 (Guest); *Labour Leader*, June 2, 23, 1905 and Oct. 5, 1906 (Guest); *Review of Reviews*, Aug. 1905.

25. *Statistics of the Transvaal Colony, 1902-07*, pp. 25, 30.

26. *P.P.*, 1905, LV, Cd. 2399, p. 50.

27. *Aborigines' Friend*, Apr. 1906, p. 547 (Molteno); *Commons*, Mar. 11, 1907, p. 1344 (Molteno); *Contemporary Rev.*, July 1906, pp. 31-33 (Pease), Jan. 1908, pp. 90-92 (Hawkin); *Labour Leader*, Mar. 16, 1906 (Guest).

28. *Aborigines' Friend*, Oct. 1908 (Bourne); *Labour Leader*, June 23, 1905 and Apr. 27, 1906 (Guest); *Positivist Rev.*, Oct. 1, 1905, p. 234 (Werner); MacDonald (1902), p. 120.

29. *P.P.*, 1905, LV, Cd. 2399, pp. 55-56.

30. South African Native Races Committee *The Natives of South Africa* (1901), p. 238.

31. *East and the West*, July 1903, pp. 279-81 (Bird); *The Times*, Feb. 16, 1903, 12e (Harcourt); *Westminster Gazette*, Aug. 5, 1902; Markham (1904), pp. 153-54; Olivier (1906), pp. 86-90.

32. *Commons*, Mar. 24, 1903, pp. 67-69 (Dilke), pp. 80-82 (Samuel), pp. 98-99 (Harcourt), pp. 113-15 (Hardie); Bourne (1903), pp. 9, 17-18, 22, 33, 43; Hobson (1905, rev. ed.), pp. 236-37.

33. *P.P.*, 1905, LV, Cd. 2399, p. 28.

34. *Clarion*, Nov. 2, 1906 (Eder); *Commons*, Mar. 11, 1907, p. 1345 (Molteno), pp. 1352-53 (Alden); *Daily News*, Jan. 30, 1908; *Manchester Guardian*, Mar. 13, 1905; *Tribune*, Mar. 12, 1906.

35. *Orange River Colony, Ordinances*, 1904, 7 pp.

36. *Clarion*, July 29, 1904 (Guest); *Economist*, Dec. 14, 1907; *International*, Feb. 1908, p. 192 (Guest); Butler (1907), pp. 83-84, 134-35.

37. Guest in *Clarion*, July 22, 29, 1904, in *Labour Leader*, Mar. 17, July 7, 1905, Oct. 5, 1906, in *Review of Reviews*, Aug. 1905, pp. 152-53.

38. *Aborigines' Friend*, Oct. 1908 (Bourne); *Daily Chronicle*, Oct. 13, 1908; *Manchester Guardian*, Oct. 10, 1906, May 14, Oct. 23, 1908; *Nation*, June 15, 1907, Apr. 18, Oct. 17, 1908; *Westminster Rev.*, Jan. 1906, pp. 43-45 (Lightbody); Bourne (1903), p. 17; MacDonald (1907), pp. 56-59.

39. *P.P.*, 1905, LV, Cd. 2400. Cf. Mansergh (1962), pp. 23-24; Pyrah (1955), p. 158ff.; Thompson (1960), pp. 22-23.

40. *Asquith Papers*, Box 19, pp. 59-73; Hancock (1962), I, pp. 207-10, 215-16; P.R.O., c.o. 879/92, No. 837. Cf. Mansergh (1962), pp. 20-27; Millin (1936), I, pp. 212-14; Pyrah (1955), pp. 164-71; Thompson (1960), pp. 25-26.

41. Ensor (1936), p. 39 n. 2; Hancock (1962), I, pp. 213-14; Mansergh (1962), pp. 127-28; Millin (1936), I, pp. 213-14; Pyrah (1955), pp. 164-65; Riddle (1934), pp. 144-45; Spender (1923), II, pp. 238-39.

42. *P.P.*, 1906, LXXX, Cd. 3250 (Transvaal), 1907, LVII, Cd. 3526 (Orange Free State); Seely (1930), p. 132.

43. *P.P.*, 1906, LXXX, Cd. 3250, pp. 2, 7-8, 10, 39 (Transvaal), 1907, LVII, Cd. 3526, pp. 2, 7-8, 10 (Orange Free State). Cf. Pyrah (1955), pp. 159-81.

44. P.R.O., c.o. 879/89, No. 800, c.o. 291/72, 84-85, 97.

45. P.R.O., c.o. 879/89, No 800, c.o. 291/88, 96.

46. P.R.O., c.o. 879/89, No. 800, c.o. 879/92, No. 840, c.o. 291/97, 112.

47. P.R.O., c.o. 291/99.

48. P.R.O., c.o. 48/580, c.o. 291/104, 112. Cf. Mansergh (1962), pp. 77-78; Marais (1939), pp. 276-78.

49. *Commons*, July 31, 1906, pp. 771-72 and Dec. 17, 1906, p. 1093 (Dilke). Cf. *Daily Chronicle*, Aug. 1, 1906; *Speaker*, Jan. 12, 1907.

50. *Empire Rev.*, June 1905, pp. 405-06 (Bruce).

51. *Aborigines' Friend*, Aug. 1906; *British Congregationalist*, Aug. 9, 1906 (Horne); *Commons*, July 31, 1906, p. 796 (MacDonald); *Economist*, Apr. 29, 1905; *Friend*, Mar. 2, 1906.

52. *Commons*, Feb. 28, 1906, 1214 (Byles), p. 1222 (Robertson), Dec. 17, 1906, p. 1095 (Dilke); *Empire Rev.*, June 1905, pp. 405-06 (Bruce); *Justice*, Apr. 21, Dec. 22, 1906; *New Age*, June 20, 1907.

53. *Empire Rev.*, Jan. 1907, p. 454 (Bruce).

54. For an analysis of Boer and Briton in their personal relations with natives see Evans (1911), pp. 50-51.

55. *Commons*, Feb. 28, 1906, pp. 1244-45 (Wyndham), Dec. 17, 1906, p. 1121 (Hills), June 20, 1907, pp. 699-700 (Fell); *Daily Telegraph*, Apr. 26, 1905; *Morning Post*, Dec. 13, 1906.

56. *Lords*, July 31, 1906, pp. 655-56 (Milner).

57. *Spectator*, July 14, 1906.

58. Headlam (1933), II, p. 353; *P.R.O.*, c.o. 291/81.

59. *Commons*, July 31, 1906, pp. 746-47 and Dec. 17, 1906, p. 1113 (Churchill); *Lords*, July 31, 1906, pp. 623-24 and Dec. 17, 1906, pp. 941-42 (Elgin).

60. *Lords*, July 31, 1906, pp. 666-67 (Ripon).

NOTES TO CHAPTER SIX

1. *P.P.*, 1907, LVII, Cd. 3564.

2. For literature on the South African national convention see Brand (1909), p. 30ff.; Pyrah (1955), pp. 109, 221-22; Thompson (1960), *passim*; Walker (1925), p. 443ff.; Walton (1912), pp. 18-30, 321-27.

3. *Asquith Papers*, Box 5, Asquith to Edward VII, July 29, 1908, p. 49, Box 46, Crewe to Asquith, Jan. 5, 1909, p. 175; Thompson (1960), p. 217; Walker (1925), p. 432.

4. *Nathan Papers*, South African National Convention, Misc. Ltrs. and Papers, Selborne to de Villiers, Oct. 20, 1908, pp. 151-58; Pyrah (1955), pp. 111-12; Thompson (1960), pp. 174, 217-18; Walker (1925), pp. 446-47.

5. *Nathan Papers*, South African National Convention, Misc. Ltrs. and Papers, Selborne to de Villiers, Oct. 22, 1908, pp. 159-61; Pyrah (1955), pp. 112-14; Thompson (1960), pp. 220-22; Walker (1925), pp. 448-49.

6. For a ready reference to the native in the constitution see Brand (1909), pp. 104-09, 137ff.

7. *Nathan Papers*, South African National Convention, Misc. Ltrs. and Papers, Selborne to de Villiers, Oct. 20, 1908, pp. 151-58 and Dec. 28, 1908 pp. 193-95; Pyrah (1955), pp. 124-34; Thompson (1960), pp. 271-78; Walker (1925), pp. 449-50, 459-60.

8. *Asquith Papers*, Box 46, Crewe to Asquith, Jan. 5, 1909, p. 175; Brand (1909), pp. 111-13; *Nathan Papers*, South African National Convention, Misc. Ltrs. and Papers, Selborne to de Villiers, Oct. 22, 1908, pp. 166-91; Pyrah (1955), pp. 128-34; Thompson (1960), pp. 272-78; Walker (1925), pp. 450, 457-62.

9. *P.R.O.*, c.o. 48/602; Thompson (1960), pp. 383-84, 403; Walker (1925), p. 479.

10. *P.R.O.*, c.o. 879/102, No. 933; Pyrah (1955), pp. 119-20, 134; Seely (1930), pp. 133-34; Thompson (1960), pp. 402, 407ff.; Walker (1925), pp. 482-84.

11. Pyrah (1955), pp. 118-19; Thompson (1960), pp. 402-04; Walker (1937), p. 323ff.

12. *Dilke Papers*, 43921, p. 2, Dilke to Seely, Mar. 2, 1909, pp. 181-82, Schreiner to Dilke, July 22, 1909; *The Times*, July 28, 1909, 9e (Abdurahman), July 27, 1909, 9d-e and Aug. 2, 1909, 4d (Schreiner), Aug. 1909, 8c (Jabavu); Pryah (1955), pp. 120-21; Thompson (1960), pp. 405-07; Walker (1937), p. 326ff.

13. *P.R.O.*, c.o. 291/125.

14. For the native provisions as they went through the British Parliament see *P.P.*, 1909, V, Bill 297, pp. 5-9, 12, 37-38, 40-43, LX, Cd. 4525, pp. 5, 8, 20-23, Cd. 4721, pp. 8-12, 24-27.

15. *Commons*, Aug. 16, 1909, pp. 958-63 (Seely); *Lords*, July 27, 1909, pp. 759-66 (Crewe).

16. *Commons*, Aug. 16, 1909, pp. 957-64 and Aug. 19, 1909, pp. 1600-01 (Seely), Aug. 19, 1909, pp. 1009-13 (Asquith); *Lords*, July 27, 1909, pp. 761-65 (Crewe).

17. *Commons*, May 27, 1909, p. 1380 (Dilke), Aug. 16, 1909, pp. 983-85 (Molteno), Aug. 19, 1909, p. 1624 (MacDonald); *Labour Leader*, Sept. 3, 1909 (Carpenter).

18. This statement of General Botha is reported in *Natal Witness*, Feb. 27, 1909, 9a.

19. *Commons*, Aug. 16, 1909, pp. 988-90 (Hardie), pp. 1028-30 (Byles), Aug. 19, 1909, pp. 1624-26 (MacDonald); *Labour Leader*, Aug. 13, 1909 (Hardie).

20. *Commons*, Aug. 16, 1909, pp. 979-80 (Dilke), Aug. 19, 1909, pp. 1540-42 (MacDonald), pp. 1580-82 (Griffith), pp. 1607-08 (Hardie); *Lords*, July 27, 1909, pp. 781-83 (Courtney).

21. *Commons*, Aug. 19, 1909, pp. 1648, 1652, 1654 (Hardie); *Daily News*, July 28, 1909; *Lords*, July 27, 1909, pp. 784-86 (Courtney); *Manchester Guardian*, Aug. 11, 1909; *Nation*, May 15, 1909; *New Age*, Feb. 18, 1909.

22. *Anti-Slavery Reporter*, Oct. 1909; *Commons*, Aug. 16, 1909, p. 995 (Griffith), Aug. 19, 1909, pp. 1594-98 (MacDonald); *Daily News*, Aug. 17, 1909; *English Rev.*, Sept. 1909, pp. 333-34 (Hobson); *The Times*, July 26, 1909, 6f (Bruce).

23. Hobson (1909), pp. 243-46.

24. Commons, Aug. 16, 1909, pp. 968-69 (Lyttelton); *Edinburgh Rev.*, July 1909, pp. 18, 27; *Lords*, July 27, 1909, p. 794 (Lansdowne); *Morning Post*, July 19, Aug. 4, 1909; *The Times*, July 17, 1909, 11e-f.

25. Commons, May 27, 1909, p. 1407 and Aug. 16, 1909, p. 967 (Lyttelton), Aug. 16, 1909, pp. 1020-21 (Parker); *Daily Telegraph*, Aug. 3, 1909.

26. *Edinburgh Rev.*, July 1909, pp. 18-19, 27; *Empire Rev.*, Sept. 1909, p. 77 (Kinloch-Cooke); *Nineteenth Century and After*, Aug. 1909, pp. 251-52 (Jones); *The Times*, July 17, 1909, 11e-f, July 26, 1909, 9e-f.

27. Commons, Aug. 16, 1909, pp. 1022-23 (Parker); *Lords*, July 27, 1909, pp. 774-75 (Curzon); *Morning Post*, July 7, 1909; *Standard*, Feb. 10, July 20, 1909; *The Times*, July 26, 1909, 9e-f.

28. *Morning Post*, July 7, 1909; *Quarterly Rev.*, Apr. 1909, p. 724; *Standard*, Aug. 17, 1909; *The Times*, July 17, 1909, 11e-f, Aug. 20, 1909, 7d-e.

29. Commons, Aug. 16, 1909, p. 1041 (Peel); *Spectator*, July 10, 1909.

30. Commons, Aug. 16, 1909, pp. 1000-03 (Balfour).

31. Commons, Aug. 19, 1909, pp. 1533-1656. Cf. Cana (1909), p. 269 n. 2; Petrie (1939), II, pp. 166-67; Riddle (1934), pp. 144-45; Thompson (1960), p. 429.

32. *Ibid.*

33. *P.R.O.*, c.o. 551/1-2; *Viscount Gladstone Papers*, 45996, Gladstone to Crewe, May 30, 1910, pp. 48-49, 46019, Bryce to Gladstone, Mar. 4, 1910, p. 123a.

34. *P.R.O.*, c.o. 551/1-2; *Viscount Gladstone Papers*, 45996, Gladstone to Crewe, May 22, 1910, p. 45a.

35. *P.R.O.*, c.o. 551/2.

36 *Viscount Gladstone Papers*, 46071, Gladstone to Burton, June 28, 1911, pp. 82-88; *Union of South Africa, Report of the Commission Appointed to Enquire Into Assaults on Women* (1913), 41 pp.

37. *British Socialist*, Dec. 15, 1912, Jan. 15, Feb. 15, and Mar. 15, 1913 (Montefiore); *Contemporary Rev.*, Mar. 1913, pp. 410-11 (Stretford); *Fabian News*, May 1911 (Guest).

38. *Contemporary Rev.*, March 1913, pp. 412-13 (Stretford); *Socialist Rev.*, Sept. 1910, pp. 61-65 (Halford); Markham (1913), pp. 280-91.

39. *Socialist Rev.*, Sept. 1910, pp. 66-67 (Halford).

40. Bryce (1910), II, p. 319.

41. *Empire Rev.*, Feb. 1913, pp. 20-23 (Neame); *The Times*, Jan. 7, 1914, 7d-e; *Westminster Gazette*, Apr. 10, 1913 (Markham); Markham (1913), pp. 301-02.

42. *Blackwood's Magazine*, Jan. 1911, pp. 62-64 (Durand); Durand (1911), pp. 169-76.

43. *Contemporary Rev.*, Mar. 1913, pp. 409-10 (Stretford); *Empire*

Rev., June 1913, p. 331 (Henry Samuel); *Fabian News*, May 1911 (Guest); *Justice*, Apr. 12, 1913; *Manchester Guardian*, Oct. 14, 1911; Bryce (1910), II, pp. 559-60.

44. For the latest reference by Lord Selborne to this favorite theme of his, delivered to a Cape University audience, see *The Times*, Mar. 1, 1909, 7d (news item).

45. *Westminster Gazette*, Apr. 7, 1913 (Markham); Markham (1913), pp. 269, 340-43, 352-58.

46. Bryce (1910), II, p. 546.

47. Markham (1913), pp. 221, 228-29.

48. *Everyman*, Aug. 22, 1913, p. 588 (Geddie).

49. *P.P.*, 1914, LIX, Cd. 7508.

50. *P.R.O.*, c.o. 551/40, 46, 56-57.

51. *Anti-Slavery Reporter*, July 1914, pp. 76-79.

52. Plaatje (1916), pp. 29ff., 149, 232-33.

53. *Commons*, July 28, 1914, pp. 1194-97 (Harcourt); *P.R.O.*, c.o. 879/114, No. 1012; *Westminster Rev.*, July 28, 1914, p. 9 (an interview with Lord Gladstone).

54. *Commons*, July 28, 1914, pp. 1167-68 (Spicer); *Daily News*, July 6, 1914; *Manchester Guardian*, July 7, 1914; *Review of Reviews*, Aug. 1914, pp. 90-92; *Westminster Gazette*, July 7, 1914.

55. *Commons*, July 28, 1914, pp. 1161-63 (Alden); *Daily News*, July 6, 1914; *Review of Reviews*, Aug. 1914, pp. 90-92; Markham (1913), pp. 264-68, 362-63.

56. Mansergh (1962), p. 76.

57. Pyrah (1955), p. 236.

58. Thompson (1960), pp. 27, 398.

59. Lord Riddle (1934), p. 145; Samuel (1945), p. 73; Seely (1930), p. 133.

60. *Commons*, July 31, 1906, pp. 757-58 (Lyttelton); Petrie (1939), II, pp. 166-67.

NOTES TO CHAPTER SEVEN

1. *P.P.*, 1903, XLV, Cd. 1684, pp. 3-4, 1905, LVI, Cd. 2239, pp. 25-26, 45. Cf. Gandhi (1954), p. 81ff.; Polak (1909), part II, pp. 7-8.

2. *P.P.*, 1903, XLV, Cd. 1684, pp. 4-6, 1904, LXI, Cd. 1986, pp. 13-18. Cf. Gandhi (1954), pp. 93-95; Palmer (1957), p. 64; Polak (1909), part II, pp. 7-9.

3. *P.P.*, 1903, LXV, Cd. 1684, pp. 4-5.

4. *P.R.O.*, c.o. 291/52.

5. *P.P.*, 1905, LVI, Cd. 2239, pp. 4-23.

6. *P.P.*, 1905, LVI, Cd. 2239, pp. 30-35.

7. *P.P.*, 1905, LVI, Cd. 2239, pp. 25-27; *P.R.O.*, c.o. 291/70.

8. *P.R.O.*, c.o 291/61, 75, co. 879/77, No. 699.

9. *P.P.*, 1905, LVI, Cd. 2239, pp. 37-48, c.o. 879/80, No. 739. Cf. Calpin (1949), pp. 27-28.

10. *P.R.O.*, c.o. 291/71-72, 82-85.

11. *P.R.O.*, c.o. 291/90-91, c.o. 879/90, No. 760.

12. *P.P.*, 1907, LVII, Cd. 3308, pp. 2-11; *P.R.O.*, c.o. 291/84, 89-90, 99. Cf. Calpin (1949), p. 30.

13. *P.P.*, 1907, LVII, Cd. 3308, p. 11; *P.R.O.*, c.o. 291/99.

14. *P.P.*, 1906, LXXX, Cd. 3251, 1907, LVII, Cd. 3308, pp. 16-20. Cf. Gandhi (1954), pp. 98-101; Hofmeyr (1952, 2nd ed., rev.), pp. 150-51.

15. *P.P.*, 1907, LVII, Cd. 3308, pp. 13-15, 20-23; *P.R.O.*, c.o. 291/102-03, 105. Cf. Gandhi (1954), p. 102ff.; Mabel (1957), pp. 65-66.

16. *P.P.*, 1907, LVII, Cd. 3308, pp. 9-11.

17. *P.P.*, 1907, LVII, Cd. 3308, pp. 31-48, 58-64; *P.R.O.*, c.o. 291/103, 105, 115. Cf. Calpin (1949), pp. 30-31; Gandhi (1954), pp. 118-20; Gangulee (1947), pp. 52-54; Polak (1909), part II, pp. 10-11.

18. *P.P.*, 1908, LXXIII, Cd. 3887, pp. 3-21, Cd. 3892, p. 3; *P.R.O.*, c.o. 291/116, 122. Cf. Gandhi (1954), p. 126; Hofmeyr (1952, 2nd ed., rev.), p. 151; Polak (1909), part II, pp. 12-14.

19. Edward Richard Henry *Classification and Use of Finger Prints* (London: 1905, 3rd ed.), pp. 6-9.

20. *P.P.*, 1908, LXXIII, Cd. 3892, p. 3, Cd. 3887, pp. 11-14; *P.R.O.*, c.o. 291/116, 123.

21. *P.P.*, 1908, LXXIII, Cd. 3887, pp. 31-37, 52-54; *P.R.O.*, c.o. 291/119, 121.

22. *P.P.*, 1908, LXXIII, Cd. 3887, pp. 43-44, 65, 74-75; *P.R.O.*, c.o. 879/97, No. 891.

23. *P.R.O.*, c.o., 48/570, 572, 574, 584-89, 591, 595, c.o. 879/78, No. 705.

24. *P.R.O.*, c.o. 48/582, 585, 595, 597.

25. *P.R.O.*, c.o. 179/227-28, 230, c.o. 879/81, No. 728.

26. *P.R.O.*, c.o. 179/236, 241, 243, 245-49. Cf. Polak (1909), part I, *passim.*

27. R. P. Patwardhan and D. V. Ambekar, eds. *Speeches and Writings of Gopal Krishna Gokhale* (Poona: 1962), I, pp. 284-94.

28. *P.R.O.*, c.o. 179/255-56, c.o. 879/101, No. 931, c.o. 879/104, No. 947.

29. *P.P.*, 1908, LXXIII, Cd 3887, pp. 37, 56-61, 66-76, Cd. 4327, pp. 4-6; *P.R.O.*, c.o. 291/120. Cf. Gandhi (1954), pp. 102-15, 127-88; Gangulee (1947), pp. 54-55; Polak (1909), part II, pp. 14-15.

30. *P.P.*, 1908, LXXIII, Cd. 4327, pp. 5-6; *P.R.O.*, c.o. 291/132.

31. *P.P.*, 1908, LXXIII, Cd. 4327, pp. 1-7, Cd. 3892, pp. 4-5. Cf. Polak (1909), part II, pp. 15-16.

32. *P.P.*, 1908, LXXIII, Cd. 4327, pp. 7-12; *P.R.O.*, c.o. 291/125.

33. *P.P.*, 1908, LXXIII, Cd. 4327, pp. 15-34, 1909, LXI, Cd. 4584, pp. 1-8; *P.R.O.*, c.o. 291/127, 132. Cf. Gandhi (1954), pp. 189-97.

34. *P.P.*, 1908, LXXIII, Cd. 4327, pp. 31-52; *P.R.O.*, c.o. 291/127-28, 130-31. Cf. Polak (1909), part II, pp. 18-19; Pyrah (1955), p. 106.

35. *P.P.*, 1909, LXI, Cd. 4584, pp. 7, 14; *P.R.O.*, c.o. 551/2. Cf. Gandhi (1954), p. 198ff.; Gangulee (1947), pp. 55-57; Palmer (1957), pp. 67-68; Polak (1909), part II, pp. 16-18.

36. *P.P.*, 1909, LXI, Cd. 4584, pp. 7-69; *P.R.O.*, c.o. 291/129, 131-32. Cf. Gandhi (1954), p. 218ff.; Polak (1909), part II, p. 22ff.; Pyrah (1955), pp. 106-08.

37. *P.P.*, 1909, LXI, Cd. 4584, 1910, LXVI, Cd. 5363; *P.R.O.*, c.o. 291/ 139, 145; *Viscount Gladstone Papers*, 45996, p. 55, Ltr. Crewe to Gladstone, June 17, 1910.

38. *Lords*, Nov. 16, 1909, pp. 601-02 (Crewe); *P.R.O.*, c.o. 291/139, 145.

39. *P.P.*, 1909, LXI, Cd. 4584, 1910, LXVI, Cd. 5363; *P.R.O.*, c.o. 291/144-45.

40. *P.R.O.*, c.o. 291/137, 140, 145, c.o. 879/104, No. 947.

41. *P.R.O.*, c.o. 291/139, 141, 144-45, c.o. 551/11.

42. Gandhi (1954), pp. 119-20; *The Times*, Nov. 30, 1906, 11c (news item).

43. *Asiatic Quarterly Rev.*, July 1903, pp. 178-79 (Griffin); *Commons*, July 21, 1904, pp. 818-20 (Dilke); *Manchester Guardian*, Aug. 27, 1904; *New Age*, Nov. 6, 1902.

44. *Asiatic Quarterly Rev.*, Jan. 1907, p. 77 (Ritch); *Lords*, May 29, 1907, pp. 1587-91 (Ampthill); *Manchester Guardian*, Jan. 2, 1908 (Ritch); *The Times*, Aug. 31, 1907, 6a-b and Jan. 1, 1908, 13a (Ritch), Feb. 3, 1908, 8b (Ampthill).

45. *Empire Rev.*, Oct. 1908, pp. 163-66 (Bruce); *Lords*, Oct. 21, 1908, pp. 1121-22 (Ampthill); *The Times*, Sept. 9, 1908, 10d (Ampthill); *Westminster Gazette*, Sept. 15, 1908 (Ritch); Bruce (1908), pp. 11-16; Bruce (1917), pp. 168-70.

46. *Indian Opinion* (Durban), Feb. 8, 1908, p. 71.

47. *Empire Rev.*, Oct. 1908, p. 172 (Bruce); *Lords*, Oct. 21, 1908, pp. 1120-23 (Ampthill); *The Times*, Sept. 9, 1908, 10d (Ampthill); *Westminster Gazette*, Sept. 15, 1908 (Ritch); Bruce (1908), pp. 11-16, 23.

48. See the petition drawn up by 100 British Indian ex-soldiers. *P.P.*, 1908, LXXII, Cd. 3887, p. 75.

49. *Daily News*, Jan. 11, 1908; *Justice*, Dec. 4, 1909 (Ritch); *Lords*, Mar. 24, 1909, pp. 518-27 (Ampthill); *Manchester Guardian*, Jan. 13, 1908; *Saturday Rev.*, Dec. 4, 1909 (Ritch).

50. *Lords*, Nov. 16, 1909, p. 593 and July 26, 1910, pp. 463-74 (Ampthill); *Manchester Guardian*, Aug. 9, 1910; *The Times*, Jan. 1, 1908, 13a (Ritch).

51. For particulars of the Imperial Conference of 1907 see *P.P.*, 1907, LV, Cd. 3523, pp. 331-32.

52. *Asiatic Quarterly Rev.*, Jan. 1907, p. 80 (Ritch); *Empire Rev.*, Jan. 1907, pp. 458-59 (Bruce); *Lords*, Feb. 4, 1908, p. 661 (Ampthill), Feb. 17, 1908, p. 390 (Elgin).

53. *Lords*, Feb. 4, 1908, p. 663 (Ampthill); *The Times*, Dec. 11, 1906, 16b (Bruce), Jan. 7, 1908, 9f (Cox); Bruce (1908), pp. 7-8, 23-24.

54. *Asiatic Quarterly Rev.*, Jan. 1907, pp. 73-75 (Ritch); *Commons*, June 20, 1907, pp. 708-09 (V. H. Rutherford); *Lords*, May 19, 1908, pp. 39-41 (Ampthill); *Morning Post*, Apr. 2, 1907 (Ritch).

55. *Asiatic Quarterly Rev.*, Jan. 1907, p. 74 (Ritch); *Lords*, May 19, 1908, p. 38 (Ampthill); *Morning Post*, Apr. 2, 1907 (Ritch). For Lord Elgin's speech see *Lords*, Oct. 21, 1908, p. 1128.

56. *Census of Tranvaal Colony and Swaziland*, Apri. 17, 1904, pp. 386-89.

57. *Asiatic Quarterly Rev.*, July 1903, p. 49 (Wedderburn); *Labour Leader*, Mar. 20, 1908 (Ritch); *Manchester Guardian*, Sept. 27, 1907 (Ritch); *The Times*, May 18, 1907, 6e-f (Ritch), Dec. 25, 1907, 8f (Cox); *Westminster Gazette*, Mar. 10, 1904 (Cox).

58. *The Times*, Jan. 7, 1908, 9f (Cox).

59. For accounts of the Indian ambulance corps see Gandhi (1954), pp. 74-79, 97-98; Gandhi (1948), pp. 264-66, 383-85.

60. *Asiatic Quarterly Rev.*, July 1903, pp. 47, 52-53 (Wedderburn), Jan. 1907, 6a (Ritch); Bruce (1908), pp. 16-19. Cf. Gangulee (1947), pp. 27-29. 39 (Ampthill); *Morning Post*, Apr. 2, 1907 (Ritch); *The Times*, Aug. 31, 1907, pp. 71-72 (Ritch), Feb. 1908, p. 9 (Bruce); *Lords*, May 19, 1908, p.

61. For an account of the Bombay demonstration see *The Times*, Jan. 31, 1908, 5d, 11f (news item).

62. For Queen Victoria's proclamation see *The Times*, Dec. 6, 1858, 7b.

63. *Empire Rev.*, Apr. 1907, pp. 215-16 (Bruce); *Lords*, Feb. 4, 1908, pp. 655-56 (Ampthill); *Tribune*, Jan. 6, 1908; Introduction by Ampthill in Doke (1909), p. v; Bruce (1908), pp. 16, 19.

64. *Empire Rev.*, Apr. 1907, pp. 215-17 (Bruce); *Journal of the Society of Arts*, Apr. 24, 1908, p. 606 (Ampthill); *Lords*, Feb. 4, 1908, pp. 659-60 (Ampthill); *Nation*, Jan. 4, 1908; *The Times*, Jan. 3, 1908, 5d (Ritch); *Tribune*, Jan. 6, 1908; Introduction by Ampthill in Doke (1909), p. v; Bruce (1908), pp. 19-24.

65. Colony of Natal, Census, April 1904, p. 672.

66. P.R.O., c.o. 476/3b, citing Tranvaal, Epitome of the Principal Statistical Figures, 1902-06, p. 273.

67. Morning Post, Mar. 28, 1908; Pall Mall Gazette, Jan. 26 and May 2, 1906 (Neame), Oct. 27, 1908 (Blackburn), Dec. 28, 1907 (ed.); Standard, Jan. 6, 1908; Neame (1907), pp. 29, 44-52.

68. Fortnightly Rev., Feb. 1907, pp. 292-300 (Stobart).

69. Journal of the Society of Arts, Apr. 24, 1908, pp. 585-90 (Jebb); Morning Post, Mar. 22, 1907 (Jebb), Nov. 6, 1907 and Mar. 28, 1908 (ed.); National Rev., Mar. 1908, pp. 158-59; Spectator, Jan. 4, 1908; Neame (1907), pp. 25, 44.

70. Willard (1923), pp. 21-23.

71. Mary Roberts Coolidge Chinese Immigration (New York: 1909), p. 302ff.

72. Journal of the Society of Arts, Apr. 24, 1908, p. 592 (Jebb); Morning Post, Dec. 31, 1907, Feb. 1, 1908; Pall Mall Gazette, Jan. 3, 1908; Standard, Jan. 25, 1908; The Times, Jan. 11, 1908, 6a (Elliott).

73. For a discussion of Gandhi's tactics see P.P., 1909, LXI, Cd. 4584, pp. 46-47.

74. Morning Post, Mar. 28, 1908; Pall Mall Gazette, Jan. 1, 29, 1908; The Times, Sept. 18, 1908, 8b and Nov. 11, 1908, 7d (Ridgeway).

75. Guardian, Jan. 8, 1908; Morning Post, Jan. 2, Nov. 3, 1908; The Times, Sept. 18, 1908, 8b (Ridgeway).

76. The Times, Nov. 10, 1906, 11e-f, Dec. 4, 1906, 9d-e, Jan. 7, 1908, 7d-e, Sept. 16, 1908, 9d-e.

77. Lords, Feb. 4, 1908, p. 666 (Roberts), pp. 668-73 (Curzon), pp. 680-83 (Lansdowne).

78. Empire Rev., Feb. 1908, pp. 10-14 (Hindlip); Journal of the Society of the Arts, Apr. 24, 1908, pp. 605-06 (Lyttelton); Morning Post, Jan. 1, 10, 29, Mar. 28, 1908; Spectator, Jan. 4, 1908; Standard, Jan. 6, 1908.

79. Journal of the Society of the Arts, Apr. 24, 1908, pp. 595-96 (Jebb).

NOTES TO CHAPTER EIGHT

1. P.P., 1909, LX, Cd. 4721, p. 24 (old Clause 140), V, Bill 297, p. 37 (new Clause 147); P.R.O., c.o. 879/100, No. 927, c.o. 879/106, No. 934; Viscount Gladstone Papers, 45996, pp. 39-41, Ltr., Crewe to Gladstone, Apr. 26, 1919. Cf. Gandhi (1954), pp. 227-28; Polak (1909), part II, pp. 33-34.

2. P.P., 1910, LXV, Cd. 5363, p. 24ff.; P.R.O., c.o. 291/141-43.

3. P.P., 1911, LII, Cd. 5579, pp 1-3.

4. *P.P.*, 1911, LII, Cd. 5579, pp. 7-8, 17.

5. *P.R.O.*, c.o. 291/144.

6. *P.R.O.*, c.o. 551/3-4, 20, c.o. 879/104, No. 947.

7. *P.P.*, 1911, Cd. 5579, pp. 9-19; *P.R.O.*, c.o. 551/20, c.o. 879/108, No. 970.

8. *P.P.*, 1912-13, LIX, Cd. 6283, pp. 1-2; *P.R.O.*, c.o. 551/14, 20, c.o. 879/108, No. 970.

9. *P.P.*, 1911, LII, Cd. 5579, pp. 9-16, 1912-13, LIX, Cd. 6283, pp. 3-14; *P.R.O.*, c.o. 551/20-22.

10. *P.P.*, 1912-13, LIX, Cd. 6283, pp. 14-22; *P.R.O.*, c.o. 551/13.

11. *P.R.O.*, c.o 551/13, 20, 34

12. *P.R.O.*, c.o. 551/27-28, 34.

13. For an account of Gokhale's visit to South Africa see Gandhi (1954), pp. 259-70.

14. *P.P.*, 1907, LVII, Cd. 3308, pp. 49-56; *P.R.O.*, c.o. 551/22. Cf. Calpin (1949), pp. 31-32; Polak (1909), part I, pp. 79-81.

15. *P.R.O.*, c.o. 551/20, 27, 43.

16. For the provisions of the *Immigrants Regulation Act* see *P.P.*, 1913, XLV, Cd. 6940, pp. 32-43.

17. *P.P.*, 1913, XLV, Cd. 6940, passim, 1914, XLIX, Cd. 7265, pp. 11-18, 24-40, LIX, Cd. 7111, pp. 1-5, 22ff. Cf. Gandhi (1954), pp. 272-73; *Round Table*, Dec. 1913, pp. 182-83.

18. *P.P.*, 1914, LXIX, Cd. 7265, pp. 18-24, LIX, Cd. 7111, pp. 24, 39-40. Cf. Gandhi (1954), pp. 276-77; Palmer (1957), p. 70.

19. *P.P.*, 1913, XLV, Cd. 6940, pp. 32-43; *P.R.O.*, c.o. 551/37-39, 49, 52.

20. *P.R.O.*, c.o. 551/35, 39-42, 49.

21. Gandhi (1954), pp. 277-85; Palmer (1957), pp. 70-71.

22. *P.P.*, 1914, LXIX, Cd. 7265, pp. 1-4, LIX, Cd. 7111, p. 65ff. Cf. Gandhi (1954), pp. 286-313; Palmer (1957), pp. 71-72.

23. *P.P.*, 1914, XLIX, Cd. 7265, pp. 5-11.

24. *P.P.*, 1914, LIX, Cd. 7111, passim; *P.R.O.*, c.o. 551/39, 42-43, 45, 49, 51.

25. *P.R.O.*, c.o. 551/43-44, 46, c.o. 879/113, No. 1009.

26. *P.P.*, 1914, LIX, Cd. 7111, pp. 2-3, XLIX, Cd. 7265, 40 pp. Cf. Gandhi (1954), pp. 321-34; Palmer (1957), pp. 72-73; *Round Table*, June 1914, pp. 477-83; *The Times*, Jan. 23, 1914, 5e (news item); Waiz (1927, 2nd ed.), pp. 270-323.

27. *P.P.*, 1914, XLIX, Cd. 7265, pp. 39-40. Cf. *Round Table*, June 1914, pp. 477-83; *The Times*, May 28, 1914, 8a (news item); Waiz (1927, 2nd ed.), pp. 270-323.

28. *P.R.O.*, c.o. 551/45-46, 49, 52-53, 56.

29. *P.P.*, 1914-16, XLV, Cd. 7644, 7 pp. Cf. Gandhi (1954), pp. 335-36; Waiz (1927, 2nd ed.), pp. 283-308.

30. Gandhi (1954), pp. 336-39; *The Times*, July 20, 1914, 7b (news item); Waiz (1927, 2nd ed.), pp. 308-23.

31. *P.R.O.*, c.o. 551/56-58.

32. *Commons*, June 29, 1910, pp. 1022-24 and Mar. 30, 1911, p. 1516 (O'Grady); *Justice*, Dec. 4, 1909 (Ritch); *Lords*, Dec. 6, 1911, pp. 666-67 (Ampthill); *Manchester Guardian*, July 13, 1910 (Ritch); *Nation*, Jan. 8, 1910 (Ritch); *Saturday Rev.*, Sept. 10, 1910 (Ritch); *The Times*, Sept. 13, 1910, 6b (Ritch).

33. *Daily News*, Sept. 26, 1913; *Empire Rev.*, Sept. 1913, pp. 103-05; *Lords*, July 30, 1913, pp. 1514-16 and July 17, 1912, pp. 565-69 (Ampthill); *Manchester Guardian*, Nov. 21, 1913; *The Times*, Aug. 4, 1913, 5b (Ampthill).

34. *Labour Leader*, Nov. 20, 1913; *Manchester Guardian*, Nov. 21, 1913; *Nation*, Nov. 22, 1913; *New Statesman*, Nov. 22, 1913.

35. *Empire Rev.*, Sept. 1913, pp. 100-03 (Ampthill); *Lords*, July 26, 1910, pp. 467-68 and July 17, 1912, pp. 570-71 (Ampthill); *Standard*, Jan. 1, 1910 (Ritch); *Westminster Gazette*, Nov. 18, 1913.

36. *The Times*, Dec. 31, 1909, 3b (news item).

37. For an account of one such frenzied meeting at Bombay on Dec. 13, 1913 attended by a vast assemblage see Waiz (1927, 2nd ed.), pp. 259-64.

38. *Lords*, July 26, 1910, p. 466, July 17, 1912, p. 568, and Feb. 11, 1913, pp. 1105-06 (Ampthill); *Nation*, Sept. 17, 1910; *New Statesman*, Nov. 22, 1913; *The Times*, Jan. 5, 1911, 6d (Ritch).

39. *Daily News*, May 29, 1914; *Lords*, July 26, 1910, pp. 467-68 (Ampthill); *Manchester Guardian*, Nov. 21, Dec. 2, 1913; *New Statesman*, Nov. 22, 1913.

40. Elizabeth Bisland *The Life and Letters of Lafcadio Hearn* (Boston: 1906), II, p. 138.

41. *Daily Mail*, Nov. 19, 1913; *Morning Post*, Sept. 26, 1913 (Jebb), Oct. 3, 1913 (ed.); *The Times*, Nov. 24, 1913, 7f (Younghusband); Fyfe (1911), p. 162ff.; Rees (1912), p. 162.

42. *The Times*, Nov. 24, 1913, 7f and Nov. 29, 1913, 8b (Younghusband).

43. *The Times*, Dec. 6, 1913, 7c-d (Ridgeway); Fyfe (1911), p. 167; Rees (1912), pp. 165-66.

44. Chirol (1910), pp. 280-87.

45. *The Times*, Jan. 4, 1911, 9e, Nov. 19, 1913, 7f 9d-e, Dec. 23, 1913, 9d-e, Dec. 31, 1913, 63d-e.

46. *The Times*, Nov. 19, 1913, 7f 9d-e, Dec. 23, 1913, 9d-e, Dec. 31, 1913, 63d-e.

47. Hardinge (1948), pp. 90-92.

48. Willard (1923), pp. 92-93.

49. Palmer (1957), p. 55.

50. Morning Post, Sept. 26, and Dec. 3, 1913 (Jebb).

51. Daily Mail, Nov. 19, 28, 1913; Daily Telegraph, Dec. 2, 1913; Morning Post, Dec. 1, 1913; Standard, Nov. 19, 25, 1913; The Times, Dec. 6, 1913, 7c-d (Ridgeway).

52. Fyfe (1911), pp. 168-70; Rees (1912), pp. 167-68.

53. The Times, Sept. 12, 1910, 9e-f and Jan. 8, 1913, 7d-e.

54. Jebb (1913), pp. 190-91.

55. Daily News, June 9, 1914; New Statesman, June 13, 1914; Standard, June 11, 1914; The Times, June 9, 1914, 9c; World's Work, July 1914, p. 145.

BIBLIOGRAPHY

I. MANUSCRIPT COLLECTIONS

Asquith Papers, Bodleian Library, Oxford.
Balfour Papers, Add. MSS, British Museum.
Campbell-Bannerman Papers, Add. MSS, British Museum.
Dilke Papers, Add. MSS, British Museum.
Viscount Gladstone Papers, Add. MSS, British Museum.
Nathan Papers, Rhodes House, Oxford.
Ripon Papers, Add. MSS, British Museum.

II. PUBLIC DOCUMENTS

A. PUBLIC RECORD OFFICE.
    African (South) Confidential Prints, 1900-14, c.o. 879 series.
    Cape Colony, Papers and Dispatches, 1902-10, c.o. 48 series.
    Natal, Papers and Dispatches, 1902-10, c.o. 179 series.
    Orange Free State (Orange River Colony), Papers and Dispatches,
    1902-10, c.o. 224 series.
    Transvaal, Papers and Dispatches, 1902-10, c.o. 291 series.
    Union of South Africa, Papers and Dispatches, 1910-14, c.o. 551 series.

B. PARLIAMENTARY DEBATES.
    House of Commons, 1902-14.
    House of Lords, 1902-14.

C. PARLIAMENTARY PAPERS
    1885, LVII, Cd. 3914, "A Convention Between Her Majesty the
    Queen of the U.K. of G.B. and Ireland and the S. African Repub-
    lic," 13 pp.
    1895, LXXI, Cd. 7911, "Papers Relating to the Grievances of Her
    Majesty's Indian Subjects in the South African Republic," 64 pp.
    1897, LIX, Cd. 1896, "Proceedings of a Conference Between the Sec-

retary of State for the Colonies and the Premiers of the Self-Governing Colonies, at the Colonial Office, London, June and July 1897,"
19 pp.

1898, LX, Cd. 8782, "Correspondence Relating to the Affairs of
Zululand," 42 pp.

1898, LX, Cd. 8797, "Correspondence Relating to Native Disturbances
in Bechuanaland," 66 pp.

1901, XLVII, Cd. 528, "Papers Relating to Negotiations Between
Commandant Louis Botha & Lord Kitchener," 7 pp.

1902, LXVII, Cd. 1163, "Further Correspondence Relating to Affairs
in South Africa," 178 pp.

1903, XLV, No. 184, "Return Showing the Rates of Taxation Now Paid
by Natives in the Several Parts of British South Africa," 8 pp.

1903, XLV, No. 345, "Return of the Statistics of Mortality, Sickness,
and Desertion Amongst the Natives Employed in the Rand Mines
During the Period October 1902 to March 1903," 6 pp.

1903, XLV, Cd. 1531, "Correspondence Relating to the Recruitment
of Labour in the British Central Africa Protectorate For Employment in the Transvaal," 19 pp.

1903, XLV, Cd. 1586, "Statement of the Estimated Financial Position of the Transvaal and the Orange River Colony," 4 pp.

1903, XLV, Cd. 1640, "Minutes of Proceedings of the South African
Customs Union Conference, Held at Bloemfontein, March 1903,"
17 pp.

1903, XLV, Cd. 1683, "Correspondence Relating to a Proposal to
Employ Indian Coolies Under Indenture On Railways in the Transvaal and the Orange River Colony," 5 pp.

1903, XLV, Cd. 1684, "Dispatch from the Governor of the Transvaal
Respecting the Position of British Indians in that Colony," 7 pp.

1904, XXXIX, Cd. 1894, "Reports of the Transvaal Labour Commission," 57 pp.

1904, XXXIX, Cd. 1896, "Reports of the Transvaal Labour Commission," 84 pp.

1904, XXXIX, Cd. 1897, "Reports of the Transvaal Labour Commission: Minutes of Proceedings and Evidence," 671 pp.

1904, LXI, No. 205, "Return of the Numbers and Rate of Mortality
from (a) Accident, (b) other Causes, among (1) the White Miners, Artisans, and Labourers employed in the Rand Mines; (2) all
classes of Natives in the Rand Mines; (3) the British Central African
Natives in the Rand Mines; (4) the Natives in the Rhodesian Mines;
and (5) the Natives in the de Beers' Mines, Kimberley, during the
last 12 months for which statistics are obtainable," 14 pp.

1904, LXI, Cd. 1844, "Report Received From Mr. Henry Birchenough, the Special Commissioner Appointed by the Board of Trade to Inquire into and Report upon the Present Position and Future Prospects of British Trade in South Africa," 160 pp.

1904, LXI, Cd. 1895, "Further Correspondence Relating to the Affairs of the Transvaal and Orange River Colony," 363 pp.

1904, LXI, Cd. 1898, "Telegraphic Correspondence Relating to the Transvaal Labour Importation Ordinance; With Appendix: The Ordinance Amended in Accordance with Telegrams," 18 pp.

1904, LXI, Cd. 1899, "Further Correspondence Regarding the Transvaal Labour Question," 23 pp.

1904, LXI, Cd. 1941, "Further Correspondence Relating to the Transvaal Labour Question," 92 pp.

1904, LXI, Cd. 1986, "Further Correspondence Relating to the Transvaal Labour Question," 18 pp.

1904, LXI, Cd. 2026, "Further Correspondence Relating to the Transvaal Labour Importation Ordinance," 56 pp.

1904, LXI, Cd. 2104, "Correspondence Relating to the Affairs in the Transvaal and Orange River Colony," 190 pp.

1904, LXII, Cd. 1945, "Correspondence Respecting the Introduction of Chinese Labour into the Transvaal," 5 pp.

1904, LXII, Cd. 1950, "Correspondence Relating to the Recruitment of Labour in the British Central Africa Protectorate For Employment in the Transvaal," 35 pp.

1904, LXII, Cd. 1956, "Convention Between the United Kingdom and China Respecting the Employment of Chinese Labour in British Colonies and Protectorates," 5 pp.

1904, LXII, Cd. 2025, "Correspondence Relating to Conditions of Native Labour Employed in Transvaal Mines," 154 pp.

1904, LXII, Cd. 2183, "Further Correspondence Relating to Labour in the Transvaal Mines," 34 pp.

1905, LV, Cd. 2399, "Report of the South African Native Affairs Commission, 1903-1905," 97 pp.

1905, LV, Cd. 2400, "Despatch Transmitting Letters Patent and Order in Council Providing for Constitutional Changes in the Transvaal," 23 pp.

1905, LV, Cd. 2401, "Further Correspondence Relating to Labour in the Transvaal Mines," 128 pp.

1905, LV, Cd. 2479, "Papers Relating to Constitutional Changes in the Transvaal," 142 pp.

1905, LV, Cd. 2563, "Further Correspondence Relating to Affairs in the Transvaal and Orange River Colony," 72 pp.

1905, LVI, Cd. 2239, "Correspondence Relating to the Position of British Indians in the Transvaal," 48 pp.

1905, XCVIII, No. 137, "Statistical Tables Relating to Emigration and Immigration from and into the United Kingdom, in the year 1904," 77 pp.

1905, CII, Cd. 2660, "Census of the British Empire, 1901." 301 pp.

1906, LXXVII, No. 357, "Coolie Labour . . . in British Possessions," 48 pp.

1906, LXXVII, Cd. 2976, "Report on the Emigrants' Information Office for the Year Ended 31st December 1905," 10 pp.

1906, LXXIX, Cd. 2905, "Correspondence Relating to Native Disturbances in Natal," 60 pp.

1906, LXXIX, Cd. 2927, "Petition to His Majesty in Council of the Twelve Natives Recently Executed in Natal and the Affidavit in Support of the Petition and Judgement," 9 pp.

1906, LXXIX, Cd. 3027, "Further Correspondence Relating to Native Disturbances in Natal," 104 pp.

1906, LXXIX, Cd. 3247, "Further Correspondence Relating to Native Disturbances in Natal," 97 pp.

1906, LXXX, No. 114, "Return of the Output of Gold from the South African Mines in the Transvaal for the five years preceding the importation of Chinese Labour," 3 pp.

1906, LXXX, No. 156, "Return of the Crimes Committed by Chinese Labourers who have deserted from the Mines of the Witwatersrand District upon the European or other Inhabitants of the Transvaal since June 1905," 19 pp.

1906, LXXX, Cd. 2786, "Further Correspondence Relating to Labour in the Transvaal Mines," 86 pp.

1906, LXXX, Cd. 2788, "Further Correspondence Relating to Labour in the Transvaal Mines," 10 pp.

1906, LXXX, Cd. 2819, "Further Correspondence Relating to Labour in the Transvaal Mines," 178 pp.

1906, LXXX, Cd. 3025, "Further Correspondence Relating to Labour in the Transvaal Mines," 190 pp.

1906, LXXX, Cd. 3250, "Transvaal Constitution, 1906; Letters Patent and Instructions Relating to the Transvaal: and Swaziland Order in Council," 40 pp.

1906, LXXX, Cd. 3251, "The Asiatic Law Amendment Ordinance No. 29, 1906," 9 pp.

1907, LV, Cd. 3253, "Minutes of Proceedings of the Colonial Conference, 1907," 622 pp.

1907, LVII, Cd. 3308, "Correspondence Relating to Legislation Affecting Asiatics in the Transvaal," 66 pp.

1907, LVII, Cd. 3338, "Annual Report of the Foreign Labour Department, 1905-6," 47 pp.

1907, LVII, Cd. 3405, "Correspondence Relating to the Introduction of Chinese Labourers Into the Transvaal in Excess of the Number of Licences Issued," 6 pp.

1907, LVII, Cd. 3526, "Letters Patent and Instructions Relating to the Orange River Colony," 47 pp.

1907, LVII, Cd. 3528, "Further Correspondence Relating to Affairs in the Transvaal and Orange River Colony," 184 pp.

1907, LVII, Cd. 3563, "Correspondence Relating to the Removal of Certain Native Prisoners From Natal," 14 pp.

1907, LVII, Cd. 3564, "Papers Relating to a Federation of the South African Colonies," 108 pp.

1907, LVII, Cd. 3621, "The Transvaal Loan Act, 1907; with papers Respecting the Finances of the Colony," 28 pp.

1908, LXXII, Cd. 3888, "Further Correspondence Relating to Native Affairs in Natal," 232 pp.

1908, LXXII, Cd. 3889, "Report of the Native Affairs Commission, 1906-7," 41 pp.

1908, LXXII, Cd. 3998, "Further Correspondence Relating to Native Affairs in Natal ," 188 pp.

1908, LXXII, Cd. 4001, "Further Correspondence Relating to Native Affairs in Natal," 16 pp.

1908, LXXII, Cd. 4194, "Further Correspondence Relating to Native Affairs in Natal," 147 pp.

1908, LXXII, Cd. 4195, "Despatch From the Governor of Natal Forwarding a Bill to Make Special Provision For the Trial of Natives Accused of Certain Crimes," 6 pp.

1908, LXXII, Cd. 4328, "Further Correspondence Relating to Native Affairs in Natal," 119 pp.

1908, LXXII, Cd. 4403, "Papers Relating to the Case of Mr. Alfred Mangena," 130 pp.

1908, LXXII, Cd. 4404, "Further Correspondence Relating to the Trial of Certain Natives in Natal," 26 pp.

1908, LXXIII, Cd. 3887, "Further Correspondence Relating to Legislation Affecting Asiatics in the Transvaal," 88 pp.

1908, LXXIII, Cd. 3892, "Further Correspondence Relating to Legislation Affecting Asiatics in the Transvaal," 5 pp.

1908, LXXIII, Cd. 3993, "Correspondence Relating to the Recruitment of Labour in the Nyasaland Protectorate For the Transvaal and Southern Rhodesia Mines," 120 pp.

1908, LXXIII, Cd. 3994, "Correspondence Relating to the Transvaal Indentured Labour Laws Temporary Continuance Act, 1907," 10 pp.

1908, LXXIII, Cd. 4120, "Statement of Mortality Amongst the Different Classes of Coloured Labourers in the Transvaal Mines From January 1906 to February 1908 Inclusive," 16 pp.

1908, LXXIII, Cd. 4121, "Papers Relating to the Form of Contract in Use in Connection With the Recruitment of Native Labourers For the Transvaal Mines in Portuguese East Africa," 4 pp.

1908, LXXIII, Cd. 4327, "Further Correspondence Relating to Legislation Affecting Asiatics in the Transvaal," 59 pp.

1908, LXXIII, Cd. 4357, "Correspondence Relating to a Proposal to Recruit Labour in Madagascar for Employment in the Transvaal Mines," 8 pp.

1909, V, Bill 297, "A Bill Intituled An Act to Constitute the Union of South Africa," 43 pp.

1909, LX, Cd. 4525, "Report to the Respective Parliaments of the Delegates to the South African Convention, 1908-1909; With Copy of the Draft South African Constitution Bill," 23 pp.

1909, LX, Cd. 2585, "Further Correspondence Relating to the Trial of Dinizulu and other Natives in Natal," 49 pp.

1909, LX, Cd. 4721, "Second Report to the Respective Parliaments of the Delegates to the South African Convention, 1908-1909; With Copy of the Draft South African Constitution Bill As Finally Passed by the Convention," 27 pp.

1909, LXI, Cd. 4584, "Further Correspondence Relating to Legislation Affecting Asiatics in the Transvaal," 69 pp.

1910, LXVI, Cd. 5363, "Further Correspondence Relating to Legislation Affecting Asiatics in the Transvaal," 136 pp.

1911, LII, Cd. 5579, "Correspondence Respecting a Bill to Regulate Immigration Into the Union of South Africa, With Special Reference to Asiatics," 33 pp.

1912-13, LIX, Cd. 6087, "Correspondence Relating to the Position of British Indians Under the Gold Law and Townships Amendment Acts, 1908, of the Transvaal," 19 pp.

1912-13, LIX, Cd. 6283, "Further Correspondence Respecting a Bill to Regulate Immigration Into the Union of South Africa; With Special Reference to Asiatics," 30 pp.

1913, XLV, Cd. 6940, "Further Correspondence Relating to a Bill to Regulate Immigration Into the Union of South Africa; With Special Reference to Asiatics," 44 pp.

1914, XLIX, Cd. 7265, "Report of the Indian Enquiry Commission," 40 pp.

1914, LIX, Cd. 7111, "Correspondence Relating to the Immigrants Regulation Act and Other Matters Affecting Asiatics in South Africa," 78 pp.

1914, LIX, Cd. 7213, "Text of the Indemnity and Undesirables Special Deportation Bill of the Union of South Africa," 4 pp.

1914, LIX, Cd. 7348, "Correspondence Relating to the Recent General Strike in South Africa," 269 pp.

1914, LIX, Cd. 7508, "Correspondence Relating to the Natives Land Act, 1913," 30 pp.

1914-16, XLV, Cd. 7644, "Correspondence Relating to the Indians Relief Act, 1914," 7 pp.

D. SOUTH AFRICAN SOURCES

Cape Hansard.

Cape of Good Hope, Debates in the House of Assembly.

Census of the Transvaal Colony and Swaziland, April 17, 1904.

Colony of Natal, Census, April 1904.

Colony of Natal, Department of Native Affairs, Annual Reports.

Handbook of Ordinances, Proclamations, Regulations, and Instructions Connected with the Importation of Foreign Labour into the Transvaal (Pretoria:1906), 91 pp.

Legislative Assembly (Natal).

Official Year Books of South Africa.

Report of the Select Committee on Asiatic Grievances, Cape of Good Hope, September 1908.

Report of the Transvaal Indigency Commission, 1906-08.

Statistical Register of the Colony of the Cape of Good Hope, 1904-06.

Statistical Year Books for Natal, 1904.

Statistical Year Books for the Union of South Africa.

The Statute Law of the Transvaal.

Transvaal Chamber of Mines, Annual Reports.

Transvaal Government Mining Engineer, Annual Reports.

Transvaal Labour Department for Asiatic Immigration, Reports, 1904-06.

Transvaal Mines Department, Detailed Statistics.

Transvaal Native Affairs Department, Annual Reports.

Union of South Africa, House of Assembly, Debates.

Union of South Africa, Mines Department, Reports.

Union of South Africa, Native Affairs Reports.

Union of South Africa, Railways and Harbours, Annual Reports.

Union of South Africa Railways, Report of a Committee Appointed to Inquire Into and to Report on Certain Matters Concerning the Railway Workshop, 1911-12.

Union of South Africa: Report of a Commission on Miners' Phthisis and Pulmonary Tuberculosis, 1912.

Union of South Africa: Report of the Commission Inquiry Into the Working of the Miners' Phthisis Acts, 1919.

Union of South Africa: Report of the Railway Commission of Inquiry, November 1914.

Union of South Africa, Senate, Debates.

Witwatersrand Native Labour Association, Annual Reports.

Year Book for South Africa.

Zululand Delimitation Commission, Report, 1905.

III. REPORTS AND PROCEEDINGS

Aborigines' Friend, Reports and monthly issues of Aborigines' Protection Society, 1902-08.

Anti-Slavery Reporter, Reports and bi-monthly issues of the British and Foreign Anti-Slavery Society, 1902-08.

Anti-Slavery Reporter and Aborigines' Friend, Reports of amalgamated Aborigines' Protection Society and British and Foreign Anti-Slavery Society, 1910-14.

General Federation of Trade Unions, Proceedings and Reports, 1902-14.

Imperial South African Association, Reports, 1902-09.

Independent Labour Party, Annual Conferences, 1902-14.

Labour Party, Annual Reports, 1906-14.

Labour Representation Committee, Annual Reports, 1901-05.

National Liberal Federation, Annual Proceedings and Reports, 1902-14.

Trades Union Congress, Annual Reports, 1902-15.

IV. NEWSPAPERS AND PERIODICALS

Albany Review (Liberal monthly), 1907-08. Suspended. Preceded by Independent.

Annual Register, (general), 1902-14.

Asiatic Quarterly Review (general), 1902-14.

Baptist Times and Freeman (weekly), 1902-14.

Blackwood's Magazine (Conservative monthly), 1902-14.
British Congregationalist and Examiner (weekly), 1906-14. Preceded by *Examiner*.
British Review (general monthly), 1913-14.
British Socialist (monthly), 1912-13.
British Weekly (Nonconformist), 1902-14.
Catholic Herald (weekly), 1902-14.
Catholic Times (weekly), 1902-14.
Church Quarterly Review (Anglican), 1902-14.
Church Times (Anglican weekly), 1902-14.
Clarion (Socialist weekly), 1902-14.
Commonwealth (Anglican weekly), 1902-14.
Conservative (monthly later known as *Conservative and Unionist* and *Our Flag*), 1902-14.
Contemporary Review (general monthly), 1902-14.
Daily Chronicle (Liberal), 1902-14.
Daily Mail (Conservative), 1902-14.
Daily News (Liberal), 1902-14.
Daily Telegraph (Conservative), 1902-14.
East and the West (Christian Missions monthly), 1903-14.
Economist (Liberal weekly), 1902-14.
Edinburgh Review (Conservative monthly), 1902-14.
Empire Review (Conservative monthly), 1902-14.
English Review (general monthly), 1908-14.
Ethics (non-Christian weekly or monthly later known as *Ethical Review* and *Ethical World*), 1902-14.
Everyman (general weekly), 1912-14.
Examiner (Congregational weekly), 1902-06. Succeeded by *British Congregationalist and Examiner*.
Fabian News (Socialist monthly), 1902-14.
Fortnightly Review (general monthly), 1902-14.
Free Church Chronicle (National Council of the Evangelical Free Churches monthly), 1902-14.
Friend (Quaker weekly), 1902-14.
Gentleman's Magazine (Conservative monthly), 1902-Sept. 1907. Suspended.
Guardian (Anglican weekly), 1902-14.
Independent Labour Party News (Socialist monthly), 1902-Dec. 1903. Suspended.
Independent Review (Liberal monthly), 1903-Mar. 1907. Succeeded by *Albany Review*.

International (general monthly), Dec. 1907-Dec. 1909. Suspended.
Investors' Review (Liberal weekly), 1902-14.
Journal of the African Society (general quarterly), 1902-14.
Journal of the East Indian Association (quarterly), 1902-14.
Journal of the Society of Arts (general weekly), 1902-14.
Justice (Socialist weekly), 1902-14.
Labour Leader (Socialist weekly), 1902-14.
Liberal Magazine (Liberal party reprints), 1902-14.
Macmillan's Magazine (general monthly), 1902-07. Suspended.
Manchester Guardian (Liberal daily), 1902-14.
Methodist Times (weekly), 1902-14.
Monthly Review, 1902-07. Suspended.
Morning Post (Conservative daily), 1902-14.
Nation (Liberal weekly), 1907-14. Preceded by *Speaker*.
National Review (Conservative monthly), 1902-14.
New Age (Guild Socialist weekly), 1902-14.
New Liberal Review (monthly), 1902-04. Suspended.
New Statesman (Fabian weekly), 1913-14.
Nineteenth Century and After (general monthly), 1902-14.
Pall Mall Gazette (Conservative daily), 1902-14.
Pilot (Anglican weekly), 1902-04. Suspended.
Positivist Review (non-Christian monthly), 1902-14.
Progress (general quarterly), 1906-14.
Quarterly Review (Conservative), 1902-14.
Reformer (Rationalist monthly), 1902-14. Suspended.
Review of Reviews (Liberal weekly), 1902-14.
Round Table (general quarterly), 1913-14.
Saturday Review (Conservative weekly), 1902-14.
Social Democrat (Socialist monthly), 1902-13. Suspended.
Socialist Annual, 1906-14.
Socialist Review (monthly and quarterly), 1908-14.
Speaker (Liberal weekly), 1902-07. Succeeded by *Nation*.
Spectator (Conservative weekly), 1902-14.
Standard (Conservative daily), 1902-14.
Tablet (Catholic weekly), 1902-14.
The Times (Conservative daily), 1902-14.
Tribune (Liberal daily), Jan. 15, 1906-May 3, 1908. Suspended.
Truth (Liberal weekly), 1902-14.
Twentieth Century Quarterly (general), 1906. Suspended.
United Empire (Royal Colonial Institute Journal, general monthly), 1910-14.

Westminster Gazette (Liberal daily), 1902-14.
Westminster Review (Liberal monthly), 1902-14.
World's Work (Liberal monthly, later known as *World's Work and Play*), 1902-14.

V.   PAMPHLETS AND BOOKS

Allsopp, Charles (Baron Hindlip), *British East Africa: Past, Present, and Future* (London: 1905), 142 pp.
Amery, Julian, *The Life of Joseph Chamberlain* (London: 1951), IV.
Ampthill, Lord, Introduction, in Joseph J. Doke M. K. *Gandhi: An Indian Patriot in South Africa* (London: 1909), pp. iii-vi.
Balfour-Browne, John Hutton, *South Africa* (London: 1905), 238 pp.
Bourne, Henry Richard Fox, *Forced Labour in British South Africa: Notes on the Condition and Prospects of South African Natives Under British Control:* (London: 1903), 56 pp.
Bruce, Sir Charles, *British Indians in the Transvaal* (London: 1908), 24 pp. Reprint of two articles in *Empire Review*, Feb. and Oct. 1908. Published by the South African British Indian Committee.
Bruce, Sir Charles, *Milestones on My Long Journey: Memories of a Colonial Governor* (Glasgow: 1917), 232 pp.
Bruce, Sir Charles, *The True Temper of Empire, with Corollary Essays* (London: 1912), 211 pp.
Bryce, James, *The American Commonwealth* (New York: 1910), 2 vols.
Burt, Thomas, *A Visit to the Transvaal; Labour: White, Black, and Yellow* (Newcastle-Upon-Tyne: 1905), 87 pp.
Butler, Sir William, *From Naboth's Vineyard: Being Impressions Formed During a Fourth Visit to South Africa Undertaken at the Request of the Tribune Newspaper* (London: 1907, 2nd ed.), 268 pp.
Butler, Sir William, *An Autobiography* (New York: 1911), 476 pp.
Buxton, Sydney Charles, *Chinese Labour* (London: 1904), 23 pp.
Buxton, Sydney Charles, *Chinese Question and Retaliation: Report of Speech Delivered by Mr. Sydney Buxton, M.P., Oxford, Mar. 12, 1904* (London: 1904), 22 pp. Eighty Club.
Campbell-Bannerman, Sir Henry, "What Is the Liberal Policy?" in William Thomas Stead, *Coming Men on Coming Questions* (1905), pp. 10-24.
Chamberlain, *An Account of the Right Hon. Joseph Chamberlain's Visit to South Africa, November, 1902—March, 1903: A Record of Unique Practical Statesmanship* (London: 1903), 76 pp.

Chirol, Valentine, *Indian Unrest* (London: 1910), 371 pp.

Colenso, Francis Ernest (pseud. Gebuza), *The Peril in Natal* (London: 1906), 29 pp.

Conservative Publication Department, *Leaflets, 1902-14.*

Davis, Alexander, *The Native Problem in South Africa* (London: 1903), 188 pp.

Dugdale, Blanche Elizabeth Campbell, *Arthur James Balfour: First Earl of Balfour* (New York: 1937), 2 vols.

Durand, Sir Henry Mortimer, *A Holiday in South Africa* (London: 1911), 275 pp.

Foster, Arnold, *Chinese Coolie Labour in South Africa* (London: 1904), 4 pp. Transvaal Pamphlet No. 82.

Fyfe, Henry Hamilton, *South Africa Today, With An Account of Modern Rhodesia* (London: 1911), 299 pp.

Gardiner, A. G., *The Life of Sir William Harcourt* (New York: 1923), 2 vols.

Gooch, George Peabody, *Life of Lord Courtney* (London: 1920), 626 pp.

Grey, Edward (Viscount of Fallodon), *Twenty-Five Years, 1892-1916* (New York: 1925), 2 vols.

Griffith, George, *With Chamberlain Through South Africa: A Narrative of the Great Trek* (London: 1903), 164 pp.

Griffith-Boscawen, Arthur Sackville Trevor, *Fourteen Years in Parliament* (London: 1907), 383 pp.

Gwynn, Stephen and Tuckwell, Gertrude Mary, *The Life of the Rt. Hon. Sir Charles W. Dilke* (New York: 1917), 2 vols.

Hardinge, Charles (Baron of Penshurst), *My Indian Years, 1910-1916* (London: 1948), 150 pp.

Headlam, Cecil, ed., *The Milner Papers: South Africa, 1897-1905* (London: 1931-33), 2 vols.

Hobhouse, Leonard Trelawney, *Democracy and Reaction* (New York: 1905), 244 pp.

Hobson, John Atkinson, *The Crisis of Liberalism: New Issues of Democracy* (London: 1909), 284 pp.

Hobson, John Atkinson, *Imperialism: A Study* (London: 1905, rev. ed.), 331 pp.

Imperial South African Association, *Leaflets on Chinese Labour Question* (London: 1902-08).

Imperial South African Association, *The Chinese Labour Question: Handy Notes* (London: 1905), 56 pp. Conservative Publication Department Leaflets, 1904-05.

Imperial South African Association, *Transvaal Labour: Unskilled Whites,*

Manager of Village Main Reef on Mr. Creswell (London: 1906), 15 pp. Written by Robert Raine.

Imperial South African Association, *A Transvaal View of the Chinese Labour Question* (London: 1906), 60 pp. Written by Raymond W. Schumacher.

Is It Slavery? (London: 1906), 15 pp. Conservative Central Office pamphlet.

Jebb, Richard, *The Britannic Question: A Survey of Alternatives* (London: 1913), 262 pp.

Jebb, Richard, *Studies on Colonial Nationalism* (London: 1905), 336 pp.

John Chinaman on the Rand: By An English Witness, with an introduction by Dr. John Clifford (London: 1905), 128 pp.

Liberal Publication Department, Pamphlets and Leaflets, 1902-14.

Kinloch-Cooke, Sir Clement, *Chinese Labour (In the Transvaal); Being a Study of Its Moral, Economic, and Imperial Aspects* (London: 1904), 39 pp.

Lee, Sir Sidney, *King Edward VII: A Biography* (1925-27), 2 vols.

Lyttelton, Edith, *Alfred Lyttelton: An Account of His Life* (London: 1917), 431 pp.

MacDonald, J. Ramsay, *Labour and The Empire* (London: 1907), 112 pp.

MacDonald, J. Ramsay, *What I saw in South Africa, September and October 1902* (London: 1902), 135 pp.

Mallet, Sir Charles, *Herbert Gladstone: A Memoir* (London: 1933), 326 pp.

Markham, Violet Rosa, *Return Passage: The Autobiography of Violet R. Markham* (London: 1953), 260 pp.

Markham, Violet Rosa, *The New Era in South Africa, With an Examination of the Chinese Labour Question* (London: 1904), 200 pp.

Markham, Violet Rosa, *The South African Scene* (London: 1913), 450 pp.

Maurice, Sir Frederick, *Haldane, 1856-1928: The Life of Viscount Haldane of Cloan* (London: 1937-39), 2 vols.

Milner, Lord, *The Nation and the Empire: Being a Collection of Speeches and Addresses* (London: 1913), 515 pp.

Munro, Dr. Aeneas, *The Transvaal (Chinese) Labour Problem* (London: 1905), 164 pp.

Native Labour in South Africa: A Report of a Public Meeting Jointly Convened by the Aborigines' Protection Society and the British and Foreign Anti-Slavery Society, Caxton Hall, Westminster, April 29, 1903 (London: 1903), 20 pp.

Naylor, Thomas, *Yellow Labour: The Truth About the Chinese in the Transvaal* (London: 1904), 31 pp.

Neame, Lawrence Elwin, "Oriental Labor in South Africa," in *Annals of The American Academy of Political and Social Sciences*, Sept. 1909, pp. 175-82.

Neame, Lawrence Elwin, *The Asiatic Danger in the Colonies* (London: 1907), 192 pp.

New Reform Club, *British Workmen or Chinese Slaves: The Labour Problem in the Transvaal* (London: 1904), 20 pp.

Olivier, Sydney, *White Capital and Coloured Labour* (London: 1906), 175 pp.

Parker, Sir Gilbert, *Our Imperial Responsibilities in the Transvaal* (London: 1904), 29 pp. Imperial South African Association pamphlet.

Parker, Sir Gilbert, *South Africa and Its Problems of Today, An Address, February 20, 1905* (London: 1905), 16 pp. Imperial South African Association pamphlet.

Petrie, Sir Charles, *The Life and Letters of the Rt. Hon. Sir Austen Chamberlain* (London: 1939-40), 2 vols.

Phillips, Lionel, *Transvaal Problems: Some Notes on Current Politics* (London: 1905), 370 pp.

Pope-Hennessy, James, *Lord Crewe, 1858-1945: The Sickness of a Liberal* (1965: reprint).

Rees, Sir John David, *Current Political Problems, With Pros and Cons* (London: 1912), 423 pp.

Riddle, Lord, *More Pages From My Diary, 1908-1914* (London: 1934), 238 pp.

Root, John Wilson, *The South African Labour Question* (Liverpool: 1903), 31 pp.

Sacks, Benjamin, *J. Ramsay MacDonald in Thought and Action: An Architect for a Better World* (Albuquerque: 1952), 592 pp.

Samuel, Viscount (Herbert Louis), *Memoirs* (London: 1945), 304 pp.

Samuel, Viscount (Herbert Louis), *Liberalism: An Attempt to State the Principles and Proposals of Contemporary Liberalism in England* (London: 1902), 396 pp.

Seely, John Edward Bernard (Lord Mottistone), *Adventure* (London: 1930), 326 pp.

Selborne Memorandum: A Review of the Mutual Relations of the British South African Colonies in 1907 (London: 1925), 184 pp. Introduction by Basil Williams.

Shaw, Thomas (Baron Craigmyle), *Narrowing the Bounds of Freedom with an Appendix Containing the Salient Clauses from the Transvaal Labour Ordinance* (London: 1904), 20 pp. New Reform Club Political Committee, Pamphlet No. 5.

Shaw, Thomas, *Letters to Isabel* (London: 1936, new ed.), 411 pp.

2

Shaw, Thomas, "South Africa's Constitutional Hope: A Liberal Forecast," in William Thomas Stead *Coming Men on Coming Questions* (London: 1905), 16 pp.

Sommer, Dudley, *Haldane of Cloan: His Life and Times, 1856-1928* (London: 1960), 448 pp.

Spender, John Alfred, *The Life of the Rt. Hon. Sir Henry Campbell-Bannerman* (London: 1923), 2 vols.

Spender, John Alfred and Asquith, Cyril, *Life of Herbert Henry Asquith, Lord Oxford and Asquith* (London: 1932), 2 vols.

Stead, William Thomas, *What I Learned in South Africa: The Open Secret of Future Peace* (London: 1904), 34 pp.

Thomson, Malcolm, *David Lloyd George: The Official Biography* (London: 1948), 470 pp.

Van Laun, Henry Theodore and Wills, Walter H. *The Labour Problem in South Africa* (London: 1904), 20 pp.

Wedgwood, Cicely Veronica, *The Last of the Radicals: Josiah Wedgwood, M.P.* (London: 1951), 252 pp.

Wolf, Lucien, *Life of the First Marquess of Ripon* (London: 1921), 2 vols.

Worsfold, William Basil, *The Reconstruction of the New Colonies Under Lord Milner* (London: 1913), 2 vols.

VI. REFERENCE MATERIALS

Andrews, Charles Freer, ed., *Mahatma Gandhi At Work: His Own Story Continued* (New York: 1931).

Bleloch, William Edwin, *The New South Africa: Its Value and Development* (London: 1920, 2nd ed., rev.).

Bosman, Walter, *The Natal Rebellion of 1906* (London: 1907).

Brand, Robert Henry, *The Union of South Africa* (Oxford: 1909).

Bryce, James, *Impressions of South Africa* (New York: 1900, 3rd ed., rev.).

Buchan, John, *The African Colony: Studies in the Reconstruction* (London: 1903).

Buell, Raymond Leslie, *The Native Problem in Africa* (New York: 1928), 2 vols.

Butterworth, Arthur Reginald, *The Immigration of Coloured Races Into British Colonies* (London: 1898).

Buxton, Sydney Charles, *General Botha* (London: 1924).

Calpin, George Harold, *Indians in South Africa* (Pietermaritzburg: 1949).

Cambridge History of the British Empire: South Africa, Rhodesia, and the High Commission Territories (Cambridge: 1936) and (Cambridge: 1963, 2nd ed.), VIII.

Campbell, Persia Crawford, *Chinese Coolie Emigration to Countries Within the British Empire* (London: 1923).

Cana, Frank Richardson, *South Africa From the Great Trek to the Union* (London: 1909).

Cory, George E., *The Rise of South Africa* (London: 1910-30), 6 vols.

Crafford, F. S., *Jam Smuts: A Biography* (New York: 1943).

Creswell, Margaret, *An Epoch of the Political History of South Africa in the Life of Frederic Hugh Page Creswell* (Capetown: 1956).

Creswell, Frederic Hugh Page, *The Chinese Labour Question From Within; Facts, Criticisms, and Suggestions; Impeachment of a Disastrous Policy* (London: 1905).

Dawson, William Harbutt, *South Africa: Peoples, Places and Problems* (London: 1925).

DeKiewiet, Cornelius William, *A History of South Africa: Social and Economic* (Oxford: 1942, reprint).

DeKock, Michael Hendrick, *The Economic Development of South Africa* (London: 1936).

Doke, Joseph John, *M. K. Gandhi: An Indian Patriot in South Africa* (London: 1909).

Emden, Paul Herman, *Randlords* (London: 1935).

Engelenburg, Frans Vredenrijk, *General Louis Botha* (London: 1929).

Evans, Maurice Smethurst, *Black and White in South East Africa: A Study in Sociology* (London: 1911).

Eybers, George Von Welfling, ed., *Select Constitutional Documents Illustrating South African History, 1795-1910* (London: 1918).

Frankel, Sally Herbert, *Capital Investment in Africa: Its Course and Effects* (London: 1938).

Fremantle, Henry Eardley Stephen, *The New Nation: A Survey of the Condition and Prospects of South Africa* (London: 1909).

Fuller, Sir Thomas E., *The Right Honourable Cecil John Rhodes: A Monograph and a Reminiscence* (London: 1910).

Galbraith, John S., *Reluctant Empire: British Policy on the South African Frontier, 1834-1854* (Berkeley and Los Angeles: 1963).

Gangulee, Nagendranath, *Indians in the Empire Overseas: A Survey* (London: 1947).

Gandhi, Mohandas Karamchand, *Gandhi's Autobiography: The Story of My Experiments with Truth* (Washington, D.C.: 1948).

Gandhi, Mohandas Karamchand, *Satyagraha in South Africa* (Stanford: 1954).

Geen, M. S., *The Making of South Africa* (Cape Town: 1958).

Goodfellow, David Martin, *A Modern Economic History of South Africa* (London: 1931).

Halévy, Elie, *Imperialism and the Rise of Labour, 1895-1905* (London: 1951, 2nd ed., rev.).

Halévy, Elie, *The Rule of Democracy, 1905-1914* (London: 1952, 2nd ed., rev.), 2 parts.

Hancock, William Keith, *Smuts: The Sanguine Years, 1870-1919* (Cambridge: 1962), I.

Hofmeyr, Jan Hendrik (rev. by J. C. Cope), *South Africa* (London: 1952, 2nd ed., rev.).

Holt, H. P., *The Mounted Police of Natal* (London: 1913).

Jacobsson, Daniel Julius, *Fifty Golden Years of the Rand, 1886-1936* (London: 1936).

Jacobsson, Daniel Julius, *Free State and New Rand Gold* (Johannesburg: 1945).

Johnston, Sir Harry Hamilton, *A History of the Colonization of Africa by Alien Races* (Cambridge: 1930, 2nd ed.).

Keith, Arthur Berriedale, *The Dominions as Sovereign States* (London: 1938).

Keith, Arthur Berriedale, *Governments of the British Empire* (New York: 1936).

Keith, Arthur Berriedale, *Imperial Unity and the Dominions* (Oxford: 1916).

Keith, Arthur Berriedale, *Responsible Government in the Dominions* (Oxford: 1928, 2nd ed.), 2 vols.

Keith, Arthur Berriedale, *South Africa: Geographical* (Oxford: 1913, rev. and new ed.).

Kennedy, William Paul McClure and Schlosberg, Herzl Joshua, *The Law and Customs of the South African Constitution* (London: 1935).

Khan, Sir Shafa' at Ahmad, *The Indian in South Africa* (Allahabad: 1946).

Kidd, Dudley, *The Essential Kafir* (London: 1904).

Kidd, Dudley, *Kafir Socialism and the Dawn of Individualism: An Introduction to the Study of the Native Problem* (London: 1908).

Knaplund, Paul, "The Unification of South Africa: A Study in British Colonial Policy," in *Transactions of the Wisconsin Academy of Sciences, Arts, and Letters*, XXI, 1924, pp. 1-21.

Knowles, Lilian Charlotte Ann and Matthews, Charles, *The Economic Development of the British Overseas Empire: South Africa* (London: 1936), III.

Kondapi, Chenchala, *Indians Overseas, 1838-1949* (Bombay: 1951).

Kraus, René, *Old Master: The Life of Jan Christian Smuts* (New York: 1944).

Lagden, Sir Godfrey, "The Native Question in South Africa," in *The Empire and the Century: A Series of Essays on Imperial Problems and Pos-*

sibilities by Various Writers, with an Introduction by Charles Sydney Goldmann (London: 1905).

Langer, William L., The Diplomacy of Imperialism, 1890-1902 (New York: 1960, 2nd ed.).

Lehfeldt, Robert Alfred, Gold, Prices, and the Witwatersrand (London: 1919).

Long, B. K., Drummond Chaplin: His Life and Times in Africa (London: 1941).

Loran, Charles Templeman, The Education of the South African Native (London: 1917).

Lovell, Colin Rhys, "Afrikaner Nationalism and Apartheid," American Historical Rev., Jan. 1956, pp. 308-29.

Lovell, Reginald Ivan, The Struggle for South Africa, 1875-1899: A Study in Economic Imperialism (1934).

Lucas, Sir Charles, South Africa: History to Union of South Africa (Oxford: 1915).

Macmillan, William Miller, Bantu, Boer, and Briton: The Making of the South African Native Problem (London: 1929).

Macmillan, William Miller, Complex South Africa: An Economic Footnote to History (London: 1930).

Macmillan, William Miller, The Cape Colour Question: A Historical Survey (London: 1927).

Marais, Johannes Stephanus, The Cape Coloured People, 1652-1947 (London: 1939).

Marais, Johannes Stephanus, The Fall of Kruger's Republic (Oxford: 1961).

Mansergh, Nicholas, South Africa, 1906-1961: The Price of Magnanimity (New York: 1962).

Marquard, Leo, The Peoples and Policies of South Africa (Oxford: 1960, 2nd ed.).

Millin, Sarah Gertrude, General Smuts (London: 1936), 2 vols.

Millin, Sarah Gertrude, Rhodes (London: 1933).

Nathan, Manfred, The South African Commonwealth (Johannesburg: 1919).

Newton, Arthur Percival, Select Documents Relating to the Unification of South Africa (London: 1924), 2 vols.

Palmer, Mabel, The History of the Indians in Natal (Cape Town: 1957), Natal Regional Survey, vol. 10.

Patterson, Sheila, Colour and Culture in South Africa: A Study of the Status of the Cape Coloured People Within the Social Structure of the Union of South Africa (London: 1953).

Payne, Enoch George, *An Experiment in Alien Labor* (Chicago: 1912).

Perham, Margery and Curtis, Lionel, *The Protectorates of South Africa: The Question of Their Transfer to the Union* (Oxford: 1935).

Plaatje, Solomon Tshekisho, *Native Life in South Africa* (London: 1916).

Polak, Henry Salomon, *The Indians of South Africa: Helots Within the Empire and How They Are Treated* (Madras: 1909), 4 parts.

Polak, Henry Salomon, Brailsford, H. N., and Pethick-Lawrence, F. W., *Mahatma Gandhi* (London: 1949).

Price, Archibald Grenfell, *White Settlers and Native Peoples* (Cambridge: 1950).

Pyrah, Geoffrey Barker, *Imperial Policy and South Africa, 1902-1910* (Oxford: 1955).

Roux, Edward, *Time Longer Than Rope: A History of the Black Man's Struggle for Freedom in South Africa* (London: 1948).

Russell, Robert C., *The Garden Colony: The Story of Natal and Its Neighbors* (London: 1903).

Smuts, Jan Christiaan (his son), *Jan Christiaan Smuts* (London: 1952).

South African Native Races Committee, *The Natives of South Africa: Their Economic and Social Condition* (London: 1901).

South African Native Races Committee, *The South African Natives: Their Progress and Present Condition* (London: 1908).

Stuart, James, *A History of the Zulu Rebellion, 1906, and of Dinizulu's Arrest, Trial, and Expatriation* (London: 1913).

Sundkler, Bengt G. M., *Bantu Prophets in South Africa* (London: 1961, 2nd ed.).

Theal, George McCall, *History of South Africa From 1795 to 1872* (London: 1927, 4th ed., rev. and enl.), 5 vols.

Theal, George McCall, *The Yellow and Dark-Skinned People of Africa South of the Zambesi* (London: 1910).

Thompson, Leonard Monteath, *The Unification of South Africa, 1902-1910* (Oxford: 1960).

Van Der Horst, Sheila Terreblanche, *Native Labour in South Africa* (Oxford: 1942).

Van Der Poel, Jean, *Railway and Customs Policies in South Africa, 1885-1910* (London: 1953).

Waiz, S. A., ed., *Indians Abroad* (Bombay: 1927, 2nd ed.). Imperial Indian Citizenship Association.

Walker, Eric Anderson, *A History of Southern Africa* (London: 1957).

Walker, Eric Anderson, *Lord De Villiers and His Times: South Africa, 1842-1914* (London: 1925).

Walker, Eric Anderson, *W. P. Schriener: A South African* (Oxford: 1937).

Walker, Eric Anderson, "Lord Milner and South Africa," in *Proceedings of the British Academy,* 1942, XXVIII, pp. 155-78.

Walton, Edgar Harris, *The Inner History of the National Convention of South Africa* (Capetown: 1912).

Willard, Myra, *History of the White Australian Policy* (Melbourne: 1923).

Worsfold, William Basil, *Lord Milner's Work in South Africa From Its Commencement in 1897 to the Peace of Vereeniging in 1902* (London: 1906).

Worsfold, William Basil, *The Reconstruction of the New Colonies Under Lord Milner* (London: 1913), 2 vols.

Worsfold, William Basil, *The Union of South Africa* (London: 1912).

Younghusband, Captain Francis, *South Africa of Today* (London: 1899).

VII. SUGGESTED READINGS ON APARTHEID AND RELATED ISSUES

Allighan, Garry, *Curtain-Up on South Africa: Presenting A National Drama* (London: 1960).

Appasamy, Bhasker, *Indians of South Africa* (Bombay: 1934).

Barlow, Arthur Godfrey, *Almost in Confidence* (Capetown: 1952).

Bate, Henry Maclear, *South Africa Without Prejudice* (Capetown: 1956).

Brookes, Edgar Harry, *South Africa in a Changing World* (London: 1953).

Brookes, Edgar Harry, *The Colour Problems of South Africa* (London: 1934).

Brookes, Edgar Harry and Macaulay, J. B., *Civil Liberty in South Africa* (Capetown: 1958).

Broomfield, Gerald Webb, *Colour Conflict: Race Relations in South Africa* (London: 1945).

Burger, Jan, *The Gulf Between* (Cape Town: 1960).

Calpin, George Harold, *Indians in South Africa* (Pietermaritzburg: 1949).

Calpin, George Harold, ed., *The South African Way of Life: Values and Ideals of a Multi-racial Society* (New York: 1953).

Calpin, George Harold, ed., *There Are No South Africans* (London: 1946).

Calvocoressi, Peter, *South Africa and World Opinion* (London: 1961).

Campbell, Alexander, *The Heart of Africa* (London: 1954).

Carter, Gwendolyn Margaret, *The Politics of Inequality: South Africa Since 1948* (New York: 1958).

Davidson, Basil, *Report on Southern Africa* (London: 1952).

DeKiewiet, Cornelius William, *The Anatomy of Misery in South Africa* (London: 1956).

Dvorin, Eugene Paul, *Racial Separation in South Africa: An Analysis of Apartheid Theory* (Chicago: 1952).

Fuller, Basil, *South Africa—Not Guilty?* (London: 1957).

Gibbs, Henry, *Twilight in South Africa* (London: 1951).

Giniewski, Paul, *The Two Faces of Apartheid* (Chicago: 1965).

Hailey, Lord, *An African Survey, Revised 1956* (London: 1957).

Hancock, William Keith, *Survey of British Commonwealth Affairs: Problems of Economic Policy, 1918-1939* (London: 1940-42), II, 2 parts.

Hatch, John, *The Dilemma of South Africa* (London: 1952).

Hellmann, Ellen, ed., *Handbook on Race Relations in South Africa* (London: 1949).

Hoernlé, F. Alfred, *Race and Reason* (Johannesburg: 1945).

Hooper, Charles, *Brief Authority* (London: 1960).

Houghton, D. Hobart, *The Tomlinson Report: A Summary of the Findings and Recommendations in the Tomlinson Commission Report* (Johannesburg: 1956).

Huddleston, Father Trevor, *Naught for Your Comfort* (London: 1956).

Joshi, Pranshanhar Someshwar, *Unrest in South Africa* (Bombay: 1958).

Keppel-Jones, Arthur, *Friends or Foes? A Point of View and a Programme for Racial Harmony in South Africa* (Pietermaritzburg: 1950).

Kruger, Daniel W., *The Age of the Generals: A Short Political History of the Union of South Africa, 1910-1948* (Johannesburg: 1958).

Kuper, Leo, *Passive Resistance in South Africa* (New Haven: 1957).

Mansergh, Nicholas, *Survey of British Commonwealth Affairs: Problems of Wartime Co-operation and Post-War Change, 1939-1952* (London: 1958).

Marquard, Leo, *The Peoples and Policies of South Africa* (Oxford: 1952).

McCord, Capt. J. J., *South African Struggle* (Pretoria: 1952), 553 pp.

Miller, John Donald Bruce, *The Commonwealth in the World* (Cambridge, Mass.: 1958).

Millin, Sarah Gertrude, *The People of South Africa* (New York: 1954).

Neame, Lawrence Elwin, *The History of Apartheid: The Story of the Colour War in South Africa* (London: 1962).

Neame, Lawrence Elwin, *White Man's Africa: The Problem of a White Nation in a Black Continent* (Capetown: 1952).

Olivier, Lord Sydney, *The Anatomy of African Misery* (London: 1927).

Patterson, Sheila, *Colour and Culture in South Africa: A Study of the Status of the Cape Coloured People Within the Social Structure of the Union of South Africa* (London: 1953).

Patterson, Sheila, *The Last Trek: A Study of the Boer People and the Afrikaner Nation* (London: 1957).

Paver, Bertram Garrett, *His Own Oppressor* (London: 1958).

Perham, Margery and Curtis, Lionel, *The Protectorates of South Africa: The Question of Their Transfer to the Union* (London: 1935).

Reeves, Ambrose (Bishop of Johannesburg), *Shooting at Sharpeville: The Agony of South Africa* (Boston: 1961).

Rhoodie, N. G. and Venter, H. J., *Apartheid: A Socio-Historical Exposition of the Origin and Development of the Apartheid Idea* (Cape Town: 1960).

Roberts, Michael and Trollip, A. E. G., *The South African Opposition, 1939-1945* (Capetown: 1947).

Robertson, Hector Menteith, *South Africa: Economic and Political Aspects* (Durham, N.C.: 1957).

Roux, Edward, *Time Longer Than Rope: A History of the Black Man's Struggle For Freedom in South Africa* (London: 1948).

Sachs, Emil Solomon, *The Choice Before South Africa* (London: 1952).

Scott, Michael, *A Time To Speak* (London: 1958).

Siegfried, André, *African Journey* (London: 1950).

Steward, Alexander, *You Are Wrong Father Huddleston* (London: 1956).

Tabata, I. B., *Education For Barbarism in South Africa: Bantu (Apartheid) Education* (London: 1960).

Tinley, James Maddison, *The Native Labor Problem of South Africa* (Chapel Hill, N.C.: 1942).

Spooner, F. P., *South African Predicament* (London: 1960).

Van Der Horst, Sheila Terreblanche, *Native Labour in South Africa* (London: 1942).

Waiz, S. A., *Indians Abroad* (Bombay: 1927, 2nd ed.).

APPENDICES

APPENDIX A—*Gold Mining Statistics for the Transvaal*

These figures are a composite based upon the following sources:

a) *Transvaal Government Mining Engineer Reports*
b) *Transvaal Chamber of Mines Reports*
c) *Witwatersrand Native Labour Association Reports*
d) *Transvaal Labour Department for Asiatic Immigration Reports*
e) *Transvaal Native Affairs Department Reports*
f) *Union of South Africa Mines Department Reports*

The attention of the reader is called to several factors that should be kept in mind in analyzing the statistics in the above sources. The statistics, where possible, relate only to the Witwatersrand gold mines. Sometimes particular statistics are available only for the Transvaal as a whole, which means including non-Rand gold-mining production near Pretoria—Barberton, Lydenburg, Pietersburg, Heidelberg, Potchefstroom. Again, the available statistics may include nonproducing gold mines (development projects) as well as the producing gold mines. Still again, the statistics may refer only to the number of workers actually at work or to the broader aggregate in service. And still again, the statistics may lump all non-Europeans as one group or break them down into native and other Coloured people (Cape Coloured). Finally, the statistics vary in point of being early tentative compilations, revision figures, or definitive tabulations.

1) NUMBER IN SERVICE

	Whites	Natives	Other Coloured	Chinese
1893	4,207	30,081		
1894	5,615	42,309		
1895	7,497	53,988		
1896	9,366	63,983		
1897	9,519	69,098		
1898	10,684	82,062		
1902				
June	6,588	28,613		
July	7,993	31,650		
Aug.	8,523	33,791		
Sep.	8,789	35,966		
Oct.	9,308	39,273		
Nov.	9,760	40,519		
Dec.	9,878	42,305		
1903				
Jan.	10,327	43,727		
Feb.	10,390	46,919		
Mar.	10,658	51,479		
Apr.	10,768	54,983		
May	10,854	58,531		
June	11,187	60,200		
July	11,208	61,906		
Aug.	11,449	63,382		
Sep.	11,805	64,089		
Oct.	11,812	65,775		
Nov.	12,104	66,643		
Dec.	12,044	67,061		
1904				
Jan.	12,118	67,994		
Feb.	12,094	70,714		
Mar.	11,991	72,608		
Apr.	12,039	72,011		
May	12,414	70,608		
June	12,730	68,174		1,004
July	13,038	65,550	1,637	1,388
Aug.	13,691	65,404	1,734	4,945
Sep.	13,775	68,042	1,545	9,020
Oct.	13,857	71,016	1,409	12,965

	Whites	Natives	Other Coloured	Chinese
Nov.	14,233	73,854	1,493	17,469
Dec.	14,346	75,742	1,467	20,885
1905				
Jan.	14,873	81,351	1,496	27,222
Feb.	15,162	89,048	1,130	31,424
Mar.	15,537	95,792	943	34,335
Apr.	15,516	97,637	961	35,575
May	15,888	96,591	719	38,111
June	16,158	94,619	690	41,340
July	16,346	93,583	709	43,191
Aug.	16,573	90,260	738	44,609
Sep.	16,903	87,537	1,073	44,538
Oct.	17,353	86,034	1,085	45,976
Nov.	17,165	85,582	1,177	45,856
Dec.	17,248	82,842	1,412	47,267
1906				
Jan.	17,696	82,525	1,430	47,166
Feb.	17,670	82,477	1,591	50,000
Mar.	17,768	82,863	1,546	49,922
Apr.	17,233	82,841	1,610	49,832
May	17,491	81,706	1,706	50,974
June	17,208	80,519	1,723	52,352
July	16,987	80,207	1,727	52,231
Aug.	16,912	81,263	2,461	52,111
Sep.	16,795	83,010	2,483	53,430
Oct.	17,003	84,103	2,376	53,163
Nov.	16,936	88,030		53,030
Dec.	16,818	90,526		52,917
1907				
Jan.	17,198	94,221		53,856
Feb.	17,103	100,371		53,764
Mar.	17,159	103,863		53,679
Apr.	17,196	104,828		53,614
May	15,118	104,245		53,434
June	16,455	102,113		51,517
July	16,587	101,318		51,472
Aug.	16722	103,129		51,283
Sep.	16,814	108,068		47,465
Oct.	16,864	112,445		44,365

	Whites	Natives	Other Coloured	Chinese
Nov.	16,918	116,832		40,055
Dec.	16,928	119,512		37,118

	Whites	Coloured	Chinese
1908			
Jan.	16,763	123,001	33,849
Feb.	16728	130,675	30,069
Mar.	16,827	136,087	27,862
Apr.	17,063	137,265	24,865
May	17,181	137,349	22,667
June	17,341	137,107	21,460
July	17,501	139,055	19,071
Aug.	17,924	141,896	17,270
Sep.	18,191	144,907	16,311
Oct.	18,379	147,139	14,314
Nov.	18,534	150,102	12,307
Dec.	18,687	154,130	12,275
1909			
Jan.	18,903	158,965	11,534
Feb.	19,225	165,765	10,025
Mar.	19,674	169,995	10,021
Apr.	19,836	170,821	8,308
May	20,290	168,984	7,710
June	20,594	164,902	7,315
Dec.	20,265	162,439	1,910
1910 (av.)	23,651	183,613	
1911 (av.)	24,708	189,912	
1912 (av.)	23,817	192,575	
1913 (av.)	23,104	184,265	
1914 (av.)	20,971	167,501	

2) Ratio of Whites to Natives and Chinese

> July 1899 — 1:8.578 (only natives)
> June 1902 — 1:4.343 (only natives)
> June 1903 — 1:5.383 (only natives)
> June 1904 — 1:5.436 (only natives)
> June 1905 — 1:8.457 (includes Chinese)
> June 1906 — 1:7.822 (includes Chinese)
> June 1907 — 1:9.336 (includes Chinese)
> June 1908 — 1:9.349 (includes Chinese)
> June 1909 — 1:8.9   (includes Chinese)
> June 1910 — 1:7.7   (includes Chinese)
> June 1911 — 1:7.7   (only natives)
> June 1912 — 1:8.1   (only natives)
> June 1913 — 1:8.0   (only natives)

3) Number of Persons Employed per Stamp at Work

> July 1899 — 15.99
> June 1903 — 14.223
> June 1905 — 20.15
> June 1906 — 18.33
> June 1907 — 19.02

4) Stamps at Work

> 1895 — 2,546
> 1896 — 3,740
> 1897 — 3,567
> 1898 — 4,765
>
> Aug. 1899 — 6,070
> June 1902 — 2,135
> June 1903 — 3,500
> June 1904 — 4,937
> June 1905 — 7,046
> June 1906 — 8,125
> June 1907 — 8,647
> June 1908 — 9,041
> June 1909 — 9,726

5) Wages (exclusive of food, lodging, and medical care)

	Natives	Chinese
1895	63s. 6d.	
1896	60s.10d.	
1897	48s. 7d.	
1898	49s. 9d.	
1901-02	26s. 8d.	
1902-03	38s. 6d.	
1903-04	48s.10d.	
1904-05	52s. 0d.	33s. 6d.
1905-06	51s.11d.	39s. 9d.
1906-07	52s. 3d.	41s. 6d.
1907-08	49s. 1d.	44s. 3d.
1908-09	46s. 4d.	47s. 3d.

6) Native Mortality Rates from Disease — Deaths per 1,000

	1903	1904	1905	1906	1907	1908
Jan.	57.88	56.09	42.23	42.32	31.3	30.3
Feb.	42.76	33.30	36.69	31.56	28.2	26.9
Mar.	45.67	31.89	36.44	29.14	29.1	
Apr.	49.53	23.61	33.32	27.06	31.0	
May	75.08	40.33	42.05	28.96	34.7	
June	83.00	33.18	51.92	29.63	32.9	
July	112.54	58.97	49.86	28.80	34.0	
Aug.	78.47	36.58	43.47	27.47	33.7	
Sep.	69.44	36.33	36.00	27.73	26.3	
Oct.	65.72	31.90	39.19	31.83	27.1	
Nov.	79.41	43.68	50.02	28.44	24.6	
Dec.	78.28	36.77	50.41	27.92	28.4	
Av.	70.07	38.38	42.59	30.12	30.10	

7) Chinese Mortality Rates from Disease — Deaths per 1,000

1904

	Present	Number of Deaths	Percentage
Aug.	4,947	6	0.12
Sep.	9,039	19	0.21
Oct.	12,968	25	0.19
Nov.	15,222	38	0.24
Dec.	20,918	49	0.23

1905

	Present	Number of Deaths	Percentage
Jan.	27,187	31	0.11
Feb.	31,389	45	0.14
Apr.-June	38,295	111	11.594
July-Sep.	44,068	113	10.256
Oct.-Dec.	46,307	132	11.40

1906

Jan.-Mar.	48,983	142	11.596
Apr.-June	51,020	151	11.838
July	52,201	45	10.3
Aug.	52,079	47	10.8
Sep.	53,400	47	10.6
Oct.	53,134	52	11.7
Nov.	53,004	45	10.2
Dec.	52,889	32	7.3

1907

Jan.	53,828	46	10.3
Feb.	53,736	38	8.5
Mar.	53,651	39	8.7
Apr.	53,588	36	8.1
May	53,406	40	9.0
June	51,497	45	10.5
July	51,441	33	7.7
Aug.	49,071	38	9.3
Sep.	46,260	30	7.8
Oct.	42,338	33	9.4
Nov.	37,728	35	11.1
Dec.	35,676	37	12.4

1908

Jan.	31,480	27	10.3
Feb.	28,406	19	8.0

8) GOLD PRODUCTION

	Fine Ounces	£ Value
1895	2,277,640	7,840,779
1896	2,280,892	7,864,341
1897	3,034,678	10,583,616
1898	3,614,385	15,141,376
Aug. 1899	392,022	1,642,025
· 1900	348,761	1,481,442
1901	258,032	1,097,219
1902		
June	139,248.089	591,488
July	146,641.000	622,892
Aug.	159,584.524	677,873
Sep.	164,180.431	697,392
Oct.	174,699.794	742,074
Nov.	177,092.208	752,237
Dec.	184,883.396	785,334
1903 (Total)	2,787,764.270	11,739,124
Jan.	188,649.730	801,335
Feb.	182,076.320	773,410
Mar.	202,345.631	859,512
Apr.	213,084.828	905,127
May	217,634.194	924,450
June	221,333.091	940,158
July	236,037.247	1,002,618
Aug.	257,335.673	1,093,093
Sep.	260,730.532	1,107,516
Oct.	268,847.695	1,141,992
Nov.	266,037.692	1,130,060
Dec.	273,051.637	1,159,853
1904 (Total)	3,603,776.438	15,307,874
Jan.	273,280.759	1,160,824
Feb.	277,146.318	1,177,236
Mar.	294,104.943	1,249,280
Apr.	294,229.035	1,249,803
May	300,459.946	1,276,276
June	294,805.773	1,252,256
July	291,559.726	1,238,465
Aug.	298,250.351	1,266,889

	Fine Ounces	£ Value
Sep.	299,089.793	1,270,447
Oct.	310,024.211	1,316,894
Nov.	324,467.774	1,378,255
Dec.	346,357.809	1,471,229
1905 (Total)	4,680,801.458	19,881,955
Jan.	356,535.214	1,514,461
Feb.	349,365.553	1,484,010
Mar.	383,483.325	1,628,937
Apr.	384,122.459	1,631,640
May	398,131.798	1,691,157
June	394,092.040	1,673,999
July	399,796.333	1,698,224
Aug.	408,207.830	1,733,965
Sep.	396,050.868	1,682,326
Oct.	395,773.267	1,681,155
Nov.	404,649.538	1,718,848
Dec.	410,393.233	1,743,233
1906 (Total)	5,534,917.860	23,510,819
Jan.	408,581.591	1,735,538
Feb.	385,806.634	1,638,794
Mar.	421,628.934	1,790,962
Apr.	417,492.400	1,773,397
May	438,978.503	1,864,660
June	454,687.097	1,931,383
July	472,213.382	2,005,838
Aug.	486,641.469	2,067,122
Sep.	484,620.804	2,058,540
Oct.	519,917.178	2,208,467
Nov.	521,042.729	2,213,253
Dec.	523,307.139	2,222,865
1907 (Total)	6,223,280.454	26,435,797
Jan.	522,359.771	2,218,841
Feb.	476,831.619	2,025,450
Mar.	519,360.330	2,206,099
Apr.	520,252.185	2,209,890
May	505,898.926	2,148,920
June	488,360.876	2,074,425
July	513,572.666	2,181,517

	Fine Ounces	£ Value
Aug.	535,419.838	2,274,315
Sep.	517,670.156	2,198,921
Oct.	533,321.155	2,265,409
Nov.	529,672.412	2,249,910
Dec.	560,560.520	2,381,110
1908 (Total)	6,734,070.712	28,805,902
Jan.	540,213.247	2,294,681
Feb.	520,500.405	2,210,944
Mar.	553,500.636	2,351,121
Apr.	543,477.721	2,308,547
May	557,431.801	2,367,821
June	552,690.063	2,347,679
July	561,702.941	2,385,962
Aug.	564,498.369	2,397,836
Sep.	565,468.865	2,401,959
Oct.	595,203.402	2,528,264
Nov.	589,189.262	2,502,717
Dec.	640,194.000	2,719,371
1909 (Total)	7,042,581.173	29,914,976
Jan.	593,659.678	2,521,706
Feb.	550,467.949	2,338,239
Mar.	593,246.296	2,519,950
Apr.	587,586.608	2,495,910
May	603,970.697	2,565,506
June	596,800.945	2,535,049
July	599,078.000	2,544,722
Aug.	590,924.000	2,510,080
Sep.	585,736.000	2,488,050
Oct.	581,132.000	2,468,493
Nov.	576,768.000	2,449,955
Dec.	583,209.000	2,477,316
1910 (Total)	7,228,311	30,703,912
1911 (Total)	7,896,802	33,543,479
1912 (Total)	8,753,568	37,182,795
1913 (Total)	8,430,998	35,812,605
1914 (Total)	8,033,570	34,124,434

APPENDIX B—*Population Statistics*

These figures are based upon the following sources:
a) *Statistical Year-Books of the Union of South Africa*
b) *Official Year-Books of the Union of South Africa*
c) Census for April-May 1904 in all colonies (*P.P.*, 1904, LXI, Cd. 2103, 22 pp.)

1) COMPOSITE FIGURES FOR SOUTH AFRICA

	1904	1911	Estimate for June 30, 1914	1951
European	1,116,806	1,276,242	1,368,959	2,641,689
Bantu	3,491,056	4,019,006	4,309,024	8,560,083
Asiatic	122,734	152,309		366,664
Mixed			737,561	
and other	445,228	525,837		1,103,016
Coloured				

2) COMPOSITE FIGURES FOR SOUTH AFRICA BY SEX

	1904 Female	1904 Male	1911 Female	1911 Male
European	481,689	635,117	591,078	685,164
Bantu	1,753,937	1,737,119	1,996,057	2,022,949
Asiatic	39,925	82,809	56,108	96,201
Mixed				
and other	218,038	227,190	260,759	265,078
Coloured				

	1951 Female	1951 Male
European	1,318,935	1,322,754
Bantu	4,190,926	4,369,157
Asiatic	177,069	189,595
Mixed		
and other	552,437	550,579
Coloured		

3) COMPOSITE FIGURES FOR EACH COLONY (PROVINCE)

Cape Colony

	1891	1904	1911	Estimate for June 30, 1914	1951
European	376,987	579,741	582,377	583,605	435,085
Bantu	838,136	1,424,728	1,519,939	1,566,252	2,492,021
Asiatic	1,700	10,242	7,690		17,818
Mixed				491,981 }	
and other Coloured	310,401	395,034	454,959		981,802

Natal

	1891	1904	1911	Estimate for June 30, 1914	1951
European	46,788	97,109	98,114	98,584	274,240
Bantu	455,983	904,041	953,398	977,220	1,810,102
Asiatic	41,142	100,918	133,439		299,491
Mixed	Incl. in			162,401 }	
and other Coloured	European	6,686	9,092		31,485

Transvaal

	1904	1911	Estimate for June 30, 1914	1951
European	297,277	420,562	494,064	1,204,712
Bantu	937,127	1,219,845	1,378,695	3,483,770
Asiatic	11,321	11,072		49,342
Mixed			51,527 }	
and other Coloured	24,226	34,762		75,014

Orange Free State

	1904	1911	Estimate for June 30, 1914	1951
European	142,679	175,189	192,706	277,652
Bantu	225,101	325,824	386,857	774,190
Asiatic	253	108		13
Mixed			31,652 }	
and other Coloured	19,282	27,053		14,715

4) COMPOSITE FIGURES FOR EACH COLONY (PROVINCE) BY SEX

Cape Colony

	1891 Female	1891 Male	1904 Female	1904 Male	1911 Female	1911 Male
European	181,031	195,956	261,197	318,544	281,109	301,268
Bantu	422,935	415,201	732,059	692,728	798,498	721,441
Asiatic	935	1,305	926	9,316	1,085	6,605
Mixed and other Coloured	155,536	154,865	196,682	198,352	228,602	226,357

	1951 Female	1951 Male
European	471,168	463,917
Bantu	1,345,617	1,146,404
Asiatic	7,669	10,119
Mixed and other Coloured	491,568	490,234

Natal

	1891 Female	1891 Male	1904 Female	1904 Male	1911 Female	1911 Male
European	21,001	25,787	40,351	56,758	45,619	52,495
Bantu	239,394	216,589	477,275	426,766	526,766	427,061
Asiatic	15,456	25,686	37,421	63,497	52,949	80,490
Mixed and other Coloured	Incl. in European		3,076	3,610	4,490	4,602

	1951 Female	1951 Male
European	137,940	136,300
Bantu	932,023	878,079
Asiatic	146,194	153,297
Mixed and other Coloured	16,230	15,255

Transvaal

	1904		1911		1951	
	Female	Male	Female	Male	Female	Male
European	119,033	178,244	183,649	236,913	597,812	606,900
Bantu	437,408	489,719	513,983	705,862	1,948,779	1,534,991
Asiatic	1,522	9,799	2,054	9,018	23,171	26,171
Mixed and other Coloured	9,419	14,807	14,971	19,762	37,550	37,464

Orange Free State

	Female	Male	Female	Male	Female	Male
European	61,108	81,571	80,701	94,488	112,015	115,637
Bantu	107,195	117,906	157,239	168,585	378,295	395,895
Asiatic	56	197	20	88	5	8
Mixed and other Coloured	8,861	10,421	12,696	14,357	7,089	7,626

5) PROTECTORATES

Basutoland

	1909	1911	1956
European		1,396	2,000
Native	347,731	403,111	631,396

Swaziland

	1904	1909	1911	1956
European	890	890	1,083	2,740
Native	84,601	84,529	98,876	143,709

Bechuanaland

	1909	1911	1946
European	1,004	1,692	1,743
Native	119,411	123,658	150,185

APPENDIX C—*Educational Statistics*

1) Overall Figures for 1904, (*P.P.*, 1905 LV, Cd. 2399, p. 50).

	Native Pop.	Est. No. of Scholars	% of Natives in School	Public Exp. on Native Education	Rate Per Head to Scholars
Cape Colony	£1,424,787	60,451	4.24	1,800	5s.6d.
Natal	904,041	10,154	1.12	£47,657	15s.9d.
Transvaal	811,753	11,683	1.13	7,265	14s.4d.
Orange River Colony	235,466	6,500	2.76	5,000	8s.7d.

Amt. Contributed by
Domiciled Natives in Direct
Taxation

Cape Colony	£105,241
Natal	162,193
Transval	280,269
Orange River Colony	42,803

2) PRIMARY AND SECONDARY EDUCATION COSTS—TOTAL AND PER SCHOLAR
Statistical Year-Book of the Union of South Africa, 1914-15, pp. 302, 307, 311-12, 316.

Natal

	1911		1912		1913		1914	
	Total Dist.	Per Scholar	Total Dist.	Per Scholar	Total Dist.	Per Scholar	Total Dist.	Per Scholar
Natives	£11,779	£0 17s. 8¾d.	£14,653	£0 18s. 6½d.	£17,304	£0 19s. 6d.	£21,889	£1 2s. 9⅓d.
Indians	6,762	2 3s. 5¼d.	7,361	2 3s. 5¼d.	7,929	2 0s. 3d.	8,373	2 0s. 2½d.
Coloured	4,581	4 0s. 11d.	5,209	4 6s. 0¾d.	5,493	4 7s. 5½d.	6,647	4 13s. 6¼d.
Whites	126,000	6 11s. 9¾d.	140,000	6 12s. 7¼d.	150,000	6 16s. 3¼d.	164,000	6 15s. 8¾d.

Transvaal

	1911		1912		1913		1914	
	Total Dist.	Per Scholar	Total Dist.	Per Scholar	Total Dist.	Per Scholar	Total Dist.	Per Scholar
Natives	£22,142	£1 8s. 3d.	£22,749	£1 7s. 4d.	£27,455	£1 11s. 5d.	£25,291	£1 9s. 4d.
Whites	595,000	9 7s. 9d.	636,000	9 4s. 11d.	685,000	9 9s. 10d.	735,000	9 10s. 11d.

Orange Free State

	1912-13	1913-14	1914-15
Natives	£ 4,759	£ 4,825	£ 4,790
Whites	247,000	297,000	339,000

Cape of Good Hope

1911-12	1912-13	1913-14
£663,662	£784,714	£853,448

No breakdown between Whites and Natives

APPENDIX D—*List of British Public Officials, 1902-14.*

1) PRIME MINISTERS

Arthur Balfour, 1902
Sir Henry Campbell-Bannerman, 1905
Herbert Asquith, 1908

2) SECRETARIES OF STATE FOR THE COLONIES

Joseph Chamberlain, 1902
Alfred Lyttelton, 1903
Earl of Elgin and Kincardine, 1905
Earl of Crewe, 1908
Lewis Harcourt, 1910

3) PARLIAMENTARY UNDER-SECRETARIES OF STATE FOR THE COLONIES

Earl of Onslow, 1900
Duke of Marlborough, 1903
Winston Spencer Churchill, 1905
John Edward Bernard Seely, 1908
Baron Lucas, 1911
Baron Emmott, 1911

4) PERMANENT UNDER-SECRETARIES OF STATE FOR THE COLONIES

Sir Montagu Frederick Ommanney, 1900
Sir Francis John Stephens Hopwood, 1907
Sir John Anderson, 1911

5) ASSISTANT UNDER-SECRETARIES OF STATE FOR THE COLONIES, SOUTH AFRICAN DEPARTMENT

Sir Frederick Graham, 1897-1907
Hugh Bertram Cox, 1897-1911
Sir George Vandeleur Fiddes, 1906-16
Sir Hartmann Wolfgang Just, 1907-16

6) PRINCIPAL CLERKS, SOUTH AFRICAN DEPARTMENT

Sir Henry Charles Miller Lambert
Sir Douglas Orme Malcolm

Sir William Arthur Robinson
Arthur Berriedale Keith
Roland Venables Vernon

7) SECRETARIES OF STATE FOR INDIA

Lord George Francis Hamilton, 1895
Earl of Middleton, 1903
Viscount Morley of Blackburn, 1905
Earl of Crewe, 1910

8) VICEROYS OF INDIA

Earl Curzon of Kedleston, 1899
Earl of Minto, 1905
Baron Hardinge of Penshurst, 1910

APPENDIX E—*List of South African Public Officials, 1902-14.*

1) CAPE COLONY

Governor
   Sir Walter Francis Hely—Hutchinson, 1901-10
Prime Ministers
   Sir John Gordon Sprigg, 1902
   Dr. Leander Starr Jameson, 1904
   John Xavier Merriman, 1908

2) NATAL

Governors
   Sir Henry McCallum, 1901-07
   Sir Matthew Nathan, 1907-09
   Baron Methuen, 1909-10

Prime Ministers

   Sir Albert Henry Hime, 1902
   George Morris Sutton, 1904
   Charles John Smythe, 1905
   Frederick Robert Moor, 1906

3) TRANSVAAL

Governors
Viscount Milner, 1901-05
Earl of Selborne, 1905-10
Lt. Governor
Sir Arthur Lawley, 1902-10
Prime Minister
Louis Botha, 1907

4) ORANGE FREE STATE

Governors
Viscount Milner, 1901-05
Earl of Selborne, 1905-10
Lt. Governor
Sir Hamilton J. Goold-Adams, 1901-10
Prime Minister
Abraham Fischer, 1902

5) UNION OF SOUTH AFRICA, 1910-14

Governor-General
Viscount Gladstone
Prime Minister
Louis Botha

INDEX

Carnarvon, Earl of (4th), 11, 12.
Carpenter, Edward, 180.
Carrington, Earl of (1st), 51, 57, 164.
Carter, Rt. Rev. William Marlborough
 (Bishop of Pretoria), 43.
Central America, 45.
Cetewayo, 105, 109, 117, 140.
Ceylon, 39, 41, 63, 76, 271.
Chaka, 105.
Chamberlain, Sir Austen, 200.
Chamberlain, Joseph, 22, 23, 24, 26-27,
 30, 34, 37, 102, 200.
Chandler, Rt. Rev. Arthur (Bishop of
 Bloemfontein), 50.
Chaplin, Sir Francis Drummond Percy,
 30, 74.
China, 34, 58, 59, 64.
Chinese Coolies (Transvaal)
 Australia, 37, 38, 42n, 44, 51, 54.
 Boers, 32, 36, 50, 85, 92, 96-97.
 Canada, 37, 51, 54.
 Cape Colony, 37, 43, 44, 50.
 Contributions, 41-42, 53-54, 73, 74-75,
  74n, 78-79, 89-90, 91-92, 93-94, 100,
  101.
 Indentured Status, 41, 43, 48, 49, 58,
  59, 60, 61, 62-64, 80-81, 90-91, 100.
 Lawlessness, 69, 70, 73, 77.
 Living Conditions, 59, 66, 71-72, 75-76,
  76n.
 Maltreatment, 67-69, 76-77, 76n, 84-86,
  89, 94-95, 98.
 Natal, 43, 43n, 44, 50-51.
 New Zealand, 38, 43n, 44, 51.
 Recruitment, 34-37, 58, 61, 65, 70, 71,
  75, 81-82, 88.
 Repatriation Program, 82-84, 88, 91, 98.
 Termination, 79-80, 81, 90, 95-96, 97-
  98, 99, 102, 103.
 Wages, 58, 60, 61,65-66, 71, 75.
 Womenfolk, 42, 48, 59, 61-62, 66-67,
  72-73, 77-78, 86, 89, 95.
Chirol, Valentine, 255.
Churchill, Sir Winston Spencer
 Bantu, 163, 163n, 174.
 British Indians, 208, 209.
 Chinese Coolies, 79, 81, 83, 84, 85-86,
  87, 88, 89, 91, 91n, 98, 100n, 101n.
 Zulu Disturbances, 111, 113n, 114, 120,
  121, 128. 129.

City and Suburban (see South Africa
 Gold Mines).
Clarkson, Thomas, 4.
Colenso, Agnes, 109, 143.
Colenso, Francis Ernest (pseud., Gebuza),
 109, 110-11, 132-33, 140.
Colenso, Harriette Emily, 109, 133, 136,
 136n, 140, 142, 143.
Colenso, Rt. Rev. John William (Bishop
 of Natal), 109.
Congo Free State, 64.
Consolidated Goldfields (see South Africa
 Gold Trust Limited).
Cotton, Sir Henry John Stedman, 209n.
Courtney of Penwith, Baron (1st), 181.
Cox, Harold, 209n, 225, 226, 227.
Cox, Hugh Bertram, 26, 111.
Creswell, Frederic Hugh Page, 49, 52-53,
 55-56, 56n, 57, 62n, 79, 92-93.
Crewe, Earl of (1st)
 Bantu, 174, 176, 177, 178, 179, 188,
  196.
 British Indians, 214, 218, 219, 221,
  235, 236, 245.
 Chinese Coolies, 91, 91n.
 Dinizulu, 133, 135, 140, 141, 142.
Curzon of Kedleston, Marquess (1st), 41,
 41n, 42, 185, 233.
Cyprus, 223.

Daniels, W. Leslie, 31.
Davidson, Dr. Randall Thomas
 (Archbishop of Canterbury), 59, 72-73,
 77, 95, 186n.
Davis, Alexander, 154-55.
Deakin, Alfred, 38, 44.
De Jongh, Jacobus Nicholas, 33.
De Kieweit, Cornelius, 9, 24.
De Villiers, Sir John Henry, 174, 175,
 176, 177, 179, 179n.
De Villiers, Melius, 16, 174.
Diefenbaker, John George, 272.
Dilke, Sir Charles Wentworth, 138, 168,
 169, 178, 181-82.
Dingaan, 105.
Dinizulu
 Arrest, 131, 135, 138.
 Biographical, 105-06.
 Health, 128, 131, 133, 135.
 Interviews, 128-30.